SCHAUM'S OUTLINE OF

CHINESE VOCABULARY

SCHAUM'S OUTLINE OF

CHINESE VOCABULARY

•

DUANDUAN LI, Ph.D.

Lecturer of Chinese,
Department of East Asian Languages and Cultures
Columbia University

YANPING XIE, M.A., M.S.

Speech and language pathologist
New York City

•

SCHAUM'S OUTLINE SERIES

MCGRAW-HILL

New York   Chicago   San Francisco
Lisbon   London   Madrid   Mexico City   Milan
New Delhi   San Juan   Seoul   Singapore
Sydney   Toronto

Duanduan Li has been teaching English and Mandarin as a foreign language in China and America for more than 20 years. She received her doctoral degree in Applied Linguistics from Teachers College, Columbia University. Her research interests include sociolinguistics, interlanguage pragmatics, cross-cultural communication, and second language acquisition. She is currently teaching Mandarin as a foreign language in the Department of East Asian Languages and Cultures at Columbia University.

Yangping Xie taught in the Department of East Asian Languages and Cultures at Columbia University for 9 years after she recieved her M.A. from Teachers College, Columbia University. She has written numerous supplementary teaching materials and coauthored *A First Reader for Advanced Beginners,* to be published by the Columbia University Press. She is now an independent contractor, working as a speech and language pathologist in New York City.

Schaum's Outline of
CHINESE VOCABULARY

McGraw-Hill

A Division of The McGraw·Hill Companies

4 5 6 7 8 9 0 CUS CUS 0 8 7 6 5

ISBN 0-07-137835-9

Sponsoring Editor: Barbara Gilson
Production Manager: Clara Stanley
Senior Editing Supervisor: Ruth W. Mannino
Project Supervision: Nicholas A. Bernini
Printed and bound by The Press of Ohio, Inc.

Contents

SCHAUM'S OUTLINE OF

CHINESE VOCABULARY

Chapter 1: At the airport

第一章：(飞)机场
(*Fēi*) *jīchǎng*

GETTING TO THE AIRPORT

这个(飞)机场有两个**登机楼**。 Zhèi ge fēijīchǎng yǒu liǎng ge *dēngjīlóu*.	terminal
东楼是**国际航班**登机楼。 *Dōng* lóu shi *guójì hángbān* dēngjīlóu.	east, international flight
西楼是**国内航班**登机楼。 *Xī* lóu shi *guónèi hángbān* dēngjīlóu.	west, domestic flight
我们可以**坐出租车**[1]去机场。 Wǒmen kěyǐ *zuò chūzūchē* qù jīchǎng.	take a taxi
我们也可以坐**公共汽车**。 Wǒmen yě kěyǐ zuò *gōnggòng qìchē*.	bus
公共汽车从**市内总站**出发。 Gōnggòng qìchē cóng *shìnèi zǒngzhàn* chūfā.	city terminal

1. Complete.

我不想坐出租车去机场。出租车太贵了。我喜欢坐 ___1___ 。公共汽车
Wǒ bùxiǎng zuò chūzūchē qù jīchǎng. Chūzūchē tài guì le. Wǒ xǐhuan zuò ___1___. Gōnggòng qìchē

从城里的 ___2___ 出发。车很多。每十五分钟就有一班车从这个
cóng chéng lǐ de ___2___ chūfā. Chē hěn duō. Měi shíwǔ fēnzhōng jiù yǒu yì bān chē cóng zhèige

总站 ___3___ 。
zǒngzhàn ___3___.

2. Complete.

A：先生，您要去哪个 登机楼?
　　Xiānsheng, nín yào qù něige dēngjīlóu?

B：飞机场有几个 ___1___ ?

---

[1] There are several terms for "Taxi" in Chinese. The formal term in Mainland is "出租车". In Taiwan it's called "计程车". In Hong Kong it's called "的士"。 "打的"means "take a taxi" which is now popularly used in Mainland too. They will be introduced in Chapter 5 "Public Transportation".

1

Fēijīchǎng yǒu jǐ ge __1__?

A：有两个。东楼是国际__2__登机楼，西楼是__3__航班登机楼。
　　Yǒu liǎng ge. Dōng lóu shi guójì __2__ dēngjīlóu. Xī lóu shi __3__ hángbān dēngjīlóu.

B：那，我要去纽约，是国际__4__。请去__5__吧。
　　Nà, wǒ yào qù Niǔyuē, shi guójì __4__. Qǐng qù __5__ ba.

CHECKING IN

Fig. 1-1

去**登机口登机**以前， Qù *dēngjīkǒu dēngjī* yǐqián,	boarding gate, board the plane
乘客们得在**航空公司**的 *Chéngkè*men děi zài *hángkōng gōngsī* de	passenger, airline company
接待柜台办理登机手续。 *jiēdài guìtái bànlǐ dēngjī shǒuxù.*	reception counter, check in
航空公司的**职员**得**检查**你的**证件**。 Hángkōng gōngsī de *zhíyuán* děi *jiǎnchá* nǐde *zhèngjiàn*.	agent, check, document(s)

人们在柜台前**排队**。   line up
Rénmen zài guìtái qián *páiduì*.

职员得看你的**机票**，   (airline) ticket
Zhíyuán děi kàn nǐde *jīpiào*.

还要看你的**护照**和**签证**。   passport, visa
hái yào kàn nǐde *hùzhào* hé *qiānzhèng*.

你可以在柜台**托运**你的大件**行李**。   check in, luggage
Nǐ kěyǐ zài guìtái *tuōyùn* nǐde dà jiàn *xíngli*.

检查你的证件以后，
Jiǎnchá nǐde zhèngjiàn yǐhòu,

职员会给你**登机牌**。   boarding pass
zhíyuán huì gěi nǐ *dēngjīpái*.

3. Complete.

我们一到飞机场，就得先到 ___1___ 去。柜台前一般总是有很多乘客在 ___2___ 。
Wǒmen yí dào fēijīchǎng, jiù děi xiān dào ___1___ qù. Guìtái qián zǒngshi yǒu hěn duō chéngkè zài ___2___ .

办理登机 ___3___ 时，我们得把 ___4___ 给职员看，要是我们坐的是国际 ___5___ ，
Bànlǐ dēngjī ___3___ shí, wǒmen děi bǎ ___4___ gěi zhíyuán kàn. Yàoshi wǒmen zuò de shi guójì ___5___ ,

就还要检查我们的 ___6___ 和 ___7___ 。
jiù hái yào jiǎnchá wǒmen de ___6___ hé ___7___ .

SPEAKING WITH THE AGENT

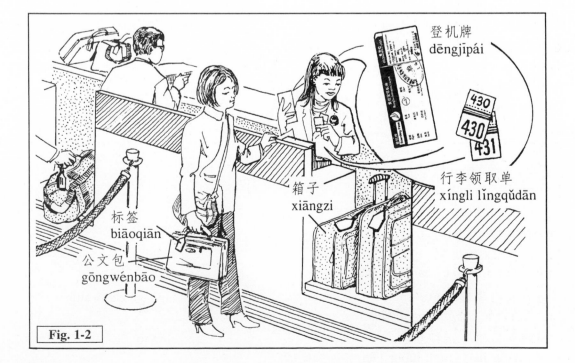

Fig. 1-2

A：您好，**请出示**您的机票。   please..., show
Nín hǎo, *qǐng chūshì* nínde jīpiào.

B：**在这儿**。   Here you are.
Zài zhèr.

A：您**去**纽约吗？可以看看您的护照吗？   go to/bound for
Nín *qù* Niǔyuē ma? Kěyǐ kànkan nínde hùzhào ma?

B：**没问题**。   No problem.
Méi wèntí.

A：谢谢。您要**靠窗的座位**还是   window seat
Xièxie. Nín yào *kàochuāng de zuòwèi* háishi

     靠走道的座位？   aisle seat
     kào zǒudào de zuòwèi?

B：我已经**预订**了一个靠走道的座位。   reserve
Wǒ yǐjīng *yùdìng*le yí ge kào zǒudào de zuòwèi.

A：噢！您的座位是**22排C座**。您有几件**行李**？   row, seat, luggage
Ò! Nínde zuòwèi shi 22 *pái* C *zuò*. Nín yǒu jǐ jiàn *xíngli*?

B：两个**箱子**。   suitcase
Liǎng ge *xiāngzi.*

A：您有**手提行李**吗？   carry-on luggage
Nín yǒu *shǒutí xíngli* ma?

B：只有这个**公文包**。   briefcase
Zhǐ yǒu zhèi ge *gōngwénbāo.*

A：很好。公文包**必须能放进**   must, fit
Hěn hǎo. Gōngwénbāo *bìxū néng fàngjìn*

     您前面的座位底下，
     nín qiánmiàn de zuòwèi dǐxia.

     或者是您**头顶上方**的行李**舱**里。   overhead, compartment,
     huòzhě shi nín tóudǐng shàngfāng de xíngli*cāng* lǐ.

     这是您的行李**标签**。   label
     Zhè shi nínde xíngli *biāoqiān.*

B：谢谢。
Xièxie.

A：不用谢。一切都办好了。
Bú yòng xiè. Yíqiè dōu bànhǎo le.

     这是您的登机牌。
     Zhè shi nínde dēngjīpái.

     去纽约的**430次班机**，22排C座。   flight
     Qù Niǔyuē de 430 cì *bānjī*, 22 pái C zuò.

     这是您的**行李领取单**。   luggage claim stub
     Zhè shi nínde *xíngli lǐngqǔdān.*

     您的两件行李将**运往**纽约。   ship to
     Nínde liǎng jiàn xíngli jiāng *yùnwǎng* Niǔyuē.

您可以在纽约**领取**。   claim
Nín kěyǐ zài Niǔyuē *lǐngqǔ*.

半小时以后机场就会**通知**   announce
Bàn xiǎoshí yǐhòu jīchǎng jiù huì *tōngzhī*

您**航班**的**起飞时间**。   flight, departure time
nín *hángbān* de *qǐfēi shíjiān*.

祝您旅途愉快!   Have a nice trip!
Zhù nín lǚtú yúkuài!

Fig. 1-3

4. Complete.

1) 史密斯太太(Mrs. Smith)要从北京去纽约。她坐的是_____航班。
   Shǐmìsī tàitai yào cóng Běijīng qù Niǔyuē. Tā zuò de shi _____ hángbān.

2) 现在她在飞机场的_____。
   Xiànzài tā zài fēijīchǎng de _____.

3) 她在跟航空公司的职员小姐说话。小姐要检查她的_____。因为
   Tā zài gēn hángkōng gōngsī de zhíyuán xiǎojiě shuōhuà. Xiǎojiě yào jiǎnchá tāde _____. Yīnwèi

   她坐的是国际航班，所以小姐也需要看她的_____和_____。
   tā zuò de shi guójì hángbān, suǒyǐ xiǎojiě yě xūyào kàn tāde _____ hé _____.

4) 在飞机上，_____必须能放进前面座位底下，或者是座位上头的行李舱里。
　　Zài fēijī shàng____ bìxū néng fàngjìn qiánmiàn zuòwèi dǐxià, huòzhě shi zuòwèi shàngtóu de xínglicāng lǐ.

5) 这对史密斯太太来说不是什么问题。她只有一个_____。
　　Zhè duì Shǐmìsī tàitai lái shuō bú shi shénme wèntí. Tā zhǐ yǒu yí ge____.

6) 航空公司小姐给了史密斯太太一张_____。没有_____乘客就不能上飞机。
　　Hángkōng gōngsī xiǎojiě gěi le Shǐmìsī tàitai yì zhāng ___. Méiyǒu ___ chéngkè jiù bù néng shàng fēijī.

7) 史密斯太太要坐430次_____去纽约。她的座位是22_____C_____。
　　Shǐmìsī tàitai yào zuò 430 cì _____ qù Niǔyuē. Tāde zuòwèi shi 22 _____ C____.

8) 史密斯太太的行李已经托运到纽约去了。她有两张_____。到纽约时
　　Shǐmìsī tàitai de xíngli yǐjīng tuōyùn dào Niǔyuē qù le. Tā yǒu liǎng zhāng _____. Dào Niǔyuē shí

　　她可以用这两张单子____行李。
　　tā kěyǐ yòng zhè liǎng zhāng dānzi _____xíngli.

9) 在飞机上，乘客得把手提行李放在前面座位的_____或者_____的行李舱里。
　　Zài fēijī shàng, chéngkè děi bǎ shǒutí xíngli fàng zài qiánmiàn zuòwèi de ___ huòzhě ___ de xínglicāng lǐ.

10) 要是行李太大，放不_____，她就得把这件行李_____。
　　Yàoshi xíngli tài dà, fàng bu_____ , tā jiù děi bǎ zhèi jiàn xíngli _____ .

5. Answer on the basis of Figure 1-4.

Fig. 1-4

1)　这位女乘客在哪儿？
　　zhèi wèi nǚ chéngkè zài nǎr?

2)　她在跟谁说话？
　　Tā zài gēn shéi shuōhuà?

3) 她给航空公司小姐的是什么？
   Tā gěi hángkōng gōngsī xiǎojiě de shi shénme?

4) 她有几件行李？
   Tā yǒu jǐ jiàn xíngli?

5) 这些行李都是手提行李吗？
   Zhèixiē xíngli dōu shi shǒutí xíngli ma?

6) 她的手提行李是什么？
   Tāde shǒutí xíngli shi shénme?

7) 这个包能放进座位底下或者是头顶上方的行李舱吗？
   Zhèige bāo néng fàngjìn zuòwèi dǐxia huòzhě shi tóudǐng shàngfāng de xínglicāng ma?

8) 航空公司小姐给她的是什么？
   Hángkōng gōngsī xiǎojiě gěi tā de shi shénme?

9) 她的座位在哪儿？
   Tāde zuòwèi zài nǎr?

10) 她要托运几件行李？
    Tā yào tuōyùn jǐ jiàn xíngli?

6. Choose the appropriate word.

1) 乘客们得出示他们的护照，因为他们坐的是＿＿＿＿航班。
   Chéngkèmen děi chūshì tāmende hùzhào, yīnwei tāmen zuò de shi _____háng bān.

   a. 国际   b. 国内   c. 长途
      guójì   guónèi   chángtú

2) C 座靠＿＿＿＿＿＿＿＿＿。
   C zuò kào _____.

   a. 窗   b. 服务台   c. 走道
      chuāng   fúwùtái   zǒudào

3) 为了识别乘客的行李，得在行李上贴上＿＿＿＿＿＿。
   Wèile shíbié chéngkè de xíngli, děi zài xíngli shàng tiēshàng ____.

   a. 标签   b. 座位   c. 包
      biāoqiān   zuòwèi   bāo

4) 没有＿＿＿＿＿就不能上飞机。
   Méiyǒu ____jiù bù néng shàng fēijī.

   a. 标签   b. 登机牌   c. 行李领取单
      biāoqiān   dēngjīpái   xíngli lǐngqǔdān

5) 我的座位在22＿＿＿＿＿C＿＿＿＿＿。
   Wǒ de zuòwèi zài 22_____C_____.

   a. 排/座   b. 座/排   c. 排/窗
      pái/zuò   zuò/pái   pái/chuāng

DEPARTURE AND ARRIVAL

离港和**到港**
Lígǎng he *dàogǎng*

航空公司**广播通知**了**飞往**纽约的	broadcast, announce, bound for
Hángkōng gōngsī *guǎngbō tōngzhī* le *fēi wǎng* Niǔyuē de	
430次班机的**离港**时间。	departure
sìsānlíng cì bānjī de *lígǎng* shíjiān.	
乘客们都得**通过安全**检查门。	pass through, security
Chéngkèmen dōu děi *tōngguò ānquán* jiǎnchá mén.	
他们也得交**机场费**[2]。	airport departure tax
Tāmen yě děi jiāo *jīchǎngfèi*.	
他们**马上**去**8号登机口**上飞机。	immediately, number 8, gate
Tāmen *mǎshàng* qù *bā hào dēngjīkǒu* shàng fēijī.	
飞机就要**起飞**了。	take off
Fēijī jiùyào *qǐfēi* le.	

7. Complete.

1) 航空公司_____通知了起飞时间。
   Hángkōng gōngsī _____tōngzhīle qǐfēi shíjiān.

2) 他们通知了430次_____的起飞时间。
   Tāmen tōngzhīle 430 cì_____ de qǐfēi shíjiān.

3) 430 次班机是_____纽约的班机。
   430 cì bānjī shi _____Niǔyuē de bānjī.

4) 乘客们都得_____安全检查门。
   Chéngkèmen dōu děi _____ānquán jiǎnchámén.

5) 机场人员在_____检查乘客们的行李。
   Jīchǎng rényuán zài _____ jiǎnchá chéngkèmen de xíngli.

6) 430次班机的乘客们要去_____登机口上飞机。
   430 cì bānjī de chéngkèmen yào qù _____dēngjīkǒu shàng fēijī.

7) 他们得马上去_____。
   Tāmen děi mǎshàng qù _____.

8) 飞机就要_____了。
   Fēijī jiù yào _____le.

---

[2] All airports in China collect departure tax, for both international and domestic flights, in Chinese yuan. Travelers should keep some Chinese cash for this purpose before departure.

An Arrival Announcement:

乘客们请**注意**，乘客们请注意，   attention, pay attention to
Chéngkèmen qǐng *zhùyì*, chéngkè men qǐng zhùyì.

从上海来的一百二十九(129)次班机已经**到达**本港，   from, arrive
Cóng shànghǎi lái de yībǎièrshíjiǔ cì bānjī yǐjīng *dàodá* běngǎng.

乘客**将**从十号登机口**出港**。   will, disembark
Chéngkè *jiāng* cóng shí hào dēngjīkǒu *chūgǎng*.

8. Complete.

A： 对不起，我没听懂这个广播。他们是在__1__我们的起飞时间吗？
   Duìbuqǐ, wǒ méi tīngdǒng zhèi ge guǎngbō. Tāmen shi zài __1__ wǒmende qǐfēi shíjiān ma?

B： 不是，他们在说另一个航班已经__2__了。
   Búshi, tāmen zài shuō lìng yī ge hángbān yǐjīng __2__ le.

A： 是哪个航班？
   Shi něige hángbān?

B： 是__3__上海来的129次__4__。
   Shi __3__ Shànghǎi lái de yìbǎièrshíjiǔ cì __4__.

9. Give the opposite of each of the following.

1) 到达
    dàodá

2) 上飞机
    shàng fēijī

3) 从...来
    cóng ...lái

CHANGING AN AIRLINE TICKET

我**误了大陆**航空公司去上海的班机。   missed, mainland
Wǒ *wùle Dàlù* Hángkōng Gōngsī qù Shànghǎi de bānjī.

好在中国航空还有一班去上海的飞机，   fortunately, China
Hǎozài Zhōngguó Hángkōng hái yǒu yì bān qù Shànghǎi de fēijī.

飞机还没有**满员**，还有**空座位**，   full, vacant seat
Fēijī hái méiyǒu *mǎnyuán*, hái yǒu *kòng zuòwèi*.

这班飞机不是**直飞**航班，   non stop
Zhèi bān fēijī bú shi *zhífēi* hángbān.

它要在南京**停**一个钟头，   stop
Tā yào zài Nánjīng *tíng* yí ge zhōngtóu.

可是我不必**转机**。   change planes/transfer
Kěshì wǒ búbì *zhuǎnjī*.

两个航空公司的**票价**都一样。   fare
Liǎng ge hángkōng gōngsī de *piàojià* dōu yíyàng.

价钱没有什么不同。   price
Jiàqián méiyǒu shénme bùtóng.

大陆航空公司可以把他们的票**转让**给中国航空公司。   endorse
Dàlù Hángkōng Gōngsī kěyǐ bǎ tāmen de piào *zhuǎnràng* gěi
Zhōngguó Hángkōng Gōngsī.

10. Complete.

A：对不起，我__1__了去上海的飞机。今天还有去上海的__2__吗？
　　Duìbuqǐ, Wǒ __1__ le qù Shànghǎi de fēijī. Jīntiān hái yǒu qù Shànghǎi de __2__ ma?

B：还有。我们还有一班三点二十分开的飞机。您是一个人吗？
　　Hái yǒu. Wǒmen hái yǒu yì bān sān diǎn èrshí fēn kāi de fēijī. Nín shi yí ge rén ma?

A：对，一个人。
　　Duì, yí ge rén.

B：我看看这班飞机__3__了没有，还有没有__4__。噢，还没满员！
　　Wǒ kànkan zhèi bān fēijī __3__ le méi yǒu. Hái yǒu méiyǒu __4__. Ò, hái méi mǎnyuán!

A：啊！太好了！__5__一样吗？
　　A! Tài hǎo le! __5__ yíyàng ma?

B：一样。这两个航空公司的机票__6__都一样。
　　Yíyàng. Zhè liǎng ge hángkōng gōngsī de jīpiào __6__ dōu yíyàng.

A：我可以就用这张票吗？
　　Wǒ kèyǐ jiù yòng zhèi zhāng piào ma?

B：可以。可是大陆航空公司得把这张票__7__给我们。
　　Kěyǐ. Kěshì Dàlù Hángkōng Gōngsī děi bǎ zhèi zhāng piào __7__ gěi wǒmen.

A：这班飞机是__8__吗？
　　Zhèi bān fēijī shi __8__ ma?

B：不是，得在南京__9__一下。
　　Búshi. Dèi zài Nánjīng __9__ yíxià.

　　史密斯先生(Mr. Smith)到了飞机场。他看见两个登机楼。东楼是国际航班楼，
　　Shǐmìsī xiānsheng dào le fēijīchǎng. Tā kànjiàn liǎng ge dēngjīlóu. Dōnglóu shi guójì hángbān lóu.

西楼是国内航班楼。他要坐国际航班，所以他去了东楼。他在航空
Xīlóu shi guónèi hángbān lóu. Tā yào zuò guójì hángbān, suǒyǐ tā qù le dōng lóu. Tā zài hángkōng

公司的柜台办理登机手续。他出示了自己的机票。航空公司的机场职员
gōngsī de guìtái bànlǐ dēngjī shǒuxù. Tā chūshì le zìjǐ de jīpiào. Hángkōng gōngsī de jīchǎng zhíyuán

也检查了他的护照。一切都很快办好了。他把他的行李交给了机场职员。他
yě jiǎnchá le tā de hùzhào. Yíqiè dōu hěn kuài bànhǎo le. Tā bǎ tāde xíngli jiāogěi le jīchǎng zhíyuán. Tā

有两个箱子要托运。职员把行李托运标签贴在他的行李上。她对史密斯
yǒu liǎng ge xiāngzi yào tuōyùn. Zhíyuán bǎ xíngli tuōyùn biāoqiān tiē zài tāde xíngli shàng. Tā duì Shǐmìsī

先生说他可以在到达纽约以后领取行李。职员也给史密斯先生要带上
xiānshen shuō tā kěyǐ zài dàodá Niǔyuē yǐhòu lǐngqǔ xíngli. Zhíyuán yě gěi Shǐmìsī xiānsheng yào dàishàng

飞机的手提行李贴了一个标签。职员说他的手提行李必须能放进座位底下
fēijī de shǒutí xíngli tiē le yí ge biāoqiān. Zhíyuán shuō tāde shǒutí xíngli bìxū néng fàng jìn zuòwèi dǐxia

或者是座位上头的行李舱里。史密斯先生说他已经预定了一个靠走道
huòzhě shi zuòwèi shàngtou de xínglicāng lǐ. Shǐmìsī xiānsheng shuō tā yǐjīng yùdìngle yí ge kào zǒudào

的座位。机场职员说电脑上没有显示他有一个预订的座位。
de zuòwèi. Jīchǎng zhíyuán shuō diànnǎo shàng méiyǒu xiǎnshì tā yǒu yí ge yùdìng de zuòwèi.

可是没问题。飞机不满，有很多靠走道的空座位。职员给了史密斯先生
kěshì méi wèntí. Fēijī bù mǎn, yǒu hěn duō kào zǒudào de kòng zuòwèi. Zhíyuán gěi le Shǐmìsī xiānsheng

一张登机牌。她说他的座位是在25排C座。飞往纽约的215次班机要在
yì zhāng dēngjīpái. Tā shuō tāde zuòwèi shi zài 25 pái C zuò. Fēiwǎng Niǔyuē de 215 cì bānjī yào zài

六号登机口离港。史密斯先生想知道这是不是直飞航班。职员说，
liù hào dēngjīkǒu lígǎng. Shǐmìsī xiānsheng xiǎng zhīdao zhè shì bu shì zhífēi hángbān, Zhíyuán shuō,

不是。飞机要在东京(Tokyo)停三个钟头，可是乘客不必转机。从那儿飞机会
bú shi, Fēijī yào zài Dōngjīng tíng sān ge zhōngtóu, kěshì chéngkè bú bì zhuǎngjī. Cóng nàr fēijī huì

一直飞到纽约。
yìzhí fēidào Niǔyuē.

　　当史密斯先生离开柜台的时候，他听到了航空公司的广播通知：
　　Dāng Shǐmìsī xiānsheng líkāi guìtái de shíhou, tā tīngdàole hángkōng gōngsī de guǎngbō tōngzhī:

飞往东京、纽 约的215次航班已经在6号登机口开始登机了。
fēi wǎng Dōngjīng, Niǔyuē de 215 cì hángbān yǐjīng zài liù hào dēngjīkǒu kāishǐ dēngjī le.

11. Complete.

1) 飞机场有两个_____，一个是国际_____，另一个是 _____登机楼。
    Fēijīchǎng yǒu liǎng ge_____ . Yí ge shi guójì_____, lìng yí ge shi _____dēngjīlóu.

2) 机场_____在_____公司的_____工作。
    Jīchǎng _____zài _____ gōngsī de _____ gōngzuò.

3) 机场职员检查乘客们的_____。
    Jīchǎng zhíyuán jiǎnchá chéngkèmen de_____.

4) 要是乘客坐的是国际航班，他们也得出示他们的 _____。
    Yàoshi chéngkè zuò de shi guójì hángbān, tāmen yě děi chūshì tāmen de _____ .

5) 史密斯先生把他的_____交给了职员，他只带了一件手提行李。
    Shǐmìsī xiānsheng bǎ tā de _____ jiāogěile zhíyuán, tā zhǐ dàile yí jiàn shǒutí xíngli.

6) 职员把_____放在机票信封里。史密斯先生要用这个_____取行李。
    Zhíyuán bǎ _____fàng zài jīpiào xìnfēng lǐ. Shǐmìsī xiānsheng yào yòng zhèi ge _____qǔ xíngli.

7) 史密斯先生的_____必须能够放进前面座位的底下。
    Shǐmìsī xiānsheng de _____ bìxū nénggòu fàngjìn qiánmian zuòwèi de dǐxia.

8) 史密斯先生想要一个_____的座位。
    Shǐmìsī xiānsheng xiǎng yào yí ge _____ de zuòwèi.

9) 电脑没显示史密斯先生_____的座位。
    Diànnǎo méi xiǎnshì Shǐmìsī xiānsheng _____ de zuòwèi.

10) 可是没问题。飞机没有＿＿＿＿，还有很多＿＿＿＿。
    Kěshì méi wèntí. fēijī méi yǒu ＿＿＿＿, hái yǒu hěn duō ＿＿＿＿ .

11) 史密斯先生拿到了他的＿＿＿＿＿＿。他的座位在25＿＿＿＿C＿＿＿＿。
    Shǐmìsī xiānsheng nádào le tā de ＿＿＿＿＿. Tā de zuòwèi zài 25＿＿＿＿C＿＿＿＿. .

12) ＿＿＿＿纽约的这班飞机得在东京＿＿＿＿三个钟头。
    ＿＿＿＿Niǔyuē de zhèi bān fēijī děi zài Dōngjīng ＿＿＿＿sān ge zhōngtóu.

13) 可是史密斯先生不必＿＿＿＿。
    Kěshì Shǐmìsī xiānsheng bú bì ＿＿＿＿ .

14) 广播通知说飞往纽约、东京的班机就要＿＿＿＿了。
    Guǎngbō tōngzhī shuō fēiwǎng Niǔyuē, Dōngjīng de bānjī jiù yào ＿＿＿＿ le.

15) 乘坐215次班机的乘客都要在6号＿＿＿＿上飞机。
    Chéngzuò 215 cì bānjī de chéngkè dōu yào zài 6 hào ＿＿＿＿ shàng fēijī.

12. Answer.

1) 史密斯先生到了什么地方？
   Shǐmìsī xiānsheng dào le shénme dìfang?

2) 这个飞机场有几个登机楼？
   Zhèi ge fēijīchǎng yǒu jǐ ge dēngjīlóu?

3) 为什么有两个登机楼？
   Wèishénme yǒu liǎng ge dēngjīlóu?

4) 在国际航班登机楼里，史密斯先生去了什么地方？
   Zài guójì hángbān dēngjīlǒu lǐ, Shǐmìsī xiānsheng qù le shénme dìfang?

5) 他为什么要去那儿？
   Tā wèishénme yào qù nàr?

6) 他有几件托运行李？
   Tā yǒu jǐ jiàn tuōyùn xíngli?

7) 他可以在哪儿领取行李？
   Tā kěyǐ zài nǎr lǐngqǔ xíngli?

8) 他领取行李的时候得出示什么？
   Tā lǐngqǔ xíngli de shíhou děi chūshì shénme?

9) 他要带什么上飞机？
   Tā yào dài shénme shàng fēijī?

10) 他得把他的手提行李放在哪儿？
    Tā děi bǎ tāde shǒutí xíngli fàng zài nǎr?

11) 他预订座位了吗？
    Tā yùdìng zuòwèi le ma?

12) 为什么职员说他没有问题？
    Wèishénme zhíyuán shuō tā méiyǒu wèntí?

13) 他得到了一个什么座位？
    Tā dédàole yí ge shénme zuòwèi?

14) 他得从哪个登机口登机？
    Tā děi cóng něige dēngjīkǒu dēngjī?

15) 这班飞机是直飞航班吗?
   Zhèi bān fēijī shi zhífēi hángbān ma?

SOME PROBLEMS YOU MAY HAVE

飞机不能**正点**起飞了。   on time
Fēijī bùnéng *zhèngdiǎn* qǐfēi le.

飞机**晚点**了。   delay
Fēijī *wǎndiǎn* le.

飞机要**推迟**45分钟起飞。   postpone
Fēijī yào *tuīchí* sìshiwǔ fēnzhōng qǐfēi.

另一个航班**取消**了。   cancel
Lìng yí ge hángbān *qǔxiāo* le.

因为**天气**问题所以航班取消了。   weather
Yīnwèi *tiānqì* wèntí suǒyǐ hángbān qǔxiāo le.

13. Answer.

1) 飞机能正点起飞吗?
   Fēijī néng zhèngdiǎn qǐfēi ma?

2) 飞机要推迟多久起飞?
   Fēijī yào tuīchí duōjiǔ qǐfēi?

3) 有被取消的航班吗?
   Yǒu bèi qǔxiāo de hángbān ma?

4) 为什么取消了?
   Wèishénme qǔxiāo le?

KEY WORDS

airline company	航空公司	hángkōng gōngsī	broadcast	广播	guǎngbō
airline ticket	飞机票	fēijīpiào	bus	公共汽车	gōnggòng qìchē
airport	飞机场	fēijīchǎng	canceled	取消	qǔxiāo
airport departure tax	机场费	jīchǎng fèi	carry-on luggage	手提行李	shǒutí xíngi
aisle seat	靠走道座位	kào zǒudào zuò wèi	change planes	转机	zhuǎn jī
			check	检查	jiǎnchá
announce	通知	tōngzhī	check in	办理登机手续	bànlǐ dēngjī shǒuxù
arrive	到达/到港	dàodá/ dàogǎng			
attention, pay attention to	注意	zhùyì	check in (luggage)	托运 (行李)	tuōyùn (xíngli)
board the plane	登机	dēngjī	China	中国	Zhōngguó
boarding gate	登机口	dēngjīkǒu	city terminal	市内总站	shìnèi zǒngzhàn
boarding pass	登机牌	dēngjīpái	claim	领取	lǐngqǔ
Bon Voyage!	旅途愉快	lǚtú yúkuài	claim stub	领取单	lǐngqǔ dān
bound for	飞往	fēiwǎng	compartment	舱	cāng
briefcase	公文包	gōngwénbāo	counter	柜台	guì tái

delay	晚点	wǎndiǎn	overhead	头顶上方	tóudǐng shàngfāng
departure time	离港时间	lígǎng shíjiān	pass through	通过	tōngguò
disembark	出港	chūgǎng	passenger	乘客	chéngkè
document(s)	文件	wénjiàn	passport	护照	hùzhào
domestic	国内	guónèi	please...	请	qǐng
endorse	转让	zhuǎnràng	postpone	推迟	tuīchí
fare	票价	piàojià	price	价钱	jiàqián
fit	能放进	néng fàngjìn	reception	接待	jiēdài
flight	航班/班机	hángbān/bānjī	reserve, book	预定	yùdìng
fortunately	好在	hǎozài	row	排	pái
from	从	cóng	seat	座	zuò
full	满员	mǎnyuán	security	安全	ānquán
Here you are.	在这儿	zài zhèr	show	出示	chūshì
immediately	马上	mǎshàng	stop	停	tíng
international	国际	guójì	suitcase	箱子	xiāngzi
label	标签	biāoqiān	take a taxi	坐出租车	zuò chūzūchē
land	着陆	zhuólù	take off	起飞	qǐfēi
line up	排队	páiduì	terminal	登机楼	dēngjīlóu
luggage	行李	xíngli	vacant seat	空座位	kòng zuòwèi
mainland	大陆	dàlù	visa	签证	qiānzhèng
missed	误了	wùle	weather	天气	tiānqì
must	必须	bìxū	will (formal), about to	将	jiāng
no problem.	没问题	méi wènti			
nonstop	直飞	zhífēi	window seat	靠窗的座位	kàochuāng de zuò wèi
number 8	8号	bā hào			
on time	正点	zhèngdiǎn			

Chapter 2: On the airplane

第二章：在飞机上
Zài fēijī shàng

WELCOME ON BOARD

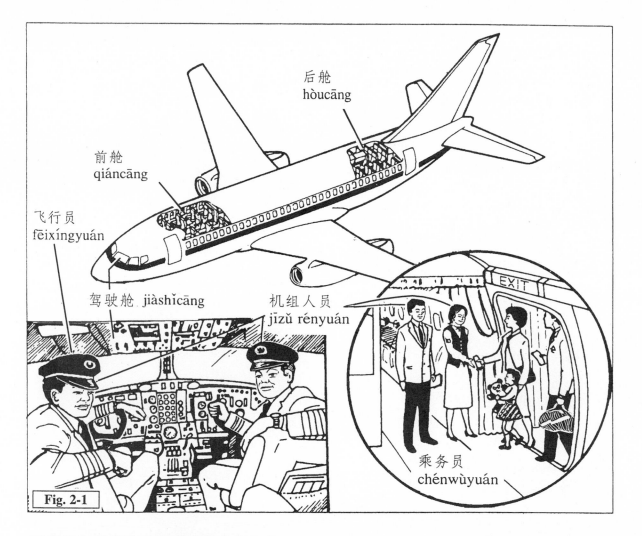

后舱
hòucāng

前舱
qiáncāng

飞行员
fēixíngyuán

驾驶舱 jiàshǐcāng

机组人员
jīzǔ rényuán

乘务员
chénwùyuán

Fig. 2-1

飞行员和**机组人员**要保证乘客的**安全**。　　　　　pilot, crew, safety
Fēixíngyuán hé *jīzǔ rényuán* yào bǎozhèng chéngkè de *ānquán*.

飞机**乘务员**在飞机上为乘客服务。　　　　　　　　flight attendants
Fēijī chéngwùyuán zài fēijī shàng wèi chéngkè fúwù.

他们在门口**欢迎**乘客。　　　　　　　　　　　　welcome
Tāmen zài ménkǒu huānyíng chéngkè.

飞机**前舱**是**头等舱**。　　　　　　　　　　front cabin, first class
Fēijī qiáncāng shi tóuděngcāng.

15

飞机**后舱**是**经济**舱。   rear cabin, economy class
Fēijī *hòucāng* shi *jīngjìcāng*.

飞行期间乘客不能进入**驾驶舱**。   cockpit
Fēixíng qījiān chéngkè bùnéng jìnrù *jiàshǐcāng*.

飞机要从北京**起飞**。   take off
Fēijī yào cóng Běijīng *qǐfēi*.

飞机要在纽约**着陆**。   land
Fēijī yào zài Niǔyuē *zhuólù*.

1. Complete.

1) 飞机上所有的工作人员都是_____。
    Fēijī shàng suǒyǒu de gōngzuò rényuán dōushi _____.

2) _____在驾驶舱工作。
    _____ zài jiàshǐcāng gōngzuò.

3) _____为乘客服务。
    _____ wèi chéngkè fúwù.

4) _____比前舱大。
    _____ bǐ qiáncāng dà.

5) 坐_____旅行的乘客坐在前舱。
    Zuò _____ lǚxíng de chéngkè zuòzài qiáncāng.

6) 坐_____旅行的乘客坐在后舱。
    Zuò _____ lǚxíng de chéngkè zuòzài hòucāng.

7) 机组人员要保证乘客的_____。
    Jīzǔ rényuán yào bǎozhèng chéngkè de _____.

8) 飞行期间乘客不准进入_____。
    Fēixíng qījiān chéngkè bùzhǔn jìnrù _____.

9) 航行开始的时候，飞机从机场_____。
    Hángxíng kāishǐ de shíhou, fēijī cóng jīchǎng _____.

10) 航行结束的时候，飞机在机场_____。
    Hángxíng jiéshù de shíhou, fēijī zài jīchǎng _____.

ANOUNCEMENTS ON BOARD

我们的**飞行时间**差不多是**16小时20分钟**。   flying time, hour, minute
Wǒmen de *fēixíng shíjiān* chàbuduō shi 16 *xiǎoshí* 20 *fēnzhōng*.

飞行**高度**是(**海拔**)10，000(一万)**米**。   altitude, above sea level, meter
Fēixíng *gāodù* shi (*hǎibá*) yíwàn *mǐ*.

飞行**速度**是一小时800(八百)**公里**。   speed, kilometer
Fēixíng *sùdù* shi yī xiǎoshí bābǎi *gōnglǐ*.

2. Complete.

　　女士们，先生们：本机机长及全体__1__ __2__你们乘坐本次班机。
　　Nǚshìmen, xiānshengmen：Běnjī jīzhǎng jí quántǐ _1_ _2_ nǐmen chéngzuò běn cì bānjī.

本次班机是从北京飞往纽约的281次航班。我们5分钟以后
Běn cì bānjī shi cóng Běijīng fēiwǎng Niǔyué de 281 cì hángbān. Wǒmen wǔ fēnzhōng yǐhòu

就要 ___3___ 了。我们从北京飞达纽约的___4___是16小时20分钟。
jiù yào _3_ le. Wǒmen cóng Běijīng fēidá Niǔyué de _4_ shi shíliù xiǎoshí èrshí fēnzhōng.

飞行___5___将是10，000米。飞行___6___是每___7___800公里。
Fēixíng _5_ jiāng shi yíwàn mǐ. Fēixíng _6_ shi měi _7_ bābǎi gōnglǐ.

SAFETY ON BOARD

救生衣　　紧急出口
jiùshēngyī　　jǐnjí chūkǒu
氧气面罩
yǎngqì miànzhào
托盘餐桌
tuōpán cānzhuō

Fig. 2-2

如果有紧急情况，　　　　　　　　　　　　if, emergency
Rúguǒ yǒu jǐnjí qíngkuàng,

救生衣就在您的座位底下。　　　　　　　　life vest
jiùshēngyī jiù zài nínde zuòwèi dǐxia.

如果空气压力有变化，　　　　　　　　　　air pressure, change
Rúguǒ kōngqì yālì yǒu biànhuà,

氧气罩会自动降下。　　　　　　　　　　　oxygen mask, automatically
yǎngqìzhào huì zìdòng jiàngxià,

飞机前舱有两个紧急出口，　　　　　　　　emergency exit
Fēijī qiáncāng yǒu liǎngge jǐnjí chūkǒu,

后舱也有两个紧急出口。
Hòucāng yě yǒu liǎngge jǐnjí chūkǒu.

机翼附近也有紧急出口。　　　　　　　　　　　wing
Jīyì fùjìn yě yǒu jǐnjí chūkǒu

在飞机起飞和着陆的时候，
Zài fēijī qǐfēi he zhuólù de shíhou,

乘客们都应该**坐好**，**系紧安全带**。　　　remain seated, fasten, seat belt
chéngkèmen dōu yīnggāi *zuòhǎo, jìjǐn ānquándài.*

在飞机飞行期间，
Zài fēijī fēixíng qījiān,

也应该**继续**系好安全带。　　　　　　　　keep (doing), continue
yě yīnggāi *jìxù* jìhǎo ānquándài.

有时候飞机会**遇上突然**的**湍流**，　　　encounter, unexpected, turbulence
Yǒu shíhou fēijī huì *yùshàng tūrán* de *tuānliú,*

遇上湍流的时候，飞机会**颠簸**。　　　　bounce/bump
Yùshàng tuānliú de shíhou, fēijī huì *diānbǒ.*

3. Answer.

1)　救生衣在飞机上的什么地方？
　　Jiùshēngyī zài fēijī shàng de shénme dìfāng?

2)　要是空气压力有变化，会发生什么事？
　　Yàoshi kōngqì yālì yǒu biànhuà, huì fāshēng shénme shì?

3)　飞机上的紧急出口都在哪儿？
　　Fēijī shàng de jǐnjí chūkǒu dōu zài nǎr?

4. Complete.

在飞机　1　和　2　的时候，飞机上的乘客们都得　3　。他们不能在飞机上
Zài fēijī 　1　 hé 　2　 de shíhou, fēijī shàng de chéngkèmen dōu děi 　3　. Tāmen bùnéng zài fēijī shàng

走动。他们不但要坐在座位上，还必须　4　安全带。在飞行期间他们也最好
zǒudòng. Tāmen búdàn yào zuò zài zuòwèi shàng, hái bìxū 　4　 ānquándài. Zài fēixíng qījiān tāmen yě zuìhǎo

继续系着　5　。我们不知道飞机什么时候会遇上突然的　6　。要是有湍流，飞机
jìxù jì zhe 　5　. Wǒmen bù zhīdao fēijī shénme shíhou huì yùshàng tūrán de 　6　, Yàoshi yǒu tuānliú, fēijī

就会　7　。
jiùhuì 　7　.

飞机上**不准抽烟**。　　　　　　　　　　　　no smoking
Fēijī shàng bù zhǔn *chōuyān.*

洗手间内装有抽烟**探测器**。　　　　　　toilet/washroom, detector
Xǐshǒujiān nèi zhuāng yǒu chōuyān *tàncèqì.*

被查出在洗手间抽烟的人会被**罚款**。　　be found out, fine
Bèi cháchū zài xǐshǒu jiān chōuyān de rén huì bèi *fákuǎn.*

飞机着陆后，乘客可以在
Fēijī zhuólù hòu, chéngkè kěyǐ zài

飞机场**指定**的**抽烟区**抽烟。   assigned, smoking area
fēijīchǎng *zhǐdìng* de *chōuyān qū* chōuyān.

5. Complete.

1) 飞机上的乘客不能_____。
    Fēijī shàng de chéngkè bù néng _____.

2) _____可以查出在_____抽烟的人。
    _____kěyǐ cháchū zài _____chōuyān de rén.

3) 在洗手间抽烟的人会被_____。
    Zài xǐshǒujiān chōuyān de rén huì bèi _____ .

4) 飞机场有指定的_____给乘客抽烟。
    Fēijīchǎng yǒu zhǐdìng de _____ gěi chéngkè chōuyān.

头顶上方的行李舱 tóudǐng shàngfāng de
xínglicāng

座椅靠背
zuòyǐ kàobèi

座位/座椅底下
zuòwèi/zuòyǐ dǐxia

Fig. 2-3

你不能把你的**手提行李**放在走道上。   carry-on luggage
Nǐ bù néng bǎ nǐde *shǒutí xíngli* fàng zài zǒudào shàng.

手提行李必须能**放进座位底下**。   fit under the seat
Shǒutí xíngli bìxū néng *fàngjìn zuòwèi dǐxia*.

要是你的行李不能放进座位底下，   if
Yàoshi nǐde xíngli bù néng fàng jìn zuòwèi dǐxia,

你就得把它放到**头顶上方**的**行李舱**里面。   overhead compartment
nǐ jiù děi bǎ tā fàngdào *tóudǐng shàngfāng* de *xínglicāng* lǐmiàn.

飞机起飞和着陆的时候，你得把**座椅靠背放直**。   seat back, straighten
Fēijī qǐfēi he zhuólù de shíhou, nǐ děi bǎ *zuòyǐ kàobèi fàngzhí*.

把**托盘餐桌收起来**。   tray table, put back

bǎ *tuōpán cānzhuō shōu qǐlai*.

6. Complete.

很多乘客都带手提行李上飞机。可是他们不能把行李放在＿＿1＿＿。
Hěnduō chéngkè dōu dài shǒutí xíngli shàng fēijī. Kěshì tāmen bù néng bǎ xíngli fàng zài ＿＿1＿＿

所有的行李都得放在＿＿2＿＿或者是＿＿3＿＿。为安全起见，在飞机起飞和
Suǒyǒu de xíngli dōu děi fàngzài ＿＿2＿＿ huòzhě shi ＿＿3＿＿. Wèi ānquán qǐjiàn, zài fēijī qǐfēi he

着陆的时候，你得把你的座椅＿＿4＿＿放直，而且，你也得把＿＿5＿＿收起来。
zhuólù de shíhou, nǐ děi bǎ nǐde zuòyǐ ＿＿4＿＿ fàngzhí. Érqiě, nǐ yě děi bǎ ＿＿5＿＿ shōu qǐlai.

SERVICE ON BOARD

飞行期间，我们会**供应饮料**和**餐点**。   serve, drink, meal
Fēixíng qījiān, wǒmen huì *gōngyìng yǐnliào* he *cāndiǎn*.

我们也有**报纸**和**杂志**。   newspaper, magazine
Wǒmen yě yǒu *bàozhǐ* he *zázhì*.

Fig. 2-4

飞机起飞以后，我们会供应**早餐**。   breakfast
Fēijī qǐfēi yǐhòu, wǒmen huì gōngyìng *zǎocān*.

想听**音乐**的乘客可以租用**耳机**。   music, headset
Xiǎng tīng *yīnyuè* de chéngkè kěyǐ zūyòng *ěrjī*.

每副耳机**租费**4元。   rent charge
Měi fù ěrjī *zūfèi* sì yuán.

我们一共有五个音乐**频道**。   channel
Wǒmen yígòng yǒu wǔ ge yīnyuè *píndào*.

我们也会放一个**电影**。   movie
Wǒmen yě huì fàng yí ge *diànyǐng*.

每个座位上都有**枕头**和**毛毯**。   pillow, blanket
Měi ge zuòwèi shàng dōu yǒu *zhěntou* he *máotǎn*.

座椅靠背上的**口袋**里有**纸袋**，   pocket, paper bag
Zuòyǐ kàobèi shàng de *kǒudài* lǐ yǒu *zhǐdài*.

给**晕机**的乘客**使用**   air sickness, use
gěi *yūnjī* de chéngkè *shǐyòng*.

7. Complete.

飞机飞行期间，乘务员会给我们供应____1____。飞机起飞以后，
Fēijī fēixíng qījiān, chéngwùyuán huì gěi wǒmen gōngyìng ____1____. Fēijī qǐfēi yǐhòu,

他们会给我们供应早餐。飞机上可以听____2____，一共有五个____3____。
tāmen huì gěi wǒmen gōngyìng zǎocān. Fēijī shàng kěyǐ tīng ____2____. Yígòng yǒu wǔ ge ____3____,

每个频道的音乐都不一样。有流行音乐，古典音乐等等。早餐后，
Měi ge píndào de yīnyuè dōu bù yíyàng. Yǒu liúxíng yīnyuè, gǔdiǎn yīnyuè děngděng. Zǎocān hòu,

他们会放一个____4____。要是你想看电影和听音乐，你可以用4元钱
tāmen huì fàng yíge ____4____. Yàoshi nǐ xiǎng kàn diànyǐng he tīng yīnyuè, nǐ kěyǐ yòng sì yuán qián

____5____一个____6____。要是你想睡觉，乘务员会给你____7____和____8____。
____5____ yí ge ____6____. Yàoshi nǐ xiǎng shuìjiào, chéngwùyuán huì gěi nǐ ____7____ he ____8____.

8. Complete.

我太累了。不想吃饭，不想听音乐，也不想看电影。我只想睡觉。
Wǒ tài lèi le. Bù xiǎng chīfàn, bù xiǎng tīng yīnyuè, yě bù xiǎng kàn diànyǐng. Wǒ zhǐ xiǎng shuìjiào.

可不可以给我一个____1____和一条____2____？
Kě bù kěyǐ gěi wǒ yí ge ____1____ he yì tiáo ____2____?

每天都有成千上万的人坐飞机旅行。乘客们上飞机的时候，
Měitiān dōu yǒu chéngqiānshàngwàn de rén zuò fēijī lǚxíng. Chéngkèmen shàng fēijī de shíhou,

乘务员和机组的其他成员都会站在门口。他们对乘客说"欢迎
chéngwùyuán he jīzǔ de qítā chéngyuán dōu huì zhànzài ménkǒu. Tāmen duì chéngkè shuō, "huānyíng

乘坐我们的飞机！"他们也检查乘客的登机牌。有时候，他们帮助乘客
chéngzuò wǒmen de fēijī." Tāmen yě jiǎnchá chéngkè de dēngjīpái. Yǒu shíhou, tāmen bāngzhu chéngkè

找到他们的座位。在豪华的大飞机上，后舱通 常是经济舱，前舱只是
zhǎodào tāmen de zuòwèi. Zài háohuá de dà fēijī shàng, hòu cāng tōngcháng shi jīngjìcāng, qián cāng zhǐ shi

给头等舱乘客坐的。飞机飞行的时候，有各种各样的通知。乘务员必须
gěi tóuděngcāng chéngkè zuòde. Fēijī fēixíng de shíhou, yǒu gèzhǒnggèyàng de tōngzhī. Chéngwùyuán bìxū

保证乘客们的舒适和安全。她们向乘客解释氧气面罩和救生衣
bǎozhèng chéngkèmen de shūshì he ānquán. Tāmen xiàng chéngkě jiěshi yǎngqì miànzhào hé jiùshēngyī

的用法。她们告诉乘客们紧急出口和洗手间在哪里。飞机上有一些重要的
de yòngfǎ. Tāmen gàosù chéngkèmen jǐnjí chūkǒu hé xǐshǒujiān zài nǎlǐ. Fēijī shàng yǒu yìxiē zhòngyào de

规则每个乘客都要遵守。所有的手提行李都得放在座位底下或者放
guīzé měi ge chéngkè dōu yào zūnshǒu. Suǒyǒu de shǒutí xíngli dōu děi fàng zài zuòwèi dǐxia huòzhě fàng

在头上的行李舱里。飞机上也不准抽烟。洗手间里装着抽烟探测器。
zài tóushang de xíngli cāng lǐ. Fēijī shàng yě bù zhǔn chōuyān. Xǐshǒujiān lǐ zhuāngzhe chōuyān tàncèqì.

要是你在洗手间抽烟被发现了，就会被罚款。飞机起飞和着陆的时候，
Yàoshi nǐ zài xǐshǒu jiān chōuyān bèi fāxiàn le, jiù huì bèi fákuǎn. Fēijī qǐfēi hé zhuǒlù de shíhou,

乘客们应该把座椅的靠背放直，系好安全带。乘务员常常强调
chéngkèmen yīnggāi bǎ zuòyǐ de kàobèi fàngzhí, jìhǎo ānquándài. Chéngwùyuán chángcháng qiángdiào

乘客们在飞机飞行期间也继续系着安全带。因为你不知道飞机什么时候会
chéngkèmen zài fēijī fēixíng qījiān yě jìxù jìzhe ānquándài. Yīnwèi nǐ bù zhīdao fēijī shénme shíhou huì

遇到湍流而颠簸。
yùdào tuānliú ér diānbǒ.

飞行期间，乘务员会供应饮料和餐点。她们也会给
Fēixíng qījiān, chéngwùyuán yěhuì gōngyìng yǐnliào he cāndiǎn. Tāmen yě huì gěi

想睡觉的乘客提供枕头和毛毯。在很多长途航班上，航空公司
xiǎng shuìjiào de chéngkè tígōng zhěntou he máotǎn. Zài hěnduō chángtú hángbān shàng, hángkōng gōngsī

会给乘客们放音乐和电影。乘务员会给想听音乐或者想看
huì gěi chéngkèmen fàng yīnyuè he diànyǐng. Chéngwùyuán huì gěi xiǎng tīng yīnyuè huòzhě xiǎng kàn

电影的乘客分发耳机。经济舱的乘客得交少量的租金才能使用耳机。
diànyǐng de chéngkè fēnfā ěrjī. Jīngjì cāng de chéngkè děi jiāo shǎoliàng de zūjīn cái néng shǐyòng ěrjī.

飞机飞行期间，乘客不准进入驾驶舱。飞行员常常通过
Fēijī fēixíng qījiān, chéngkè bù zhǔn jìnrù jiàshǐcāng. Fēixíngyuán chángcháng tōngguò

广播告诉乘客他们这次飞行大概需要的时间，通过的航线，
guǎngbō gàosù chéngkè tāmen zhècì fēixíng dàgài xūyào de shíjiān, tōngguò de hángxiàn,

飞机的飞行高度和速度等等。他们也会很客气地祝乘客们旅途愉快。
fēijī de fēixíng gāodù hé sùdù děngděng. Tāmen yě huì hěn kèqì de zhù chéngkèmen lǚtú yúkuài.

9. Complete.

1) 在豪华的大飞机上，一般有两个_____。
    Zài háohuá de dà fēijī shàng, yìbān yǒu liǎng ge _____.

2) _____舱是给头等_____的客人坐的。后舱是给_____舱的客人坐的。
    _____cāng shi gěi tóuděng _____de kèrén zuò de, hòucāng shi gěi _____cāng de kèrén zuò de .

3) 飞机_____在乘客们上飞机的时候检查他们的_____。
    Fēijī _____zài chéngkèmen shàng fēijī de shíhou jiǎnchá tāmen de _____ .

4) 要是气压发生变化，乘客们就要用_____来呼吸。
   Yàoshi qìyā fāshēng biànhuà, chéngkèmen jiù yào yòng _____ lái hūxī .

5) _____一定要能放进座位底下或者_____。
   _____ yīdìng yào néng fàng jìn zuòwèi dǐxia huòzhě _____.

6) 在飞机上乘客不准_____。洗手间里也装有_____。
   Zài fēijī shàng chéngkè bù zhǔn _____. Xǐshǒujiān lǐ yě zhuāng yǒu _____.

7) 被发现抽烟的人会被_____。
   Bèi fāxiàn chōuyān de rén huì bèi _____ .

8) 飞机起飞和_____的时候，乘客们得把他们的座椅靠背_____。
   Fēijī qǐfēi hé _____ de shíhou, chéngkè men děi bǎ tāmen de zuòyǐ kàobèi _____ .

9) 机组人员总是告诉乘客飞机飞行时在座位上要系好_____。
   Jīzǔ rényuán zǒngshi gàosù chéngkè fēijī fēixíng shí zài zuòwèi shàng yào jìhǎo _____ .

10) 飞机长途飞行时，乘务员会供应_____和_____。
    Fēijī chángtú fēixíng shí, chéngwùyuán huì gōngyìng _____ hé _____ .

11) 乘客需要用_____来听音乐或者看电影。
    Chéngkè xūyào yòng _____ lái tīng yīnyuè huòzhě kàn diànyǐng .

12) 飞机飞行时，任何人都不准进入_____。
    Fēijī fēixíng shí, rènhé rén dōu bù zhǔn jìnrù _____ .

10. Answer.

1) 乘客上飞机的时候飞机上的乘务员会做什么？
   Chéngkè shàng fēijī de shíhou, fēijī shàng de chéngwùyuán huì zuò shénme?

2) 豪华大飞机上的前舱是什么舱? 后舱是什么舱?
   Háohuá dà fēijī shàng de qiáncāng shi shénme cāng? Hòucāng shi shénme cāng?

3) 乘客们得学会用什么？
   Chéngkèmen děi xuéhuì yòng shénme?

4) 他们把手提行李放在哪儿？
   Tāmen bǎ shǒutí xíngli fàng zài nǎr?

5) 乘客可以在飞机上抽烟吗？
   Chéngkè kěyǐ zài fēijī shàng chōuyān ma?

6) 洗手间里为什么要装探测器？
   Xǐshǒujiān lǐ wèishénme yào zhuāng tàncèqì?

7) 飞机起飞和着陆的时候，乘客们得做什么？
   Fēijī qǐfēi he zhuólù de shíhou, chéngkèmen děi zuò shénme?

8) 为什么飞机飞行的时候乘客们最好系上安全带？
   Wèishénme fēijī fēixíng de shíhou, chéngkèmen zuìhǎo jìshàng ānquándài?

9) 乘务员会给乘客们供应什么？
   Chéngwùyuán huì gěi chéngkèmen gōngyìng shénme?

10) 飞行员会给乘客们广播哪些通知？
    Fēixíngyuán huì gěi chéngkèmen guǎngbō nǎxiē tōngzhī?

11. Match.

1) 飞机上的所有工作人员叫_____。
   Fēijī shàng de suǒyǒu gōngzuò rényuán jiào _____.

2) 气压发生变化时，_____会自动降下。
   Qìyā fāshēng biànhuà shí, _____huì zìdòng jiàngxià.

3) 乘客们必须有_____才能上飞机。
   Chéngkèmen bìxū yǒu _____ cái néng shàng fēijī.

4) 飞机起飞和着陆时_____必须放直。
   Fēijī qǐfēi hé zhuólù shí _____bìxū fàngzhí.

5) 飞机起飞和着陆时乘客必须系好_____。
   Fēijī qǐfēi hé zhuólù shí chéngkè bìxū jìhǎo _____.

6) _____为乘客供应餐点和饮料。
   _____wèi chéngkè gōngyìng cāndiǎn hé yǐnliào.

7) 要是有紧急情况，乘客们就得去_____。
   Yàoshi yǒu jǐnjí qíngkuàn, chéngkèmen jiù děi qù _____.

8) 你可以把手提行李放在_____。
   Nǐ kěyǐ bǎ shǒutí xíngli fàng zài _____.

9) 飞机飞行的路线叫_____。
   Fēijī fēixíng de lùxiàn jiào _____.

10) 在驾驶舱工作的人员叫_____。
    Zài jiàshǐcāng gōngzuò de rényuán jiào _____.

a. 座椅靠背
   zuòyǐ kàobèi

b. 飞行员
   fēixíngyuán

c. 乘务员
   chéngwùyuán

d. 航线
   hángxiàn

e. 紧急出口
   jǐnjí chūkǒu

f. 座位底下
   zuòwèi dǐxia

g. 安全带
   ānquándài

h. 登机牌
   dēngjīpái

i. 氧气面罩
   yǎngqì miànzhào

j. 机组人员
   jīzǔ rényuán

KEY WORDS

air pressure	气压	qìyā	encounter	遇上	yùshàng
airplane	飞机	fēijī	fasten	系紧	jìjǐn
air sickness	晕机	yūnjī	fine	罚款	fákuǎn
above sea level	海拔	hǎibá	first class	头等(舱)	tóuděng (cāng)
altitude, height	高度	gāodù	fit	能放进	néng fàngjìn
assigned	指定的	zhǐdìng de	flight attendants	乘务员	chéngwùyuán
automatically	自动	zìdòng	flying time	飞行时间	fēixíng shíjiān
be found out	被发现	bèi fāxiàn	forward	前	qián
blanket	毛毯	máotǎn	headset	耳机	ěrjī
bounce/bump	颠簸	diānbǒ	hour	小时/钟头	xiǎoshí/zhōngtóu
breakfast	早餐	zǎocān	if	要是	yàoshì
carry-on luggage	随身行李	suíshēn xíngli	in case of	如果	rúguǒ
change	换	huàn	keep (doing)	继续	jìxù
channel	频道	píndào	kilometer	公里	gōnglǐ
cockpit	驾驶舱	jiàshǐcāng	land	着陆	zhuólù
crew	机组人员	jīzǔ rényuán	life vest	救生衣	jiùshēngyī
detector	探测器	tàncèqì	magazine	杂志	zázhì
drink	饮料	yǐnliào	meal	餐点	cāndiǎn
economy class	经济(舱)	jīngjì (cāng)	meter	米	mǐ
emergency	紧急情况	jǐnjí qíngkuàng	minute	分钟	fēnzhōng
emergency exit	紧急出口	jǐnjí chūkǒu	movie	电影	diànyǐng

music	音乐	yīnyuè	seat back	座椅靠背	zuòyǐ kàobèi
newspaper	报纸	bàozhǐ	seat belt	安全带	ānquándài
no smoking	不准抽烟	bùzhǔn chōuyān	seated	坐好	zuòhǎo
on	在...上	zài...shàng	serve	供应	gōngyìng
original position	原来位置	yuánlái wèizhì	smoking area	抽烟区	chōuyān qū
overhead compartment	头顶舱	tóudǐngcāng	speed	速度	sùdù
			straighten	放直	fàngzhí
oxygen mask	氧气罩	yǎngqìzhào	take off	起飞	qǐfēi
paper bag	纸袋	zhǐdài	toilet/washroom	洗手间	xǐshǒujiān
pillow	枕头	zhěntou	tray table	托盘餐桌	tuōpán cānzhuō
pilot	飞行员	fēixíngyuán	turbulence	湍流	tuānliú
pocket	口袋	kǒudài	under the seat	座位/座椅	zuòwèi/zuòyǐ
put back	收起来	shōu qǐlai	unexpected	突然	tūrán
rear cabin	后舱	hòucāng	use	用	yòng
remain	继续,保持	jìxù, bǎochí	welcome	欢迎	huānyíng
rent charge	租金	zūjīn	wing	机翼	jīyì
safety	安全	ānquán			

Chapter 3: Passport control and customs

第三章：入境检查和海关
Rùjìng jiǎnchá he hǎiguān

AT THE PASSPORT CONTROL OFFICE

A：这是我的**护照**。   passport
Zhèi shi wǒ de *hùzhào*.

　　　签证   visa
　　　qiānzhèng

B：您**打算**在这儿**呆多久**?   plan, stay, how long
Nín *dǎsuàn* zài zhèr *dāi duō jiǔ*?

A：**只**有几天。   only
Zhí yǒu jǐ tiān.

　　　一个**星期**   week
　　　yí ge *xīngqī*

　　　一个**月**   month
　　　yí ge *yuè*

B：您来这儿是**有公务**还是**旅游**?   on business, tour
Nín lái zhèr shi *yǒu gōngwù* háishi *lǚyóu*?

A：我只是**路过**。   pass through, pass by
Wǒ zhǐ shi *lùguò*.

1. Complete.

在入境检查处
Zài rùjìng jiǎnchá chù

A：请给我看看您的__1__。
Qǐng gěi wǒ kànkan nín de __1__.

B：这是我的__2__。
Zhè shi wǒ de __2__.

A：您打算在这儿呆__3__?
Nín dǎsuan zài zhèr dāi __3__?

B：我只在这儿__4__一个星期。
Wǒ zhǐ zài zhèr __4__ yí ge xīngqī.

26

A：您打算__5__在哪儿?
Nín dǎsuàn __5__ zài nǎr?

B：北京饭店。
Běijīng Fàndiàn.

A：您来这儿是__6__还是旅游?
Nín lái zhèr shi __6__ háishi lǚyóu?

B：__7__。我是来度假的。
__7__. Wǒ shi lái dùjià de .

AT CUSTOMS

我没有要**申报**的**物品**。 Wǒ méiyǒu yào *shēnbào* de *wùpǐn*.	declare, thing/article
我有要申报的物品。 Wǒ yǒu yào shēnbào de wùpǐn.	
要是没有申报物品，请走**绿色通道**。 Yàoshi méiyǒu shēnbào wùpǐn, qǐng zǒu *lǜsè tōngdào*.	green channel
要是你有申报物品，请走**红色通道**。 Yàoshi nǐ yǒu shēnbào wùpǐn, qǐng zǒu *hóngsè tōngdào*.	red channel
海关官员会问： *Hǎiguān guānyuán* huì wèn:	customs agent
你带**香烟**了吗? Nǐ dài *xiāngyān* le ma?	cigarettes
酒 *jiǔ*	alcohol
水果 *shuǐguǒ*	fruit
蔬菜 *shūcài*	vegetables
我只带了**个人**物品。 Wǒ zhǐ dàile *gèrén wùpǐn*.	personal
请给我看看你的**海关申报**单。 Qǐng gěi wǒ kànkan nǐ de *hǎiguān shēnbàodān*.	customs declaration
我想申报三瓶**威士忌**。 Wǒ xiǎng shēnbào sān píng *wēishìjì*.	whiskey
请打开你的**包**。 Qǐng dǎ kāi nǐ de *bāo*.	bag
箱子 *xiāngzi*	suitcase

要是你带了三瓶**以上**的威士忌，   more than
Yàoshi nǐ dàile sān píng *yǐshàng* de wēishìjì,

你就得**交税**。   pay duty

nǐ jiù děi *jiāo shuì*.

2. Complete.

1) 要是乘客没有要_____的物品，他们可以从绿色_____出去。
  Yàoshi chéngkè méiyǒu yào _____de wùpǐn, tāmen kěyǐ cóng lùsè _____ chūqù.

2) 有申报物品的乘客得从_____出去。
  Yǒu shēnbào wùpǐn de chéngkè děi cóng _____ chūqù.

3) 游客只可以带_____瓶威士忌入关。
  Yóukè zhǐ kěyǐ dài _____ píng wēishìjì rùguān.

4) 要是你带了三瓶，你就得_____一瓶，并且交_____。
  Yàoshi nǐ dài le sān píng, nǐ jiù děi _____ yì píng, bìngqiě jiāo _____.

5) 海关官员要看我的_____。
  Hǎiguān guānyuán yào kàn wǒde _____.

6) 我没有要申报的物品，因为我只带了_____。
  Wǒ méiyǒu yào shēnbào de wùpǐn, yīnwèi wǒ zhǐ dàile _____.

KEY WORDS

a few	几	jǐ	only	只	zhǐ
alcohol	酒	jiǔ	pass through	路过	lùguò
article, thing	物品	wùpǐn	passport	护照	hùzhào
bag	包	bāo	pay duty	交税	jiāo shuì
cigarettes	香烟	xiāngyān	personal	个人(的)	gèrén (de)
customs officer	海关官员	hǎiguān guānyuán	plan	打算	dǎsuàn
day	天	tiān	red channel	红色通道	hóngsè tōngdào
declaration	申报	shēnbào	stay	呆	dāi
declare	申报	shēnbào	suitcase	手提箱	shǒutíxiāng
fruit	水果	shuǐguǒ	tour	旅游	lǚyóu
green channel	绿色通道	lùsè tōngdào	vegetables	蔬菜	shūcài
how long (time)	多久	duōjiǔ	visa	签证	qiānzhèng
month	月	yuè	week	星期	xīngqī
more than	多/超过	duō/chāoguò	whiskey	威士忌	wēishìjì
on business	公务	gōngwù			

Chapter 4: At the train station

第四章：在火车站
Zài huǒchēzhàn

GETTING A TICKET

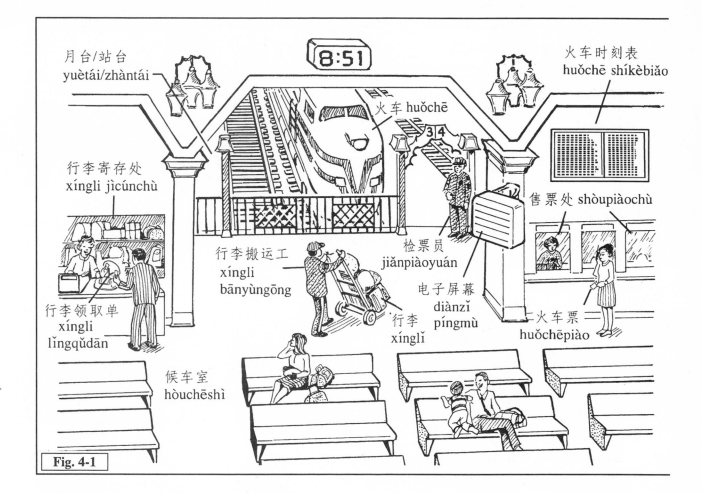

月台/站台
yuètái/zhàntái

火车时刻表
huǒchē shíkèbiǎo

火车 huǒchē

行李寄存处
xíngli jìcúnchù

售票处 shòupiàochù

行李搬运工
xíngli
bānyùngōng

检票员
jiǎnpiàoyuán

行李领取单
xíngli
lǐngqǔdān

电子屏幕
diànzǐ
píngmù

行李
xínglǐ

火车票
huǒchēpiào

候车室
hòuchēshì

Fig. 4-1

在**火车站**买**票**   train station; buy tickets
Zài *huǒchēzhàn mǎi piào*

A: 请问有明天去上海的**火车票**吗？   train ticket
   Qǐng wèn yǒu míngtiān qù Shànghǎi de *huǒchēpiào* ma?

B: 要几张？**软卧**、**硬卧**还是**硬座**？   soft sleeper; hard sleeper; hard seat
   Yào jǐ zhāng? *ruǎnwò, yìngwò* háishi *yìngzuò*?

A: 要两张硬卧。
   Yào liǎng zhāng yìngwò.

B：对不起，只有一张**上铺**了。软卧行吗？　　　　　　upper berth
　　Duìbuqǐ, zhǐyǒu yì zhāng *shàngpù* le. Ruǎnwò xíng ma?

A：软卧太贵了。后天有票吗？
　　Ruǎnwò tài guì le. Hòutiān yǒu piào ma?

B：让我看看。噢！后天还有硬卧。
　　Ràng wǒ kànkan, Ò!　Hòutiān háiyǒu yìngwò.

A：可以买**来回票**吗？　　　　　　　　　　　　　round trip ticket
　　Kěyǐ mǎi *láihuípiào* ma?

B：对不起，我们不**卖**来回票，只卖**单程票**。　　sell, one-way ticket
　　Duìbuqǐ, wǒmen bú *mài* láihuípiào, zhǐ mài *dānchéngpiào*.

A：那我就买两张单程票吧。要**下铺**。　　　　　　lower berth
　　Nà wǒ jiù mǎi liǎng zhāng dānchéngpiào ba. Yào *xiàpù*.

1. Complete.

我们想坐火车去上海，所以到＿＿1＿＿去买票。我们不想买＿＿2＿＿，因为太
Wǒmen xiǎng zuò huǒchē qù Shànghǎi, suǒyǐ dào ＿＿1＿＿ qù mǎi piào. Wǒmen bù xiǎng mǎi ＿＿2＿＿, yīnwèi tài

贵。可是明天的＿＿3＿＿票只有一张了，而且是＿＿4＿＿铺。我只好买后天的。火车站
guì. Kěshì míngtiān de ＿＿3＿＿piào zhǐyǒu yìzhāng le, érqiě shi ＿＿4＿＿pù. Wǒ zhǐhǎo mǎi hòutiān de. Huǒchēzhàn

也不卖来回票，所以我们买了两张后天的＿＿5＿＿票。好在他们还有＿＿6＿＿铺。
yě bú mài láihuí piào, suǒyǐ wǒmen mǎile liǎng zhāng hòutian de ＿5＿piào. Hǎozài tāmen hái yǒu ＿6＿pù.

2. Complete.

在北京火车站
Zài Běijīng Huǒchēzhàn

A：请问有明天去上海的＿＿1＿＿吗？
　　Qǐngwen yǒu míngtiān qù Shànghǎi de ＿＿1＿＿ma?

B：对不起，没有了。后天还有。
　　Duìbuqǐ, méiyǒu le. Hòutiān hái yǒu.

A：后天的也可以。要两张硬卧。
　　Hòutiān de yě kěyǐ. Yào liǎng zhāng yìngwò.

B：对不起，只有＿＿2＿＿了。
　　Duìbuqǐ, zhī yǒu ＿＿2＿＿le.

A：是上铺还是＿＿3＿＿？
　　Shi shàngpù háishi ＿＿3＿＿?

B：都有。您要＿＿4＿＿张？
　　Dōu yǒu. Nín yào ＿＿4＿＿zhāng?

A：要两张下铺。＿＿5＿＿。
　　yào liǎng zhāng xiàpù. ＿＿5＿＿.

B：对不起，我们只卖＿＿6＿＿票。
　　Duìbuqǐ, wǒmen zhǐ mài ＿＿6＿＿piào.

A：好吧，那就买两张__7__吧。
　　Hǎo ba. Nà jiù mǎi liǎng zhāng __7__ba.

买票得去**售票处**。   ticket office
Mǎi piào děi qù *shòupiàochù*.

售票处是**卖票**的地方。   sell tickets
Shòupiàochù shi *mài piào* de dìfang.

特快的**票价**比较贵。   express train; fare
Tèkuài de *piàojià* bǐjiào guì.

慢车的票价便宜一点儿。   local train
Mànchē de piàojià piányì yìdiǎnr,

我们不必**换车**。   change trains
Wǒmen búbì *huànchē*.

3. Complete.

我想去上海，可是我没有票。我得去__1__站买票。可是__2__处在哪儿呢？
Wǒ xiǎng qù Shànghǎi, kěshì wǒ méiyǒu piào. Wǒ děi qù __1__zhàn mǎi piào. Kěshì __2__ chù zài nǎr ne?

噢！在那儿。好象人不太多。
Ò! Zài nàr. Hǎoxiàng rén bú tài duō.

(在__3__处)
(Zài __3__ chù)

A：请买一张去上海的火车票。
　　Qǐng mǎi yì zhāng qù Shànghǎi de huǒchēpiào.

B：您要__4__还是__5__?
　　Nín yào __4__ háishi __5__?

A：__6__太贵，我要__7__吧。多少钱？
　　__6__ tài guì, Wǒ yào __7__ba. Duōshǎo qián?

B：您坐__8__还是慢车？
　　Nín zuò __8__ háishi mànchē?

A：慢车？不要不要。我要__9__。
　　Màn chē? Bú yào, bú yào. Wǒ yào __9__ .

B：好。去上海的特快__10__票一张，450块。
　　Hǎo. Qù Shànghǎi de tèkuài __10__ piào yì zhāng, sìbǎiwǔshí kuài.

WAITING FOR THE TRAIN

Fig. 4-2

在比较**现代**的火车站里，	modern
Zài bǐjiào *xiàndài* de huǒchēzhàn lǐ,	
你可以在**电子屏幕**上看到火车**时刻表**。	electronic screen; time schedule
Nǐ kěyǐ zài *diànzǐ píngmù* shàng kàndào huǒchē *shíkèbiǎo*.	
比较老的车站里，一般都有火车时刻**牌**。	board
Bǐjiào lǎo de chēzhàn lǐ, yìbān dōu yǒu huǒchē shíkè *pái*.	
一个牌子上是**长途**车次，	long distance
yí ge páizi shàng shi *chángtú* chēcì,	
一个牌子上是**短途**车次。	short distance
yí ge páizi shàng shi *duǎntú* chēcì.	
从北京去上海的长途火车	
Cóng Běijīng qù Shànghǎi de chángtú huǒchē	
应该是下午2:00开。	
yīnggāi shi xiàwǔ liǎng diǎn kāi.	
可是今天因为有个**事故**，不能**正点**开车。	accident; on time
Kěshì jīntiān yīnwèi yǒu ge *shìgù*, bù néng *zhèngdiǎn* kāichē.	
可能要3:00才能开。	
Kěnéng yào sān diǎn cái néng kāi.	
火车要**推迟**一个钟头开车。	postpone
Huǒchē yào *tuīchí* yí ge zhōngtóu kāichē.	

火车要**晚点**了。   delay
Huǒchē yào *wǎndiǎn* le.

我们得在**候车室**里**等候**。   waiting room; wait
Wǒmen děi zài *hòuchēshì* lǐ *děnghòu*.

4. Answer

1) 从北京去上海的火车是长途还是短途？
   Cóng Běijīng qù Shànghǎi de huǒchē shi chángtú hái shi duǎntú?

2) 在哪儿可以看到火车时刻表？
   Zài nǎr kěyǐ kàndao huǒchē shíkèbiǎo?

3) 去上海的火车应该什么时候开？
   Qù Shànghǎi de huǒchē yīnggāi shénme shíhou kāi?

4) 今天它会正点开吗？为什么？
   Jīntiān tā huì zhèngdiǎn kāi ma? Wèishénme?

5) 今天它要什么时候才能开？
   Jīntiān tā yào shénme shíhou cái néng kāi?

6) 它会不会晚点？
   Tā huì bu huì wǎndiǎn?

7) 它要晚点多久？
   Tā yào wǎndiǎn duō jiǔ?

8) 乘客们得在什么地方等候？
   Chéngkèmen děi zài shénme dìfāng děnghòu?

5. Complete.

今天去上海的火车因为 __1__ 不能 __2__ 开车。它本来应该下午2:00开车。
Jīntiān qù Shànghǎi de huǒchē yīnwèi __1__ bù néng __2__ kāichē. Tā běnlái yīnggāi xiàwǔ 2:00 kāichē.

可是现在它要到3:00才能开车。它要推迟 __3__ 钟头开车。乘客们可以
Kěshì xiànzài tā yào dào 3:00 cái néng kāichē. Tā yào tuīchí __3__ zhōngtóu kāichē. Chéngkèmen kěyǐ

在 __4__ 等候。
zài __4__ děnghòu.

GETTING ON THE TRAIN

去上海的火车就要开了。
Qù Shànghǎi de huǒchē jiù yào kāi le.

去上海的乘客在8号**站台/月台**上车。   platform
Qù Shànghǎi de chéngkè zài bā hào *zhàntái/yuètái* shàngchē.

我的座位在第三**车厢**12号下铺。   car
Wǒde zuòwèi zài dì sān *chēxiāng* shíèr hào xiàpù.

列车员在车门口**检票**。   conductor; check ticket
Lièchēyuán zài chē ménkǒu *jiǎnpiào*.

很多乘客**上车**，也有很多乘客**下车**。　　　　　　　　　　get on; get off
Hěn duō chéngkè *shàngchē*, yě yǒu hěn duō chéngkè *xiàchē*.

6. Complete.

1) 去上海的乘客在8号_____上车。
　　Qù Shànghǎi de chéngkè zài bā hào _____shàngchē.

2) 我的座位在第3_____12_____下铺。
　　Wǒde zuòwèi zài dì sān _____shíèr _____xiàpù.

3) 在车门口，乘客们得把车票给_____检查。
　　Zài chē ménkǒu, chéngkèmen děi bǎ chēpiào gěi_____ jiǎnchá.

4) 从北京到上海去的乘客在北京_____，在上海_____。
　　Cóng Běijīng dào Shànghǎi qù de chéngkè zài Běijīng _____, zài Shànghǎi _____.

ON THE TRAIN

列车员是火车上的**服务人员**。　　　　　　　　　　service; personnel
Lièchēyuán shi huǒchē shàng de *fúwù rényuán*.

他们要检查乘客的车票，
Tāmen yào jiǎnchá chéngkè de chēpiào.

他们也**打扫**车厢，**整理卧具**。　　　　　　　　　clean; tidy up; bedding
Tāmen yě *dǎsǎo* chēxiāng, *zhěnglǐ wòjù*.

有时候他们也卖报纸、杂志、**零食**和饮料。　　　　　snacks
Yǒushíhou tāmen yě mài bàozhǐ, zázhì, *língshí* he yǐnliào.

吃饭的时候，乘客们可以去**餐车用餐**。　　　　　　dinning car; have a meal
Chīfàn de shíhou, chéngkèmen kěyǐ qù *cānchē yòngcān*.

列车员也会给各个车厢送**盒饭**。　　　　　　　　　boxed meal
Lièchēyuán yě huì gěi gè ge chēxiāng sòng *héfàn*.

7. Complete.

1) 在火车上为乘客服务的人叫_____。
　　Zài huǒchē shàng wèi chéngkè fúwù de rén jiào _____ .

2) 列车员_____车厢，_____卧具。
　　Lièchēyuán _____chēxiāng, _____wòjù .

3) 要是乘客饿了，他们可以去_____用餐。
　　Yàoshi chéngkè è le, tāmen kěyǐ qù _____yòngcān.

4) 不想去餐车吃饭的乘客可以在自己的车厢买_____吃。
　　Bù xiǎng qù cānchē chīfàn de chéngkè kěyǐ zài zìjǐ de chēxiāng mǎi _____ chī.

史密斯先生和他太太要坐火车去旅行。他们在北京火车站前面下了
Shǐmìsī xiānsheng hé tā tàitai yào zuò huǒchē qù lǚxíng. Tāmen zài Běijīng huǒchē zhàn qiánmian xiàle

出租车。进车站以后，他们发现他们要坐的那趟火车不能正点发车。
chūzūchē. Jìn chēzhàn yǐhòu, tāmen fāxiàn tāmen yào zuò de nà tàng huǒchē bù néng zhèngdiǎn fāchē.

因为那天出了一个事故，火车得推迟发车。可能要晚点1.5小时。史密斯
Yīnwèi nà tiān chūle yí ge shìgù, huǒchē děi tuīchí fāchē. Kěnéng yào wǎndiǎn yí ge bàn xiǎoshí. Shǐmìsī

先生到售票处买了两张去上海的硬卧票。因为售票处不卖
xiānsheng dào shòupiàochù mǎile liǎng zhāng qù Shànghǎi de yìngwòpiào. Yīnwèi shòupiàochù bú mài

来回票，他只能买单程票。回来的票还得在上海买。他们在候车室
láihuípiào, tā zhǐ néng mǎi dānchéngpiào. Huílái de piào hái děi zài Shànghǎi mǎi. Tāmen zài hòuchēshì

等了一个多小时，总算能上车了。他们从电子屏幕上看到，去上海
déngle yí ge duō xiǎoshí, zǒngsuàn néng shàngchē le. Tāmen cóng diànzǐ píngmù shàng kàndào, qù Shànghǎi

的乘客在第8月台上车。他们的座位在第三车厢，是硬卧车厢。列车员
de chéngkè zài dì bā yuètái shàngchē. Tāmende zuòwèi zài dì sān chēxiāng, shi yìngwò chēxiāng. Lièchēyuán

在车厢门口欢迎乘客，检查乘客的车票。史密斯先生和太太上车
zài chēxiāng ménkǒu huāngyíng chéngkè, jiǎnchá chéngkè de chēpiào. Shǐmìsī xiānsheng he tàitai shàngchē

以后，找到了他们的座位，是七、八号两个下铺。因为从北京到上海很远，
yǐhòu, zhǎodàole tāmende zuòwèi,.shi qī, bā hào liǎng ge xiàpù. Yīnwèi cóng Běijīng dào Shànghǎi hěn yuǎn,

所以乘客们一般都买卧铺票，这样可以在火车上睡觉。火车开了以后，
suǒyǐ chéngkèmen yìbān dōu mǎi wòpù piào, zhèyàng kěyǐ zài huǒchē shàng shuìjiào. Huǒchē kāile yǐhòu,

列车员送来了报纸、杂志、零食和饮料。他们也常常来打扫车厢。到吃饭
lièchēyuán sòngláile bàozhǐ, zázhì, língshí he yǐnliào. Tāmen yě chángcháng lái dǎsǎo chēxiāng. Dào chīfàn

的时候，很多乘客都到餐车去用餐。列车员也会给各车厢送盒饭，
de shíhou, hěn duō chéngkè dōu dào cānchē qù yòngcān. Lièchēyuán yě huì gěi gè chēxiāng sòng héfàn.

不想去餐车用餐的乘客可以在自己的车厢买盒饭吃。
Bù xiǎng qù cānchē yòngcān de chéngkè kěyǐ zài zìjǐ de chēxiāng mǎi héfàn chī.

8. Mark the following statements true (T) or false (F) based on the story above:

1) 史密斯先生和太太要坐火车去旅行。
   Shǐmìsī xiānsheng he tàitai yào zuò huǒchē qù lǚxíng.

2) 他们坐公共汽车去火车站。
   Tāmen zuò gōnggòng qìchē qù huǒchēzhàn.

3) 他们要坐的那趟火车会正点发车。
   Tāmen yào zuò de nà tàng huǒchē huì zhèngdiǎn fāchē.

4) 他们买了两张去上海的来回票。
   Tāmen mǎile liǎng zhāng qù Shànghǎi de láihuípiào.

5) 去上海的乘客应该在第8月台上车。
   Qù Shànghǎi de chéngkè yīnggāi zài dì bā yuètái shàngchē.

6) 他们的车厢是软卧车厢。
   Tāmende chēxiāng shi ruǎnwò chēxiāng.

7) 从北京到上海要坐很久的火车。
   Cóng Běijīng dào Shànghǎi yào zuò hěn jiǔ de huǒchē.

8) 列车员在车厢门口给乘客送报纸和杂志。
   Lièchēyuán zài chēxiāng ménkǒu gěi chéngkè sòng bàozhǐ he zázhì.

9) 餐车是乘客们吃饭的地方。
   Cānchē shi chéngkèmen chīfàn de dìfang.

10) 吃了饭乘客们得打扫车厢。
    Chīle fàn chéngkè men děi dǎsǎo chēxiāng.

9. Answer:

1) 史密斯先生和太太是怎么到火车站去的?
   Shǐmìsī xiānsheng he tàitai shi zěnme dào huǒchēzhàn qù de?

2) 火车会正点发车吗?
   Huǒchē huì zhèngdiǎn fāchē ma?

3) 火车要晚点多久?
   Huǒchē yào wǎndiǎn duō jiǔ?

4) 他们在哪儿买票?
   Tāmen zài nǎr mǎi piào?

5) 他们买了什么票?
   Tāmen mǎile shénme piào?

6) 他们在哪儿等车?
   Tāmen zài nǎr děng chē?

7) 他们在哪儿上车?
   Tāmen zài nǎr shàngchē?

8) 为什么他们要买卧铺票?
   Wèishénme tāmen yào mǎi wòpùpiào?

9) 火车上的列车员都做些什么?
   Huǒchē shàng de lièchēyuán dōu zuò xiē shénme?

10) 火车上的乘客在哪儿吃饭?
    Huǒchē shàng de chéngkè zài nǎr chīfàn?

10. Match.

1) 售票处   a. 车站里乘客上火车的地方
   shòupiàochù   chēzhàn lǐ chéngkè shàng huǒchē de dìfang

2) 来回票   b. 火车上乘客可以睡觉的地方
   láihuípiào   huǒchē shàng chéngkè kěyǐ shuìjiào de dìfang

3) 晚点   c. 买票的地方
   wǎndiǎn   mǎi piào de dìfang

4) 卧铺   d. 在火车上工作的人
   wòpù   zài huǒchē shàng gōngzuò de rén

5) 月台   e. 不正点
   yuètái   bú zhèngdiǎn

6) 餐车   f. 火车上吃饭的车厢
   cānchē   huǒchēshàng chīfàn de chēxiāng

7) 候车室   g. 乘客等火车的地方
   hòuchē shì   chéngkè děng huǒchē de dìfang

8) 列车员　　　　　　　h. 可以去也可以回来的票
　　lièchēyuán　　　　　kěyǐ qù yě kěyǐ huílái de piào

KEY WORDS

(train) car	车厢	chēxiāng	
accident	事故	shìgù	
bedding	卧具	wòjù	
board	上车	shàngchē	
boxed meal	盒饭	héfàn	
buy	买	mǎi	
change train	换车	huànchē	
check ticket	查票	chápiào	
clean	打扫	dǎsǎo	
conductor	列车员	lièchēyuán	
delay	晚点	wǎndiǎn	
dining car	餐车	cānchē	
display	显示	xiǎnshì	
electronic screen	电子屏幕	diànzǐ píngmù	
express train	特快	tèkuài	
fare	票价	piàojià	
get off	下车	xiàchē	
get on	上车	shàngchē	
hard seat	硬座	yìngzuò	
hard sleeper	硬卧	yìngwò	
have a meal	用餐	yòngcān	
local train	慢车	mànchē	
long distance	长途	chángtú	

lower berth	下铺	xiàpù	
modern	现代	xiàndài	
on time	准时/正点	zhǔnshí/zhèngdiǎn	
one way ticket	单程票	dānchéngpiào	
personnel	人员	rényuán	
platform	站台/月台	zhàntái/yuètái	
postpone	推迟	tuīchí	
round trip ticket	来回票	láihuípiào	
sell	卖	mài	
service	服务	fúwù	
short distance	短途	duǎntú	
sleeper	卧铺	wòpù	
snacks	小吃/零食	xiǎochī/língshí	
soft sleeper	软卧	ruǎnwò	
ticket	票	piào	
ticket office	售票处	shòupiàochù	
tidy up	整理	zhěnglǐ	
time schedule	时刻表	shíkèbiǎo	
train station	火车站	huǒchēzhàn	
upper berth	上铺	shàngpù	
wait	等	děng	
waiting room	候车室	hòuchēshì	

Chapter 5: Public transportation

第五章：公共交通
Gōnggòng jiāotōng

TAKING BUSES AND THE SUBWAY

请问**公共汽车站**在哪儿？	bus, stop/station
Qǐngwèn *gōnggòng qìchēzhàn* zài nǎr?	
电车站	trolley
*diànchē*zhàn	
地铁站	subway
*dìtiě*zhàn	
公共汽车上有**司机**，也有**售票员**。	driver, conductor
Gōnggòng qìchē shàng yǒu *sījī,* yě yǒu *shòupiàoyuán*	
乘客上车以后向售票员买票。	passenger, get on
Chéngkè shàngchē yǐhòu xiàng shòupiàoyuán mǎi piào.	
地铁上没有售票员，	
Dìtiě shàng méiyǒu shòupiàoyuán.	
乘客在**地铁站**买票。	subway station
Chéngkè děi zài *dìtiězhàn* mǎi piào.	
去**天安门广场**应该**坐**什么车？	Tian'anmen Square, take
Qù *Tiānānmén Guǎngchǎng* yīnggāi zuò shénme chē?	
去北京饭店应该坐**几路**公共汽车？	which route
Qù Běijīng Fàndiàn yīnggāi zuò *jǐ lù* gōnggòng qìchē?	
这是**去**北京大学的车吗？	bound for/to
Zhè shi *qù* Běijīng Dàxué de chē ma?	
什么时候**开**？	leave
Shénme shíhòu kāi?	
头班/末班地铁什么时候开？	first /last subway
Tóu bān/mò bān dìtiě shénme shíhòu kāi?	
这路车**多久来一趟**？	how often does it come
Zhèi lù chē *duōjiǔ lái yí tàng?*	
这路车在西山公园**停**吗？	stop
Zhè lù chē zài Xīshān Gōngyuán *tíng* ma?	
我应该坐哪个**方向**的车？	direction
Wǒ yīnggāi zuò něige *fāngxiàng* de chē?	
要坐几**站**？	stop
Yào zuò jǐ *zhàn?*	

在哪儿**下车**？   get off
Zài nǎr *xiàchē*?

在哪儿**换车**？   transfer
Zài nǎr *huànchē*?

在哪儿买**票**？   ticket
Zài nǎr mǎi *piào*?

到站时请告诉我。   arrive
*Dào*zhàn shí qǐng gàosù wǒ.

买一张到天安门的车票。
Mǎi yì zhāng dào Tiānānmén de chēpiào.

我要买一张**月票**。   monthly pass
Wǒ yào mǎi yì zhāng *yuèpiào*.

地铁票在一**天以内**都可以用。   within a day
Dìtiěpiào zài *yì tiān yǐnèi* dōu kěyǐ yòng.

对不起，**下一站**是火车站吗？   next stop
Duìbuqǐ, *xià yí zhàn* shi huǒchēzhàn ma?

对不起，**先下后上**。   let people get off first
Duìbuqǐ, *xiān xià hòu shàng*.

1. Complete.

1) 公共汽车、地铁、电车都是＿＿＿＿工具。
     Gōnggòng qìchē, dìtiě, diànchē dōu shi ＿＿＿＿gōngjù.

2) ＿＿＿＿是乘客上下公共汽车的地方。
     ＿＿＿＿shi chéngkè shàng xià gōnggòng qìchē de dìfāng.

3) 在地下行驶的火车叫＿＿＿＿。
     Zài dìxià xíngshǐ de huǒchē jiào ＿＿＿＿.

4) 我要去北京大学，应该坐几＿＿＿＿公共汽车？
     Wǒ yào qù Běijīng Dàxué, yīnggāi zuò jǐ ＿＿＿＿gōnggòng qìchē?

5) 从这儿坐302路电车去北京饭店，要坐几＿＿＿＿？
     Cóng zhèr zuò 302 lù diànchē qù Běijīng Fàndiàn, yào zuò jǐ ＿＿＿＿?

6) 这是＿＿＿＿天安门广场的车吗？
     Zhè shi ＿＿＿＿ Tiānānmén Guǎngchǎng de chē ma?

7) 这辆车在友谊饭店＿＿＿＿吗？
     Zhèi liàng chē zài Yǒuyì Fàndiàn ＿＿＿＿ma?

8) 我天天要坐车，可是不想天天买票，我要买一张＿＿＿＿。
     Wǒ tiāntiān yào zuò chē, kěshì bù xiǎng tiāntiān mǎi piào, wǒ yào mǎi yì zhāng ＿＿＿＿.

9) 火车站在西边，这辆车往东开，你坐错了＿＿＿＿。
     Huǒchēzhàn zài xībiān, zhèi liàng chē wǎng dōng kāi, nǐ zuòcuòle ＿＿＿＿.

10) 我不知道应该在哪儿下车，请你＿＿＿＿时告诉我一下。
     Wǒ bù zhīdào yīnggāi zài nǎr xiàchē, qǐng nǐ ＿＿＿＿shí gàosù wǒ yíxià.

2. Complete.

A： 我买一张去北京大学的__1__。
Wǒ mǎi yì zhāng qù Běijīng Dàxué de __1__.

B： 这辆车不__2__北京大学。
Zhèi liàng chē bú __2__ Běijīng Dàxué.

A： 什么？我__3__错车了吗？
Shénme? wǒ __3__ cuò chē le ma?

B： 不要紧，你在下一站__4__，__5__十五路就行了。
Búyàojǐn, nǐ zài xià yí zhàn __4__, __5__ shíwǔ lù jiù xíng le.

A： 谢谢。那我应该买多少钱的票呢？
Xièxie, Nà wǒ Yīnggāi mǎi duōshǎo qián de piào ne?

B： 一块。
Yí kuài.

A： 谢谢。
Xièxie.

B： 北京书店__6__了。到北京书店的__7__请下车。
Běijīng Shūdiàn __6__ le. Dào Běijīng Shūdiàn de __7__ qǐng xiàchē.

A： 对不起，我要__8__。
Duìbuqǐ, wǒ yào __8__.

3. Complete.

A： 小王，我想去天安门__1__，你说坐什么__2__好？
Xiǎo wáng, wǒ xiǎng qù Tiānānmén __1__. Nǐ shuō zuò shénme __2__ hǎo?

B： 坐__3__吧。地铁又快又方便。
Zuò __3__ ba. Dìtiě yòu kuài yòu fāngbiàn.

A： 地铁贵不贵？
Dìtiě guì bú guì?

B： 很便宜。不管去哪儿都是三块。
Hěn piányì, bùguǎn qù nǎr dōu shi sān kuài.

A： 那太好了。我得在__4__买票吗？
Nà tài hǎo le, wǒ děi zài __4__ mǎi piào ma?

B： 不行，地铁车上没有__5__。你得在__6__买票。
Bùxíng, dìtiěchē shàng méiyǒu __5__. Nǐ děi zài __6__ mǎi piào.

A： 谢谢你告诉我。
Xièxie nǐ gàosù wǒ.

B： 你回来也__7__地铁吗？
Nǐ huílái yě __7__ dìtiě ma?

A： 会。
Huì.

B： 那你最好一次买两张__8__。地铁票在一天__9__都可以用。
Nà nǐ zuìhǎo yí cì mǎi liǎng zhāng __8__. Dìtiěpiào zài yì tiān __9__ dōu kěyǐ yòng.

TAKING A TAXI

坐**出租车**又叫**"打的"**。   taxi, take a taxi
Zuò *chūzūchē* yòu jiào "*dǎdī*".

在台湾，出租车也叫**"计程车"**。   taxi
Zài Táiwān, chūzūchē yě jiào "*jìchéngzhē*".

在香港，出租车叫**"的士"**。   taxi
Zài Xiānggǎng, chūzūchē jiào "*dīshì*".

你可以打个电话**叫**出租车。   call
Nǐ kěyǐ dǎ ge diànhuà *jiào* chūzūchē.

师傅，请去火车站。   master[3] (skilled worker)
Shīfu, qǐng qù huǒchēzhàn.

　　　　飞机场
　　　　fēijīchǎng

　　　　友谊宾馆
　　　　Yǒuyì Bīnguǎn

去长城多少钱？
Qù Chángchéng duōshǎo qián?

按计程表算。   according to, meter
Àn jìchéngbiǎo suàn.

三公里以内十块钱，
Sān gōnglǐ yǐnèi shí kuài qián.

三公里以外，每公里一块六。
Sān gōnglǐ yǐwài, měi gōnglǐ yí kuài liù.

包一天多少钱？   hire/charter
Bāo yì tiān duōshǎo qián?

租一辆车多少钱？要交**押金**吗？   rent, deposit
Zū yí liàng chē duōshǎo qián? yào jiāo *yājīn* ma?

请在这儿等一下，我五分钟就回来。
Qǐng zài zhèr děng yíxià, wǒ wǔ fēnzhōng jiù huílái.

请**开慢**一点儿。   drive, slow
Qǐng *kāi màn* yìdiǎnr.

　　　　快   fast
　　　　kuài

这是给你的**小费**[4]。   tip
Zhè shi gěi nǐ de *xiǎofèi*.

---

[3] "Shifu" is a general address term now used for skilled workers or service people (mostly male) instead of the dated term "comrade" in service encounters. "Xiaojie" (miss) is a preferred term for young females.

[4] Tipping was not a convention in China. However, it is starting to become a fashion in some service business, such as luxurious hotels, restaurants, and taxis.

4. Complete.

1) 坐出租车又叫_____。
   Zuò chūzūchē yòu jiào _____.

2) 出租车司机按_____收车费。
   Chūzūchē sījī àn _____shōu chēfèi.

3) 要是你需要用一天的出租车，你可以_____一辆车。
   Yàoshi nǐ xūyào yòng yì tiān de chūzūchē, nǐ kěyǐ _____yí liàng chē.

4) 要是你需要用车，可是不需要司机，你可以_____一辆车。
   Yàoshi nǐ xūyào yòng chē, kěshì bù xūyào sījī, nǐ kěyǐ _____yí liàng chē.

5) 在出租车公司租车得先交_____。
   Zài chūzūchē gōngsī zūchē děi xiān jiāo _____.

6) 我们可以叫出租车司机_____。
   Wǒmen kěyǐ jiào chūzūchē sījī _____.

7) 要是你觉得车开得太快，你可以请他开_____一点。
   Yàoshi nǐ juéde chē kāi de tài kuài, nǐ kěyǐ qǐng tā kāi _____yìdiǎn.

8) 车费是28块，你给司机30块，多给的那两块钱就是_____。
   Chēfèi shi 28 kuài, nǐ gěi sījī 30 kuài, duō gěi de nà liǎng kuài qián jiùshi _____.

5. Complete.

A：喂，请问是出租__1__服务公司吗?
   Wéi, qǐngwèn shi chūzū__1__fúwù gōngsī ma?

B：是的。先生，您什么时间要__2__?
   Shìde. Xiānsheng, nín shénme shíjiān yào __2__?

A：我现在就__3__。
   Wǒ xiànzài jiù __3__.

B：您现在在__4__? 要到哪儿__5__?
   Nín xiànzài zài __4__? Yào dào nǎr __5__?

A：我现在在友谊饭店。要到机场去。
   Wǒ xiànzài zài Yǒuyì Fàndiàn. Yào dào jīchǎng qù.

B：请等一下。__6__ 5分钟就到。
   Qǐng děng yíxià, __6__wǔ fēnzhōng jiù dào.

6. Complete.

A：师傅，请__1__北京饭店。
   Shīfu, qǐng __1__Běijīng Fàndiàn.

B：上车吧。
   Shàngchē ba.

A：请问从这儿去北京饭店要__2__?
   Qǐngwèn cóng zhèr qù Běijīng Fàndiàn yào __2__?

B：得看__3__情况怎么样。要是不塞车，15分钟就到了。
   Děi kàn __3__qíngkuàng zěnmeyàng. Yàoshi bù sāichē, shíwǔ fēnzhōng jiù dào le.

A：我有急事，可不可以请你开__4__一点儿?
　　Wǒ yǒu jí shì, kě bù kěyǐ qǐng nǐ kāi __4__ yìdiǎnr?

B：先生，北京饭店__5__。
　　Xiānsheng, Běijīng Fàndiàn __5__.

A：请问__6__钱?
　　Qǐngwèn __6__ qián?

B：二十七块。
　　Èrshíqī kuài.

A：这是三十块，不用找了。
　　Zhè shi sānshí kuài, bú yòng zhǎo le.

B：先生，我们不收__7__，找您三块。
　　Xiānsheng, wǒmen bù shōu __7__. Zhǎo nín sān kuài.

KEY WORDS

according to	按	àn	
arrive	到站	dàozhàn	
bound for/to	去	qù	
bus stop	公共汽车站	gōnggòng qìchē zhàn	
call	叫	jiào	
conductor	售票员	shòupiàoyuán	
deposit	押金	yājīn	
direction	方向	fāngxiàng	
drive	开	kāi	
driver	司机	sījī	
fast	快	kuài	
first	先	xiān	
first /last subway	头班/末班地铁	tóubān/mòbān dìtiě	
get off	下(车)	xiàchē	
get on	上(车)	shàngchē	
hire/charter	包	bāo	
How often does it come?	多久来一趟?	Duōjiǔ lái yí tàng?	
later	后	hòu	
leave/drive	开	kāi	
master (skilled worker)	师傅	shīfu	

meter	计程表	jìchéngbiǎo	
monthly pass	月票	yuè piào	
next stop	下一站	xià yí zhàn	
passenger	乘客	chéngkè	
price	价钱	jiàqián	
rent	租	zū	
slow	慢	màn	
stop	停	tíng	
stop, station	站	zhàn	
subway	地铁	dìtiě	
subway station	地铁站	dìtiězhàn	
take (vehicle)	坐(车)	zuò (chē)	
take a taxi	打 "的"	dǎdī	
taxi	出租车/计程车/的士	chūzūchē, jìchéngchē, dīshì	
Tian'anmen Square	天安门广场	Tiānānmén Guǎngchǎng	
ticket	票	piào	
tip	小费	xiǎofèi	
transfer	换车	huàn chē	
transportation	交通，运输	jiāotōng, yùnshū	
trolley	电车	diànchē	
which route	几路	jǐ lù	
within	以内	yǐnèi	

Chapter 6: The automobile

第六章：汽车
   Qìchē

RENTING A CAR

我想**租一辆车**。	rent a car
Wǒ xiǎng *zū yí liàng chē*.	
请问**租一天**多少钱？	rent for a day
Qǐngwèn *zū yì tiān* duōshǎo qián?	
有**里程限制**吗？	mileage limits
Yǒu *lǐchéng xiànzhì* ma?	
按**公里收费**吗？	kilometer; charge
Àn *gōnglǐ shōufèi* ma?	
包括汽油钱吗？	include; gas
Bāokuò qìyóu qián ma?	
有**自动挡**的车吗？	automatic transmission
Yǒu *zìdòngdǎng* de chē ma?	
都是**手排挡**的吗？	manual transmission
Dōu shi *shǒupáidǎng* de ma?	
我们要不要付**押金**？	deposit
Wǒmen yào bú yào fù *yājīn*?	
我想买**保险**。	insurance
Wǒ xiǎng mǎi *bǎoxiǎn*.	
这是我的**驾(驶执)照**。	driver's license
Zhè shi wǒde *jià (shǐ zhí) zhào*.	
我想用**信用卡付帐**。	credit card; pay (bill)
Wǒ xiǎng yòng *xìnyòngkǎ fùzhàng*.	
请在**合同**上**签字**。	contract; sign
Qǐng zài *hétóng* shàng *qiānzì*.	

1. Complete.

1) 我想租一辆_____的车，因为我不会开手排挡的。
   Wǒ xiǎng zū yí liàng _____de chē, yīnwèi wǒ bú huì kāi shǒupáidǎng de.

2) 你想_____几天？
   Nǐ xiǎng _____ jǐ tiān?

3) 限制_____吗?

Xiànzhì _____ma?

4) 按天收费, 不按_____收费。

Àn tiān shōufèi, bú àn _____shōufèi.

5) 你可以付现金, 你也可以用_____。

Nǐ kěyǐ fù xiànjīn, nǐ yě kěyǐ yòng _____.

6) 开车的人一定要带上自己的_____。

Kāichē de rén yídìng yào dàishàng zìjǐ de _____.

2. Complete.

A：我要__1__一辆车。

　　Wǒ yào __1__ yí liàng chē.

B：你要大__2__还是小__3__?

　　Nǐ yào dà __2__ háishi xiǎo __3__?

A：小车。

　　Xiǎo chē.

B：你要__4__多久?

　　Nǐ yào __4__ duō jiǔ?

A：租一天得__5__?

　　Zū yì tiān děi __5__?

B：一天300块, 一个月8,000块。

　　Yì tiān sānbǎi kuài, yí ge yuè bāqiān kuài.

A：有__6__限制吗?

　　Yǒu __6__ xiànzhì ma?

B：没有。

　　Méiyǒu.

A：好, 我租一个星期。我还要买保险吗?

　　Hǎo, wǒ zū yí ge xīngqī. Wǒ hái yào mǎi bǎoxiǎn ma?

B：租金里已经包括__7__费了。

　　Zūjīn lǐ yǐjīng bāokuò __7__ fèi le.

A：太好了。

　　Tài hǎo le.

B：我看一下你的__8__。

　　Wǒ kàn yíxia nǐde __8__.

A：给你。

　　Gěi nǐ.

B：好, 驾照没有问题, 那就请你付__9__吧。

　　Hǎo, jiàozhào méi yǒu wèntí, nà jiù qǐng nǐ fù __9__ ba.

A：我可以用__10__卡付押金吗?

　　Wǒ kěyǐ yòng __10__ kǎ fù yājīn ma?

B：可以。还得请你在合同上__11__。

　　Kěyǐ. Hái děi qǐng nǐ zài hétóng shàng __11__.

CHECKING OUT THE CAR

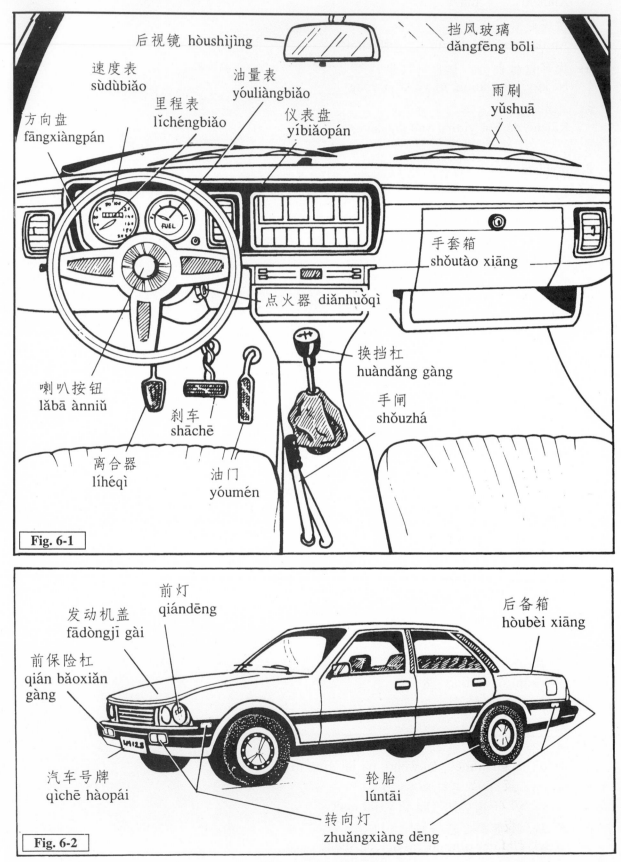

后视镜 hòushìjìng

挡风玻璃
dǎngfēng bōli

速度表
sùdùbiǎo

油量表
yóuliàngbiǎo

里程表
lǐchéngbiǎo

雨刷
yǔshuā

方向盘
fāngxiàngpán

仪表盘
yíbiǎopán

手套箱
shǒutào xiāng

点火器 diǎnhuǒqì

换挡杆
huàndǎng gàng

喇叭按钮
lǎbā ànniǔ

手闸
shǒuzhá

刹车
shāchē

离合器
líhéqì

油门
yóumén

Fig. 6-1

前灯
qiándēng

发动机盖
fādòngjī gài

后备箱
hòubèi xiāng

前保险杠
qián bǎoxiǎn
gàng

汽车号牌
qìchē hàopái

轮胎
lúntāi

转向灯
zhuǎngxiàng dēng

Fig. 6-2

不要**踩刹车**。   step on the break
Bú yào *cǎi shāchē*.

请踩**离合器**。   clutch
Qǐng cǎi *líhéqì*.

现在**点火/熄火**。   start the engine/stop the engine
Xiànzài *diǎnhuǒ/ xīhuǒ*.

现在**加速**。   accelerate
Xiànzài *jiāsù*.

轻轻地踩**油门**。   gas pedal
Qīngqing de cǎi *yóumén*.

打左**转向灯**。   turn signal
Dǎ zuǒ *zhuǎngxiàngdēng*.

这是**前(大)灯**。   headlight
Zhè shi *qián(dà)dēng*.

这是**高光灯**。   high beam
Zhè shi *gāoguāngdēng*.

　　　低光灯   low beam
　　　dīguāngdēng

按一下**喇叭**。   press, horn
Àn yíxià *lǎbā*.

怎么**起动雨刷**?   start, windshield wiper
Zěnme *qǐdòng yǔshuā?*

你能告诉我怎么**换挡**吗?   change gear
Nǐ néng gàosù wǒ zěnme *huàn dǎng* ma?

　　　　　挂一挡   put in first gear
　　　　　guà yīdǎng

　　　　　挂空档   neutral gear
　　　　　guà kōngdǎng

　　　　　挂倒档   reverse gear
　　　　　guà dàodǎng

后备箱里有**千斤顶**吗?   trunk, jack
Hòubèixiāng lǐ yǒu *qiānjīndǐng* ma?

有没有**备用轮胎**?   spare tire
Yǒu méi yǒu *bèiyòng lúntāi?*

开车时请系上**安全带**。   seatbelt
Kāi chē shí qǐng jìshàng *ānquán dài*.

调整一下**后视镜**。   adjust, rearview mirror
Tiáozhěng yíxià *hòushìjìng*.

　　　左反光镜   left mirror
　　　zuǒ fǎnguāngjìng

　　　右反光镜   right
　　　yòu fǎnguāngjìng

3. Choose the appropriate word.

1) 换挡的时候，我应该脚踩＿＿＿。　　　　　a 刹车　　　　b 离合器　　　c 油门
   Huàn dǎng de shíhou, wǒ yīnggāi jiǎo cǎi ＿＿＿.　　shāchē　　　líhéqì　　　yóumén

2) 停车时要脚踩＿＿＿。　　　　　　　　　　a 刹车　　　　b 离合器　　　c 油门
   Tíng chē shí yào jiǎo cǎi ＿＿＿.　　　　　shāchē　　　líhéqì　　　yóumén

3) 转弯前，我得先＿＿＿。　　　　　　　　　a 挂空档　　　b 按喇叭　　　c 打转向灯
   Zhuǎngwān qián, wǒ děi xiān ＿＿＿.　　　guà kōngdǎng　àn lǎbā　　dǎ zhuǎngxiàng
   　　　　　　　　　　　　　　　　　　　　　　　　　　　　　　　　　　　　dēng

4) 夜里开车，我得开＿＿＿。　　　　　　　　a 前灯　　　　b 喇叭　　　c 转向灯
   Yèlǐ kāichē, wǒ děi kāi ＿＿＿.　　　　　qiándēng　　lǎbā　　　zhuǎngxiàng
   　　　　　　　　　　　　　　　　　　　　　　　　　　　　　　　　　　　dēng

5) 马路上有人时，我得＿＿＿。　　　　　　　a 踩油门　　　b 系安全带　c 按喇叭
   Mǎlù shàng yǒu rén shí, wǒ děi ＿＿＿.　　cǎi yóumén　jì ānquándài　àn lǎbā

6) 倒车时，我得＿＿＿。　　　　　　　　　　a 熄火　　　　b 挂倒档　　c 按喇叭
   Dǎochē shí, wǒ děi ＿＿＿.　　　　　　　xīhuǒ　　　guà dàodǎng　àn lǎbā

7) 下雨了，我得＿＿＿。　　　　　　　　　　a 刹车　　　　b 熄火　　　c 起动雨刷
   Xiàyǔ le, wǒ děi ＿＿＿.　　　　　　　　shāchē　　　xīhuǒ　　　qǐdòng yǔshuā

8) ＿＿＿可以告诉你一共走了多少里。　　　　a 方向盘　　　b 里程表　　c 油量表
   ＿＿＿kěyǐ gàosù nǐ yígòng zǒu le duōshǎo lǐ.　fāngxiànpán　líchéngbiǎo　yóuliàngbiǎo

9) 发动车时，你得＿＿＿。　　　　　　　　　a 点火　　　　b 开前灯　　c 踩油门
   Fādòng chē shí, nǐ děi ＿＿＿.　　　　　diǎnhuǒ　　kāi qiándēng　cǎi yóumén

10) 夜里开车，要是车不多，我可以开＿＿＿。　a 雾灯　　　　b 喇叭　　　c 高光灯
    Yèlǐ kāi chē, yàoshi chē bù duō, wǒ kěyǐ kāi ＿＿＿.　wùdēng　　lǎbā　　gāoguāngdēng

4. Complete.

1) 我得学会怎么挂一挡，怎么挂＿＿＿。
   Wǒ děi xuéhuì zěnme guà yī dǎng, zěnme guà ＿＿＿.

2) 转弯的时候，我得先打＿＿＿。
   Zhuǎnwān de shíhòu, wǒ děi xiān dǎ ＿＿＿.

3) 点火以前，我得先系好＿＿＿。
   Diǎnhuǒ yǐqián, wǒ děi xiān jìhǎo ＿＿＿.

4) 要是路上轮胎坏了，我可以先换上后备箱里的＿＿＿。
   Yàoshi lù shàng lúntāi huài le, wǒ kěyǐ xiān huànshàng hòubèixiāng lǐ de ＿＿＿.

5) 从＿＿＿里，我可以看到后面的车。
   Cóng ＿＿＿lǐ, wǒ kěyǐ kàndào hòumiàn de chē.

5. Put the following actions in starting a car on the proper order. Omit any item that does not belong.

a. 踩刹车
   cǎi shāchē

b. 踩油门
   cǎi yóumén

c. 踩离合器
    cǎi líhéqì

d. 按喇叭
    àn lǎbā

e. 点火
    diǎnhuǒ

f. 起动雨刷
    qǐdòng yǔshuā

g. 挂一挡
    guà yīdǎng

AT THE GAS STATION

我要去**加油站**。 Wǒ yào qù *jiāyóuzhàn*.	gas station
车得**加油**了。 Chē děi *jiāyóu* le.	fill, gas
油箱空了。 *Yóuxiāng kōng* le.	tank, empty
请给我加20**立升**的油。 Qǐng gěi wǒ jiā èrshí *lìshēng* de yóu.	liter
要**无铅**的。 Yào *wúqiān* de.	unleaded
请**查**一下**电池**。 Qǐng *chá* yíxia *diànchí*.	check, battery
冷却液 *lěngquèyè*	coolant
发动机油 *fādòngjī yóu*	engine oil
变速箱润滑油 *biànsùxiāng rùnhuáyóu*	transmission oil
轮胎的**气足**不足 lúntāi de *qì zú* bù zú	air, enough
请**擦**一下**挡风玻璃**。 Qǐng *cā* yíxia *dǎngfēng bōli*.	wipe (clean), windshield

6. Complete.

1) 车得加油了。_____空了。我得找个_____。
    Chē děi jiāyóu le. _____ kōng le. Wǒ děi zhǎo ge _____.

2) 请帮我查一下散热器里的_____够不够。
    Qǐng bāng wǒ chá yíxia sànrèqì lǐ de _____ gòu bú gòu.

3) 发动机好像有问题。请你帮我查一下_____。
   Fādòngjí hǎoxiàng yǒu wèntí. Qǐng nǐ bāng wǒ chá yíxia _____.

4) 再检查一下_____的气足不足。
   Zài jiǎnchá yíxia _____de qì zú bù zú.

5) 我得擦一下_____。太脏了，我什么都看不清。
   Wǒ děi cā yíxia _____. Tài zāng le, wǒ shénme dōu kàn bù qīng.

6) 开了5,000公里以后，最好换一下_____油和_____油。
   Kāile wǔqiān gōnglǐ yǐhou, zuìhǎo huàn yíxia _____yóu hé _____yóu.

SOME MINOR CAR PROBLEMS

车**坏**了。   breakdown
Chē *huài* le.

车**抛锚**了。   stalled
Chē *pāomáo* le.

车**打不着火**了。   won't start
Chē *dǎ bù zháo huǒ* le.

发动机**过热**。   overheating
Fādòngjī *guò rè*.

油箱**漏油**了。   leaking/dripping
Yóuxiāng *lòu yóu* le.

车胎瘪了。   tire, flat
Chētāi biěle.

你能帮我叫一辆**拖车**吗？   tow truck
Nǐ néng bāng wǒ jiào yí liàng *tuōchē* ma?

我需要把车**拖走**。   tow away
Wǒ xūyào bǎ chē *tuōzǒu.*

你能帮我**修**吗？   repair
Nǐ néng bāng wǒ *xiū* ma?

现在就能修吗？   now, right away
Xiànzài jiù néng xiū ma?

您有**备用零件**吗？   spare parts
Nín yǒu *bèiyòng língjiàn* ma?

7. Complete.

一天，在高速公路上，我们的车突然__1__了。车怎么都打不着__2__。我们只
Yì tiān, zài gāosù gōnglù shàng, wǒmen de chē tūrán __1__ le. Chē zěnme dōu dǎ bùzháo __2__. Wǒmen zhǐ

好叫了一辆__3__，把我们的车__4__到了附近的一个车行。我问车行的
hǎo jiào le yí liàng __3__, bǎ wǒmen de chē __4__dào le fùjìn de yí ge chēháng. Wǒ wèn chēháng de

人能不能马上就修，车行的人说只要有__5__，马上就可以__6__。
rén néng bù néng mǎshàng jiù xiū, chēháng de rén shuō zhǐyào yǒu __5__, mǎshàng jiù kěyǐ __6__.

ROAD SIGNS AND REGULATIONS

交通标志和交通规则
jiāotōng biāozhì he jiāotōng guēizé

1. 禁止通行
   jìnzhǐ tōngxíng

1. No thoroughfare

2. 禁止机动车通行
   jìnzhǐ jīdòngchē tōngxíng

2. No thoroughfare for vehicles

3. 禁止驶入
   jìnzhǐ shǐrù

3. Do not enter

4. 禁止停车
   jìnzhǐ tíngchē

4. No parking

5. 禁止鸣喇叭
   jìnzhǐ míng lǎbā

5. No horn

6. 禁止左转弯
   jìnzhǐ zuǒ zhuǎnwān

6. No left turn

7. 禁止调头
jìnzhǐ diàotóu

7. No U turn

8. 禁止超车
jìnzhǐ chāochē

8. No passing

9. 限制速度
xiànzhì sùdù

9. Speed limit (40 km/h)

10. 向右转弯
xiàng yòu zhuǎnwān

10. Right turn

11. 双向交通
zhuāngxiàng jiāotōng

11. Two way traffic

12. 减速让行
jiǎnsù ràngxíng

12. Yield

13. 停车(场)
tíngchē (chǎng)

13. Parking

14. 注意交通信号灯
zhùyì jiāotōng xìnhàodēng

14.   Traffic light

15. 向左急转弯
xiàng zuǒ jí zhuǎnwān

15.   Sharp left turn

16. 道路变窄
dàolù biàn zhǎi

16.   Road narrows

17. 路滑
lù huá

17.   Slippery road

18. 铁路道口
tiělù dàokǒu

18.   Railroad crossing

19. 施工
shīgōng

19.   Under construction

20. 高速公路入口
gāosù gōnglù rùkǒu

20.   Expressway entrance

KEY WORDS

accelerate	加速	jiāsù	manual transmission	手排挡	shǒupáidǎng
adjust	调整	tiáozhěng			
air	气	qì	mileage	里程	lǐchéng
automatic transmission	自动挡	zìdòngdǎng	neutral gear	空档	kōngdǎng
			No honking!	禁止鸣喇叭!	jìnzhǐ míng lǎbā
battery	电池	diànchí			
brake	刹车	shāchē	No left turn!	禁止左转弯!	jìnzhǐ zuǒ zhuǎnwān
brake pedal	刹车闸	shāchē zhá			
breakdown	坏	huài	No parking!	禁止停车!	jìnzhǐ tíngchē
bumper	前保险杠	qián bǎoxiǎngàng	No passing!	禁止超车!	jìnzhǐ chāochē
car	车	chē	No thoroughfare for vehicles!	禁止机动车通行!	jìnzhǐ jīdòngchē tōngxíng
change gears	换挡	huàn dǎng			
charge	收费	shōufèi	No thoroughfare!	禁止通行!	jìnzhǐ tōngxíng
check	查	chá			
clutch	离合器	líhéqì	No U turn!	禁止调头!	jìnzhǐ diàotóu
clutch pedal	离合器踏板	líhéqì tàbǎn	now; right away	现在	xiànzài
			odometer	里程表	lǐchéngbiǎo
contract	合同	hétóng	overheating	过热	guò rè
coolant	冷却液	lěngquèyè	Parking	停车(场)	tíngchē (chǎng)
credit card	信用卡	xìnyòngkǎ	parts	零件	língjiàn
dashboard	仪表盘	yíbiǎopán	pay	付帐	fù zhàng
deposit	押金	yājīn	press	按	àn
Do not enter!	禁止驶入	jìnzhǐ shǐrù	put in first gear	挂一挡	guà yīdǎng
driver's license	驾(驶执)照	jià(shǐ zhí) zhào	Railroad crossing!	铁路道口	tiělù dàokǒu
empty	空	kōng			
engine oil	发动机油	fādòngjīyóu	rearview mirror	后视镜	hòushìjìng
enough	足	zú	regulation	规则	guīzé
fill	加	jiā	rent	租	zū
flat	瘪	biě	rent for a day	租一天	zū yì tiān
fuel gauge	油量表	yóuliàngbiǎo	repair	修	xiū
gas	汽油	qìyóu	reverse gear	倒档	dàodǎng
gas pedal	油门	yóumén	right	右	yòu
gas station	加油站	jiāyóuzhàn	Right turn	向右转弯	xiàng yòu zhuǎnwān
gear shift lever	换挡杆	huàndǎnggǎn			
glove compartment	手套箱	shǒutào xiāng	Road narrows!	道路变窄	dàolù biàn zhǎi
			safety belt	安全带	ānquándài
hand brake	手闸	shǒuzhá	Sharp left turn!	向左急转弯	xiàng zuǒ jí zhuǎnwān
headlight	前(大)灯	qián (dà) dēng			
high beam	高光灯	gāoguāng dēng	sign (a name)	签字	qiān zì
highway entrance	高速公路入口	gāosù gōnglù rùkǒu	Slippery road!	路滑!	lù huá
			spare	备用	bèiyòng
hood of a car	发动机盖	fādòngjī gài	Speed limit (40km/h)	限制速度	xiànzhì sùdù
horn	喇叭	lǎbā			
ignition switch	点火器	diǎnhuǒqì	speedometer	速度表	sùdù biǎo
include	包括	bāokuò	stalled	抛锚	pāomáo
insurance	保险	bǎoxiǎn	start	起动	qǐdòng
jack	千斤顶	qiānjīndǐng	start the engine	点火	diǎn huǒ
kilometer	公里	gōnglǐ	steering wheel	方向盘	fāngxiàngpán
leaking/dripping	漏油	lòu yóu	step on	踩	cǎi
left mirror	左反光镜	zuǒ fǎnguāngjìng	stop the engine	熄火	xī huǒ
license plate	汽车号牌	qìchēhàopái	tank	油箱	yóuxiāng
limits	限制	xiànzhì	tire	轮胎	lúntāi
liter	立升	lìshēng	tow away	拖走	tuōzǒu
low	低	dī	tow truck	拖车	tuōchē

Traffic light!	注意交通 信号灯!	zhùyì jiāotōng xìnhàodēng	Under construction!	施工	shīgōng
traffic sign	交通标志	jiāotōng biāozhì	unleaded	无铅	wúqiān
transmission oil	变速箱润 滑油	biànsùxiāng rùnhuáyóu	windshield windshield wiper	挡风玻璃 雨刷	dǎngfēng bōli yǔshuā
trunk	后备箱	hòubèixiāng	wipe (clean)	擦	cā
turn signal	转向灯	zhuǎnxiàngdēng	won't start	打不着火	dǎ bù zháo huǒ
Two-way traffic	双向交通	shuāngxiàng jiāotōng	Yield!	减速让行!	jiǎnsù ràngxíng

Chapter 7: Asking for directions

第七章：问路
    Wènlù

ASKING FOR DIRECTIONS WHILE ON FOOT

我没有**市区地图**。 Wǒ méiyǒu *shìqū dìtú*.	city map
对不起，先生，我**迷路**了。 Duìbuqǐ, xiānsheng, wǒ *mílù* le.	get lost
请问十四**街**跟北京**大道交叉**的地方在哪儿？ Qǐngwèn shísì jiē gēn Běijīng *Dàdào jiāochā* de dìfang zài nǎr?	street, avenue, cross
离这儿**远**不**远**？ *Lí* zhèr *yuǎn* bù yuǎn?	from, far
不**远**，很**近**，可以**走路**去。 Bù yuǎn, hěn *jìn*. Kěyǐ *zǒulù* qù.	near, walk/on foot
要**过**几个**路口**？ Yào *guò* jǐ ge *lùkǒu*?	pass, crossroad, intersection
向左转还是**向右转**？ *Xiàng zuǒ zhuǎn* háishi *xiàng yòu zhuǎn*?	turn to the left, turn to the right
正好是**相反**的**方向**。 Zhènghǎo shi *xiāngfǎn* de *fāngxiàng*.	opposite, direction
从这儿**向后转**，一**直往前**走， Cóng zhèr *xiàng hòu zhuǎn*, *yìzhí wǎng qián* zǒu,	turn back, straight ahead
过三个路口。 guǒ sān ge lùkǒu.	
向左转/拐，再过两个路口，**就到**了。 *Xiàng zuǒ zhuǎn/guǎi, zài guò* liǎng ge lùkǒu, *jiù dào le*.	turn left, pass again, you'll be there
请问**厕所**在哪儿？ Qǐngwèn *cèsuǒ* zài nǎr?	toilet
洗手间 *xǐshǒujiān*	washroom
在**餐厅**的**后面**。 Zài *cāntīng* de *hòumiàn*.	restaurant, back
请问**附近**有**公共厕所**吗？ Qǐngwèn *fùjìn* yǒu *gōnggòng cèsuǒ* ma?	nearby, public restroom
前面路口向左转就是。 Qiánmiàn lùkǒu xiàng zuǒ zhuǎn jiù shi.	

1. Complete.

A：对不起，先生。我不知道这是什么地方。我＿＿1＿＿了。
   Duìbuqǐ, xiānsheng, Wǒ bù zhīdao zhè shi shénme dìfang, Wǒ ＿＿1＿＿ le.

B：没关系，我可以帮你。你要去哪条＿＿2＿＿？
   Méiguānxì, wǒ kěyǐ bāng nǐ. Nǐ yào qù nǎ tiáo ＿＿2＿＿?

A：我要去十四街。
   Wǒ yào qù shísì jiē.

B：噢！十四街很长。你要去十四街的什么地方？你知道那个地方的街道号码吗？
   Ò! Shísì jiē hěn cháng, Nǐ yào qù shísì jiē de shénme dìfang? Nǐ zhīdao nèige dìfang de jiēdào hàomǎ ma?

A：不知道。我要去十四街跟北京＿＿3＿＿交叉的那个地方。
   Bù zhīdao, Wǒ yào qù shísì jiē gēn Běijīng ＿＿3＿＿ jiāochā de nèige dìfang.

B：啊，我知道了。
   Ā, Wǒ zhīdao le.

A：很＿＿4＿＿吗？
   Hěn ＿＿4＿＿ ma?

B：不＿＿5＿＿，很＿＿6＿＿。你可以＿＿7＿＿去。可是是在相反的＿＿8＿＿。你得向＿＿9＿＿转，
   Bù ＿＿5＿＿, hěn ＿＿6＿＿. Nǐ kěyǐ ＿＿7＿＿qù. Kěshì shi zài xiāngfǎn de ＿＿8＿＿. Nǐ děi xiàng ＿＿9＿＿zhuǎn,

   一直＿＿10＿＿走。过三个＿＿11＿＿，向右＿＿12＿＿，＿＿13＿＿过两个路口，就＿＿14＿＿。
   Yìzhí ＿＿10＿＿ zǒu. Guò sān ge ＿＿11＿＿, xiàng yòu ＿＿12＿＿, ＿＿13＿＿ guò liǎng ge lùkǒu, jiù ＿＿14＿＿.

A：谢谢你，先生。我重复一次好吗？从＿＿15＿＿向＿＿16＿＿转，＿＿17＿＿往前走，
   Xièxie nǐ, xiānsheng, Wǒ chóngfù yí cì hǎo ma? Cóng ＿＿15＿＿ xiàng ＿＿16＿＿ zhuǎn, ＿＿17＿＿wǎng qián zǒu,

   到第三个＿＿18＿＿向＿＿19＿＿转，再＿＿20＿＿两个路口就是十四街。对吗？
   dào dì sān ge ＿＿18＿＿ xiàng ＿＿19＿＿ zhuǎn, zài ＿＿20＿＿ liǎng ge lùkǒu jiù shi shísì jiē. Duìma?

B：一点不错！
   Yìdiǎn búcuò!

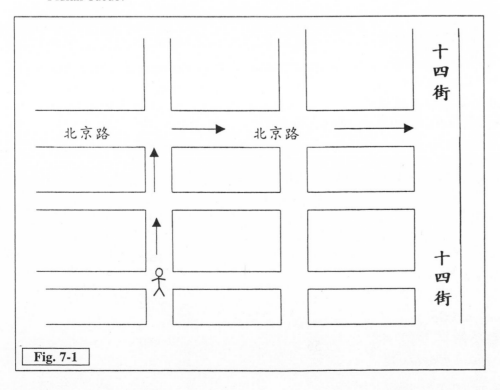

Fig. 7-1

请问，上海大道在哪儿？
Qǐng wèn, Shànghǎi Dàdào zài nǎr?

很远。你得坐**公共汽车**去。   bus
Hěn yuǎn, nǐ děi zuò *gōnggòng qìchē* qù.

公共汽车站就在**下一个街口**。   bus stop, next, street corner
Gōnggòng qìchē zhàn jiù zài *xià yí ge jiēkǒu*.

你得坐**十路**公共汽车。   Number 10/Route 10
Nǐ děi zuò *shí lù* gōnggòng qìchē.

到第六站**下车**就是上海大道。   get off
Dào dì liù zhàn *xià chē* jiùshi Shànghǎi Dàdào.

2. Complete.

A：对不起，先生，您知道上海___1___在哪儿吗？
　　Duìbuqǐ, xiānsheng, nín zhīdao Shànghǎi ___1___ zài nàr ma?

B：知道。很远。你不能___2___去。你得坐___3___。
　　Zhīdao. Hěnyuǎn. Nǐ bù néng ___2___ qù. Nǐ děi zuò ___3___.

A：我在哪儿坐公共汽车呢？
　　Wǒ zài nǎr zuò gōnggòng qìchē ne?

B：___4___就在下一个___5___。
　　___4___ jiù zài xià yí ge ___5___.

A：我应该坐几___6___公共汽车呢？
　　Wǒ yīnggāi zuò jǐ ___6___ gōnggòng qìchē ne?

B：那个___7___有两趟公共汽车经过。你得坐___8___。过六站以后___9___，
　　Nèi ge ___7___ yǒu liǎng tàng gōnggòng qìchē jīngguò. Nǐ děi zuò ___8___. Guò liù zhàn yǐhòu ___9___,

　　你就到了上海大道了。
　　nǐ jiù dàole Shànghǎi Dàdào le.

A：太谢谢您了！
　　Tài xièxie nín le!

B：不客气。
　　Bú kèqi.

ASKING FOR DIRECTIONS WHILE IN A CAR

请问去西山**公园怎么走**？   park, how to go to
Qǐng wèn qù Xīshān *Gōngyuán zěnme zǒu?*

西山公园在**郊区**。   suburb
Xīshān gōngyuán zài *jiāoqū*.

你得走二号**国道**。   national highway
Nǐ děi zǒu èr hào *guódào*.

你也可以走**高速公路**去。   expressway
Nǐ yě kěyǐ zǒu *gāosù gōnglù* qù.

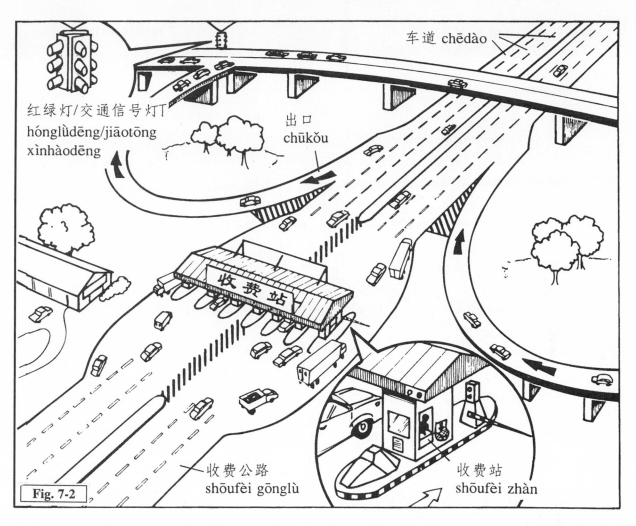

车道 chēdào

红绿灯/交通信号灯
hónglǜdēng/jiāotōng
xìnhàodēng

出口
chūkǒu

收费站

收费公路
shōufèi gōnglù

收费站
shōufèi zhàn

Fig. 7-2

我怎么上高速公路呢？　　　　　　　　　　　　　　get (on)to
Wǒ zěnme *shàng* gāosù gōnglù ne?

从这儿**开**到第二个**红绿灯**向左转，　　　　　　drive, traffic light
Cóng zhèr *kāi* dào dì èr ge *hónglǜdēng* xiàng zuǒ zhuǎn,

再一直往前开。
zài yìzhí wǎng qián kāi.

这不是一条**单行道**。　　　　　　　　　　　　　　one-way street
Zhè bú shi yì tiáo *dānxíngdào*.

这是一条**收费公路**。　　　　　　　　　　　　　　turnpike
Zhè shi yì tiáo *shōufèi gōnglù*.

在**收费站**付了高速**公路费**以后，　　　　　　　tollbooth, toll
Zài *shōufèi zhàn* fùle gāosù *gōnglù fèi* yǐhòu,

继续走右边的**车道**，　　　　　　　　　　　　keep, lane
jìxù zǒu yòubiān de *chēdào*,

从第二个**出口**出去就上高速公路了。　　　　　　exit
cóng dì èr ge *chūkǒu* chūqu jiù shàng gāsù gōnglù le.

高速公路上车很多。
Gāosù gōnglù shàng chē hěn duō.

高峰时期常常**堵车/塞车**。   rush hour, traffic jam
Gāofēng shíqī chángcháng *dǔchē/sāichē*.

3. Complete.

1) 西山公园在北京的_____。
   Xīshān Gōngyuán zài Běijīng de _____.

2) 开车去西山公园得走_____或者_____。
   Kāichē qù Xīshān Gōngyuán děi zǒu _____ huòzhě _____.

3) 高速公路上车很多，_____时期常常_____。
   Gāosù gōnglù shàng chē hěn duō, _____ shíqī chángcháng _____.

4) 大家上班和下班的时候就是_____。
   Dàjiā shàngbān hé xiàbān de shíhou jiù shi _____.

5) 我觉得走二号_____比走高速公路更快。
   Wǒ juéde zǒu èr hào _____ bǐ zǒu gāosù gōnglù gèng kuài.

6) 走收费公路得付_____。
   Zǒu shōu fèi gōnglù děi fù _____.

7) 高速公路上通常有三条_____，
   Gāosù gōnglù shàng tōngcháng yǒu sān tiáo _____.

8) 我们得继续走右边的_____，因为我们要在下一个_____出高速公路。
   Wǒmen děi jìxù zǒu yòubiān de _____, yīnwèi wǒmen yào zài xià yí ge _____ chū gāosù gōnglù.

9) 我们不能进这条街，因为这是一条_____。
   Wǒmen bù néng jìn zhèi tiáo jiē, yīnwèi zhè shi yì tiáo _____.

10) 你没看见_____吗？红灯亮的时候我们应该停车。
    Nǐ méi kànjiàn _____ ma? Hóngdēng liàng de shíhou wǒmen yīnggāi tíngchē.

4. Identify each item in figure 7-3.

5. Match.

1) 付高速公路费的地方叫_____。   a. 单行道
   Fù gāosù gōnglù fèi de dìfang jiào _____.   dān xíng dào

2) 告诉你停车或者是继续开车的信号灯叫_____。   b. 高峰时期
   Gàosù nǐ tíng chē huòzhě shì jìxù kāi chē de xìnhàodēng jiào _____.   gāo fēng shíqī

3) 汽车不能朝两个方向开的街叫_____。   c. 出口
   Qìchē bù néng cháo liǎng ge fāngxiàng kāi de jiē jiào _____.   chūkǒu

4) 在_____你会看见两条街。   d. 收费站
   Zài _____ nǐ huì kànjiàn liǎng tiáo jiē.   shōu fèi zhàn

5) 交通很忙的时候叫_____。   e. 一直往前走
   Jiāotōng hěn máng de shíhou jiào _____.   yìzhí wǎng qián zǒu

6) 不在城里，可是离城市不远的地方叫_____。   f. 红绿灯
   Bú zài chéng lǐ, kěshì lí chéngshì bù yuǎn de dìfang jiào _____.   hóng lǜ dēng

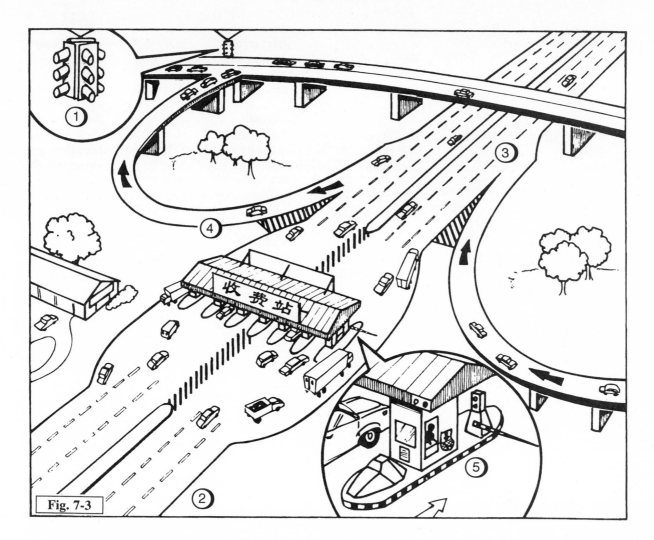

Fig. 7-3

7) 不向左转也不向右转就是_____。
   Bú xiàng zuǒ zhuǎn yě bú xiàng yòu zhuǎn jiùshi _____.

   g. 街角
      jiējiǎo

8) 可以出去的地方叫_____。
   Kěyǐ chūqù de dìfang jiào _____.

   h. 郊区
      jiāoqū

Key Words

again	再	zài	drive	开车	kāi chē
ask for direction	问路	wènlù	exit	出口	chūkǒu
avenue	大道	dàdào	express way	高速公路	gāosù gōnglù
back	后面	hòumiàn	far	远	yuǎn
bus	公共汽车	gōnggòng qìchē	from	离	lí
bus stop	汽车站	qìchēzhàn	get (on)to	上	shàng
city map	市区地图	shìqū dìtú	get off	下	xià
cross	交叉	jiāochā	how to go	怎么走	zěnme zǒu
cross road/	路口	lùkǒu	keep, continue	继续	jìxù
intersection			lane	车道	chēdào
direction	方向	fāngxiàng	lost	迷路	mílù

national highway	国道	guódào	street	街	jiē
near	近	jìn	street corner	街口/街角	jiēkǒu/jiējiǎo
nearby	附近	fùjìn	suburb	郊区	jiāoqū
next	下一个	xià yī ge	toilet	厕所	cèsuǒ
Number 10/ Route 10(bus)	十路	shí lù	toll	高速公路费	gāosù gōnglù fèi
one-way street	单行道	dānxíngdào	tollbooth	收费站	shōufèi zhàn
opposite	相反	xiāngfǎn	traffic jam	堵车/塞车	dǔchē/sāichē
park	公园	gōngyuán	traffic light	红绿灯	hónglùdēng
pass	经过	jīngguò	turn back	向后转	xiàng hòu zhuǎn
public	公共	gōnggòng	turn to the left	向左转/拐	xiàng zuǒ zhuǎn/guǎi
public restroom	公共厕所	gōnggòng cèsuǒ	turnpike	收费公路	shōufèi gōnglù
restaurant	餐厅	cāntīng	walk/on foot	走路	zǒu lù
right	右	yòu	washroom	洗手间	xǐshǒujiān
rush hour	高峰期	gāofēngqī	You'll be there.	你就到了	Nǐ jiù dào le.
straight ahead	一直向前	yìzhí xiàngqián			

Chapter 8: Making a phone call

第八章：打电话
Dǎdiànhuà

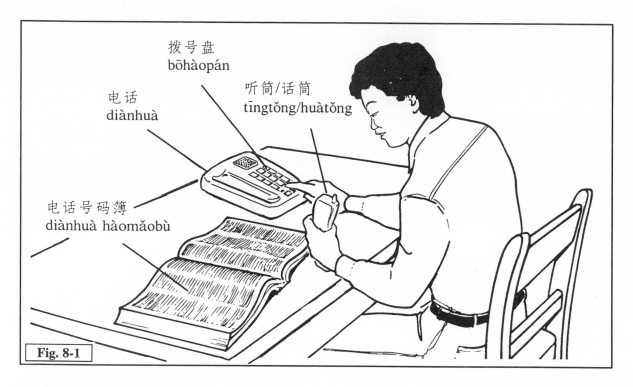

拨号盘
bōhàopán

电话
diànhuà

听筒/话筒
tīngtǒng/huàtǒng

电话号码簿
diànhuà hàomǎobù

Fig. 8-1

MAKING A LOCAL CALL

我想**打一个电话**， Wǒ xiǎng *dǎ yí ge diànhuà*,	make a phone call
可是我不知道**号码**。 Kěshì wǒ bù zhīdao *hàomǎ*.	number
我得**查**电话**号码簿**。 Wǒ děi *chá* diànhuà *hàomabù*.	consult; directory
地区号(码)是多少？ *Dìqū hào(mǎ)* shi duōshǎo?	area code
打**市内**电话你不必**拨**地区号码。 Dǎ *shìnèi* diànhuà nǐ bú bì *bō* dìqū hàomǎ.	local; dial
你拿起**听筒**，听到**拨号音**， Nǐ ná qǐ *tīngtǒng*, tīng dào *bōhào yīn*,	receiver; dial tone
就可以在**拨号盘**上**按**电话号码。 jiù kěyǐ zài *bōhàopán* shàng *àn* diànhuà hàomǎ.	dial pad; press

电话铃一响。   ring
Diànhuà líng yì xiǎng,

对方就会**接**电话。   the other party; receive
Duìfāng jiū huì *jiē* diànhuà.

1. Complete.

史密斯先生想给朋友王小姐打一个＿＿1＿＿，可是他不知道她的电话＿＿2＿＿。
Shǐmìsī xiānsheng xiǎng gěi péngyǒu Wáng xiǎojiě dǎ yí ge ＿1＿, kěshì tā bù zhīdao tā de diànhuà ＿2＿.

他得查＿＿3＿＿。他查到了她的电话号码是8789986。因为王小姐就住在本市，
Tā děi chá ＿3＿. Tā chádào le tā de diànhuà hàomǎ shi 8789986. Yīnwèi Wáng xiǎojiě jiù zhù zài běn shì,

所以史密斯先生只要打一个＿＿4＿＿电话。他不必拨＿＿5＿＿。他拿起＿＿6＿＿，听到＿＿7＿＿以后，
suǒyǐ Shǐmìsī xiānsheng zhǐyào dǎo yí ge ＿4＿ diànhuà. Tā búbì bō ＿5＿. Tā ná qǐ ＿6＿, tīngdào ＿7＿ yǐhòu,

就在＿＿8＿＿上＿＿9＿＿了王小姐的电话号码。他听到了对方的＿＿10＿＿。他希望
jiù zài ＿8＿ shàng ＿9＿ le Wáng xiǎojiě de diànhuà hàomǎ. Tā tīngdào le duìfāng de ＿10＿. Tā xīwàng

王小姐在家，可以＿＿11＿＿他的电话。
Wáng xiǎojiě zài jiā, kěyǐ ＿11＿ tā de diànhuà.

MAKING A LONG-DISTANCE CALL

我要打一个**长途**电话。   long distance
Wǒ yào dǎ yí ge *chángtú* diànhuà.

这是一个**国际**电话，不是**市外**电话。   international; out-of-town
Zhè shi yí ge *guójì* diànhuà, bú shi *shì wài* diànhuà.

打长途电话可以**直拨**，不必**通过接线员**。   direct dial; go through; operator
Dǎ chángtú diànhuà kěyǐ *zhíbō*, bú bì *tōngguò jiēxiànyuán*.

你得先拨**国家号码**，再拨地区号码。   country code
Nǐ děi xiān bō *guójiā hàomǎ*, zài bō dìqū hàomǎ.

要是你不想**付电话费**，   pay; telephone fare/charge
Yàoshi nǐ bù xiǎng *fù diànhuà fèi*,

你可以打**对方付费的电话**。   collect call
Nǐ kěyǐ dǎ *duìfāng fùfèi de diànhuà*.

喂！   Hello!
wéi/wèi.

2. Complete.

1) 这不是本市电话。这是＿＿＿＿＿＿＿电话。
   Zhè bú shi běn shì diànhuà. Zhè shi ＿＿＿＿＿＿diànhuà.

2) 打市外电话时，你得先拨＿＿＿＿＿＿＿号码。
   Dǎ shì wài diànhuà shí, nǐ děi xiān bō ＿＿＿＿＿＿ hàomǎ.

3) 打国际电话时，你得先拨＿＿＿＿＿＿＿号码。
   Dǎ guójì diànhuà shí, nǐ děi xiān bō ＿＿＿＿＿＿ hàomǎ.

4) 这个电话不能直拨国际电话。你得通过_____拨你要的号码。
    Zhèi ge diànhuà bù néng zhí bō guójì diànhuà. Nǐ děi tōngguò _____ bō nǐ yào de hàomǎ.

5) 我没有钱，我只能打_____的电话。
    Wǒ méiyǒu qián, wǒ zhǐ néng dǎ _____ de diànhuà.

CELLULAR PHONES

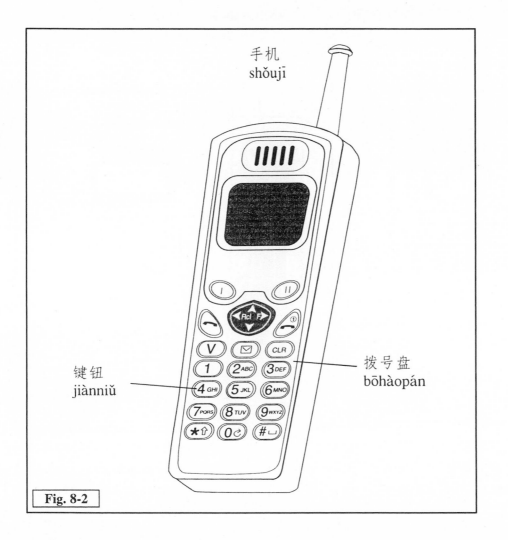

手机
shǒujī

键钮
jiànniǔ

拨号盘
bōhàopán

Fig. 8-2

手机   cellular phone
shǒujī

无绳电话   cordless phone
wúshéng diànhuà

3. Complete.

现在很多人都喜欢用__1__。这种电话没有__2__，所以叫__3__电话。
Xiànzài hěn duō rén dōu xǐhuan yòng __1__. Zhèi zhǒng diànhuà méi yǒu __2__, suǒyǐ yòu jiào __3__ diànhuà.

可是用__4__比用无绳电话更方便。因为不管你在哪儿都可以打__5__。
Kěshì yòng __4__ bǐ yòng wúshéng diànhuà gèng fāngbiàn, Yīnwèi bùguǎn nǐ zài nǎr dōu kěyǐ dǎ __5__.

USING A PUBLIC PHONE

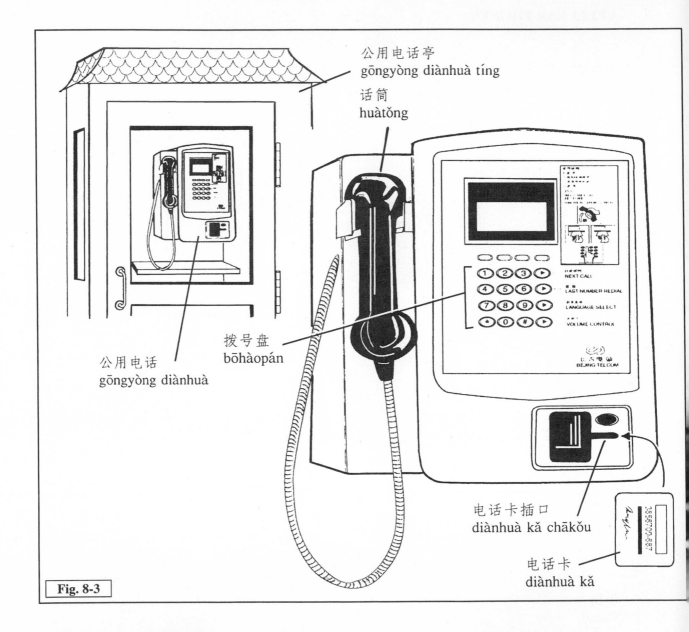

公用电话亭
gōngyòng diànhuà tíng

话筒
huàtǒng

公用电话
gōngyòng diànhuà

拨号盘
bōhàopán

电话卡插口
diànhuà kǎ chākǒu

电话卡
diànhuà kǎ

Fig. 8-3

请问这儿有没有**公用电话**?   public phone
Qǐngwèn zhèr yǒu méiyǒu *gōngyòng diànhuà*?

请问公用**电话亭**在哪儿?   phone booth
Qǐngwèn gōngyòng *diànhuàtíng* zài nǎr?

你有没有**电话卡**？   prepaid phone card
Nǐ yǒu méiyǒu *diànhuàkǎ*?

要是你没有电话卡，
Yàoshi nǐ méiyǒu diànhuàkǎ,

你也可以用**硬币**。   coins
nǐ yě kěyǐ yòng *yìngbì*.

要是你不知道对方的电话号码，
Yàoshi nǐ bù zhīdao duìfāng de diànhuà hàomǎ,

你可以问**查号台**。   phone directory service
Nǐ kěyǐ wèn *cháhàotái*.

打公用电话时，你得：
Dǎ gōngyòng diànhuà shí, nǐ děi:

1) **拿起**电话听筒   pick up
   náqǐ diànhuà tīngtǒng,

2) **插入**电话卡 (或者**投入**硬币)   insert; feed; coin
   chārù diànhuàkǎ (huòzhě *tóurù* yìngbì)

3) 听到拨号音时，拨你需要的号码
   tīngdào bōhàoyīn shí, bō nǐ xūyào de hàomǎ

4) 等对方的电话铃响
   děng duìfāng de diànhuàlíng xiǎng

5) 听到对方的**回答**时，开始说话。   answer
   tīngdào duìfāng de *huídá* shí, kāishǐ shuōhuà.

4. Complete.

朋友们，你们好！我现在在一个__1__亭。这是我第一次用__2__打电话。
Péngyǒumen, nǐmen hǎo! Wǒ xiànzài zài yí ge __1__ tíng. Zhè shi wǒ dì yī cì yòng __2__ dǎ diànhuà.

我怎么打呢？啊，对了！我有一张__3__。我先__4__电话听筒，__5__我的电话卡，
Wǒ zěnme dǎ ne? Ā, duì le! Wǒ yǒu yì zhāng __3__. Wǒ xiān __4__ diànhuà tīngtǒng, __5__ wǒde diànhuàkǎ.

现在我来听听--噢！我听到了__6__音！那我就可以开始__7__了。现在我听到了
Xiànzài wǒ lái tīngting,...Ò! wǒ tīngdào le __6__ yīn! Nà wǒ jiù kěyǐ kāishǐ __7__ le. Xiànzài wǒ tīngdào le

__8__的电话铃声。诶，对方__9__电话了！"喂！..."
__8__ de diànhuà líng shēng. Éi, duìfāng __9__ diànuhà le! "wéi! ..."

SPEAKING ON THE PHONE

喂！
Wéi!

请问史密斯先生在吗？   May I please speak to Mr. Smith?
Qǐngwèn Shǐmìsī xiānsheng zài ma?

请问您是哪一位？   May I ask who is calling?
Qǐngwèn nín shi nǎ yí wèi?

我姓王，是他的朋友。
Wǒ xìng Wáng, shi tāde péngyǒu.

请稍等。别挂电话。   Hold on please; hang up
Qǐng shāoděng, bié guà diàhuà.

对不起，他不在。   He is not in.
Duìbùqǐ, *tā bú zài.*

我可以留话吗？   leave a message
Wǒ kěyǐ *liú huà* ma?

当然可以。
Dāngrán kěyǐ.

5. Use the following as a guide to make up your own telephone conversation.

A：喂！
　　Wéi!

B：__1__！__2__王先生__3__？
　　__1__！__2__Wáng xiānsheng __3__?

A：请问__4__？
　　Qǐngwèn __4__?

B：__5__。
　　__5__.

A：请__6__。(After a moment) 对不起，__7__。
　　Qǐng __6__. (After a moment) Duìbuqǐ, __7__.

B：请先别__8__，我可以__9__吗？
　　Qǐng xiān bié __8__. Wǒ kěyǐ __9__ma?

A：当然可以。
　　Dāngrán kěyǐ.

SOME PROBLEMS YOU MAY HAVE

怎么没有拨号音？   dial tone
Zěnme méiyǒu bōhàoyīn?

电话坏了。   broken
Diànhuà huài le.

你拨错了号码。   dialed wrong number
Nǐ bōcuòle hàomǎ.

电话占线。   (line is) busy
Diànhuà zhàn xiàn.

电话里有很多杂音/干扰音。   static/noise
Diànhuà lǐ yǒu hěnduō záyīn/gānrǎoyīn.

电话**线断**了。   line, disconnected
Diànhuà*xiàn duàn*le.

没有人接(电话)。   No one answers
Méiyǒu rén jiē (diànhuà).

我过一会儿再**打回去**。   call back
Wǒ guò yíhuìr zài *dǎ huíqù*.

电话**接不通**。   cannot connect
Diànhuà *jiē bù tōng*.

请问**分机号码**是多少?   extension number
Qǐngwèn *fēnjī hàomǎ* shi duōshǎo?

6. Complete.

我拿起话筒，可是电话没有___1___。
Wǒ náqǐ huàtǒng, kěshì diànhuà méiyǒu ___1___.

这个电话可能___2___。
Zhèi ge diànhuà kěnéng ___2___.

每次我给他打电话都是___3___。他在给谁打电话呢?
Měi cì wǒ gěi tā dǎ diànhuà dōushi ___3___. Tā zài gěi shéi dǎ diànhuà ne?

A：我们这儿没有姓王的。B：对不起，我___4___。
A: Wǒmen zhèr méiyǒu xìng Wáng de. B: Duìbuqǐ, wǒ ___4___.

没有人接电话。我过一会儿___5___。
Méiyǒu rén jiē diànhuà. Wǒ guò yí huìr ___5___.

我听不清楚，___6___太多了。
Wǒ tīng bù qīngchǔ, ___6___ tài duō le.

我们正在谈话，可是忽然没声音了。电话线___7___了。
Wǒmen zhèngzài tánhuà, kěshì hūrán méi shēngyīng le. Diànhuà xiàn ___7___ le.

7. Put the following in the proper order for making a phone call.

a. 拿起电话话筒
   Náqǐ diànhuà huàtǒng

b. 挂上电话
   Guàshàng diànhuà

c. 拨电话号码
   Bō diànhuà hàomǎ

d. 在电话号码簿上查号码
   Zài diànhuà hàomǎbù shàng chá hàomǎ

e. 听拨号音
   Tīng bōhàoyīn

f. 等对方接电话
   Děng duìfāng jiē diànhuà

g. 开始说话
   Kāishǐ shuōhuà

BEEPING

有的人没有手机，可是有**呼机**。   beeper
Yǒude rén méiyǒu shǒujī, kěshì yǒu *hūjī*.

要是你想**呼**一个朋友，   beep
Yàoshi nǐ xiǎng *hū* yí ge péngyǒu,

你得知道他的**呼机号码**。   beeper number
Nǐ děi zhīdào tā de *hūjī hàomǎ*.

他**收到**你在呼机上的**留言**以后，   receive, message
Tā *shōudào* nǐ zài hūjī shàng de *liúyán* yǐhòu,

可以很快给你**回电话**。   return call
Kěyǐ hěn kuài gěi nǐ *huí diànhuà*.

8. Complete

你朋友的__1__是86045566-12345
Nǐ péngyǒu de __1__ shi 86045566-12345.

你得先打电话给860455566
Nǐ děi xiān dǎ diànhuà gěi 860455566.

A：您好!
    Nín hǎo.

B：请__2__12345。
    Qǐng __2__ 12345.

A：您贵__3__?
    Nín guì __3__?

B：我姓王。
    Wǒ xìng wáng.

A：请说全名。
    Qǐng shuō quán míng.

B：王大明。
    Wáng Dàmíng.

A：您的__4__?
    Nín de __4__?

B：请给86542366__5__。
    Qǐng gěi 86542366 __5__.

KEY WORDS

again	再	zài	
answer a phone	接电话	jiē diànhuà	
area code	地区号(码)	dìqūhào(mǎ)	
beep	呼	hū	
beeper	呼机	hūjī	
beeper number	呼机号码	hūjī hàomǎ	
broken	坏了	huài le	
busy signal	忙音	mángyīn	
cellular	手机	shǒujī	
coin	硬币	yìngbì	
collect call	对方付费电话	duìfāng fùfèi diànhuà	
connect	接	jiē	
connection	连通	liántōng	
cordless	无绳	wúshéng	
country code	国家号码	guójiā hàomǎ	
dial	拨	bō	
dial pad	拨号盘	bōhào pán	
dial tone	拨号音	bōhàoyīn	
disconnected	断了	duànle	
extension	分机	fēnjī	
extension number	分机号码	fēnjī hàomǎ	
hang up	挂	guà	
hold on	稍等	shāoděng	
international call	国际电话	guójì diànhuà	
leave a message	留话	liúhuà	
line	线	xiàn	
local call	本市电话	běnshì diànhuà	
long-distance call	长途电话	chángtú diànhuà	
make (a call)	打(电话)	dǎ diànhuà	
message	留言	liúyán	
operator	接线员	jiēxiànyuán	
phone book	电话号码簿	diànhuà hàomǎbù	
phone number	电话号码	diànhuà hàomǎ	
pick up	拿起	náqǐ	
receive	收到	shōudào	
return call	回电话	huí diànhuà	
ring	响	xiǎng	
rotary dial	转盘电话	zhuànpán diànhuà	
static	杂音/干扰音	záyīn/gānrǎoyīn	
switchboard	总机	zǒngjī	
telephone card	电话卡	diànhuàkǎ	
telephone booth	公共电话亭	gōnggòng diànhuà tíng	
the line is busy	占线	zhànxiàn	
the other party	对方	duìfāng	
touchtone	按键电话	ànjiàn diànhuà	
try	试	shì	
who's calling?	请问是哪位?	qǐngwèn shi nǎwèi	
wrong number	号码错了	hàomǎ cuòle	

Chapter 9: At the hotel[5]

第九章：旅馆
Lǚguǎn

CHECKING IN

办理入住手续
Bànlǐ rùzhù shǒuxù

前台
qiántái

前台

行李员
xínglǐyuán

客房钥匙
kèfáng
yàoshi

前台服务员
qiántái
fúwùyuán

客人
kèrén

信用卡
xìngyòngkǎ

旅客登记表
lǚkè dēngjì biǎo

Fig. 9-1

这位**客人**在**饭店前台**。	guest; hotel; reception desk
Zhèi wèi *kèrén* zài *fàndiàn qiántái.*	
他说，我在你们这儿**预定**了一个**单人房间**。	reserve; single room
Tā shuō, wǒ zài nǐmen zhèr *yùdìng*le yí ge *dānrén fángjiān.*	
双人房间	double room
shuāngrén fángjiān	
套间	suite
tàojiān	

---

[5] There are different terms for different kinds of hotels: the more luxurious ones are called "酒店jiǔdiàn,"
"饭店fàndiàn," or "宾馆bīnguǎn." "旅馆lǚguǎn" is a more general term for midrange hotels.

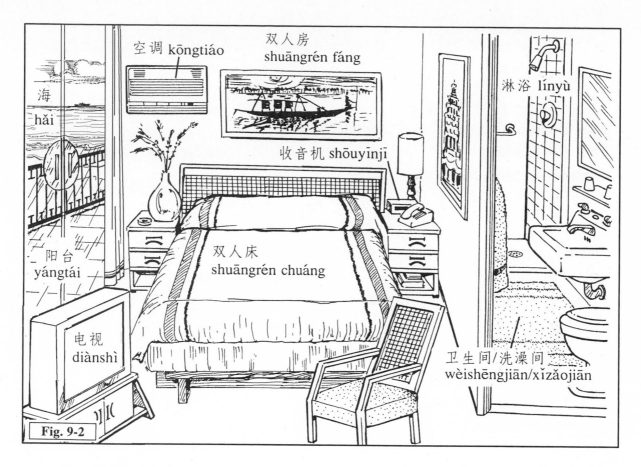

空调 kōngtiáo

双人房
shuāngrén fáng

海
hǎi

淋浴 línyù

收音机 shōuyīnjī

双人床
shuāngrén chuáng

阳台
yángtái

电视
diànshì

卫生间/洗澡间
wèishēngjiān/xǐzǎojiān

Fig. 9-2

我想要一个**带阳台**的房间。   with, balcony
Wǒ xiǎng yào yí ge *dài yángtái* de fángjiān.

       卫生间   bathroom
       wèishēngjiān

我想要一个**朝海**的房间。   face, the sea
Wǒ xiǎng yào yí ge *cháo hǎi* de fángjiān

       山   mountain
       shān

       大街   the street
       dàjiē

       院子   courtyard
       yuànzi

我想要一个**安静的**房间。   quiet
Wǒ xiǎng yào yí ge *ānjìng* de fángjiān.

       光线好的   bright
       guāngxiàn hǎo de

这个房间有**暖气**吗？   heat
Zhèi ge fángjiān yǒu *nuǎnqì* ma?

       空调   air conditioner
       kōngtiáo

电视   TV
diànshì

淋浴   shower
línyù

这个房间**房价**多少？**包早餐**吗？   room charge; including breakfast
Zhèi ge fángjiān *fángjià* duōshǎo? *Bāo zǎocān* ma?

全天供应热水吗？   all day long, hot water
Quán tiān gōngyìng *rèshuǐ* ma?

我先看一下房间，好吗？
Wǒ xiān kàn yíxià fángjiān, hǎo ma?

我不太喜欢这间。有**别的**吗？   other
Wǒ bú tài xǐhuan zhèi jiān. Yǒu *biéde* ma?

能不能再**加**一张**床**？   add; bed
Néng bu néng zài *jiā* yì zhāng *chuáng*?

这个饭店有**游泳池**吗？   swimming pool
Zhèi ge fàndiàn yǒu *yóuyǒngchí* ma?

请把我的行李**送**到我的房间去。   deliver
Qǐng bǎ wǒde xíngli *sòng* dào wǒde fángjiān qù.

我们要在这儿**呆到**下星期三。   stay until
Wǒmen yào zài zhèr *dāidào* xià xīngqīsān.

前台服务员说：   receptionist
Qiántái fúwùyuán shuō,

我们今天**客满**了，没有**空**房间了。   full; empty/vacant
Wǒmen jīntiān *kèmǎn* le. Méiyǒu *kōng* fángjiān le.

我们还有空房间。
Wǒmen hái yǒu kōng fángjiān.

这个房间有两张**单人床**。   single bed
Zhèi ge fángjiān yǒu liǎng zhāng *dānrénchuáng*.

那个房间有一张**双人床**。   double bed
Nèi ge fángjiān yǒu yí zhāng *shuāngrénchuáng*.

请您**填**一下这张**表**。   fill in; form
Qǐng nín *tián* yíxià zhèi zhāng biǎo.

对不起，您的**证件**呢？   ID
Duìbuqǐ, nínde *zhèngjiàn* ne?

您用现金还是**信用卡**付帐？   credit card
Nín yòng xiànjīn háishi *xìnyòngkǎ* fù zhàng?

这是您的房间**钥匙**，604号房间。   key
Zhè shi nínde fángjiān *yàoshi*, liùlíngsì hào fángjiān.

行李员会把行李送到您的房间去。   porter
Xíngliyuán huì bǎ xíngli sòngdào nínde fángjiān qù.

您**退房**的时候，请把钥匙**留**在前台。   check out; leave
Nín *tuìfáng* de shíhou, qǐng bǎ yàoshi *liú* zài qiántái.

1. Complete

1) 上个月我就打电话_____了房间。
   Shàng ge yuè wǒ jiù dǎ diànhuà _____le fángjiān.

2) _____是给一个人住的房间。
   _____shi gěi yí ge rén zhù de fángjiān.

3) 给两个人住的房间是_____。
   Gěi liǎng ge rén zhù de fángjiān shi _____.

4) 朝_____的房间比朝_____的房间安静。
   Cháo _____de fángjiān bǐ cháo _____de fángjiān ānjìng.

5) 因为这个旅馆在海边，我希望我的房间朝_____。
   Yīnwèi zhèi ge lǚguǎn zài hǎibiān, wǒ xīwàng wǒde fángjiān cháo _____.

6) 因为这家旅馆的房费_____，所以我不必出去吃早饭。
   Yīnwèi zhèi jiā lǚguǎn de fángfèi _____, suǒyǐ wǒ búbì chūqù chī zǎofàn.

7) 夏天我想要一个带_____的房间。
   Xiàtiān wǒ xiǎngyào yí ge dài _____de fángjiān.

8) 冬天我想要一个带_____的房间。
   Dōngtiān wǒ xiǎngyào yí ge dài _____de fángjiān.

9) 要是旅馆_____了，就没有_____房间了。
   Yàoshi lǚguǎn _____le, jiù méiyǒu _____fángjiān le.

10) 客人入住以前，得在总台_____，而且得出示_____。
   Kèrén rùzhù yǐqián, děi zài zǒngtái _____, érqiě děi chūshì _____.

11) 要是客人是外国人，他就得出示_____。
   Yàoshi kèrén shi wàiguórén, tā jiù děi chūshì _____.

12) _____会帮助客人把行李拿到房间去。
   _____huì bāngzhù kèrén bǎ xíngli nádào fángjiān qù.

13) 很多人都不带太多现金。他们用_____付帐。
   Hěn duō rén dōu bú dài tài duō xiànjīn. Tāmen yòng _____fù zhàng.

14) 客人离开的时候，应该留下房间的_____。
   Kèrén líkāi de shíhòu, yīnggāi liúxià fángjiān de _____.

2. At the hotel's reception desk.

A：您好!
   Nín hǎo!

B：您好! 你们还有双人__1__吗?
   Nín hǎo! Nǐmen hái yǒu shuāngrén __1__ma?

A：你们__2__了吗?
   Nǐmen __2__le ma?

B：没有。
   Méiyǒu.

A：我来看看。我们今天差不多__3__了。噢! 还有两个__4__的双人房。
   Wǒ lái kànkan. Wǒmen jīntiān chàbuduō __3__le. Ò. Hái yǒu liǎng ge __4__de shuāngrénfáng.

B：太好了!
　　Tài hǎo le.

A：您想要带两张__5__的还是要带一张__6__的?
　　Nín xiǎng yào dài liǎng zhāng __5__ de háishi yào dài yì zhāng __6__ de?

B：带两张__7__的。这个房间是朝街的还是朝院子的?
　　Dài liǎng zhāng __7__ de. Zhèi ge fángjiān shi cháo jiē de háishi cháo yuànzi de?

A：这些房间都是__8__街的。
　　Zhèixiē fángjiān dōu shi __8__ jiē de.

B：没问题。__9__多少?
　　Méi wènti. __9__ duōshǎo?

A：二百五十块一天，__10__早餐。
　　Èrbǎi wǔshí kuài yì tiān, __10__ 早餐

B：这几天真热，房间里有__11__吗?
　　Zhèi jǐ tiān zhēn rè. Fángjiān lǐ yǒu __11__ ma?

A：有。也有收音机和电视。您打算住__12__?
　　Yǒu. Yě yǒu shōuyīnjī hé diànshi. Nín dǎsuan zhù __12__?

B：我们要住__13__下星期二。
　　Wǒmen yào zhù __13__ xià xīngqīèr.

A：现在请您__14__一下这张表。可以看看您的__15__吗?
　　Xiànzài qǐng nín __14__ yíxia zhèi zhāng biǎo. Kěyǐ kànkan nín de __15__ ma?

B：在这儿。
　　Zài zhèr.

A：谢谢。这是您的钥匙。
　　Xièxie. Zhè shi nínde yàoshi.

B：谢谢你!
　　Xièxie nǐ.

A：不客气。行李员会把您的__16__送到房间去。
　　Bú kèqi. Xíngliyuán huì bǎ nínde __16__ sòngdào fángjiān qù.

SPEAKING WITH THE HOUSEKEEPER

客房服务员!   (hotel) housekeeper
Kèfáng fúwùyuán!

请进!
Qǐng jìn!

我可以现在**打扫**房间吗?   clean
Wǒ kěyǐ xiànzài *dǎsǎo* fángjiān ma?

可以。谢谢。我们马上就要出去。
Kěyǐ, Xièxie. Wǒmen mǎshàng jiùyào chūqù.

你们有没有**洗衣服务**?   laundry service
Nǐmen yǒu méyǒu *xǐyī fúwù*.

衣架
yījià

衣橱
yīchú

毛巾
máojīn

浴巾
yùjīn

电插座
diànchāzuò

淋浴
línyù

枕头
zhěntou

毛毯 máotǎn

盥洗池
guànxǐchí

床
chuáng

卫生纸
wèishēnzhǐ

马桶
mǎtǒng

Fig. 9-3

你们可以**洗烫**衣服吗？   wash and iron
Nǐmen kěyǐ *xǐ tàng* yīfu ma?

我想**干洗**这套**西装**。   dry clean, suit
Wǒ xiǎng *gānxǐ* zhèi tào *xīzhuāng*.

什么时候可以洗好？
Shénme shíhou kěyǐ xǐ hǎo?

要是你今天就要，得付**加急费**。   fee for express service
Yàoshi nǐ jīntiān jiùyào, děi fù *jiājí fèi*.

我还需要一个**枕头**   pillow
Wǒ hái xūyào yí ge *zhěntou*.

　　　一条**毛巾**   towel
　　　yì tiáo *máojīn*

　　　　浴巾   bath towel
　　　　yùjīn

　　　　毛毯   blanket
　　　　máotǎn

　　　几个**衣架**   hanger
　　　jǐ ge *yījià*

请问，**剃须刀**的**插座**在哪儿？   electric razor; socket
Qǐngwèn, *tìxūdāo* de *chāzuò* zài nǎr?

      电吹风   hair drier
      diànchuīfēng

请给我一瓶开水[6]。   bottle; boiled water
Qǐng gěi wǒ yì *píng kāishuǐ*.

      一卷卫生纸   roll; toilet paper
      yì *juǎn wèishēngzhǐ*

      一块香皂   bar; soap
      yí *kuài xiāngzào*

3. Complete.

1) _____每天打扫我的房间。
    _____měi tiān dǎosǎo wǒde fángjiān.

2) 我有很多衣服要洗。饭店有_____吗？
    Wǒ yǒu hěn duō yīfu yào xǐ. Fàndiàn yǒu _____ma?

3) 小姐，可以请你帮我_____一下这件衬衣吗？
    Xiǎojiě, kěyǐ qǐng nǐ bāng wǒ _____yíxia zhèi jiàn chènyī ma?

4) 你们可以帮我_____这套西装吗？
    Nǐmen kěyǐ bāng wǒ _____zhèi tào xīzhuāng ma?

5) 要是我付_____，他们今天就能把我的衣服洗好。
    Yàoshi wǒ fù _____, tāmen jīntiān jiù néng bǎ wǒde yīfu xǐhǎo.

6) 我要用电动剃须刀，_____在哪儿？
    Wǒ yào yòng diàndòng tìxūdāo, _____zài nǎr?

7) 这几天晚上很冷，我床上还需要一条_____。
    Zhèi jǐ tiān wǎnshang hěn lěng, Wǒ chuáng shàng hái xūyào yì tiáo _____.

8) 洗澡的大毛巾就是_____。
    Xǐzǎo de dà máojīn jiùshi _____.

9) 我常常带很多衣服，所以饭店的_____总是不够。
    Wǒ chángcháng dài hěn duō yīfu, suǒyǐ fàndiàn de _____zǒngshi bú gòu.

10) 饭店一般都会在洗手间多放一卷_____。
    Fàndiàn yìbān dōu huì zài xǐshǒujiān duō fàng yì juǎn _____.

4. Identify each item in Fig. 9-4.

    1)   2)   3)   4)   5)   6)

    7)   8)   9)   10)   11)   12)

---

[6] It is not safe to drink tap water in China. People usually drink boiled water--"开水kāishuǐ".

Fig. 9-4

SOME PROBLEMS YOU MAY HAVE

水龙头坏了。   faucet, broke/doesn't work
Shuǐlóngtou huài le.

电灯   lamp
diàndēng

开关   light switch
kāiguān

电视
diànshì

收音机
shōuyīnjī

马桶堵住了。   toilet, clogged
Mǎtǒng dǔzhù le.

盥洗池   basin
guànxǐchí

没有热水。
Méiyǒu rèshuǐ.

窗户打不开。   window; can't open
Chuānghu dǎ bù kāi.

灯坏了
dēng huài le

开关坏了
kāiguān huài le

盥洗池堵了
guànxǐchí dǔ le

Fig. 9-5

门关不上。   can't close
Mén *guān bú shàng*.

我的钥匙丢了。   lost
Wǒde yàoshi *diū le*.

请小声点儿。   be quiet
Qǐng *xiǎoshēng* diǎnr.

5. Complete.

1) 我房间的灯_____，
    Wǒ fángjiān de dēng _____.

2) 我打开_____，可是没有水。
    Wǒ dǎkāi _____, kěshì méiyǒu shuǐ.

3) 盥洗池里还有那么多水，一定是_____了。
    Guànxǐchí lǐ hái yǒu nàme duō shuǐ, yídìng shi _____ le.

4) 没有_____我就不能洗澡。
    Méiyǒu _____ wǒ jiù bù néng xǐzǎo.

5) 这把钥匙不对，门打_____。
    Zhèi bǎ yàoshi búduì. Mén dǎ _____.

6) 我找不到我的钥匙，一定是_____。
    Wǒ zhǎo bú dào wǒde yàoshi, yídìng shi _____.

Fig. 9-6

6. Identify each item in Fig. 9-6.

1)   2)   3)   4)   5)

CHECKING OUT

我们今天要**退房**。   check out
Wǒmen jīntiān yào *tuìfáng*.

几点我得**腾出**房间？   vacate
Jǐ diǎn wǒ děi *téngchū* fángjiān?

我们要**结帐**。我们住在604号房间。   settle the bill
Wǒmen yào *jiézhàng*. Wǒmen zhù zài liùlíngsì hào fángjiān

这个电话**帐单**不是我的。   bill
Zhèi ge diànhuà *zhàngdān* bú shi wǒde.

你们**收信用卡**吗？   accept; credit card
Nǐmen *shōu xìnyòngkǎ* ma?

你们打电话了吗？
Nǐmen dǎ diànhuà le ma?

请**让人**把我们的行李拿下去。   have someone (do something)
Qǐng *ràng rén* bǎ wōmen de xíngli ná xiàqù.

请**替**我们**叫**一辆出租车。   for; call
Qǐng *tì* wǒmen *jiào* yí liàng chūzūchē.

这是我们房间的钥匙。
Zhē shi wǒmen fángjiān de yàoshi.

7. Complete.

A：您好，我们今天要离开了。请给我们＿＿1＿＿。
    Nín hǎo, wǒmen jīntiān yào líkāi le. Qǐng gěi wǒmen ＿＿1＿＿.

B：请问您的＿＿2＿＿号码?
    Qǐng wèn nínde ＿＿2＿＿hàomǎ?

A：604 号房间。
    Liùlíngsì hào fángjiān.

B：很好。这是您的＿＿3＿＿。一共1,350 元。
    Hěn hǎo. Zhè shi nínde ＿＿3＿＿. Yígòng yìqiān sānbǎi wǔshí yuán.

A：这个＿＿4＿＿帐单不是我们的。我们没打过德国长途电话。
    Zhèi ge ＿＿4＿＿zhàngdān bú shi wǒmen de. Wǒmen méi dǎ guò Déguó chángtú diànhuà.

B：噢，对不起。这是605 房间的。
    Ò, duìbuqǐ. Zhē shi liùlíngwǔ fángjiān de.

A：我们没有很多现金，你们收＿＿5＿＿吗?
    Wǒmen méi yǒu hěnduō xiànjīn. Nǐmen shōu ＿＿5＿＿ma? .

B：收。您是用什么＿＿6＿＿?
    Shōu. Nín shi yòng shénme ＿＿6＿＿?

B: Visa.

8. Complete.

1) 客人来到一个饭店，得先去＿＿＿＿＿＿办理＿＿＿＿＿＿。
    Kèrén láidào yí ge fàndiàn, děi xiān qù ＿＿＿＿＿＿bànlǐ ＿＿＿＿＿＿.

2) 你得＿＿＿＿＿＿一个表，还得向前台服务员出示你的＿＿＿＿＿＿。
    Nǐ děi ＿＿＿＿＿＿yí ge biǎo, hái děi xiàng qiántái fúwùyuán chūshì nǐde ＿＿＿＿＿＿.

3) 要是只有一位客人，他只需要一个＿＿＿＿＿＿房间。
    Yàoshi zhǐ yǒu yí wèi kèrén, tā zhǐ xūyào yí ge ＿＿＿＿＿＿fángjiān.

4) 要是有两位客人，他们一般需要一个＿＿＿＿＿＿房间。
    Yàoshi yǒu liǎng wèi kèrén, tāmen yìbān xūyào yí ge ＿＿＿＿＿＿fángjiān.

5) 双人房间可能有两个＿＿＿＿＿＿床，也可能有一个＿＿＿＿＿＿床。
    Shuānrén fángjiān kěnéng yǒu liǎng ge ＿＿＿＿＿＿chuáng, yě kěnéng yǒu yí ge ＿＿＿＿＿＿chuáng.

6) 很多饭店的房费都＿＿＿＿＿＿早餐。
    Hěn duō fàndiàn de fángfèi dōu ＿＿＿＿＿＿zǎocān.

7) ＿＿＿＿＿＿院子的房间比＿＿＿＿＿＿街的房间＿＿＿＿＿＿。
    ＿＿＿＿＿＿yuànzi de fángjiān bǐ ＿＿＿＿＿＿jiē de fángjiān ＿＿＿＿＿＿.

8) 很多人去饭店以前就已经＿＿＿＿＿＿好了房间。
    Hěn duō rén qù fàndiàn yǐqián jiù yǐjīng ＿＿＿＿＿＿hǎo le fángjiān.

9) 要是饭店没有_____房间了。这个饭店就是_____了。
   Yàoshi fàndiàn méiyǒu _____fángjiān le, zhèige fàndiàn jiùshi _____le.

10) _____帮助客人把他们的行李拿到房间去。
    _____bāngzhù kèrén bǎ tāmende xíngli nádào fángjiān qù.

11) _____打扫饭店的房间。
    _____dǎsǎo fàndiàn de fángjiān.

12) 冬天饭店里差不多都有_____，夏天都会有_____。
    Dōngtiān fàndiàn lǐ chàbuduō dōu yǒu _____, xiàtiān dōu huì yǒu _____.

13) 要是客人睡觉时觉得冷，他可以再加一条_____。
    Yàoshi kèrén shuìjiào shí juéde lěng, tā kěyǐ zài jiā yì tiáo _____.

14) 饭店的衣橱里有_____给客人挂衣服用。
    Fàndiàn de yīchú lǐ yǒu _____gěi kèrén guà yīfu yòng.

15) 很多饭店都有_____服务，替客人洗烫衣服。
    Hěn duō fàndiàn dōu yǒu _____fúwù, tì kèrén xǐ tàng yīfu.

16) 客人离开饭店以前，应该去前台_____。
    Kèrén líkāi fàndiàn yǐqián, yīnggāi qù qiántái _____.

17) 除了付房费以外，要是你用了饭店的电话，你也得付_____。
    Chúle fù fángfèi yǐwài, yàoshi nǐ yòng le fàndiàn de diànhuà, nǐ yě děi fù _____.

18) 现在很多人都喜欢用_____付帐。
    Xiànzài hěn duō rén dōu xǐhuan yòng _____fùzhàng.

19) 可是有的饭店不_____信用卡。
    Kěshì yǒude fàndiàn bù _____xìnyòngkǎ.

20) 饭店服务员可以帮你_____出租车。
    Fàndiàn fúwùyuán kěyǐ bāng nǐ _____ chūzūchē.

9. Answer on the basis of Figure 9-7.

1) 这个房间朝街吗?
   Zhèi ge fángjiān cháo jiē ma?

2) 这个房间有没有阳台?
   Zhèi ge fángjiān yǒu méiyǒu yángtái?

3) 这个房间有一张什么床?
   Zhèi ge fángjiān yǒu yí zhāng shénme chuáng?

4) 这是一个什么房间?
   Zhè shi yí ge shénme fángjiān?

5) 这个房间有卫生间吗?
   Zhèi ge fángjiān yǒu wèishēngjiān ma?

6) 卫生间里有什么?
   Wèishēngjiān lǐ yǒu shénme?

7) 房间里有什么天气热的时候要用的东西?
   Fángjiān lǐ yǒu shénme tiānqi rè de shíhou yào yòng de dōngxi?

Fig. 9-7

8) 床上有什么？

  Chuáng shang yǒu shénme?

10. Look at Figure 9-8 and correct each false statement.

1) 这些人在飞机场。

  Zhèi xiē rén zài fēijīchǎng.

2) 他们要买飞机票。

  Tāmen yào mǎi fēijī piào.

3) 他们在跟行李员说话。

  Tāmen zài gēn xíngliyuán shuōhuà.

4) 那个女的在填表。

  Nèi ge nǚde zài tián biǎo.

5) 前台服务员手里拿着客房钥匙。

  Qiántái fúwùyuán shǒu li názhe kèfáng yàoshi.

6) 那个男的手里拿着信用卡。

  Nèi ge nánde shǒu li názhe xìnyòngkǎ.

Fig. 9-8

Fig. 9-9

11. Answer questions on the basis of Figure 9-9.

1) 这是什么地方？
   Zhè shi shénme dìfang?

2) 床上有什么？
   Chuáng shàng yǒu shénme?

3) 谁在房间里工作？
   Shéi zài fángjiān lǐ gōngzuò?

4) 她在做什么？
   Tā zài zuò shénme?

5) 壁橱里有什么？
   Bìchú lǐ yǒu shénme?

6) 盥洗池是在房间里还是在卫生间里？
   Guànxǐchí shi zài fángjiān lǐ háishi zài wèishēngjiān lǐ?

7) 卫生间里有没有淋浴？
   Wèishēngjiān lǐ yǒu méiyǒu línyù?

8) 卫生间里有没有电动剃须刀插座？
   Wèishēngjiān lǐ yǒu méiyǒu diàndòng tìxūdāo chāzuò?

9) 卫生间里有几条毛巾？
   Wèishēngjiān lǐ yǒu jǐ tiáo máojīn?

10) 卫生间里有几卷卫生纸？
    Wèishēngjiān lǐ yǒu jǐ juǎn wèishēngzhǐ?

KEY WORDS

accept	收	shōu	clogged	堵住	dǔzhù
add	加	jiā	courtyard	院子	yuànzi
air conditioner	空调	kōngtiáo	credit card	信用卡	xìnyòngkǎ
all day long	全天	quán tiān	deliver	送	sòng
balcony	阳台	yángtái	doesn't work	坏了	huàile
bar	块	kuài	double bed	双人床	shuāngrén chuáng
basin	盥洗池	guànxǐchí	double room	双人房	shuāngrénfáng
bath towel	浴巾	yùjīn	dry clean	干洗	gānxǐ
bathroom	卫生间	wèishēngjiān	electric razor	剃须刀	tìxūdāo
be quiet	小声	xiǎoshēng	empty/vacant	空	kōng
bed	床	chuáng	face	朝	cháo
bill	帐单	zhàngdān	faucet	水龙头	shuǐlóngtou
blanket	毛毯	máotǎn	fee for express service	加急费	jiājífèi
boiled water	开水	kāishuǐ	figure out the bill	结帐	jié zhàng
bottle	瓶	píng			
breakfast	早餐	zǎocān			
bright	光线好	guāngxiàn hǎo	fill in	填	tián
call	叫	jiào	for	替	tì
can't close	关不上	guān bú shàng	form	表	biǎo
can't open	打不开	dǎ bù kāi	full (no vacancy)	客满	kèmǎn
check out	退房	tuì fáng			
clean	打扫	dǎsǎo	guest	客人	kèrén

hair drier	电吹风	diànchuīfēng	reserve	预订	yùdìng
hanger	衣架	yījià	roll (of paper)	卷	juǎn
have someone (do sth.)	让人	ràng rén	room charge	房价	fángjià
			sea	海	hǎi
heat	暖气	nuǎnqì	service	服务	fúwù
hot	热	rè	shower	淋浴	línyù
hotel	饭店	fàndiàn	single bed	单人床	dānrénchuáng
(hotel) housekeeper	客房服务员	kèfáng fúwùyuán	single room	单人房	dānrénfáng
			soap	香皂	xiāngzào
ID	证件	zhèngjiàn	socket	插座	chāzuò
including	包	bāo	stay	待	dāi
iron, press	烫	tàng	street	大街	dàjiē
key	钥匙	yàoshi	suit	西装	xīzhuāng
lamp	电灯	diàndēng	suite	套间	tàojiān
laundry	洗衣	xǐyī	swimming	游泳	yóuyǒng
leave	留	liú	toilet	马桶	mǎtǒng
light switch	开关	kāiguān	toilet paper	卫生纸	wèishēngzhǐ
lost	丢了	diūle	towel	毛巾	máojīn
mountain	山	shān	TV	电视	diànshì
other	别的	biéde	until	到	dào
pillow	枕头	zhěntou	vacate	腾出	téngchū
pool	池	chí	wash	洗	xǐ
porter	行李员	xíngliyuán	water	水	shuǐ
quiet	安静	ānjìng	window	窗户	chuānghu
reception	前台	qiántái	with	带	dài
receptionist	前台服务员	qiántái fúwùyuán			

Chapter 10: At the bank

第十章：银行
     Yínháng

EXCHANGING MONEY

出纳窗口
chūnà chuāngkǒu

支票
zhīpiào

硬硬币 yìngbì

纸币
zhǐbì

银行 yínháng

Fig. 10-1

请问**银行**在哪儿？	bank
Qǐngwèn *yínháng* zài nǎr?	
请问**外币兑换处**在哪儿？	foreign currency; exchange bureau
Qǐngwèn *wàibì duìhuànchù* zài nǎr?	
我需要**人民币**。	RMB(Chinese currency)
Wǒ xūyào *rénmínbì.*	
我要**换**100**美元**的人民币。	exchange; dollar
Wǒ yào *huàn* yìbǎi *měiyuán* de rénmínbì.	
您用**旅行支票**换还是用**现金**换？	traveler's check; cash
Nín yòng *lǚxíng zhīpiào* huàn háishi yòng *xiànjīn* huàn?	

今天的**兑换率**是多少？   exchange rate
Jīntiān de *duìhuàn lù* shi duō shǎo?

一美元换8.25元人民币。
Yì měiyuán huàn bā diǎn èr wǔ yuán rénmínbì.

你们**收**多少钱**手续费**？   charge; commission
Nǐmen *shōu* duōshǎo qián *shǒuxùfèi*?

现在您可以去**出纳窗口**了。   cashier's window
Xiànzài nin kěyǐ qù *chūnà chuāngkǒu* le.

1. Complete.

史密斯先生在中国。他想去买东西，可是他没有中国的__1__。他想去
Shǐmìsī xiānsheng zài Zhōngguó. Tā xiǎng qù mǎi dōngxi, kěshì tā méiyǒu Zhōngguó de __1__. Tā xiǎng qù

__2__100美元的人民币。他不想在旅馆换，因为他知道旅馆收的__3__太
__2__ yì bǎi měiyuán de rénmínbì. Tā bù xiǎng zài lǚguǎn huàn, yīnwèi tā zhīdao lǚguǎn shōu de __3__ tài

高。他想去__4__换钱。他知道银行不会收旅馆那么高的__5__。
gāo. Tā xiǎng qù __4__ huàn qián. Tā zhīdao yínháng bú huì shōu nàme gāo de __5__.

2. Complete.

A：您好！我想__1__100美元的人民币。
　　Nín hǎo! Wǒ xiǎng __1__ yìbǎi měiyuán de rénmínbì.

B：好的。
　　Hǎo de.

A：今天的__2__是多少?
　　Jīntiān de __2__ shi duōshǎo?

B：您是用__3__还是用现金换?
　　Nín shi yòng __3__ háishi yòng xiànjīn huàn?

A：旅行支票。
　　Lǚxíng zhīpiào.

B：今天的__4__是1美元换8.25元人民币。
　　Jīntiān de __4__ shi yī měiyuán huàn bā diǎn èr wǔ yuán rénmínbì.

A：很好。
　　Hén hǎo.

B：您带护照了吗?
　　Nín dài hùzhào le ma?

A：带了。你看。
　　Dài le. Nǐ kàn.

B：您可以去__5__了。您在那儿取钱。
　　Nín kěyǐ qù __5__ le. Nín zài nàr qǔ qián.

MAKING CHANGE

我不能再**用现金付帐**了。   in cash, pay a bill
Wǒ bù néng zài *yòng xiànjīn fù zhàng* le.

我得去**兑现**这张**旅行支票**。   cash, traveler's check
Wǒ děi qù *duìxiàn* zhèi zhāng *lǚxíng zhīpiào*.

我没有**零钱**。   small change
Wǒ méiyǒu *língqián*.

您能**换开**这张500块的**大票子**吗？   break, large bill
Nín néng *huàn kāi* zhèi zhāng wǔbǎi kuài de *dà piàozi* ma?

3. Complete.

史密斯先生一直是用现金___1___。可是现在他没有___2___了。他得去银行___3___一
Shǐmìsī xiānsheng yìzhí shi yòng xiànjīn ___1___. Kěshì tā xiànzài méiyǒu ___2___ le. Tā děi qù yínháng ___3___ yì

张旅行支票。
zhāng lǚxíng zhīpiào.

4. Complete.

(在银行里)

A：您好，我想兑现这张___1___。
   Nín hǎo, wǒ xiǎng duìxiàn zhèi zhāng ___1___.

B：是美元还是英镑？
   Shi měiyuán háishi yīngbàng?

A：是美元。请问今天的___2___是多少？
   Shi měiyuán. Qǐng wèn jīntiān de ___2___ shi duōshǎo?

B：1美元___3___8.25元人民币。
   Yì měiyuán ___3___ bā diǎn èr wǔ yuán rénmínbì.

A：很好。这是我的护照。
   Hěn hǎo. Zhē shi wǒde hùzhào.

B：好了，现在您可以去___4___取钱了。
   Hǎo le, xiànzài nín kěyǐ qù ___4___ qǔ qián le.

(在出纳窗口)

A：一共8250元___5___。请点清。
   Yígòng bāqiān'èrbǎiwǔshí yuán ___5___. Qǐng diǎnqīng.

B：对不起，可不可以多给我一些十块一张的？我需要___6___。
   Duìbùqǐ, kě bù kěyǐ duō gěi wǒ yìxiē shí kuài yì zhāng de? Wǒ xūyào ___6___.

A：好吧，这是25张十块的。还有80张100块的。
   Hǎo ba, zhē shi èrshíwǔ zhāng shí kuài de. Hái yǒu bāshí zhāng yìbǎi kuài de.

B：谢谢！
   Xièxie.

OPENING A SAVINGS ACCOUNT

出纳员
chūnàyuán

存款

存款台窗口
cúnkuǎntái
chuāngkǒu

存折
cúnzhé

Fig. 10-2

我想开一个**存款户头**。 Wǒ xiǎng *kāi* yí ge *cúnkuǎn hùtóu*.	open, savings account
我要**存**一笔钱。 Wǒ yào *cún* yì bǐ *qián*.	make a deposit
我要**存**100块钱。 Wǒ yào *cún* yìbǎi kuài *qián*.	deposit money
我想**取钱**。 Wǒ xiǎng *qǔ qián*.	withdraw money
在存款台的**窗口**, Zài cúnkuǎntái de *chuāngkǒu*.	window
我把我的**银行存折**和钱交给**出纳员**。 Wǒ bǎ wǒde *yínháng cúnzhé* hé qián jiāo gěi *chūnàyuán*.	bankbook, teller
现在很多银行都有**自动提款机**。 Xiànzài hěn duō yínháng dōu yǒu *zìdòng tíkuǎnjī*.	ATM
你可以在自动提款机上存钱、取钱、 Nǐ kěyǐ zài zìdòng tíkuǎnjī shàng cún qián, qǔ qián.	

查你的户头结余。   check, balance
chá nǐde hùtóu *jiéyú.*

你得有一张银行卡和密码才可以用自动提款机。   bank card, PIN
Nǐ děi yǒu yì zhāng *yínhángkǎ* hé *mìmǎ* cái kěyǐ yòng
zìdòng tíkuǎnjī.

5. Complete.

我喜欢存钱。我在银行里开了一个___1___。明天我要去银行___2___100块钱。
Wǒ xǐhuān cún qián. Wǒ zài yínháng lǐ kāi le yí ge ___1___. Míngtiān wǒ yào qù yínháng ___2___ yìbǎi kuài qián.

我每个月都存___3___。在银行里，我去存款台把我的___4___和钱交给出纳员。你看，
Wǒ měi ge yuè dōu cún ___3___. Zài yínháng lǐ, wǒ qù cúnkuǎntái bǎ wǒ de ___4___ hé qián jiāo gěi chūnàyuán. Nǐ kàn,

我喜欢___5___，可是我不喜欢从我的存款户头里___6___。有时候，我不想在
wǒ xǐhuan ___5___, kěshì wǒ bù xǐhuan cóng wǒde cúnkuǎn hùtóu lǐ ___6___. Yǒushíhou, wǒ bù xiǎng zài

出纳窗口排队，就用银行的___7___。可是你得有一张___8___和___9___才能
chūnà chuāngkǒu páiduì, jiù yòng yínháng de ___7___. Kěshì nǐ děi yǒu yì zhāng ___8___ he ___9___ cái néng

用自动提款机。
yòng zìdòng tíkuǎnjī.

6. Complete each item with the appropriate verb:

1)   我需要钱。我得去银行_____这张旅行支票。
     Wǒ xūyào qián. Wǒ děi qù yínháng _____ zhèi zhāng lǚxíng zhīpiào.

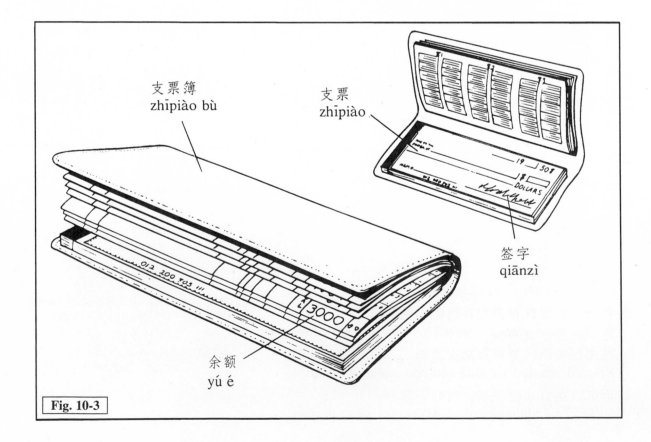

支票簿
zhīpiào bù

支票
zhīpiào

签字
qiānzì

余额
yú é

Fig. 10-3

2) 我要去银行换钱，因为旅馆_____的手续费太高。
   Wǒ yào qù yínháng huàn qián, yīnwèi lǚguǎn _____de shǒuxù fèi tài gāo.

3) 在这儿你得用现金_____。
   Zài zhèr nǐ děi yòng xiànjīn _____.

4) 我没有零钱了。您能_____这张500块的钞票吗？
   Wǒ méi yǒu língqián le. Nín néng _____zhèi zhāng wǔbǎi kuài de chāopiào ma?

5) 我在银行里_____了一个存款户头。
   Wǒ zài yínháng lǐ _____le yí ge cún kuǎn hùtóu.

6) 这些钱我现在不用，所以我想把它_____到我的存款户头里去。
   Zhèi xiē qián wǒ xiànzài bú yòng, suǒyǐ wǒ xiǎng bǎ tā _____dào wǒde cúnkuǎn hùtóu lǐ qù.

7) 我的人民币用完了。我得去银行用美元_____一点人民币。
   Wǒ de rénmínbì yòng wán le. Wǒ děi qù yínháng yòng měiyuán _____yìdiǎn rénmínbì.

8) 我没有钱了。得去银行里我的存款户头里_____一点钱。
   Wǒ méi yǒu qián le. Děi qù yínháng lǐ wǒde cúnkuǎn hùtóu lǐ _____yìdiǎn qián.

9) 你可以在自动提款机上_____、_____和_____。
   Nǐ kěyǐ zài zìdòng tíkuǎnjī shàng _____, _____he _____.

10) 我需要现金。我要用自动提款机_____。
    Wǒ xūyào xiànjīn. Wǒ yào yòng zìdòng tíkuǎnjī _____.

KEY WORDS

account	户头	hùtóu	exchange	换	huàn
ATM	自动提款机	zìdòng tíkuǎnjī	exchange bureau	兑换处	duìhuànchù
			exchange rate	兑换率	duìhuànlǜ
balance	结余	jiéyú	foreign currency	外币	wàibì
bank	银行	yínháng	in cash	用现金	yòng xiànjīn
bank card	银行卡	yínhángkǎ	large bills	大票子	dà piàozi
bankbook	存折	cúnzhé	make a deposit	存一笔钱	cún yì bǐ qián
break (a large bill),	换开	huànkāi	open	开	kāi
make change			pay a bill	付帐	fù zhàng
cash	现金	xiànjīn	PIN	密码	mìmǎ
cash (a check)	兑现(支票)	duìxiàn (zhīpiào)	RMB(Chinese currency)	人民币	rénmínbì
cashier's window	出纳窗口	chūnà chuāngkǒu	savings	存款	cúnkuǎn
			small change	零钱	língqián
charge	收(费)	shōu (fèi)	teller	出纳	chūnà
check	查	chá	traveler's check	旅行支票	lǚxíng zhīpiào
commission	手续费	shǒuxù fèi	window	窗口	chuāngkǒu
deposit money	存钱	cún qián	withdraw money	取钱	qǔ qián
dollar (U. S.)	美元	měiyuán			

Chapter 11: At the post office

第十一章：邮局
       Yóujú

SENDING A LETTER

窗口 chuāngkǒu

邮箱 yóuxiāng

明信片
míngxìnpiàn

信
xìn

Fig. 11-1

我要**寄**一封**信**。	send, letter
Wǒ yào *jì* yì fēng *xìn*.	
一张**明信片**	postcard
yì zhāng *míngxìnpiàn*	
我得把它投进**邮筒/信筒**。	postbox
Wǒ děi bǎ tā tóujìn *yóutǒng/xìntǒng*.	
可是我要先买**邮票**，才能**寄出去**。	stamp, send out
Kěshì wǒ yào xiān mǎi *yóupiào*, cái néng *jì chūqu*.	

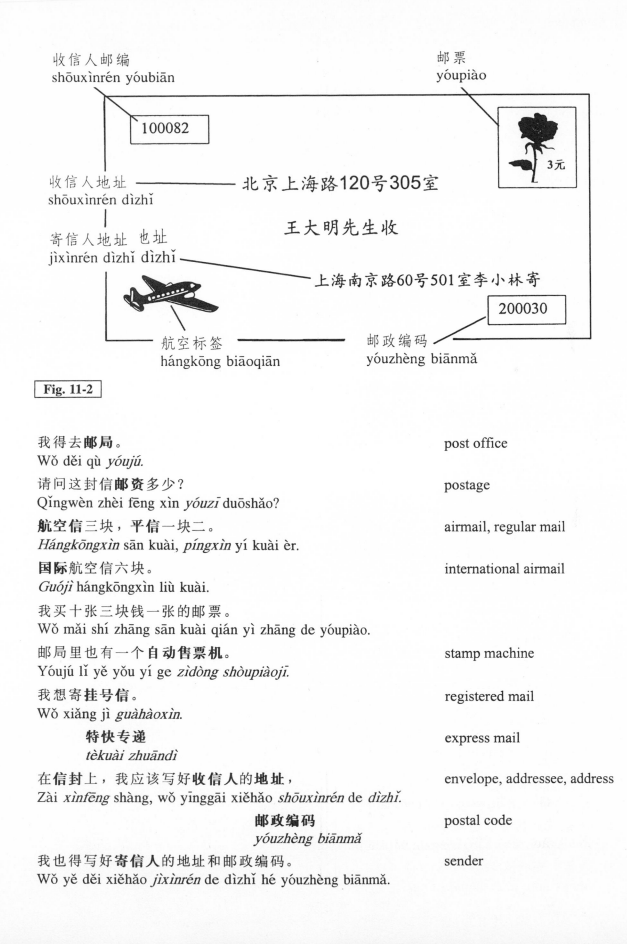

收信人邮编
shōuxìnrén yóubiān

邮票
yóupiào

100082

北京上海路120号305室

王大明先生收

收信人地址
shōuxìnrén dìzhǐ

寄信人地址 也址
jìxìnrén dìzhǐ dìzhǐ

上海南京路60号501室李小林寄

200030

航空标签
hángkōng biāoqiān

邮政编码
yóuzhèng biānmǎ

Fig. 11-2

我得去**邮局**。 Wǒ děi qù *yóujú*.	post office
请问这封信**邮资**多少？ Qǐngwèn zhèi fēng xìn *yóuzī* duōshǎo?	postage
航空信三块，**平信**一块二。 *Hángkōngxìn* sān kuài, *píngxìn* yí kuài èr.	airmail, regular mail
国际航空信六块。 *Guójì* hángkōngxìn liù kuài.	international airmail
我买十张三块钱一张的邮票。 Wǒ mǎi shí zhāng sān kuài qián yì zhāng de yóupiào.	
邮局里也有一个**自动售票机**。 Yóujú lǐ yě yǒu yí ge *zìdòng shòupiàojī*.	stamp machine
我想寄**挂号信**。 Wǒ xiǎng jì *guàhàoxìn*.	registered mail
特快专递 *tèkuài zhuāndì*	express mail
在**信封**上，我应该写好**收信人**的**地址**， Zài *xìnfēng* shàng, wǒ yīnggāi xiěhǎo *shōuxìnrén* de *dìzhǐ*.	envelope, addressee, address
邮政编码 *yóuzhèng biānmǎ*	postal code
我也得写好**寄信人**的地址和邮政编码。 Wǒ yě děi xiěhǎo *jìxìnrén* de dìzhǐ hé yóuzhèng biānmǎ.	sender

1. Complete.

我想＿＿1＿＿这封信。可是我不能把它投进＿＿2＿＿去。我得到＿＿3＿＿去。因为我不
Wǒ xiǎng ＿＿1＿＿ zhèi fēng xìn. Kěshì wǒ bù néng bǎ tā tóujìn ＿＿2＿＿ qù. Wǒ děi dào ＿＿3＿＿ qù. Yīnwèi wǒ bù

知道这封信的＿＿4＿＿应该是多少，而且我也没有＿＿5＿＿。我得去＿＿6＿＿买＿＿7＿＿。
zhīdao zhèi fēng xìn de＿＿4＿＿ yīnggāi shi duōshǎo, érqiě wǒ yě měi yǒu ＿＿5＿＿. Wǒ děi qù ＿＿6＿＿ mǎi ＿＿7＿＿.

2. Complete.

在邮局里 (zài yóujú lǐ)

A：我想把这封信＿＿1＿＿到美国去，请问＿＿2＿＿应该是多少？
　　Wǒ xiǎng bǎ zhèi fēng xìn ＿＿1＿＿ dào Měiguó qù. Qǐngwèn ＿＿2＿＿ yīnggāi shi duōshǎo?

B：您想寄＿＿3＿＿还是平信？
　　Nín xiǎng jì ＿＿3＿＿ háishi píngxìn?

A：航空信。
　　Hángkōng xìn.

B：去美国的＿＿4＿＿得六块钱＿＿5＿＿。
　　Qù Měiguó de ＿＿4＿＿ děi liù kuài qián ＿＿5＿＿.

A：几天可以到？
　　Jǐ tiān kěyǐ dào?

B：大概得十天。
　　Dàgài děi shítiān.

A：十天太慢了。
　　Shítiān tài màn le.

B：你可以寄＿＿6＿＿。两、三天就到了。
　　Nǐ kěyǐ jì ＿＿6＿＿. Liǎng sān tiān jiù dào le.

A：特快专递要多少钱？
　　Tèkuài zhuāndì yào duōshǎo qián?

B：一百二十块。
　　Yībǎi èrshí kuài.

A：好吧，我寄＿＿7＿＿吧。再买十张六块钱一张的邮票。
　　Hǎo ba, wǒ jì ＿＿7＿＿ ba. Zài mǎi shí zhāng liù kuài qián yìzhāng de yóupiào.

3. Answer on the basis of Figure 11-3.

1). 这封信的邮资是多少？
　　Zhèi fēng xìn de yóuzī shi duōshǎo?

2). 这是一封航空信还是平信？
　　Zhè shi yì fēng hángkōngxìn hái shi píngxìn?

3). 收信人叫什么名字？
　　Shōuxìnrén jiào shéme míngzi?

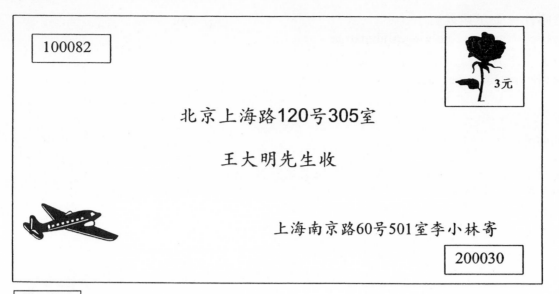

Fig. 11-3

4). 收信人的邮政编码是多少?
   Shōuxìnrén de yóuzhèng biānmǎ shi duōshǎo?

5). 寄信人叫什么名字?
   Jìxìnrén jiào shénme míngzi?

6). 信要寄到什么地方去?
   Xìn yào jìdào shénme dìfang qù?

7). 寄信人的邮政编码是多少?
   Jìxìnrén de yóuzhèng biānmǎ shi duōshǎo?

SENDING A PACKAGE

我要寄一个**包裹**。 Wǒ yào jì yí ge *bāoguǒ*.	package/parcel
这个包裹**多重**? Zhèi ge bāoguǒ duō *zhòng*?	how much does it weigh
我不知道。可不可以请你**称**一下? Wǒ bù zhīdào, kě bù kěyǐ qǐng nǐ *chēng* yíxià?	weigh
这个包裹要**保险**吗? Zhèi ge bāoguǒ yào *bǎoxiǎn* ma?	insurance
是不是**易碎**物品? 比方说,**瓷器**,**玻璃器皿**? Shì bú shì *yìsuì* wùpǐn? Bǐfāngshuō, cíqì, bōli qìmǐn?	fragile, ceramics, glassware
请你**填**一下这张**表**。 Qǐng nǐ *tián* yíxià zhèi zhāng *biǎo*.	fill, form
要多久才能**到**? Yào duō jiǔ cái néng *dào*?	arrive

寄**航空邮件**一个星期就到了。   airmail
Jì *hángkōng yóujiàn* yí ge xīngqī jiù dào le.

海运得要两个月。   by sea
Hǎiyùn děi yào liǎng ge yuè.

4. Complete.

1) 我想寄一個_____去美國，可是我不知道這個包裹_____。
   Wǒ xiǎng jì yí ge _____ qù Měiguó, kěshì wǒ bù zhīdao zhèi ge bāoguǒ _____.

2) 我得去郵局_____一下。
   Wǒ děi qù yóujú _____ yíxià.

3) 這個包裹裡沒有什麼貴重的東西，不必_____。
   Zhèi ge bāoguǒ lǐ méiyǒu shénme guìzhòng de dōngxi, búbì _____.

4) 這個包裹裡有_____物品，是瓷器。
   Zhèi ge bāoguǒ lǐ yǒu _____ wùpǐn, Shì cíqì.

5) 要是寄_____郵件，這個包裹一個星期就到了。
   Yàoshi jì _____ yóujiàn, zhèi ge bāoguǒ yí ge xīngqī jiù dào le.

6) 要是你用_____，得兩個月才到。
   Yàoshi nǐ yòng _____, děi liǎng ge yuè cái dào.

7) 當然，_____比_____便宜多了。
   Dāngrán, _____ bǐ _____ piányì duō le.

OTHER WORDS YOU MAY NEED

今天有我的**邮件**吗？   mail
Jīntiān yǒu wǒde *yóujiàn* ma?

除了星期天**以外**，每天都有人**送**邮件。   except for, deliver
Chúle xīngqītiān *yǐwài*, měi tiān dōu yǒu rén *sòng* yóujiàn.

邮递员每天早上送邮件。   mail carrier
Yóudìyuán měi tiān zǎoshang sòng yóujiàn.

你们家有**信箱**吗？   mailbox
Nǐmen jiā yǒu *xìnxiāng* ma?

哪儿可以买到**邮政汇票**？   money order
Nǎr kěyǐ mǎidào *yóuzhèng huìpiào*?

5. Complete.

我不必去__1__取我的邮件。每天__2__会把信送到我家来。
Wǒ bú bì qù __1__ qǔ wǒde yóujiàn. Měi tiān __2__ huì bǎ xìn sòngdào wǒ jiā lái.

要是你交一些钱，就可以在邮局里有一个自己的＿＿3＿＿。
Yàoshi nǐ jiāo yìxiē qián, jiù kěyǐ zài yóujú lǐ yǒu yí ge zìjǐ de ＿＿3＿＿.

你要是想寄钱的话，可以去买＿＿4＿＿。
Nǐ yàoshi xiǎng jì qián de huà, kěyǐ qù mǎi ＿＿4＿＿.

KEY WORDS

address	地址	dìzhǐ	mail	邮件	yóujiàn
addressee	收信人	shōuxìnrén	mail carrier	邮递员	yóudìyuán
airmail	航空信	hángkōngxìn	mailbox	邮箱/信箱	yóuxiāng/xìnxiāng
arrive	到	dào	money order	汇票	huìpiào
by sea	海运	hǎiyùn	package	包裹	bāoguǒ
ceramics	瓷器	cíqì	post office	邮局	yóujú
deliver	送	sòng	postage	邮资	yóuzī
envelope	信封	xìnfēng	postal code	邮政编码	yóuzhèng biānmǎ
except for	除了...以外	chúle...yǐwài	postbox	邮筒/信筒	yóutǒng/xìntǒng
express mail	特快专递	tèkuài zhuāndì	postcard	明信片	míngxìnpiàn
fill (a form)	填	tián	registered mail	挂号信	guàhàoxìn
form	表	biǎo	regular mail	平信	píngxìn
fragile	易碎	yìsuì	send	寄	jì
glassware	玻璃器皿	bōli qìmǐn	send out	寄出去	jì chūqù
how heavy	多重	duōzhòng	sender	寄信人	jìxìnrén
insurance	保险	bǎoxiǎn	stamp	邮票	yóupiào
international	国际	guójì	stamp machine	售邮票机	shòuyóupiàojī
letter	信	xìn	weigh	称	chēng

Chapter 12: At the clothing store

第十二章：在服装店
Zài fúzhuāng diàn

BUYING SHOES

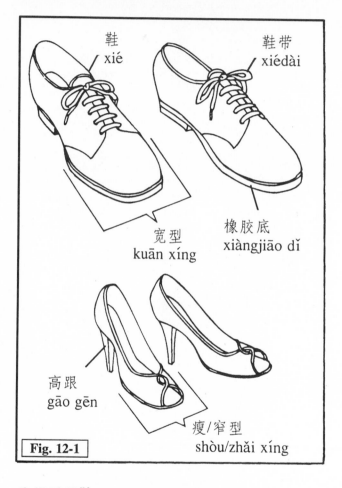

鞋
xié

鞋带
xiédài

宽型
kuān xíng

橡胶底
xiàngjiāo dǐ

高跟
gāo gēn

瘦/窄型
shòu/zhǎi xíng

Fig. 12-1

我想买**双鞋**。	pair, shoe
Wǒ xiǎng mǎi *shuāng xié*.	
您想买什么样的鞋呢？	
Nín xiǎng mǎi shénmeyàng de xié ne?	
我想买一双**皮**鞋。	leather
Wǒ xiǎng mǎi yì shuāng *píxié*.	
靴子	boot
xuēzi	
凉鞋	sandal
liángxié	

拖鞋	slipper
tuōxié	
旅游鞋	sneaker
lǚyóuxié	
您穿**多大号**的？	what size
Nín chuān *duō dà hào* de?	
我穿**40** 号的。	size 40
Wǒ chuān *sìshí hào* de.	
这**鞋跟**太**高**了。	heel, high
Zhè *xiégēn* tài *gāo* le.	
我不喜欢**高跟**鞋。	high heel
Wǒ bù xǐhuān *gāogēn* xié.	
我只能穿**平跟**鞋。	flat heel
Wǒ zhǐ néng chuān *pínggēn* xié.	
我不要**(橡)胶底**的。	rubber sole
Wǒ bú yào *(xiàng)jiāo dǐ* de.	
您喜欢什么**颜色**的？	color
Nín xǐhuan shénme *yánsè* de?	
我喜欢**黑**的。	black
Wǒ xǐhuan *hēi* de.	
白	white
bái	
红	red
hóng	
咖啡色	brown
kāfēisè	
蓝	blue
lán	
这双大小不**合适**。	fit
Zhèi shuāng dàxiǎo bù *héshì*.	
太**瘦**了。	narrow
Tài *shòu* le.	
肥	wide (for clothing only)
féi	
这双鞋**挤脚**。	hurt the feet
Zhè shuāng xié *jǐ jiǎo*.	
我还要一副**鞋带**。	shoelace
Wǒ hái yào yí fù *xiédài*.	
一盒**鞋油**	shoe polish
yì hé *xiéyóu*	

Fig. 12-2

1. Answer on the basis of Figure 12-2.

1) 这是什么鞋？皮鞋、凉鞋还是靴子？
   Zhè shi shénme xié? píxié, liángxié háishi xuēzi?

2) 这双鞋是高跟还是平跟？
   Zhèi shuāng xié shi gāogēn háishi pínggēn.

3) 这双鞋有鞋带吗？
   Zhèi shuāng xié yǒu xiédài ma?

2. Complete.

A：小姐，买鞋吗？
   Xiǎojiě, mǎi xié ma?

B：我想买一双___1___。
   Wǒ xiǎng mǎi yì shuāng ___1___.

A：请问您穿多少___2___的?
   Qǐng wèn nín chuān duōshǎo___2___de?

B：我穿37___3___的。
   Wǒ chuān sānshíqī___3___de.

A：您要高跟的还是平跟的？
   Nín yào gāogēn de háishi pínggēn de?

B：平跟的。我不喜欢___4___。
   Pínggēn de. Wǒ bù xǐhuan ___4___.

A：那您想要什么___5___的呢？
   Nà nín xiǎng yào shénme ___5___de ne?

B：咖啡色的吧。
   Kāfēisè de ba.

A：这双怎么样？
   Zhèi shuāng zěnmeyàng?

B：还不错，可是___6___不合适，
   Hái búcuò, kěshì ___6___bù héshi.

A: 是肥了还是瘦了?
   Shì féi le háishi shòu le?

B: 有点儿挤脚。我想这双太__7__了。有没有__8__一点儿的?
   Yǒu diǎnr jǐjiǎo. Wǒ xiǎng zhèi shuāng tài __7__ le. Yǒu méiyǒu __8__ yìdiǎnr de?

BUYING MEN'S CLOTHING

请问您要买什么?
Qǐngwèn nín yào mǎi shénme?

我想买一条**牛仔裤**。 Wǒ xiǎng mǎi yì tiáo *niúzǎikù.*	jeans
长裤 *chángkù*	pants/trousers
短裤 *duǎnkù*	shorts
内短裤/三角裤 *nèiduǎnkù/sānjiǎokù*	underwear, briefs
领带 *lǐngdài*	tie
皮带 *pídài*	belt
一件**大衣** *yí jiàn dàyī*	coat
游泳衣 *yóuyǒngyī*	bathing suit
背心 *bèixīn*	vest
汗衫/汗背心 *hànshān/hànbèixīn*	undershirt
T恤 *tīxù*	T shirt
夹克 *jiákè*	jacket
风衣 *fēngyī*	trench coat
雨衣 *yǔyī*	raincoat
毛衣 *máoyī*	sweater
一套**西装** *yí tào xīzhuāng*	suit

睡衣   pajamas
shuìyī

内衣   underclothes
nèiyī

一双手套   gloves
yìshuāng *shǒutào*

袜子   socks
wàzi

一顶帽子   hat
yì dǐng *màozi*

我想买一件纯棉衬衫。   (all) cotton, shirt
Wǒ xiǎng mǎi yí jiàn *chúnmián chènshān*.

真丝   (pure) silk
zhēnsī

法兰绒   flannel
fǎlánróng

混纺   blend fabric
hùnfǎng

尼龙   nylon
nílóng

灯芯绒   corduroy
dēngxīnróng

人(造)棉   rayon
rén (zào) mián

化纤料的衣服能防皱。   synthetic fabric; wrinkle resistant
Huàxiān liào de yīfu néng *fáng zhòu*.

我想买一件呢子大衣   heavy woolen
Wǒ xiǎng mǎi yí jiàn *nízi* dàyī.

我喜欢格子衬衫。   checked
Wǒ xǐhuan *gézi* chènshān.

条纹   striped
tiáowén

花   patterned
huā

单色的   solid colored
dānsè de

扣子的颜色跟衣服不配。   button; match
Kòuzi de yánsè gēn yīfu bú *pèi*.

您要长袖还是短袖?   long sleeve, short sleeve
Nín yào *chángxiù* háishi *duǎnxiù*?

您穿多大号的衣服?   what size
Nín chuān *duō dà hào* de yīfu?

我不知道，你能不能量一量我的尺寸？   measure; measurement
Wǒ bù zhīdao, nǐ néng bùnéng *liáng* yì liáng wǒde *chǐcùn*?

这件衣服不**合身**，太**紧**了。   fit; tight
Zhèi jiàn yīfu bù *héshēn*, tài *jǐn* le.

3. List complete outfit of a man.

4. Complete.

A： 您好，先生，想买点__1__？
    Nín hǎo, xiānsheng. Xiǎng mǎi diǎn __1__?

B： 我想买件衬衫。
    Wǒ xiǎng mǎi jiàn chènshān.

A： 这件怎么样？
    Zhèi jiàn zěnmeyàng?

B： 我不太喜欢这种料子。现在天气这么热，__2__的穿着不舒服。
    Wǒ bú tài xǐhuan zhèi zhǒng liàozi. Xiànzài tiānqi zhème rè, __2__ de chuānzhe bù shūfu.

A： 我们也有纯__3__的和真__4__的。
    Wǒmen yě yǒu chún __3__ de hé zhēn __4__ de.

B： 我喜欢棉的。好洗。
    Wǒ xǐhuan mián de. Hǎo xǐ.

A： 您穿__5__的衬衫？
    Nín chuān __5__ de chènshān?

B： 我穿41__6__。
    Wǒ chuān 41 __6__.

A： 您要长袖还是__7__？
    Nín yào chángxiù háishi __7__?

B： 长__8__。
    cháng __8__.

A： 您要格子的还是__9__的？
    Nín yào gézi de háishi __9__ de?

B： 我不要__10__的，也不要__11__的。我只要单色的。
    Wǒ bú yào __10__ de, yě bú yào __11__ de. Wǒ zhǐ yào dānsè de.

A： 您喜欢什么__12__呢？
    Nín xǐhuan shénme __12__ ne?

B： 白的和蓝的。可以__13__我的西装。
    Bái de hé lán de. Kěyǐ __13__ wǒde xīzhuāng.

A： 还要什么吗？
    Hái yào shénme ma?

B： 还要一条__14__，配我的衬衫。
    Hái yào yì tiáo __14__. Pèi wǒde chènshān.

5. Choose the word that *does not* belong.

1) 我想买一条____长裤。 a. 纯棉 b. 呢子 c. 灯芯绒 d. 领带
  Wǒ xiǎng mǎi yì tiáo ____chángkù. chúnmián nízi dēngxīnróng lǐngdài

2) 我想买一件____衬衫。 a. 真丝 b. 纯棉 c. 呢子 d. 化纤
  Wǒ xiǎng mǎi yí jiàn ____chènshān. zhēnsī chúnmián nízi huàxiān

3) 我想买一件____夹克。 a. 扣子 b. 法兰绒 c. 尼龙 d. 皮
  Wǒ xiǎng mǎi yí jiàn ____jiákè. kòuzi fǎlánróng nílóng pí

4) 我想买一件____风衣。 a. 尼龙 b. 袜子 c. 化纤 d. 纯棉
  Wǒ xiǎng mǎi yí jiàn ____fēngyī. nílóng wàzi huàxiān chúnmián

6. Complete.

1) 这件格子衬衫跟我的条纹领带不_____。
  Zhèi jiàn gézi chènshān gēn wǒde tiáowén lǐngdài bú_____.

2) 我不喜欢穿鞋跟太_____的鞋子。
  Wǒ bù xǐhuan chuān xiégēn tài _____de xiézi.

3) 下雨天我得穿_____。
  Xiàyǔ tiān wǒ děi chuān _____.

4) 我需要内衣。我得去买六条_____和六件_____。
  Wǒ xūyào nèiyī. Wǒ děi qù mǎi liù tiáo _____hé liù jiàn _____.

5) 我不知道我穿多大号的衣服。请你_____我的_____。
  Wǒ bù zhīdao wǒ chuān duō dà de hào yīfu. Qǐng nǐ _____wǒde _____.

6) 纯棉的衣服穿着舒服，可是不_____。
  Chúnmián de yīfu chuānzhe shūfu, kěshì bù _____.

7) _____的衣服能防皱，可是穿着不_____。
  _____de yīfu néng fángzhòu, kěshì chuānzhe bù _____.

8) 这件夹克我穿太_____了。我要一件大一点儿的。
  Zhèi jiàn jiákè wǒ chuān tài _____le. Wǒ yào yí jiàn dà yìdiǎnr de.

BUYING WOMEN'S CLOTHING

小姐，您要买什么？
Xiǎojiě, nín yào mǎi shénme?

我想买一条真丝**围巾**。   scarf
Wǒ xiǎng mǎi yì tiáo zhēnsī *wéijīn*.

  一件**衬衫**   blouse
  yí jiàn *chènshān*

   旗袍   Mandarin dress
   qípáo

  一条**裙子**   skirt
  yì tiáo *qúnzi*

连衣裙 *liányīqún*	dress
衬裙 *chènqún*	slip
紧身裤 *jǐnshēnkù*	tights
一个胸罩 yí ge *xiōngzhào*	brassiere
一双长丝袜/连裤袜 yì shuāng *chángsīwà/liánkùwà*	panty hose

您要长裙还是短裙?
Nín yào *cháng* qún háishi *duǎn* qún?   long, short

我想要棉毛混纺的料子。
Wǒ xiǎng yào mián máo *hùnfǎng* de *liàozi*.   blend, fabric

这件带点儿的衬衫配这条红裙子正好。
Zhèi jiàn *dài diǎnr* de chènshān pèi zhèi tiáo hóng qúnzi zhèng hǎo.   polka-dotted

带花边儿的 dài *huābiānr* de	lace

您穿多少号?
Nín chuān duōshǎo hào?

我穿小号。   small
Wǒ chuān *xiǎohào*.

中号 *zhōnghào*	medium
大号 *dàhào*	large
加大号 *jiādàhào*	extra-large

7. List items for a complete outfit for a woman.

————————————————   ————————————————
————————————————   ————————————————
————————————————   ————————————————
————————————————   ————————————————

8. Answer based on Figure 12-3.

1) 这是一件____衬衫。
    Zhè shi yí jiàn ____chènshān.

2) 这是一件____短袖衣。
    Zhè shi yí jiàn ____duǎnxiù yī.

3) 这是一条____围巾。
    Zhè shi yì tiáo ____wéijīn.

Fig. 12-3

9. Complete.

1) 我的内衣不够。我得去买几条_____，几双_____，和一个_____。
    Wǒde nèiyī bú gòu. Wǒ děi qù mǎi jǐ tiáo _____, jǐ shuāng _____, he yíge _____.

2) 这件条纹衬衫____这条格子裙不好看。
    Zhèi jiàn tiáowén chènshān _____zhèi tiáo gézi qún bù hǎokàn.

3) 这件中号衣服我穿太小。你们有没有_____的?
    Zhèi jiàn zhōnghào yīfu wǒ chuān tài xiǎo. Nǐmen yǒu měiyǒu _____de?

4) 我不想要棉衬衫，因为棉的不_____。
    Wǒ bù xiǎng yào mián chènshān, yīnwèi mián de bù _____.

10. Choose the appropriate word.

1) 我想买一条_____连衣裙。   a. 橡胶   b. 真丝   c. 皮
    Wǒ xiǎng mǎi yì tiáo _____liányīqún.   xiàngjiāo   zhēnsī   pí

2) 我不喜欢穿裙子。我喜欢穿_____。   a. 长裤   b. 丝巾   c. 胸罩
    Wǒ bù xǐhuan chuān qúnzi. Wǒ xǐhuan chuān ____.   chángkù   sījīn   xiōngzhào

3) 你们有没有尼龙_____?   a. 短袖   b.长丝袜   c. 鞋
    Nǐmen yǒu méiyǒu nílóng _____?   duǎnxiù   cháng sīwà   xié

4) 我买了一条_____围巾。   a. 皮   b. 高跟   c. 真丝
    Wǒ mǎile yì tiáo _____wéijīn   pí   gāogēn   zhēnsī

5) 天气太冷了，我要再穿一件_____。   a. 毛衣   b. 游泳衣   c. 衬裙
    Tiānqì tài lěng le, wǒ yào zài chuān yí jiàn _____.   máoyī   yóuyǒngyī   chènqún

KEY WORDS

(all) cotton	纯棉	chúnmián	patterned	花	huā
bathing suit	游泳衣	yóuyǒngyī	polka-dotted	带点儿的	dài diǎnr de
belt	皮带	pídài	rain coat	雨衣	yǔyī
black	黑	hēi	rayon	人(造)棉	rén (zào) mián
blend	混纺	hùnfǎng	red	红	hóng
blouse	衬衫/衬衣	chènshān/chènyī	rubber	(橡)胶	(xiàng)jiāo
blue	蓝	lán	sandal	凉鞋	liángxié
boot	靴子	xuēzi	scarf	围巾	wéijīn
brassiere	胸罩	xiōngzhào	shirt	衬衫/衬衣	chènshān/chènyī
brown	咖啡色	kāfēisè	shoe	鞋	xié
button	扣子	kòuzi	shoe polish	鞋油	xiéyóu
checked	格子	gézi	shoelace	鞋带	xiédài
clothing store	服装店	fúzhuāng diàn	short	短	duǎn
coat	大衣	dàyī	short sleeve	短袖	duǎnxiù
color	颜色	yánsè	shorts	短裤	duǎnkù
corduroy	灯芯绒	dēngxīnróng	size	号	hào
dress	连衣裙	liányīqún	(pure) silk	真丝	zhēnsī
extra-large	加大号	jiādàhào	size 40	40 号	sìshíhào
fabric	料子	liàozi	skirt	裙子	qúnzi
fit	合身,合适	héshēn, héshì	slip	衬裙	chènqún
flannel	法兰绒	fǎlánróng	slipper	拖鞋	tuōxié
flat heel	平跟	pínggēn	small (size)	小号	xiǎohào
gloves	手套	shǒutào	sneaker	旅游鞋	lǚyóuxié
hat	帽子	màozi	socks	袜子	wàzi
heavy woolen	呢子	nízi	sole	底	dǐ
heel	鞋跟	xiégēn	solid colored	单色	dānsè
high	高	gāo	striped	条纹	tiáowén
high heel	高跟	gāogēn	suit	西装	xīzhuāng
hurt the feet	挤脚	jǐjiǎo	sweater	毛衣	máoyī
jacket	夹克	jiákè	synthetic fabric	化纤料	huàxiānliào
jeans	牛仔裤	niúzǎikù	T shirt	T恤	tīxù
lace	花边儿	huābiānr	tie	领带	lǐngdài
large	大号	dàhào	tight	紧	jǐn
leather	皮	pí	tights	紧身裤	jǐnshēnkù
long	长	cháng	trench coat	风衣	fēngyī
long sleeve	长袖	chángxiù	underclothes	内衣	nèiyī
Mandarin dress	旗袍	qípáo	undershirt	汗衫/汗背心	hànshān/hàn
match	配	pèi			bèixīn
measure	量	liáng	underwear,	内短裤/三角	nèiduǎnkù/
measurement	尺寸	chǐcùn	briefs	裤	sānjiǎokù
medium (size)	中号	zhōnghào	vest	背心	bèixīn
narrow	瘦	shòu	what size	多大(号)	duōdà (hào)
nylon	尼龙	nílóng	white	白	bái
pair	双	shuāng	wide/big (for	肥	féi
pajamas	睡衣	shuìyī	clothing)		
pants/trousers	长裤	chángkù	wrinkle-resistant	防皱	fángzhòu
panty hose	长丝袜/连裤	chángsīwà/			
	袜	liánkùwà			

Chapter 13: At the dry cleaner[7]

第十三章：在干洗店
Zài gānxǐ diàn

我有很多**脏衣服**。   dirty clothes
Wǒ yǒu hěn duō *zāng yīfu*.

我要去**干洗店**。   dry cleaner's
Wǒ yào qù *gānxǐ diàn*.

这件衣服请你给我**洗**一洗，   wash
Zhèi jiàn yīfu qǐng nǐ gěi wǒ *xǐ* yi xǐ,

烫一下，不用**浆**。   iron, starch
tàng yíxià, bú yòng *jiāng*.

什么时候可以**取**？   pick up
Shénme shíhou kěyǐ *qǔ?*

这件西服能**干洗**吗？   dry clean
Zhèi jiàn xīfú néng *gānxǐ* ma?

这件毛衣水洗了会不会**缩水**？   shrink
Zhèi jiàn máoyī shuǐ xǐle huì bú huì *suōshuǐ?*

这儿有个**洞**，能**补**一下吗？   hole; mend
Zhèr yǒu ge *dòng*, néng *bǔ* yíxià ma?

这块**污渍/脏东西**能**去掉**吗？   stain; remove
Zhèi kuài *wūzì/zāng dōngxi* néng *qùdiào* ma?

掉了一个**扣子**。   lost, button
*Diào*le yí ge *kòuzi*.

这条**缝开线**了，能**缝**一下吗？   seam, torn, sew
Zhèi tiáo *fèng kāixiàn* le, néng *féng* yíxià ma?

对不起，今天**裁缝师傅**不在。   tailor
Duìbuqǐ, jīntiān *cáifeng shīfu* bú zài.

1. Complete.

1) 这件毛衣用水洗了会_____，你只能_____。
   Zhèi jiàn máoyī yòng shuǐ xǐle huì _____, nǐ zhǐ néng _____.

2) 请你先把这件衣服_____一下，然后再_____一烫。
   Qǐng nǐ xiān bǎ zhèi jiàn yīfu _____ yíxià, ránhòu zài _____ yí tàng.

---

[7] For articles of clothing and fabrics, see Chapter 12.

3) 这件衣服的这个地方_____线了，你能_____一下吗？
   Zhèi jiàn yīfu de zhèi ge dìfang _____ xiàn le, nǐ néng _____ yíxià ma?

4) 这条裙子上有一个洞，能_____一下吗？
   Zhèi tiáo qúnzi shàng yǒu yí ge dòng., néng _____ yíxià ma?

5) 这个_____掉了，请你替我_____上。
   Zhèi ge _____ diào le, qǐng nǐ tì wǒ _____ shàng.

6) 这件衬衫上有一块_____，你能_____吗？
   Zhèi jiàn chènshān shàng yǒu yí kuài _____, nǐ néng _____ ma?

2. Complete.

   (At the Dry Cleaner's shop)

A：您好！请你把这件衬衣给我__1__，再__2__。
   Nín hǎo! Qǐng nǐ bǎ zhèi jiàn chènyī gěi wǒ __1__, zài __2__.

B：好，要__3__吗？
   Hǎo, yào __3__ ma?

A：稍微__4__一下。这儿有一块__5__，你能不能__6__？
   Shāowēi __4__ yíxià. Zhèr yǒu yí kuài __5__, nǐ néng bu néng __6__?

B：是油渍吗？
   Shi yóuzì ma?

A：不是，是咖啡。
   Bú shi, shi kāfēi.

B：我可以试试。不过不知道能不能全部__7__，因为咖啡渍很难__8__。
   Wǒ kěyǐ shìshi. Búguò bù zhīdao néng bu néng quánbù __7__, yīnwèi kāfēi zì hěn nán __8__.

A：我知道。这件毛衣也要洗一下。
   Wǒ zhīdao. Zhèi jiàn máoyī yě yào xǐ yíxià.

B：这件毛衣不能水__9__，洗了会__10__，最好__11__。
   Zhèi jiàn máoyī bù néng shuǐ __9__, xǐ le huì __10__, zuìhǎo __11__.

A：好，那我明天能__12__吗？
   Hǎo, nà wǒ míngtiān néng __12__ ma?

B：衬衣明天就能__13__。毛衣不行，因为干洗得两天。
   Chènyī míngtiān jiù néng __13__. Máoyī bù xíng, yīnwèi gānxǐ děi liǎng tiān.

A：那好吧，谢谢。
   Nà hǎo ba, xièxie.

KEY WORDS

button	扣子	kòuzi	remove	去掉	qùdiào
clothes	衣服	yīfu	seam	缝	fèng
dirty	脏	zāng	sew	缝	féng
dry clean	干洗	gānxǐ	shrink	缩水	suōshuǐ
dry cleaner's	干洗店	gānxǐdiàn	stain	污渍/脏东西	wūzì/zāng dōngxi
hole	洞	dòng	starch	浆	jiāng
iron	烫	tàng	tailor	裁缝师傅	cáiféng shīfu
lost	掉了	diào le	torn	开线	kāixiàn
mend	补	bǔ	wash	洗	xǐ
pick up	取	qǔ			

Chapter 14: At the restaurant

第十四章：在饭馆
Zài fànguǎn

GETTING SETTLED

墙角 qiángjiǎo

菜单
càidān

饮料
yǐnliào

服务员
fúwùyuán

窗户
chuānghu

Fig. 14-1

这是一家**高级酒楼** Zhè shi yì jiā *gāojí jiǔlóu*.	high class/fancy restaurant
豪华酒家 *háohuá jiǔjiā*	luxurious restaurant
普通 饭馆 *pǔtōng fànguǎn*	ordinary, restaurant,
普通**餐厅** pǔtōng *cāntīng*	restaurant /diner
普通**餐馆** pǔtōng *cānguǎn*	restaurant /diner
比较**便宜的小吃店** bǐjiào *piányi* de *xiǎochīdiàn*	inexpensive, snack shop

112

中餐馆   Chinese food/meal
zhōngcān guǎn

西餐馆   Western food/meal
xīcān guǎn

快餐店   fast food
kuàicān diàn

咖啡厅   café
kāfēitīng

请问，几位？
Qǐngwèn, jǐ wèi?

四位。
Sì wèi.

对不起，没有**空位**了。   available seat/table
Duìbuqǐ, méiyǒu *kōng wèi* le.

我们已经**订位**了。   make reservation
Wǒmen yǐjīng *dìngwèi* le.

我们要**靠窗**的那张**桌子**。   by the window, table
Wǒmen yào *kào chuāng* de nèi zhāng *zhuōzi*.

靠墙角   at the corner
kào qiángjiǎo

我们想坐在**外头**。   outside
Wǒmen xiǎng zuò zài *wàitou*.

我们想要一个**包间**。   private room
Wǒmen xiǎng yào yí ge *bāojiān*.

服务员来了。   waiter
Fúwùyuán lái le.

请把**菜单**拿过来好吗？   menu
Qǐng bǎ *càidān* ná guòlái hǎo ma?

酒单   wine list
jiǔdān

现在可以**点菜**了吗？   order (dishes)
Xiànzài kěyǐ *diǎncài* le ma?

1. Complete.

1) 我没有_____位。我在等空_____。
   Wǒ méiyǒu _____wèi. Wǒ zài děng kōng _____.

2) 这是一家_____酒楼。这儿的菜特别贵。
   Zhè shi yì jiā _____jiǔlóu. Zhèr de cài tèbié guì.

3) 这是一家_____餐厅，这儿的菜比那家大酒楼的菜便宜多了。
   Zhè shi yì jiā _____cāntīng, zhèr de cài bǐ nèi jiā dà jiǔlóu de cài piányì duō le.

4) 今天天气真好。我们坐在_____好吗?
Jīntiān tiānqi zhēn hǎo. Wǒmen zuò zài _____ hǎo ma?

5) _____! 请把_____拿过来给我们看看。
_____! Qǐng bǎ _____ná guòlái gěi wǒmen kànkan.

6) 我们几个人想安静地说说话。你们有_____吗?
Wǒmen jǐ ge rén xiǎng ānjìng de shuōshuo huà. Nǐmen yǒu _____ma?

7) 我们想喝点儿酒。你们的_____呢?
Wǒmen xiǎng hē diǎnr jiǔ. Nǐmen de _____ne?

8) 你不想吃_____吗? 那我们就去西_____吧。
Nǐ bù xiǎng chī _____mā? Nà wǒmen jiù qù xī _____ ba.

2. Complete.

(In the restaurant)

A：您好! __1__位?
Nín hǎo, __1__wèi?

B：三 __2__ 。
Sān __2__ .

A：您__3__了吗?
Nín __3__le ma?

B：订了。
Dìng le.

A：用的哪位的名字?
Yòng de nǎ wèi de míngzì?

B：李小平。
Lǐ Xiǎopíng.

A：请问先生喜欢__4__在这儿还是喜欢__5__窗户坐?
Qǐngwèn xiānsheng xǐhuan __4__zài zhèr háishi xǐhuan __5__chuānghu zuò?

B：我们想要一个__6__间。
Wǒmen xiǎng yào yí ge __6__jiān.

A：请这边来。
Qǐng zhèibiān lái.

3. Complete.

美美在一家__1__工作。她是餐厅的__2__小姐。客人来了以后，她会给客人
Měiměi zài yì jiā __1__gōngzuò. Tā shi cāntīng de __2__xiǎojiě. Kèren láile yǐhòu, tā huì gěi kèren

安排__3__，然后给每位客人一份__4__。客人看了__5__以后就会点菜。
ānpái __3__, ránhòu gěi měi wèi kèren yí fèn __4__. Kèren kànle __5__yǐhòu jiù huì diǎncài.

LOOKING AT THE CHINESE MENU[8]

凉菜 *liángcài*	cold dish
拼盘 *pīnpán*	starters, assorted cold dishes
凉拌黄瓜 *liángbàn huángguā*	cold and dressed with sauce, cucumber
五香牛肉 *wǔxiāng niúròu*	five spiced beef
醉鸡 *zuì jī*	drunken chicken
素鸭 *sù yā*	vegetarian duck
汤 *tāng*	soup
云吞(馄饨)汤 *yúntūn (húntun)* tāng	wonton
酸辣汤 *suānlà* tāng	hot and sour
蛋花汤 *tànhuā* tāng	egg drop
火腿冬瓜汤 *huǒtuǐ dōngguā* tāng	ham and winter melon
肉 *ròu*	meat
红烧猪肉 *hóngshāo zhūròu*	pork braised in soy sauce
清炖牛肉 *qīngdùn niúròu*	beef stew
葱爆羊肉片 *cōngbào yángròu piàn*	sliced lamb quick fried with scallions
宫保鸡丁 *gōngbǎo jī dīng*	diced chicken stir-fried with chili and peanuts
香酥鸡 *xiāngsū jī*	crispy chicken
北京烤鸭 *Běijīng kǎoyā*	Beijing roast duck
海鲜 *hǎixiān*	seafood

---

[8] For more food items, spices, and cooking methods, please refer to Appendix 3: Food .

糖醋鱼 *tángcù yú*	sweet and sour fish
油焖大虾 *yóumèn dà xiā*	sautéed shrimp
葱姜龙虾 *cōng jiāng lóngxiā*	lobster with scallion and ginger
清蒸螃蟹 *qīngzhēng pángxiè*	steamed crab
炒鱿鱼丝 *chǎo yóuyú sī*	stir-fried shredded squid
蔬菜 *shūcài*	vegetables
炒青菜 *chǎo qīngcài*	stir-fried green-leaf vegetables
干煸四季豆 *gānbiān sìjìdòu*	dry sautéed string beans
鱼香茄子 *yúxiāng qiézi*	eggplant with garlic sauce
家常豆腐 *jiācháng dòufu*	fried tofu homestyle
主食 *zhǔshí*	staple/principal food
米 *mǐ*	rice
米饭 *mǐfàn*	cooked rice
蛋炒饭 *dàn chǎofàn*	stir-fried rice with eggs
河粉/米粉 *héfěn/mǐfěn*	rice noodles
炒年糕 *chǎo niángāo*	stir-fried rice cake
面食 *miànshí*	wheat-based food
馒头 *mántou*	steamed bun
包子 *bāozi*	steamed meat bun
饺子 *jiǎozi*	dumpling
锅贴 *guōtiē*	fried dumplings, pot stickers

葱油饼 *cōngyóubǐng*	scallion pancake
面条 *miàntiáo*	noodle
炒面 *chǎomiàn*	fried noodles
汤面 *tāngmiàn*	noodle soup
甜点 *tiándiǎn*	dessert
芝麻汤圆 *zhīmá tāngyuán*	rice ball with sesame paste
拔丝苹果 *básī píngguǒ*	toffee apple

LOOKING AT THE WESTERN MENU

开胃菜 *kāiwèicài*	appetizer
什锦水果 *shíjǐn shuǐguǒ*	fruit cup
虾拼盘 *xiā pīnpán*	shrimp cocktail
汤 *tāng*	soup
鸡汤 *jītāng*	chicken soup
奶油蘑菇汤 *nǎiyóu mógū* tāng	cream, mushroom
牛尾汤 *niúwěi* tāng	oxtail
沙拉 *shālā*	salad
拌沙拉 *bàn shālā*	tossed salad
土豆沙拉 *tǔdòu* shālā	potato salad
主菜 *zhǔcài*	entree/main course
烤三文鱼 *kǎo sānwényú*	grilled salmon

熏火鸡 *xūn huǒjī*	smoked turkey
炸鸡 *zhá jī*	deep-fried chicken
牛排 *niúpái*	steak
西兰花 *xīlánhuā*	broccoli
火腿三明治 *huǒtuǐ sānmíngzhì*	ham sandwich
肉丸意大利粉 *ròuwán yìdàlì fěn*	spaghetti with meatballs
烤土豆/马铃薯 *kǎo tǔdòu/mǎlíngshǔ*	baked potato
煮鸡蛋 *zhǔ jīdàn*	boiled eggs
面包 *miànbāo*	bread
快餐 *kuàicān*	fast food
汉堡包 *hànbǎobāo*	hamburger
匹萨饼 *pǐsàbǐng*	pizza
热狗 *règǒu*	hot dog
炸薯条 *zhá shǔtiáo*	French fries
炸薯片 *zhá shǔpiàn*	potato chips
番茄酱 *fānqié jiàng*	ketchup
泡菜 *pàocài*	pickles
芥末 *jièmò*	mustard

ORDERING FOOD

客人说：
Kèrén shuō:

我不知道**点**什么。   order
Wǒ bù zhīdao diǎn shénme.

你能给我们**推荐**几个菜吗？   recommend
Nǐ néng gěi wǒmen *tuījiàn* jǐ ge cài ma?

请问这里的**拿手菜/招牌**菜是什么？   house specialty
Qǐngwèn zhèlǐ de *náshǒu cài /zhāopái cài* shi shénme?

我想**来**一个宫保鸡丁。   have (in ordering dishes)
Wǒ xiǎng *lái* yí ge gōngbǎo jīdīng.

　　　一个酸辣汤
　　　yí ge suānlà tāng

　　　一**碗**米饭   bowl
　　　yì *wǎn* mǐfàn

我不太**饿**，   hungry
Wǒ bú tài *è*,

一个菜就行了。   one dish
yí ge cài jiù xíng le.

你们有没有葱爆羊肉？
Nǐmen yǒu méiyǒu cōngbào yángròu?

我要一份**牛排**。   steak
Wǒ yào yí fèn *niúpái*.

　　　我喜欢**嫩**一点儿的。   rare
　　　Wǒ xǐhuan *nèn* yìdiànr de.

　　　老一点儿的   well done
　　　lǎo yì diǎnr de

我不吃肉，我**吃素**。你们有什么**素菜**？   vegetarian, vegetarian dish
Wǒ bù chī ròu, wǒ *chī sù*. Nǐmen yǒu shénme *sùcài?*

服务员说：
Fúwùyuán shuō,

您**决定**点什么了吗？   decide
Nín *juédìng* diǎn shénme le ma?

我给您推荐...
Wǒ gěi nín tuījiàn...

您慢慢吃。   Take your time! (Enjoy!)
Nín mànmàn chī.

4. Answer on the basis of Figure 14-2.

1)　这是一家豪华酒楼还是一家普通餐馆？
　　Zhè shi yì jiā háohuá jiǔlóu háishi yì jiā pǔtōng cānguǎn.

2)　一共有几位客人?
　　Yígòng yǒu jǐ wèi kèrén?

Fig. 14-2

3) 桌子在哪儿?
   Zhuōzi zài nǎr?

4) 谁在为他们服务?
   Shéi zài wèi tāmen fúwù?

5) 服务员拿的那个盘子里有什么?
   Fúwùyuán ná de nèi ge pánzi lǐ yǒu shénme?

6) 服务员另一只手里拿的是什么?
   Fúwùyuán lìng yì zhī shǒu lǐ ná de shi shénme?

7) 他们吃的是中餐还是西餐?
   Tāmen chī de shi zhōngcān háishi xīcān?

5. Complete.

1) 在中国有_____餐馆也有_____餐馆。
   Zài Zhōngguó yǒu _____cānguǎn yě yǒu _____cānguǎn.

2) _____常常先问你要点什么饮料。
   _____chángcháng xiān wèn nǐ yào diǎn shénme yǐngliào.

3) 我向您_____这个菜。这是我们这儿的_____菜。
   Wǒ xiàng nín _____zhèi ge cài, zhè shi wǒmen zhèr de _____cài.

4) 我不太饿的时候，常常只要一个_____。
   Wǒ bú tài è de shíhou, chángcháng zhǐ yào yí ge _____.

5) 我不知道点什么菜好，我得先看看_____。
   Wǒ bù zhīdao diǎn shénme cài hǎo, wǒ děi xiān kànkàn _____.

6) 有的人不吃肉，只吃_____。
　　Yǒude rén bù chī ròu, zhǐ chī _____.

7) A：我吃素，请问你们这儿有些什么_____?
　　A: Wǒ chīsù. Qǐngwèn nǐmen zhèr yǒu xie shénme _____?

6. How do you say the following in Chinese?

1) cooked on a grill

2) baked in the oven

3) cooked slowly in liquid on top of the stove

4) smoked

5) well done

6) rare

7. Complete.

1) _____鱼得用很多油。
　　_____yú děi yòng hěn duō yóu.

2) _____牛肉要用很长的时间。
　　_____niúròu yào yòng hěng cháng de shíjiān.

3) _____丸子吃起来又酸又甜。
　　_____wánzi chī qǐlai yòu suān yòu tián.

4) _____的菜不是热的。
　　_____de cài bú shi rè de.

5) 吃_____的人不吃肉。
　　chī _____de rén bù chī ròu.

6) _____汤的味道又酸又辣。
　　_____tāng de wèidào yòu suān yòu là.

7) 做_____肉要用很多酱油。
　　zuò _____ròu yào yòng hěn duō jiàngyóu

8) 中国人最常用的做菜方法是_____。
　　Zhōngguó rén zuì chángyòng de zuòcài fāngfǎ shi _____.

8. Match.

1) 鸡丁							a. shredded meat
　　jīdīng

2) 羊肉片						b. meatballs
　　yángròu piàn

3) 肉丝							c. sliced lamb
　　ròusī

4) 肉丸子   d. diced chicken
    ròu wánzi

ORDERING BEVERAGES

我要一壶绿茶。   pot, green tea
Wǒ yào yì *hú lǜchá*.

    红茶   black tea
    hóngchá

    茉莉花茶   jasmine tea
    mòlì huāchá

    乌龙茶   Woolong tea
    wūlóngchá

    菊花茶   chrysanthemum tea
    júhuāchá.

请问你们有什么洋酒？   foreign
Qǐngwèn nǐmen yǒu shénme *yáng* jiǔ?

有威士忌。   whiskey
Yǒu *wēishìjì*

    白兰地   brandy
    báilándì

    伏特加   vodka
    fútèjiā

    香槟   champagne
    xiāngbīn

有什么中国酒呢？   Chinese wine
Yǒu shénme Zhōngguó jiǔ ne?

有茅台   Maotai
yǒu *máotái*

    干红葡萄酒   dry, red wine
    gān hóng pútaojiǔ

    白葡萄酒   white wine
    bái pútaojiǔ

请给我们来一瓶青岛啤酒。   Qingdao, beer
Qǐng gěi wǒmen lái yì píng *Qīngdǎo píjiǔ*.

    一听可乐   can, coke
    yì *tīng kělè*

    七喜   Seven Up
    qīxǐ

一杯桔子汁/橙汁 yì bēi *júzi zhī/chéngzhī*	orange juice
果汁 *guǒzhī*	fruit juice
矿泉水 *kuàngquánshuǐ*	mineral water

请加冰。 Qǐng jiā *bīng.*	ice
我要一杯咖啡。 Wǒ yào yì bēi *kāfēi.*	coffee
别放糖和牛奶。 Bié fàng *táng* he *niúnǎi.*	sugar, milk

9. Name three beverages that contain alcohol, three cold beverages that are nonalcohol, and three beverages that are normally served hot.

1) _____ _____ _____

2) _____ _____ _____

3) _____ _____ _____

SOME SPECIAL REQUIREMENTS FOR THE DISHES

请少放盐，我不爱吃咸的。 Qǐng shǎo fàng *yán*, wǒ bú ài chī *xián* de.		salt, salty
醋 *cù*	酸 *suān*	vinegar, sour
辣椒 *làjiāo*	辣 *là*	chili/hot pepper, spicy/hot
糖 *táng*	甜 *tián*	sugar, sweet
油 *yóu*	油腻 *yóunì*	oil, oily/greasy
请不要放味精，我对味精过敏。 Qǐng bú yào fàng *wèijīng*, wǒ duì wèijīng *guòmǐn.*		MSG, allergic
请不要放猪油。 Qǐng bú yào fàng *zhūyóu.*		lard

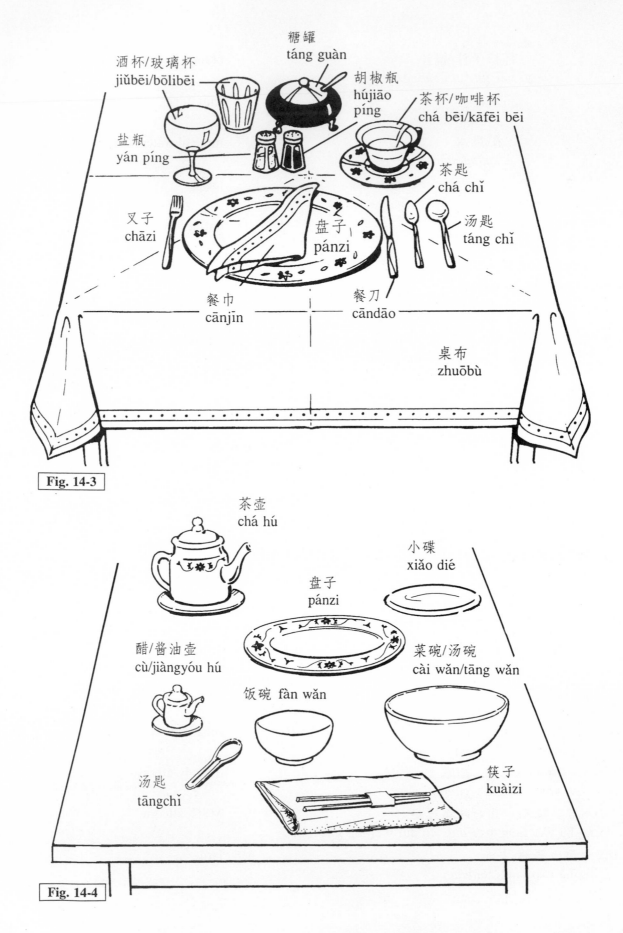

酒杯/玻璃杯
jiǔbēi/bōlibēi

糖罐
táng guàn

胡椒瓶
hújiāo
píng

茶杯/咖啡杯
chá bēi/kāfēi bēi

盐瓶
yán píng

茶匙
chá chǐ

叉子
chāzi

盘子
pánzi

汤匙
táng chǐ

餐巾
cānjīn

餐刀
cāndāo

桌布
zhuōbù

Fig. 14-3

茶壶
chá hú

小碟
xiǎo dié

盘子
pánzi

醋/酱油壶
cù/jiàngyóu hú

菜碗/汤碗
cài wǎn/tāng wǎn

饭碗 fàn wǎn

汤匙
tāngchǐ

筷子
kuàizi

Fig. 14-4

SOME PROBLEMS YOU MAY HAVE

对不起，少了一双筷子。 Duìbuqǐ, *shǎo* le yì shuāng *kuàizi*.	lack, chopsticks
一个杯子 yí ge *bēizi*	cup
盘子 *pánzi*	plate
碗 *wǎn*	bowl
一把刀 yì bǎ *dāo*	knife
叉(子) *chā(zi)*	fork
勺(子) *sháo(zi)*	spoon
请拿些餐巾纸来好吗？ Qǐng ná xie *cānjīnzhǐ* lái hǎo ma?	napkin
请你拿点儿酱油来，好吗？ Qǐng nǐ ná diǎnr *jiàngyóu* lái, hǎo ma?	soy sauce
胡椒 *hújiāo*	pepper
能给我们一点儿辣椒酱吗？ Néng gěi wǒmen yìdiǎnr *làjiāojiàng* má?	chili sauce
有牙签吗？ Yǒu *yáqiān* ma?	toothpick
我们点的菜好了没有？ Wǒmen diǎn de cài *hǎo* le méiyǒu?	ready
能快一点儿吗？ Néng kuài yìdiǎnr ma?	
你忘了我们要的饮料了吧？ Nǐ *wàngle* wǒmen yào de *yǐnliào* le ba?	forget, drinks
这个盘子太脏了。 Zhèi ge pánzi tài *zāng* le.	dirty
肉太生了。 Ròu tài *shēng* le.	too rare
老 *lǎo*	overdone
硬 *yìng*	tough
菜太淡(咸/辣/甜/酸)了。 Cài tài *dàn* (xián/là/tián/suān) le.	not salty enough, bland

汤太**冷**了。   cold

Tāng tài *lěng* le.

这鱼不**新鲜**了。   fresh

Zhè yú bù *xīnxiān* le.

10. Match.

1) 醋   a. 甜

   cù   tián

2) 糖   b. 咸

   táng   xián

3) 辣椒   c. 辣

   làjiāo   là

4) 盐   d. 酸

   yán   suān

11. Complete.

1) 小姐，_____了一个杯子。我们五个人，只有四个杯子。

   Xiǎojiě, _____le yí ge bēizi. Wǒmen wǔ ge rén, zhǐ yǒu sì ge bēizi.

2) 请把_____拿过来好吗？这个菜不够咸。

   Qǐng bǎ _____ná guòlai hǎo ma? Zhèige cài bú gòu xián.

3) 小姐，_____放多了吧？怎么这么酸啊？

   Xiǎojiě, _____fàng duō le ba? Zěnme zhème suān a?

4) 请别放_____，我过敏。

   Qǐng bié fàng _____, wǒ guòmǐn.

5) 我们的菜怎么还没_____啊？我们已经等了三十分钟了。

   Wǒmen de cài zěnme hái méi _____a? Wǒmen yǐjīng děngle sānshí fēnzhōng le.

6) 这肉太_____了。是不是炸得时间太长了？

   Zhè ròu tài _____le. Shì bu shì zhá de shíjiān tài cháng le?

12. Identify each item in Figure 14-5 and 14-6.

1)_____   2)_____   3)_____   4)_____   5)_____

6)_____   7)_____   8)_____   9)_____   10)_____

11)_____   12)_____   13)_____   14)_____   15)_____

16)_____   17)_____   18)_____   19)_____   20)_____

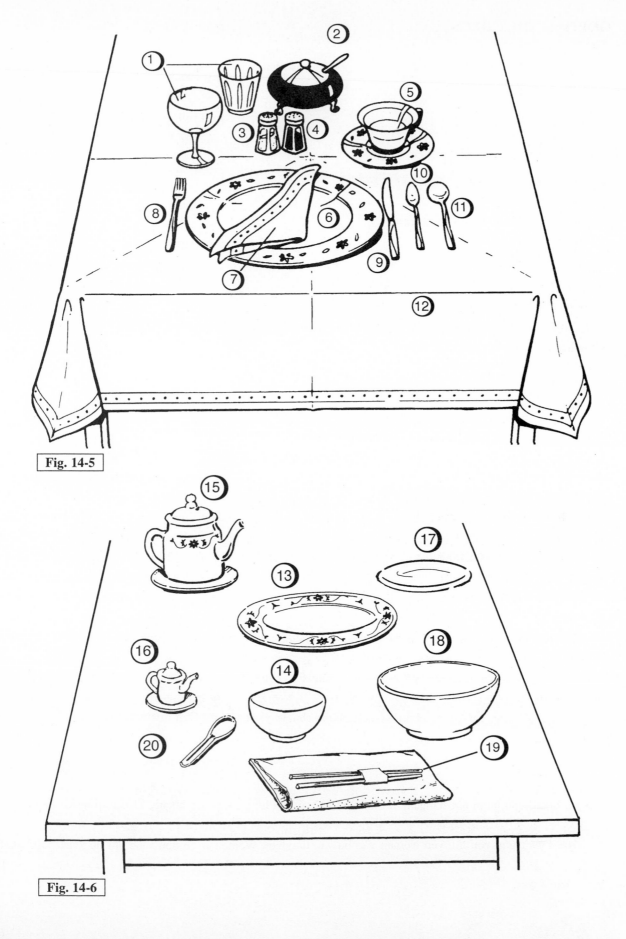

Fig. 14-5

Fig. 14-6

GETTING THE CHECK

小姐，**结帐/买单**。   pay check/bill
Xiǎojiě, *jiézhàng/mǎidān*.

我们要**分开算**。   split bill/go Dutch
Wǒmen yào *fēnkāi suàn*.

请给我**帐单**。我们**一起算**。   bill, one check for everyone
Qǐng gěi wǒ *zhàngdān*. Wǒmen *yìqǐ suàn*.

这顿饭吃得很好，谢谢。
Zhè dùn fàn chī de hěn hǎo, xièxie.

这个帐**算**得不对吧？   calculate
Zhèige zhàng *suàn* de bú duì ba?

好象没有这么多钱啊。
Hǎoxiàng méiyǒu zhème duō qián a.

先生，我们这儿得**收**10% 的**服务费**。   charge, service fee
Xiānsheng, wǒmen zhèr děi *shōu*
bǎi fēn zhī shí de *fúwù fèi*.

一天我跟几个朋友到一家饭馆去吃饭。到了那儿以后，我告诉服务员小姐
Yì tiān wǒ gen jǐ ge péngyou dào yì jiā fànguǎn qù chīfàn. Dàole nàr yǐhòu, wǒ gàosù fúwùyuán xiǎojiě

我们已经事先订位了。所以她给了我们一个很好的靠窗的桌子。那天
wǒmen yǐjīng shìxiān dìngwèi le. Suǒyǐ tā gěile wǒmen yí ge hěn hǎo de kào chuāng de zhuōzi. Nà tiān

我们不想坐在外头，因为风有点儿大。坐好以后，服务员小姐给我们拿来
wǒmen bù xiǎng zuòzài wàitou, yīnwèi fēng yǒu diǎnr dà. Zuòhǎo yǐhòu, fúwùyuán xiǎojiě gěi wǒmen nálái

了酒单和菜单，问我们要不要喝酒。我喜欢喝红酒，可是我的朋友都喜欢
le jiǔdān he càidān, wèn wǒmen yào bu yào hējiǔ. Wǒ xǐhuan hē hóng jiǔ, Kěshì wǒde péngyǒu dōu xǐhuan

洋酒，所以我们要了一瓶白兰地，点了两个凉菜下酒。接着我们又开始点
yáng jiǔ. suǒyǐ wǒmen yàole yì píng báilandì, diǎnle liǎng ge liángcài xiàjiǔ. Jiēzhe wǒmen yòu kāishǐ diǎn

热菜。小王点了一个清蒸鱼，小李点的是服务员小姐推荐的这家饭馆
rè cài. Xiǎo Wáng diǎnle yí ge qīngzhéng yú, Xiǎo lǐ diǎn de shi fúwùyuán xiǎojiě tuījiàn de zhèi jiā fànguǎn

的招牌菜：红烧牛肉。我要的是宫保鸡丁。最后我们又要了一个炒青菜
de zhāopáicài: hóngshāo niúròu. Wǒ yào de shi gōngbǎo jīdīng. Zuìhòu wǒmen yòu yàole yí ge chǎo qīngcài

和一个酸辣汤。酒来了，可是我们发现少了一个酒杯。跟服务员说了以后，她很
hé yí ge suānlà tāng. Jiǔ lái le, kěshì wǒmen fāxiàn shǎole yí ge jiǔbēi. Gēn fúwùyuán shuōle yǐhòu, tā hěn

快就给我们送来了。
kuài jiù gěi wǒmen sònglái le.

我们边喝酒，边吃凉菜。一会儿，热菜也好了。菜做得不错，只是青菜咸了
Wǒmen biān hējiǔ, biān chī liángcài. Yì huǐr, rè cài yě hǎo le. Cài zuò de búcuò, Zhǐshi qīngcài xiánle

一点儿。服务员又来问我们要不要甜点。我们几个都说吃不下了，只要了
yì diǎnr. Fúwùyuán yòu lái wèn wǒmen yào bu yào tiándiǎn. Wǒmen jǐ ge dōu shuō chī bú xià le, zhǐ yàole

一壶菊花茶。
yì hú júhuāchá.

13. Complete the following statements according to the above passage.

1) 他们在一家_____吃饭。
   Tāmen zài yì jiā ____chīfàn.

2) 他们去饭馆前已经_____了。
   Tāmen qù fànguǎn qián yǐjīng ____le.

3) 他们没有坐在_____，因为那天风太大了。
   Tāmen méiyǒu zuòzài ____, yīnwèi nèi tiān fēng tài dà le.

4) 他们坐的是_____的桌子。
   Tāmen zuò de shi ____de zhuōzi.

5) 他们坐下以后，服务员拿来了_____和_____。
   Tāmen zuòxià yǐhòu, fúwùyuán náláile ____he ____.

6) 他的朋友不爱喝_____，所以他们要了一瓶白兰地。
   Tā de péngyou bú ài hē ____, suǒyǐ tāmen yàole yì píng báilándì.

7) 他们一共点了两个_____菜，四个_____菜，还有一个_____。
   Tāmen yígòng diǎnle liǎng ge ____cài, sì ge ____cài, hái yǒu yí ge ____.

8) 四个菜里只有一个是_____菜。
   Sì ge cài lǐ zhǐ yǒu yí ge shi ____cài.

9) 小李点的菜是服务员_____的。
   Xiǎo Lǐ diǎn de cài shi fúwùyuán ____de.

10) 他们没点红烧鱼，他们点的是_____鱼。
    Tāmen méi diǎn hóngshāoyú, tāmen diǎn de shi ____yú.

14. Answer.

1) 他们坐在哪儿？
   Tāmen zuò zài nǎr?

2) 为什么服务员给他们那么好的桌子？
   Wèishénme fúwùyuán gěi tāmen nàme hǎo de zhuōzi?

3) 他们为什么没要红酒？
   Tāmen wèishénme méi yào hóng jiǔ?

4) 他们的桌子上少了什么？
   Tāmen de zhuōzi shàng shǎo le shénme?

5) 他们喝酒的时候吃什么了？
   Tāmen hējiǔ de shǐhou chī shénme le?

6) 这家饭馆的菜怎么样？
   Zhèi jiā fànguǎn de cài zěnmeyàng?

7) 哪个菜做得不太好？
   Něi ge cài zuò de bú tài hǎo?

8) 他们点汤了吗？
   Tāmen diǎn tāng le ma?

9) 他们点甜食了吗?
Tāmen diǎn tiánshí le ma?

10) 吃饭以后他们点了什么饮料?
Chīfàn yǐhòu tāmen diǎn le shénme yǐnliào?

KEY WORDS

allergic	过敏	guòmǐn	
appetizer	开胃菜	kāiwèi cài	
at the corner	靠墙角	kào qiángjiǎo	
available seat/table	空位	kōng wèi	
baked	烤	kǎo	
beef	牛肉	niúròu	
beer	啤酒	píjiǔ	
bill	帐单	zhàngdān	
black tea	红茶	hóngchá	
boiled	煮	zhǔ	
bowl	碗	wǎn	
braise in soy sauce	红烧	hóngshāo	
brandy	白兰地	báilándì	
bread	面包	miànbāo	
by the window	靠窗	kào chuāng	
calculate	算	suàn	
can	听	tīng	
champagne	香槟	xiāngbīn	
charge	收	shōu	
chicken	鸡	jī	
chili sauce	辣椒酱	làjiāo jiàng	
chili/hot pepper	辣椒	làjiāo	
Chinese meal	中餐	zhōngcān	
chopsticks	筷子	kuàizi	
chrysanthemum	菊花	júhuā	
coffee	咖啡	kāfēi	
coke	可乐	kělè	
cold	冷	lěng	
cold and dressed with sauce	凉拌	liángbàn	
cold dish	凉菜	liángcài	
cooked rice	米饭	mǐfàn	
crab	螃蟹	pángxiè	
crispy duck	香酥鸭	xiāngsū yā	
cucumber	黄瓜	huángguā	
cup/glass	杯子	bēizi	
decide	决定	juédìng	
deep fry	炸	zhá	
dessert	甜点	tiándiǎn	
dirty	脏	zāng	
drinks	饮料	yǐnliào	
dry	干	gān	
duck	鸭	yā	

dumplings	饺子	jiǎozi	
eggs	(鸡)蛋	(jī)dàn	
Enjoy!	您慢慢吃	nín mànmàn chī	
entrée	主菜	zhǔcài	
first class	高级	gāojí	
fish	鱼	yú	
foreign drinks	洋酒	yáng jiǔ	
forget	忘	wàng	
fork	叉(子)	chā(zi)	
fresh	新鲜	xīnxiān	
fried dumplings	锅贴	guōtiē	
fried noodles	炒面	chǎo miàn	
fried rice	炒饭	chǎo fàn	
fried rice noodles	炒粉	chǎo fěn	
fruit juice	果汁	guǒzhī	
green tea	绿茶	lǜchá	
green-leaf vegetables	青菜	qīngcài	
grilled	烤	kǎo	
ham	火腿	huǒtuǐ	
house specialty	拿手菜/招牌菜	náshǒu cài/zhāopáicài	
hungry	饿	è	
ice	冰	bīng	
inexpensive	便宜	piányi	
jasmine	茉莉花	mòlìhuā	
knife	刀	dāo	
lack	少	shǎo	
lamb	羊肉	yángròu	
lard	猪油	zhūyóu	
lobster	龙虾	lóngxiā	
luxurious	豪华	háohuá	
Maotai (a strong Chinese spirit)	茅台	máotái	
meat	肉	ròu	
meatballs	丸子	wánzi	
menu	菜单	càidān	
milk	牛奶	niú nǎi	
mineral water	矿泉水	kuàngquánshuǐ	
MSG	味精	wèijīng	
napkin	餐巾纸	cānjīn zhǐ	
noodle soup	汤面	tāng miàn	
noodles	面条	miàntiáo	
oil	油	yóu	

oily/greasy	油腻	yóunì	
one check for everyone	一起算	yìqǐ suàn	
one dish	一个菜	yí ge cài	
orange juice	桔子汁/橙汁	júzi zhī/ chéngzhī	
order dishes	点菜	diǎncài	
ordinary	普通	pǔtōng	
outside	外头	wàitou	
overdone	老	lǎo	
pay check/bill	结帐/买单	jiézhàng/mǎidān	
pepper	胡椒	hújiāo	
plain, bland	淡	dàn	
plate	盘子	pánzi	
pork	猪肉	zhūròu	
pot	壶	hú	
potato	土豆	tǔdòu	
private room	包间	bāojiān	
Qingdao	青岛	qīngdǎo	
quick-fry	爆	bào	
rare	嫩	nèn	
rare	生	shēng	
ready	好	hǎo	
recommend	推荐	tuījiàn	
red wine	红葡萄酒	hóng pútaojiǔ	
restaurant	酒楼/酒家	jiǔlóu/jiǔjiā	
restaurant	饭馆/餐厅/餐馆	fànguǎn/cāntīng/ cānguǎn	
roast	烤	kǎo	
salad	沙拉	shālā	
salmon	三文鱼	sānwényú	
salt	盐	yán	
salty	咸	xián	
sandwich	三明治	sānmíngzhì	
scallion	葱	cōng	
seafood	海鲜	hǎixiān	
service fee	服务费	fúwù fèi	
seven up	七喜	Qīxǐ	
shredded meat	肉丝	ròusī	
shrimp	虾	xiā	
sliced	片	piàn	
smoked	熏	xūn	

snack shop	小吃店	xiǎochīdiàn	
soup	汤	tāng	
sour	酸	suān	
sour and spicy	酸辣	suānlà	
soy sauce	酱油	jiàngyóu	
spicy diced chicken with peanuts	宫保鸡丁	gōngbǎo jīdīng	
spicy/hot	辣	là	
split the bill/ go Dutch	分开算	fēn kāi suàn	
spoon	勺	sháo	
squid	鱿鱼	yóuyú	
staple	主食	zhǔshí	
principal food			
starter, assorted cold dishes	拼盘	pīnpán	
steak	牛排	niúpái	
steamed buns	馒头	mántou	
steamed meat bun	包子	bāozi	
stew	炖	dùn	
stir fry	炒	chǎo	
sugar	糖	táng	
sweet	甜	tián	
sweet and sour	糖醋	tángcù	
table	桌子	zhuōzi	
tenderloin	里脊	lǐjī	
toothpick	牙签	yáqiān	
tough	硬	yìng	
turkey	火鸡	huǒjī	
vegetarian	吃素	chīsù	
vegetarian dish	素菜	sùcài	
vinegar	醋	cù	
vodka	伏特加	fútèjiā	
waiter	服务员	fúwùyuán	
well done	老	lǎo	
Western meal	西餐	xīcān	
whiskey	威士忌	wēishìjì	
white wine	白葡萄酒	bái pútaojiǔ	
wine list	酒单	jiǔ dān	
Woolong tea	乌龙茶	wūlóng chá	

Chapter 15: Shopping for food

第十五章：购买食品

Gòumǎi shípǐn

TYPES OF STORES AND MARKETS

我要去菜店/菜市场。 green grocer
Wǒ yào qù *cài diàn/cài shìchǎng.*

肉店 meat market
ròu diàn

超市(超级市场) supermarket
chāoshì (chāojí shìchǎng)

超市**糕点部** bakery, section
chāoshì *gāodiǎn bù*

糖果 candy
tángguǒ

水果 fruit
shuǐguǒ

熟食 cooked food
shóushí

饮料 beverage
yǐnliào

蔬菜 vegetables
shūcài

冷冻食品 frozen food
lěngdòng shípǐn

水产 seafood
shuǐchǎn

肉食 meat product
ròushí

豆制品 soybean product
dòu zhìpǐn

粮食 grain
liángshi

调味品 spice
tiáowèipǐn

烟酒 cigarettes and alcohol
yān jiǔ

132

超级市场里什么**食品**都有。   food
Chāojí shìchǎng lǐ shénme *shípǐn* dōu yǒu.

超市门口有**购物推车**和**篮子**。   shopping cart, basket
Chāoshì ménkǒu yǒu *gòuwù tuīchē* hé *lánzi.*

人们用**塑料袋**装东西。   plastic bag
Rénmen yòng *sùliào dài* zhuāng dōngxi.

副食品店就象一个小超市。   grocery store
Fùshípǐn diàn jiù xiàng yí ge xiǎo chāoshì.

自由市场卖的东西都很**新鲜**。   free market,   fresh
Zìyóu shìchǎng mài de dōngxi dōu hěn *xīnxiān.*

1. Complete.

1)   _____店又卖面包又卖蛋糕。
     _____diàn yòu mài miànbāo yòu mài dàngāo.

2)   在_____店可以买到牛肉和猪肉。
     Zài _____diàn kěyǐ mǎidào niúròu hé zhūròu.

3)   买苹果香蕉请去_____店。
     Mǎi píngguǒ xiāngjiāo qǐng qù _____diàn.

4)   超市_____部卖做熟了的鱼、肉等。
     Chāoshì _____bù mài zuòshóu le de yú, ròu děng.

5)   买可口可乐、啤酒、果汁应该去超市的_____部。
     Mǎi kěkǒu kělè、píjiǔ、guǒzhī yīnggāi qù chāoshì de _____ bù.

6)   要买鱼请去_____部。
     Yào mǎi yú qǐng qù _____ bù.

7)   买蔬菜得去_____店。
     Mǎi shūcài děi qù _____ diàn.

8)   买酱油、盐、胡椒应该去超市的_____部。
     Mǎi jiàngyóu、yán、hújiāo yīnggāi qù chāoshì de _____bù.

9)   自由市场卖豆腐，超市的_____部也卖豆腐。
     Zìyóu shìchǎng mài dòufu, chāoshì de _____bù yě mài dòufu.

10) 超市的_____部卖大米、面粉等等。
     Chāoshì de _____bù mài dàmǐ, miànfěn děngděng.

11) 要是你要买很多东西，最好去超市门口拿一个购物_____。
     Yàoshi nǐ yào mǎi hěnduō dōngxi, zuìhǎo qù chāoshì ménkǒu ná yí ge gòuwù _____.

12) _____市场卖的菜很新鲜。
     _____ shìchǎng mài de cài hěn xīnxiān.

2. Identify the sections in a supermarket you would find the following.

1)   面包 (bread)
     miànbāo

2) 口香糖 (chewing gum)
   kǒuxiāngtáng

3) 菠菜 (spinach)
   bōcài

4) 苹果 (apple)
   píngguǒ

5) 可口可乐 (coke)
   kěkǒu kělè

6) 虾 (shrimp)
   xiā

7) 鸡肉 (chicken)
   jīròu

8) 香肠 (sausage)
   xiāngcháng

9) 米 (rice)
   mǐ

10) 冰淇淋(ice cream)
    bīngqílín

3. Complete.

在中国，要是你想买吃的__1__，你可以去超级__2__，那儿什么__3__都有。
Zài Zhōngguó, yàoshi nǐ xiǎng mǎi chīde __1__, nǐ kěyǐ qù chāojí __2__, nàr shénme __3__ dōuyǒu.

__4__ 就象一个小超市，也卖不少__5__。要是你想买新鲜的东西，
__4__ jiù xiàng yí ge xiǎo chāoshì, yě mài bù shǎo __5__. Yàoshi nǐ xiǎng mǎi xīnxian de dōngxi,

最好去__6__。
zuìhǎo qù __6__.

AT THE FREE MARKET

在自由市场
Zài zìyóu shìchǎng

您好，**想买点什么**？	May I help you?
Nín hǎo, xiǎng mǎi diǎn shénmē?	
我想买点**水果**。	fruit
Wǒ xiǎng mǎi diǎn shuǐguǒ.	
香蕉怎么卖？	How do you sell bananas?
Xiāngjiāo zěnme mài?	
桃多少钱一**公斤**？	peach, kilo
Táo duōshǎo qián yì *gōngjīn?*	
梨多少钱一**斤**？	pear, half-kilo.
Lí duōshǎo qián yì *jīn?*	

荔枝   lychee
lìzhī

怎么这么**贵**啊？   expensive
Zěnme zhème *guì* a?

太贵了！
Tài guì le!

能不能**少一点儿**[9]？   (in bargaining) lower the price
Néng bù néng *shǎo yìdiǎnr*?

能不能**便宜一点儿**？   sell it cheaper
Néng bù néng *piányì yìdiǎnr*?

能**尝**吗？   taste
Néng *cháng* ma?

挑   select
tiāo

对不起，**苹果卖完了**。   apple, sold out
Duìbuqǐ, *píngguǒ màiwánle*.

一共三十五块六毛。   altogether
Yígòng sānshíwǔ kuài liù máo.

找你四块四毛钱。   give change
Zhǎo nǐ sì kuài sì máo qián.

4. Complete.

A：您好，__1__？
　　Nín hǎo, __1__?

B：我想买点__2__，有苹果吗？
　　Wǒ xiǎng mǎi diǎn __2__, yǒu píngguǒ ma?

A：没有__3__，可是我们有新鲜的桃，还有香蕉。
　　Méiyǒu __3__, Kěshì wǒmen yǒu xīnxiān de táo, hái yǒu xiāngjiāo.

B：这是什么？
　　Zhè shi shénme?

A：噢！这是刚从广东来的新鲜__4__。
　　Ò! Zhē shi gāng cóng guǎngdōng lái de xīnxiān __4__.

B：荔枝多少钱一斤？
　　Lìzhī duōshǎo qián yì jīn?

A：十八块。
　　Shíbā kuài.

B：十八块？太__5__了！能不能__6__？
　　Shíbā kuài? Tài __5__ le! Néng bù néng __6__?

---

[9] Bargaining is usually allowed (or even expected) in free markets or small stores. How to cut the price varies according to situations. Generally speaking, negotiating is accepted if you are sincere in buying. In big department stores, however, bargaining is very rare unless the counter is rented to private business owners.

A：要是你买两斤，就给三十块好了。
　　Yàoshi nǐ mǎi liǎng jīn, jiù gěi sānshí kuài hǎo le.

B：我要两斤吧。香蕉 ___7___？
　　Wǒ yào liǎng jīn ba. Xiāngjiāo ___7___？

A：三块五一斤。两斤六块。
　　Sān kuài wǔ yì jīn, liǎng jīn liù kuài.

B：也来两斤吧。有没有梨？
　　Yě lái liǎng jīn ba. Yǒu méiyǒu lí?

A：对不起，梨今天 ___8___。还要别的吗？
　　Duìbuqǐ, Lí jīntiān ___8___. Hái yào biéde ma?

B：不要了。谢谢。
　　Bú yào le. Xièxie.

A：___9___ 三十六块。___10___ 您四块。谢谢！
　　___9___ sānshíliù kuài, ___10___ nín sì kuài. Xièxie.

KEY WORDS

alcohol	酒	jiǔ	lower the price (in bargaining)	少一点儿	shǎo yìdiǎnr
altogether	一共	yígòng	lychee	荔枝	lìzhī
apple	苹果	píngguǒ	market	市场	shìchǎng
bakery	糕点	gāodiǎn	May I help you?	想买点什么？	xiǎng mǎi diǎn shénme?
banana	香蕉	xiāngjiāo			
basket	篮子	lánzi	meat	肉	ròu
beverage	饮料	yǐnliào	meat product	肉食	ròushí
candy	糖果	tángguǒ	peach	桃	táo
cart	推车	tuīchē	pear	梨	lí
cigarette	烟	yān	plastic bag	塑料袋	sùliào dài
cooked food	熟食	shóu shí	seafood	水产	shuǐchǎn
expensive	贵	guì	section	部	bù
food	食品	shípǐn	select	挑	tiāo
free	自由	zìyóu	sell it cheaper	便宜一点儿	piányi yìdiǎnr
fresh	新鲜	xīnxiān	shopping	购物	gòuwù
frozen	冷冻	lěngdòng	sold out	卖完了	màiwán le
fruit	水果	shuǐguǒ	soybean product	豆制品	dòu zhìpǐn
give change	找	zhǎo	spice	调味品	tiáowèipǐn
grain	粮食	liángshi	supermarket	超级市场 (超市)	chāojí shìchǎng
green grocer	菜店	cài diàn			
grocery store	副食品店	fùshípǐn diàn	taste	尝	cháng
half-kilo	斤	jīn	vegetable	蔬菜	shūcài
How do you sell .	...怎么卖？	...zěnme mài?			
kilo	公斤	gōngjīn			

Chapter 16: At home

第十六章：家
 jiā

THE KITCHEN[10]

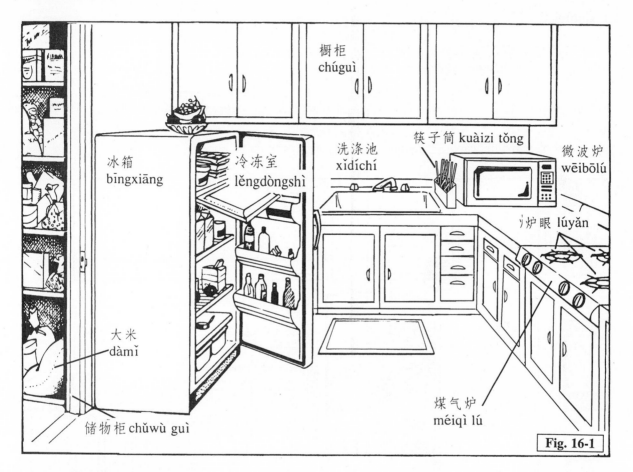

橱柜 chúguì
筷子筒 kuàizi tǒng
微波炉 wēibōlú
洗涤池 xǐdíchí
炉眼 lúyǎn
冰箱 bīngxiāng
冷冻室 lěngdòngshì
大米 dàmǐ
煤气炉 méiqì lú
储物柜 chǔwù guì

Fig. 16-1

WASHING THE DISHES[11]

把**盘子**和**碗**放到**洗涤池**里   plate, bowl, sink
Bǎ *pángzi* hé *wǎn* fàngdào *xǐdí chí* lǐ,

打开水龙头   turn on, faucet
Dǎkāi shuǐlóngtóu

把**洗碗剂**倒在**海绵**上，   dishwashing liquid, sponge
Bǎ *xǐwǎnjì* dàozài *hǎimián* shàng

---

[10] Refer to Appendix 3 for the food mentioned in this unit.
[11] In China, people say "洗碗"(wash bowls) rather than "wash dishes"

137

用海绵**洗**碗和盘子。   wash
Yòng hǎimián *xǐ* wǎn hé pánzi.

用水把碗和盘子**冲洗**干净。   rinse
Yòng shuǐ bǎ wǎn hé pánzi *chōngxǐ* gānjìng,

再用**洗碗布**把它们**擦干**。   dish towel, towel dry
Zài yòng *xǐwǎn bù* bǎ tāmen *cāgān*.

1. Complete.

吃饭以后有很多脏盘子脏碗。我得__1__了。我先把__2__和碗放到__3__里，
Chīfàn yǐhòu yǒu hěn duō zāng pánzi zāng wǎn. Wǒ děi __1__ le. Wǒ xiān bǎ __2__ hé wǎn fàngdào __3__ lǐ,

然后打开__4__，开始洗碗。我把__5__倒在海绵上，用海绵__6__一遍以后，再
Ránhòu dǎkāi __4__, kāishǐ xǐ wǎn. Wǒ bǎ __5__ dào zài hǎimián shàng, yòng hǎimián __6__ yí biàn yǐhòu, zài

用水把盘子和碗__7__干净。最后用洗碗布把它们__8__。
yòng shuǐ bǎ pánzi hé wǎn __7__ gānjìng, Zuìhòu yòng xǐwǎn bù bǎ tāmen __8__.

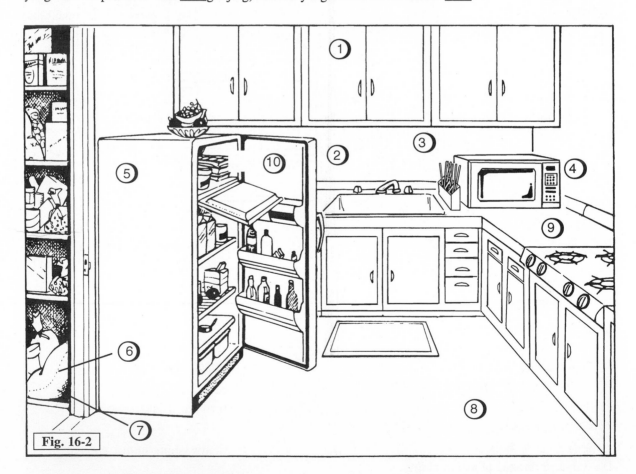

Fig. 16-2

2. Answer on the basis of Figure 16-2.

1) 厨房里有洗涤池吗？
    Chúfáng lǐ yǒu xǐdíchí ma?

2) 水从什么地方出来？
    Shuǐ cóng shénme dìfāng chūlái?

3) 筷子放在哪儿?
   Kuàizi fàng zài nǎr?

4) 大米放在哪儿?
   Dàmǐ fàng zài nǎr?

5) 厨房里有洗碗机吗?
   Chúfáng lǐ yǒu xǐwǎn jī ma?

6) 炉子是电炉还是煤气炉?
   Lúzi shi diànlú háishi méiqìlú?

7) 有几个炉眼?
   Yǒu jǐ ge lúyǎn?

8) 冰箱有冷冻室吗?
   Bīngxiāng yǒu lěngdòngshì ma?

COOKING

我要**做饭**了。 Wǒ yào *zuòfàn* le.	cook
我用**电饭锅做米饭**。 Wǒ yòng *diàn fànguō zuò mǐfàn.*	electric rice cooker, cook rice
开水壶烧水 *kāishuǐhú shāo shuǐ*	kettle, boil water
炒锅炒菜 *chǎoguō chǎo* cài	wok, stir fry
炸鱼 *zháo* yú	fry
蒸锅蒸馒头 *zhēngguō zhēng mántou*	steamer, steam, steamed buns
大锅煮汤 *dàguō zhǔ tāng*	pot, boil, soup
燉肉 *dùn* ròu	stew
平底锅烙饼 *píngdǐ guō lào bǐng*	frying pan, make pancake
我用**大火**炒菜 Wǒ yòng *dà huǒ* chǎo cài	high heat
我**盖上锅盖**，用**小火熬**汤。 Wǒ *gài shàng guōgài*, yòng *xiǎo huǒ áo* tāng.	cover, lid, low heat, simmer
我用**擀面杖擀饺子皮**。 Wǒ yòng *gǎnmiànzhàng gǎn jiǎozi pí.*	rolling pin, roll, dumpling wrap
菜刀在案板(切菜板)上**切**菜 *càidāo* zài *ànbǎn* (qiēcài bǎn) shàng *qiē* cài	kitchen knife, chopping board, chop/cut

锅铲
guōchǎn

汤勺
tāngsháo

打蛋器
dǎdànqì

开水壶
kāishuǐ hú

电饭锅
diàn fànguō

洗菜盆
xǐcàipén

沥水盆
lìshuǐpén

菜刀
càidāo

案板
ànbǎn

搅拌器
jiǎobànqì

平底锅
píngdǐguō

开罐刀
kāiguàndāo

启瓶器
qǐpíngqì

锅柄/把
guōbǐng/bà

锅盖
guōgài

锅
guō

擀面杖
gǎnmiànzhàng

炒菜锅
chǎocàiguō

Fig. 16-3

削皮刀削皮   peeler, peel, skin
xiāopídāo xiāo pí

洗菜盆洗菜   wash bowl
xǐcài pén xǐ cài

沥水盆沥水   strainer, strain
lìshuǐ pén lìshuǐ

3. Tell which utensil one will need in doing the following things:

1) 烧水
    shāo shuǐ

2) 炒菜
    chǎo cài

3) 做米饭
    zuò mǐfàn

4) 蒸鱼
    zhēng yú

5) 煮汤
    zhǔ tāng

6) 烙饼
    lào bǐng

7) 削土豆皮
    xiāo tǔdòu pí

8) 切肉
    qiē ròu

9) 洗菜
    xǐ cài

10) 沥干青菜的水
    lì gān qīngcài de shuǐ

11) 开罐头
    kāi guàntóu

12) 打开酒瓶
    dǎkāi jiǔ píng

4. Identify each item in Figure 16-4.

1)_____   2)_____   3)_____   4)_____   5)_____

6)_____   7)_____   8)_____   9)_____   10)_____

11)_____   12)_____   13)_____   14)_____   15)_____

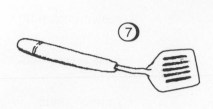

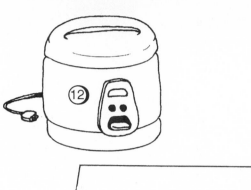

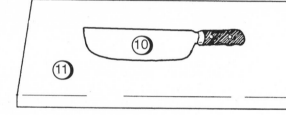
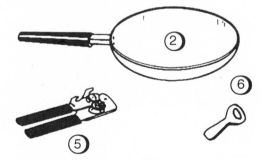

Fig. 16-4

5. Complete.

a) 我先用__1__把土豆皮削掉，再用水把它__2__干净，然后我就把土豆放
 Wǒ xiān yòng __1__ bǎ tǔdòu pí xiāo diào, zài yòng shuǐ bǎ tā __2__ gānjìng, ránhòu wǒ jiù bǎ tǔdòu fàng

在__3__上，用__4__把它切成片。
zài __3__ shàng, yòng __4__ bǎ tā qiē chéng piàn.

b) 我先把青菜放在 __1__ 里，用水 __2__ 干净。再放到 __3__ 里沥水。然后我

Wǒ xiān bǎ qīngcài fàng zài __1__ lǐ, yòng shuǐ __2__ gānjìng. Zài fàng dào __3__ lǐ lì shuǐ. Ránhòu wǒ

在 __4__ 里放一点花生油。等油热了以后，我就把 __5__ 倒进锅里翻炒。

zài __4__ lǐ fàng yìdiǎn huāshēng yóu. Děng yóu rè le yǐhòu, wǒ jiù bǎ __5__ dàojìn guō lǐ fānchǎo.

6. Give the Chinese verb for:

1) steam something in a steamer

2) deep fry something in a wok

3) stir fry something in a wok

4) boil something in liquid

5) make pancakes in a frying pan

THE BATHROOM

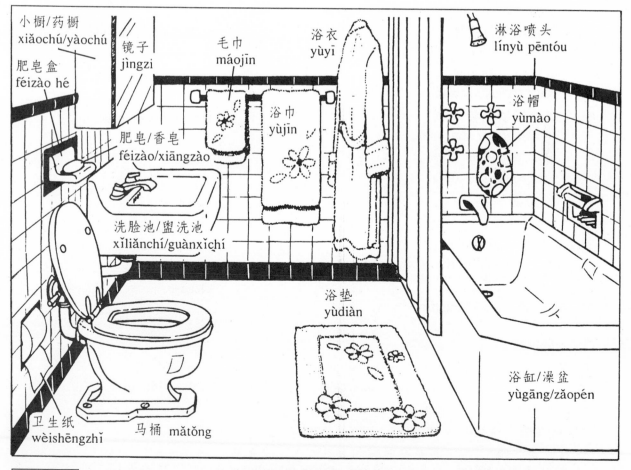

Fig. 16-5

浴室里可以洗淋浴，   bathroom, shower
Yùshì lǐ kěyǐ xǐ línyù,

也可以在浴缸里泡澡。   bathtub, take a bath
yě kěyǐ zài yùgāng lǐ pàozǎo.

洗澡时得用肥皂/香皂或沐浴液   soap, body wash lotion
Xǐzǎo shí děi yòng féizào/xiāngzào huò mùyùyè.

肥皂放在肥皂盒里。   soapdish
Féizào fàngzài féizào hé lǐ

洗头发时要用洗发香波。   hair, shampoo
Xǐ tóufà shí yào yòng xǐfà xiāngbō.

洗澡后要用浴巾把身体擦干，   bath towel
Xǐzǎo hòu yào yòng yùjīn bǎ shēntǐ cāgān

然后穿上浴衣。   bath robe
ránhòu chuānshàng yùyī.

我们可以在盥洗池里洗脸，洗手，   washbasin, face, hand
Wǒmen kěyǐ zài guànxǐchí lǐ xǐliǎn, xǐshǒu.

　　用毛巾擦干手，脸   towel
　　yòng máojīn cāgān shǒu, liǎn.

　　用牙刷牙膏刷牙   toothbrush, tooth paste, brush teeth
　　yòng yáshuā yágāo shuāyá.

　　用剃须刀刮胡子   razor, shave
　　yòng tìxūdāo guā húzi

　　对着镜子化妆   mirror, put on make up
　　duìzhe jìngzi huàzhuāng

　　用梳子梳头发   comb
　　yòng shūzi shū tóufà.

　　　发刷   brush
　　　fàshuā

卫生小橱里有卫生用品。   medicine cabinet, hygiene, articles
Wèishēng xiǎo chú lǐ yǒu wèishēng yòngpǐn.

　　　洗涤用品   cleanse
　　　xǐdí yòngpǐn

7. Complete.

1) 我在＿＿＿里洗手。我的手很脏，所以我得用一点＿＿＿。
　　 Wǒ zài ＿＿＿ lǐ xǐshǒu. Wǒde shǒu hěn zāng, suǒyǐ wǒ děi yòng yìdiǎn ＿＿＿.

2) 用完肥皂以后，我把肥皂放回＿＿＿里去。
　　 Yòngwán féizào yǐhòu, wǒ bǎ féizào fànghuí ＿＿＿ lǐ qù.

3) 有时候我洗＿＿＿，可是有时候我喜欢在＿＿＿里泡澡。
　　 Yǒu shíhòu wǒ xǐ ＿＿＿, kěshì yǒu shíhou wǒ xǐhuān zài ＿＿＿ lǐ pàozǎo.

4) 洗完澡，我用＿＿＿擦干身体，然后穿上＿＿＿。
　　 Xǐwán zǎo, wǒ yòng ＿＿＿ cāgān shēntǐ, ránhòu chuānshàng ＿＿＿.

5) 我一边照____，一边梳_____。
   Wǒ yìbiān zhào _____, yìbiān shū_____.

6) 我用牙刷牙膏_____。刷完牙后，又把牙刷牙膏放进小_____里去。
   Wǒ yòng yáshuā yágāo _____. Shuāwán yá hòu, yòu bǎ yáshuā yágāo fàngjìn xiǎo _____ lǐ qù.

8. Identify each item in Figure 16-6.

1)_____   2)_____   3)_____   4)_____   5)_____

6)_____   7)_____   8)_____   9)_____   10)_____

11)_____   12)_____   13)_____   14)_____   15)_____

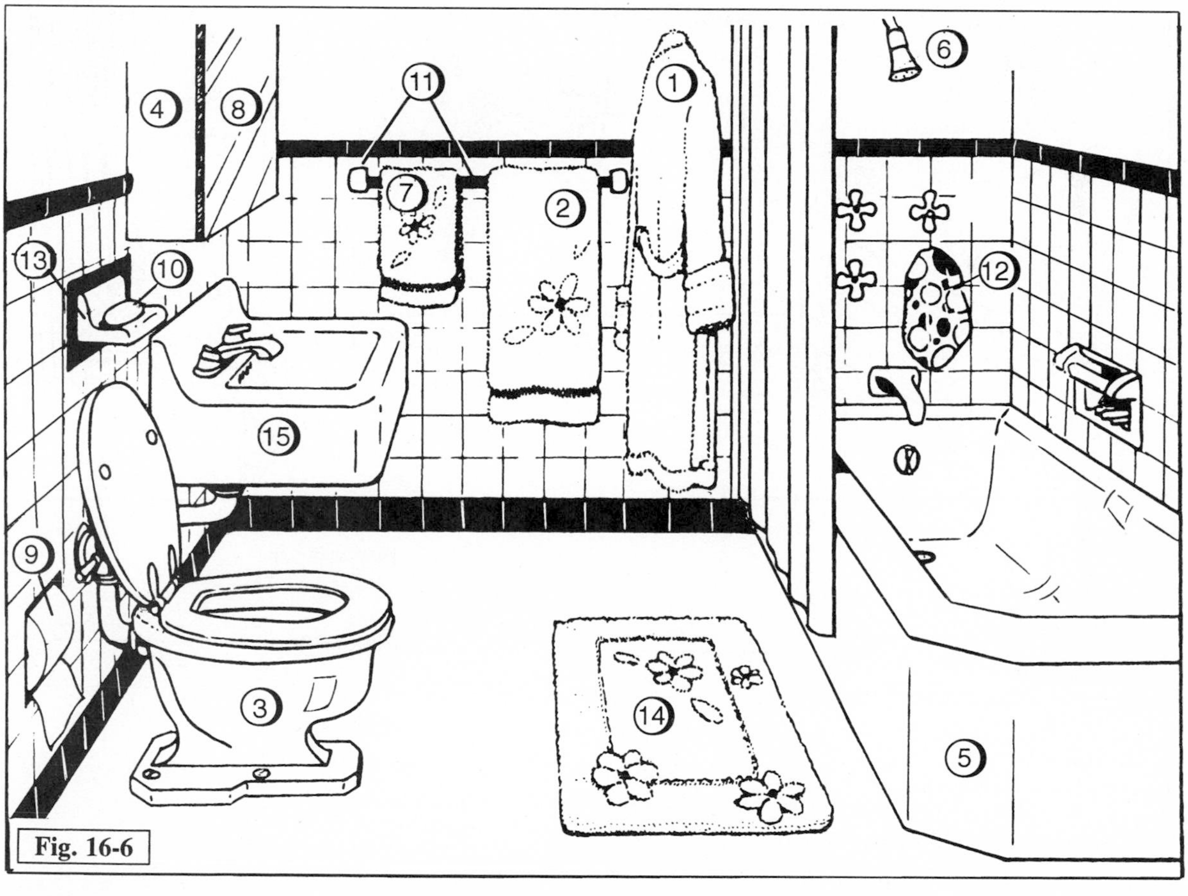

Fig. 16-6

THE LIVING ROOM

一家人坐在**客厅**里 Yì jiā rén zuò zài kètīng lǐ,	living room
他们跟**客人轻松**地**聊天** Tāmen gēn kèrén qīngsōng de liáotiān	guests, relax, chat
请客人**喝茶** qǐng kèrén hē chá	drink tea
打开**音响**听**音乐** dǎkāi yīnxiǎng tīng yīnyuè	stereo, music

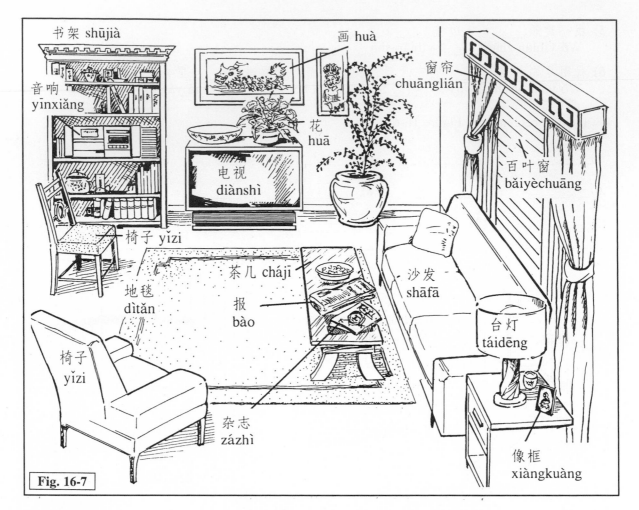

书架 shūjià

音响
yīnxiǎng

画 huà

窗帘
chuānglián

花
huā

电视
diànshì

百叶窗
bǎiyèchuāng

椅子 yǐzi

茶几 chájī

沙发
shāfā

地毯
dìtǎn

报
bào

台灯
táidēng

椅子
yǐzi

杂志
zázhì

像框
xiàngkuàng

Fig. 16-7

看**报(纸)** kàn *bào(zhǐ)*	newspaper
杂志 *zázhì*	magazine
电视 *diànshì*	television

9. Complete on the basis of Figure 16-7.

1) 我打开_____，让阳光照进客厅。
Wǒ dǎkāi _____, ràng yángguāng zhàojìn kètīng.

2) 晚上，我打开_____看书。
Wǎnshang, wǒ dǎkāi _____kànshū.

3) _____上有很多书，还有一个_____。
_____shàng yǒu hěn duō shū, hái yǒu yí ge _____.

4) 报纸和杂志在_____上。
Bàozhǐ he zázhì zài _____shàng.

5) 墙上挂着一幅_____。
Qiáng shàng guàzhe yì fú _____.

6) ＿＿＿＿上放着一瓶花。台灯旁边放着一个＿＿＿＿。
　　＿＿＿＿ shàng fàng zhe yì píng huā. Táidēng pángbiān fàng zhe yí ge ＿＿＿＿.

7) 书架前有一把＿＿＿＿。
　　Shūjià qián yǒu yì bǎ ＿＿＿＿.

8) ＿＿＿＿只能坐一个人。
　　＿＿＿＿zhǐ néng zuò yí ge rén.

9) ＿＿＿＿可以坐两个人。
　　＿＿＿＿kěyǐ zuò liǎng ge rén.

10) ＿＿＿＿可以坐三个人。
　　＿＿＿＿kěyǐ zuò sān ge rén.

11) 客厅中间的地板上铺着＿＿＿＿。
　　Kètīng zhōngjiān de dìbǎn shàng pūzhe ＿＿＿＿.

THE BEDROOM

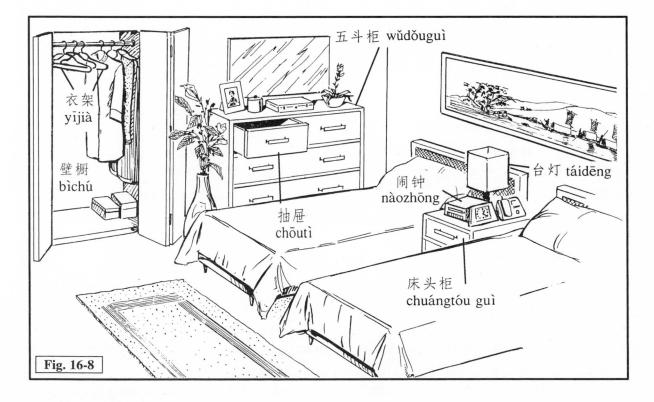

Fig. 16-8

我要去**卧室睡觉**了。　　　　　　　　　　　　　bedroom, go to bed
Wǒ yào qù *wòshì shuìjiào* le.

我把**闹钟拨**到七点。　　　　　　　　　　　　　alarm clock, set
Wǒ bǎ *nàozhōng bō*dào qī diǎn.

我每天**睡**八个钟头。　　　　　　　　　　　　　sleep
Wǒ měi tiān *shuì* bā ge zhōngtóu.

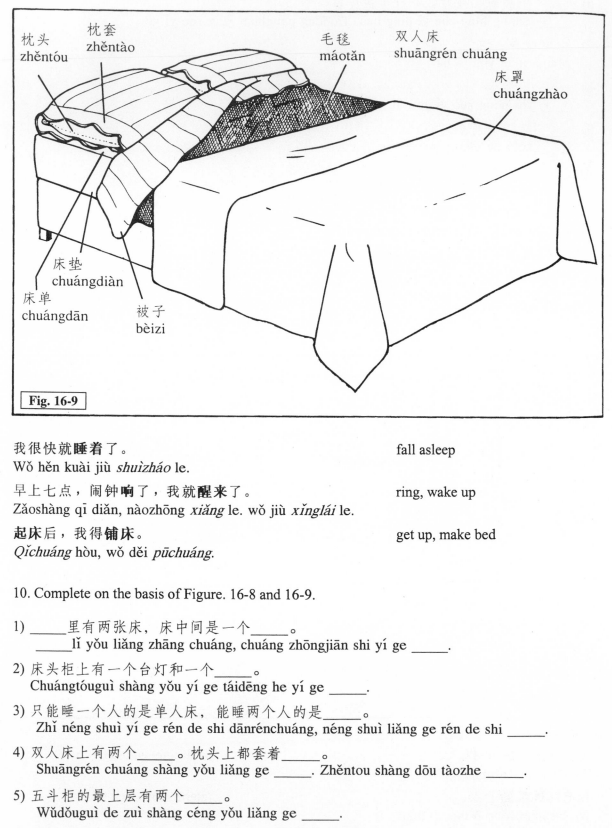

枕头   枕套   毛毯   双人床
zhěntóu   zhěntào   máotǎn   shuāngrén chuáng

                                                                  床罩
                                                                  chuángzhào

床垫
chuángdiàn

床单   被子
chuángdān   bèizi

Fig. 16-9

我很快就**睡着**了。   fall asleep
Wǒ hěn kuài jiù *shuìzháo* le.

早上七点，闹钟**响**了，我就**醒来**了。   ring, wake up
Zǎoshàng qī diǎn, nàozhōng *xiǎng* le. wǒ jiù *xǐnglái* le.

起床后，我得**铺床**。   get up, make bed
Qǐchuáng hòu, wǒ děi *pūchuáng*.

10. Complete on the basis of Figure. 16-8 and 16-9.

1) _____里有两张床，床中间是一个_____。
   _____lǐ yǒu liǎng zhāng chuáng, chuáng zhōngjiān shi yí ge _____.

2) 床头柜上有一个台灯和一个_____。
   Chuángtóuguì shàng yǒu yí ge táidēng he yí ge _____.

3) 只能睡一个人的是单人床，能睡两个人的是_____。
   Zhǐ néng shuì yí ge rén de shi dānrénchuáng, néng shuì liǎng ge rén de shi _____.

4) 双人床上有两个_____。枕头上都套着_____。
   Shuāngrén chuáng shàng yǒu liǎng ge _____. Zhěntou shàng dōu tàozhe _____.

5) 五斗柜的最上层有两个_____。
   Wǔdǒuguì de zuì shàng céng yǒu liǎng ge _____.

6) 壁橱里有六个_____。
   Bìchú lǐ yǒu liù ge _____.

11. Name six items that go on a bed.

12. Answer.

1) 你晚上在哪个房间睡觉？
   Nǐ wǎnshang zài něige fángjiān shuìjiào?

2) 你什么时候上床睡觉？
   Nǐ shénme shíhou shàngchuáng shuìjiào?

3) 你睡觉前得拨好什么？
   Nǐ shuìjiào qián děi bōhǎo shénme?

4) 你每天睡几个小时？
   Nǐ měi tiān shuì jǐ ge xiǎoshí?

5) 你很快就能睡着还是很久睡不着？
   Nǐ hěn kuài jiù néng shuìzháo háishi hěn jiǔ shuì bù zháo?

6) 你每天怎么醒来？
   Nǐ měi tiān zěnme xǐnglái?

7) 你早上几点起床？
   Nǐ zǎoshang jǐ diǎn qǐchuáng?

8) 你起床后铺不铺床？
   Nǐ qǐchuáng hòu pū bù pūchuáng?

HOUSEWORK

我有很多**脏衣服**， Wǒ yǒu hěn duō *zāng yīfu.*	dirty clothes
我得**洗衣服**了。 Wǒ děi *xǐ yīfu* le.	do laundry
我把脏衣服放到**洗衣机**里， Wǒ bǎ zāng yīfu fàngdào *xǐyījī* lǐ,	washing machine
衣服洗了以后常常得**烫/熨**。 Yīfu xǐle yǐhòu chángcháng děi *tàng/yùn.*	to iron
烫衣服得有**熨斗**和**烫衣板**。 Tàng yīfu děi yǒu *yùndǒu* he *tàngyībǎn.*	iron, ironing board
我得**打扫房间**， Wǒ děi *dǎsǎo fángjiān.*	clean, room
用**抹布抹家具** yòng *mābù mā jiājù*	rag, wipe, furniture
用**吸尘器**给**地毯吸尘** yòng *xīchénqì* gěi *dìtǎn xīchén*	vacuum machine, carpet, vacuum clean
用**扫帚扫地** yòng *sàozhǒu sǎodì*	broom, sweep the floor
用**拖把拖地板** yòng *tuōbǎ tuō dìbǎn*	mop, to mop, floor

我把**垃圾**倒在**垃圾筒**里。   garbage, garbage can
Wǒ bǎ *lājī* dàozài *lājītǒng* lǐ.

13. Complete.

今天我有很多事情要做。第一件事是___1___。衣服洗好以后还要放到烫衣板
Jīntiān wǒ yǒu hěn duō shìqing yào zuò. Dì yī jiàn shì shi ___1___. Yīfu xǐhǎo yǐhòu hái yào fàngdào tàngyībǎn

上用___2___烫平。第二件事是给地毯___3___。我打算把衣服放进___4___里就开始
shàng yòng ___2___ tàngpíng. Dì èr jiàn shì shi gěi dìtǎn ___3___. Wǒ dǎsuàn bǎ yīfu fàngjìn ___4___ lǐ jiù kāishǐ

用___5___吸尘。我还要___6___家具，倒___7___。
yòng ___5___ xīchén. Wǒ hái yào ___6___ jiājù, dào ___7___.

14. Match the housework and the tool you need to do the housework.

1) 烫衣服   a. 抹布
   tàng yīfu   mābù

2) 扫地   b. 烫衣板
   sǎodì   tàngyībǎn

3) 拖地板   c. 洗衣机
   tuō dìbǎn   xǐyījī

4) 抹家具   d. 扫帚
   mā jiājù   sàozhǒu

5) 吸地毯   e. 拖把
   xī dìtǎn   tuōbǎ

6) 洗衣服   f. 吸尘器
   xǐ yīfu   xīchénqì

SOME PROBLEMS YOU MAY HAVE

我要**开灯**。   turn on the light
Wǒ yào *kāi dēng*

我**按下**电灯**开关**，   press, light switch
Wǒ *ànxià* diàndēng *kāiguān*,

灯**不亮**，   not on
dēng *bú liàng*

灯泡烧坏了。   light bulb, blown out
dēngpào shāohuài le.

我要**插上**台灯的**电源插头**，   plug in, plug
Wǒ yào *chāshàng* táidēng de *diànyuán chātóu*,

可是**保险丝烧断**了。   fuse, blown
kěshì *bǎoxiǎnsī shāoduàn le.*

我得请**电工**来**修(理)**一下。   electrician, repair
Wǒ děi qǐng *diàngōng* lái *xiū(lǐ)* yíxià.

水池不**排水**了，　　　　　　　　　　　　　　　drain
Shuǐchí bù *pái shuǐ* le.

下水道堵住了。　　　　　　　　　　　　　drainage pipe, clogged up
xiàshuǐdào dǔzhù le.

水管漏水了，　　　　　　　　　　　　　pipe, dripping/leaking
Shuǐguǎn lòushuǐ le.

我得请**水管工**来修一下。　　　　　　　plumber
Wǒ děi qǐng *shuǐguǎngōng* lái xiū yíxià.

15. Complete.

灯不亮了。不知道是＿1＿烧坏了，还是＿2＿没插好，还是＿3＿烧断了。
Dēng bú liàng le. Bù zhīdao shi ＿1＿shāohuài le, háishi ＿2＿méi chāhǎo, háishi ＿3＿shāoduàn le.

得请＿4＿来看看。
Děi qǐng ＿4＿lái kànkan.

16. Complete.

盥洗池不＿1＿了！一定是＿2＿堵住了。得赶快请＿3＿来给我们＿4＿一下。
Guànxǐchí bù ＿1＿le! Yídìng shi ＿2＿dǔzhù le. Děi gǎnkuài qǐng ＿3＿lái gěi wǒmen ＿4＿yíxià.

KEY WORDS

alarm clock	闹钟	nàozhōng
articles	用品	yòngpǐn
basin	盥洗池	guànxǐchí
bath cap	浴帽	yùmào
bath mat	浴垫	yùdiàn
bath robe	浴衣	yùyī
bath towel	浴巾	yùjīn
bathroom	浴室	yùshì
bathtub	浴缸	yùgāng
bed	床	chuáng
bed sheet	床单	chuángdān
bedroom	卧室	wòshì
bedside table	床头柜	chuángtóuguì
bedspread	床罩	chuángzhào
blender	搅拌机	jiǎobànjī
blow (fuse)	烧断	shāoduàn
body wash lotion	沐浴液	mùyùyè
boil water	烧水	shāo shuǐ
boil, cook	煮	zhǔ
bookcase	书架	shūjià
bottle opener	启瓶器	qǐpíngqì
bowl	碗	wǎn
broom	扫帚	sàozhǒu
brush	刷	shuā
burn out	烧坏	shāohuài
burner	炉眼	lúyǎn
can opener	开罐刀	kāiguàndāo
carpet	地毯	dìtǎn
chair	椅子	yǐzi
chat	聊天	liáotiān
chest of drawers	五斗柜	wǔdǒuguì
chop/cut	切	qiē
chopping board	案板，切菜板	ànbǎn, qiēcàibǎn
chopstick holder	筷子筒	kuàizi tǒng
clean	打扫	dǎsǎo
cleanse	洗涤	xǐdí
clogged up	堵住	dǔzhù
closet	壁橱	bìchú
clothes	衣服	yīfu
coffee table	茶几	chájī
comb	梳子	shūzi
cook	做饭	zuòfàn
cook rice	做米饭	zuò mǐfàn
cover	盖上	gàishang
curtain	窗帘	chuānglián
desk lamp	台灯	táidēng
dirty	脏	zāng
dish towel	洗碗布	xǐwǎn bù
dishwashing liquid	洗碗剂	xǐwǎn jì
do laundry	洗衣服	xǐ yīfu

drain	排水	pái shuǐ
drainage pipe	下水道	xiàshuǐdào
drawer	抽屉	chōutì
drink	喝	hē
dripping/leaking	漏水	lòushuǐ
dry	擦干	cā gān
dumpling wrap	饺子皮	jiǎozi pí
electric rice cooker	电饭锅	diàn fànguō
electric stove	电炉	diànlú
electrician	电工	diàngōng
face	脸	liǎn
face cloth	洗脸巾	xǐliǎnjīn
fall asleep	睡着	shuìzháo
faucet	水龙头	shuǐlóngtóu
fish	鱼	yú
flowers	花	huā
freezer	冷冻室	lěngdòngshì
fry	炸	zhá
frying pan	平底锅	píngdǐguō
furniture	家具	jiājù
fuse	保险丝	bǎoxiǎnsī
garbage	垃圾	lājī
garbage can	垃圾筒	lājītǒng
gas stove	煤气炉	méiqìlú
get up	起床	qǐchuáng
go to bed	睡觉	shuìjiào
guests	客人	kèren
hair	头发	tóufa
hairbrush	发刷	fàshuā
hand	手	shǒu
hanger	衣架	yījià
high heat	大火	dà huǒ
hygiene	卫生	wèishēng
iron	熨斗	yùndǒu
ironing board	烫衣板	tàngyībǎn
kettle	开水壶	kāishuǐhú
kitchen	厨房	chúfáng
kitchen knife	菜刀	càidāo
lid	锅盖	guōgài
light	灯	dēng
light bulb	灯泡	dēngpào
light switch	开关	kāiguān
living room	客厅	kètīng
low heat	小火	xiǎo huǒ
magazine	杂志	zázhì
make pancakes	烙饼	làobǐng
make the bed	铺床	pūchuáng
mattress	床垫	chuāngdiàn
meat	肉	ròu
medicine cabinet, kitchen closet	小橱/柜	xiǎochú/guì
microwave	微波炉	wēibōlú
mirror	镜子	jìngzi
mop	拖把	tuōbǎ
mop the floor	拖地板	tuō dìbǎn
music	音乐	yīnyuè
newspaper	报	bào
oven	烤箱	kǎoxiāng
painting	画	huà
peel	削	xiāo
peeler	削皮刀	xiāopídāo
picture frame	像框	xiàngkuàng
pillow	枕头	zhěntou
pillowcase	枕套	zhěntào
pipe	水管	shuǐguǎn
plate	盘子	pánzi
plug	电源插头	diànyuán chātóu
plug in	插上	chāshang
plumber	水管工	shuǐguǎngōng
pot	锅	guō
press down	按下	ànxià
put on make-up	化妆	huàzhuāng
quilt	被子	bèizi
rag (to wipe things)	抹布	mābù
razor	剃须刀	tìxūdāo
refrigerator	冰箱	bīngxiāng
relax	轻松	qīngsōng
repair	修(理)	xiū(lǐ)
ring	响	xiǎng
rinse	冲洗	chōngxǐ
roll	擀	gǎn
rolling pin	擀面杖	gǎnmiànzhàng
room	房间	fángjiān
set to (clock time)	拨到	bōdào
shampoo	洗发香波	xǐfà xiāngbō
shave	刮胡子	guā húzi
shine/on	亮	liàng
shower	淋浴	línyù
simmer	熬	áo
sink, basin	洗涤池	xǐdíchí
skin	皮	pí
sleep	睡	shuì
soap	肥皂/香皂	féizào/xiāngzào
soapdish	肥皂盒	féizào hé
sofa	沙发	shāfā
soup	汤	tāng
soup ladle	汤勺	tāng sháo
sponge	海绵	hǎimián
steam	蒸	zhēng
steamed buns	馒头	mántou
steamer	蒸锅	zhēngguō
stereo	音响	yīnxiǎng
stew	炖	dùn
stir fry	炒	chǎo
strain	沥水	lìshuǐ
strainer	沥水盆	lìshuǐpén
sweep the floor	扫地	sǎo dì
take a bath	泡澡	pào zǎo
tea	茶	chá
television	电视	diànshì

to iron	烫/熨	tàng/yùn	vacuum cleaner	吸尘器	xīchénqì
tooth	牙	yá	vacuum-clean	吸尘	xīchén
toothbrush	牙刷	yáshuā	wake up	醒来	xǐng lái
toothpaste	牙膏	yágāo	wardrobe	衣橱/柜	yīchú/guì
towel	毛巾	máojīn	wash	洗	xǐ
towel bar	毛巾架	máojīn jià	washbowl	洗菜盆	xǐcài pén
towel dry	擦干	cā gān	washing machine	洗衣机	xǐyījī
turn on	(打)开	(dǎ) kāi	wipe	抹	mā
turner, spatula	锅铲	guōchǎn	wok	炒锅	chǎoguō

Chapter 17: At the hospital

第十七章：在医院里
Zài yīyuàn lǐ

ADMITTANCE

你是来**看病**的吗？   see a doctor
Nǐ shi lái *kànbìng* de ma?

请先到**挂号处**去**挂号**。   registration (office), register
Qǐng xiān dào *guàhàochù* qù *guàhào*.

这张**表**请你**填**一下。   form, fill in
Zhèi zhāng *biǎo* qǐng nǐ *tián* yíxià.

写上你的**医疗保险**号。   medical insurance
Xiěshàng nǐde *yīliáo bǎoxiǎn hào*.

请坐在**候诊室**等**护士叫号**。   waiting room, nurse, call number
Qǐng zuò zài *hòuzhěnshì* děng *hùshì jiào hào*.

医生会给你看病。   doctor
Yīshēng huì gěi nǐ kànbìng.

1. Complete.

去医院 __1__ 时，一般先要到挂号处去 __2__ 。挂号的时候，护士会要你 __3__ 表。
Qù yīyuàn __1__ shí, yìbān xiān yào dào guàhàochù qù __2__ . Guàhào de shíhòu, hùshì huì yào nǐ __3__ biǎo.

然后你就坐在 __4__ 里等。听到叫你的 __5__ 时，你就可以进去见 __6__ 了。
Ránhòu nǐ jiù zuò zài __4__ lǐ děng. Tīng dào jiào nǐde __5__ shí, nǐ jiù kěyǐ jìnqù jiàn __6__ le.

I HAVE A COLD

病人说：   patient
Bìngrén shuō:

我觉得很**难受**。   sick
Wǒ juéde hěn *nánshòu*.

我有点**恶心**。   nauseous
Wǒ yǒu diǎn *ěxīn*.

我**感冒**了。   have a cold
Wǒ *gǎnmào* le.

我得了**流感**。　　　　　　　　　　　catch, flu
Wǒ *déle liúgǎn*.

我**嗓子/喉咙**很疼。　　　　　　　　throat, hurt/sore
Wǒ *sǎngzi/hóulóng* hěn *téng*.

　　耳朵　　　　　　　　　　　　　　ear
　　ěrduō

　　头　　　　　　　　　　　　　　　head
　　tóu

我**发烧**了。　　　　　　　　　　　fever
Wǒ *fāshāo* le.

　　发冷　　　　　　　　　　　　　　chills
　　fālěng

　　淋巴肿了　　　　　　　　　　　　glands, swollen
　　línbā zhǒng le

　　咳嗽　　　　　　　　　　　　　　cough
　　késou

　　鼻子不通　　　　　　　　　　　　nose, congested
　　bízi bù tōng

　　流鼻涕　　　　　　　　　　　　　running nose
　　liú bítì

　　拉肚子/腹泻　　　　　　　　　　　diarrhea
　　lā dùzi/fùxiè

　　吐　　　　　　　　　　　　　　　vomit
　　tù

医生说：
Yīshēng shuō:

你什么地方**不舒服**？　　　　　　　uncomfortable
Nǐ shénme dìfang *bù shūfu*?

有什么**症状**？　　　　　　　　　　symptoms
Yǒu shénme *zhèngzhuàng*?

头晕吗？　　　　　　　　　　　　dizzy
Tóuyūn ma?

恶心不恶心？
Ěxīn bù ěxīn?

张开嘴　　　　　　　　　　　　　open, mouth
Zhāngkāi zuǐ

我**检查**一下你的喉咙。　　　　　　examine
Wǒ *jiǎnchá* yíxià nǐde hóulóng.

喉咙很红，
hóulóng hěnhóng

好象有点**发炎**。　　　　　　　　　inflammation
Hǎoxiàng yǒu diǎn *fāyán*.

深深地吸一口气   take a deep breath
Shēnshēn de xī yì kǒu qì

呼气   exhale
Hūqì

胸口疼吗？   chest
Xiōngkǒu téng ma?

小腹   abdomen
xiǎofù

胃疼   stomachache
wèiténg

量一下体温   take temperature
Liáng yíxià tǐwēn

你青霉素过敏吗？   penicillin, allergic
Nǐ qīngméisù guòmǐn ma?

打一针   give an injection
Dǎ yì zhēn

卷起袖子   roll up one's sleeve
Juǎnqǐ xiùzi

给你开一点抗生素。   prescribe, antibiotics
Gěi nǐ *kāi* yìdiǎn *kàngshēngsù.*

每天吃三次，每次两片。   tablet/pill
Měi tiān chī sān cì, měi cì liǎng *piàn.*

这种药，饭后吃。   medicine
Zhèi zhǒng *yào*, fàn hòu chī.

每隔四小时吃一次。   every four hours
Měi gé sì xiǎoshí chī yí cì.

2. Complete.

王先生病了。他觉得恶心，头＿＿1＿＿，嗓子也疼。浑身＿＿2＿＿，鼻子＿＿3＿＿，他还咳嗽。
Wáng xiānshēng bìng le. Tā juéde ěxīn, tóu ＿＿1＿＿, sǎngzi yě téng. Húnshēn ＿＿2＿＿, bízi ＿＿3＿＿, tā hái késou.

淋巴也＿＿4＿＿了。王先生不知道自己得的是＿＿5＿＿还是＿＿6＿＿。他决定去医院＿＿7＿＿。
Línbā yě ＿＿4＿＿ le. Wáng xiānsheng bù zhīdào zìjǐ dé de shì ＿＿5＿＿ háishi ＿＿6＿＿. Tā juédìng qù yīyuàn ＿＿7＿＿.

3. Complete.

（在医生的办公室里。）
(zài yīshēng de bàngōngshì lǐ.)

A：大夫，您好！
　　Dàifu, nín hǎo!

B：你好！你怎么了？
　　Nǐ hǎo! Nǐ zěnme le?

A：我不知道我是__1__了还是得__2__了。

　　Wǒ bù zhīdao wǒ shi __1__le hǎishi dé le__2__.

B：你有什么__3__呢?

　　Nǐ yǒu shénme __3__ ne?

A：我头__4__，流__5__。

　　Wǒ tóu __4__, liú __5__.

B：好，张开__6__，我检查一下你的__7__。

　　Hǎo, zhāngkāi __6__. wǒ jiǎnchá yíxià nǐde __7__.

A：我喉咙很__8__。

　　Wǒ hóulóng hěn __8__.

B：嗯，很红。嗓子有点发炎。你__9__吗?

　　Ēn. Hěn hóng. Sǎngzi yǒudiǎn fāyán. Nǐ __9__ ma?

A：咳得很厉害。

　　Ké de hěn lìhai.

B：现在我给你量一下__10__。38度，有点高。

　　Xiànzài wǒ gěi nǐ liáng yíxià __10__. Sānshíbā dù, yǒu diǎn gāo.

A：我感冒了吗?

　　Wǒ gǎnmào le ma?

B：你是感冒了。你对药物__11__吗?

　　Nǐ shi gǎnmào le. Nǐ duì yàowù __11__ ma?

A：我不过敏。

　　Wǒ bú guòmǐn.

B：那好，卷起__12__，我先给你打一__13__青霉素。

　　Nà hǎo. Juǎnqǐ __12__, wǒ xiān gěi nǐ dǎ yì __13__ qīngméisù.

A：我还得吃__14__吗?

　　Wǒ hái děi chī __14__ ma?

B：对。我再给你开一些__15__。你一天吃三__16__，一次两__17__。过几天就好了。

　　Duì. Wǒ zài gěi nǐ kāi yìxiē __15__. Nǐ yì tiān chī sān __16__, yí cì liǎng __17__. Guò jǐ tiān jiù hǎo le.

4. Complete.

1) 一般人在感冒时常常不发烧，而是____疼，_____不通。

　　Yìbān rén zài gǎnmào shí chángcháng bù fāshāo, érshì ____téng, ____bùtōng.

2) 人在发烧时，常常一会儿觉得_____，一会儿觉得热。

　　Rén zài fāshāo shí, chángcháng yìhuǐr juéde ____, yìhuǐr juéde rè.

3) 医生检查_____的时候，病人得张开嘴。

　　Yīshēng jiǎnchá ____ de shíhou, bìngrén děi zhāngkāi zuǐ.

4) 医生要在你胳膊上_____的时候，你得把_____卷起来。

　　Yīshēng yào zài nǐ gēbo shàng ____ de shíhou, nǐ děi bǎ ____ juǎn qǐlai.

A PHYSICAL EXAMINATION

病史   Medical History
Bìngshǐ

你或者你家里人有**关节炎**吗?   arthritis
Nǐ huòzhě nǐ jiālǐ rén yǒu guānjiéyán ma?

      哮喘   asthma
      xiàochuǎng

      癌(症)   cancer
      ái(zhèng)

      糖尿病   diabetes
      tángniàobìng

      心脏病   heart disease
      xīnzàngbìng

      精神病   mental illness
      jīngshénbìng

      性病   venereal disease
      xìngbìng

      癫痫   epilepsy
      diānxián

      肺结核   tuberculosis
      fèijiéhé

      肠炎   enteritis
      chángyán

      过敏症   allergy
      guòmǐnzhèng

你小时候得过**小儿麻痹症**吗?   polio
Nǐ xiǎo shíhou déguo xiǎoér mábìzhèng ma?

      麻疹   measles
      mázhěn

      水痘   chicken pox
      shuǐdòu

      流行性腮腺炎   mumps
      liúxíngxìng sāixiànyán

THE VITAL ORGANS OF A HUMAN BODY

人体**主要脏器**   vital organs
Réntǐ zhǔyào zàngqì

你是什么**血型**?   blood type
Nǐ shi shénme xuèxíng?

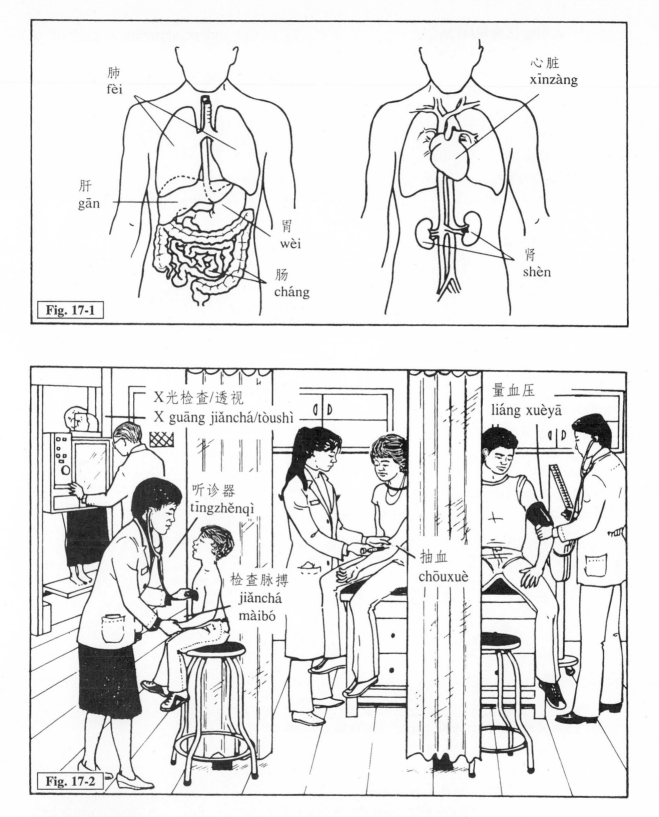

Fig. 17-1

Fig. 17-2

你月经正常吗？   menstrual periods, regular
Nǐ *yuèjīng zhèngcháng* ma?

你以前做过手术吗？   operation
Nǐ yǐqián zuòguo shǒushù ma?

做过。我**切除**过**阑尾/盲肠**。   remove, appendix
Zuòguo. Wǒ *qiēchú*guo *lánwěi/mángcháng*.

　　　　　　　　扁桃腺   tonsils
　　　　　　　　biǎntáoxiàn

医生说：
Yīshēng shuō:

把袖子卷起来，
Bǎ xiùzi juǎn qǐlái.

我来给你**量**一下**血压**。   measure, blood pressure
Wǒ lái gěi nǐ *liáng* yíxià *xuèyā*.

　　　　　　　抽点血   collect, blood
　　　　　　　chōu diǎn *xuè*

　　　　　　　验血   blood test
　　　　　　　yànxuè

　　　　　　　测一下**脉搏**   check, pulse
　　　　　　　cè yíxià *màibó*

我用**听诊器**听一下你**的心脏**。   stethoscope, heart
Wǒ yòng *tīngzhěnqì* tīng yíxià nǐde *xīnzàng*.

你的**肾脏**有问题。   kidney
Nǐde *shènzàng* yǒu wèntí.

　　　　　肝脏   liver
　　　　　gānzàng

现在你去做**肺部X光检查/透视**。   lungs, X-ray
Xiànzài nǐ qù zuò *fèibù X guāng jiǎnchá/tòushì*.

　　　　　　做一个**心电图**   electrocardiogram
　　　　　　zuò yí ge *xīndiàntú*

　　　　　　化验一下**小便**   lab test, urine
　　　　　　huàyàn yíxià *xiǎobiàn*

　　　　　　　　大便   feces
　　　　　　　　dàbiàn

5. Complete.

1) 他不能打青霉素针，因为他对青霉素_____。
   Tā bù néng dǎ qīngméisù zhēn, yīnwèi tā duì qīngméisù _____.

2) 有_____的人呼吸很困难。
   Yǒu _____de rén hūxī hěn kùnnan.

3) 心脏、肝脏和肾脏都是人体的重要_____。
   Xīnzàng, gānzàng hé shènzàng dōu shi réntǐ de zhòngyào _____.

4) 我是O型血，你知道你的血_____吗?
   Wǒ shi O xíng xuè, nǐ zhīdao nǐde xuè _____ma?

5) 她的月经不太_____。
   Tāde yuèjīng bú tài _____.

6) 医生给我作了_____检查，看我有没有肺_____。
   Yīshēng gěi wǒ zuò le _____jiǎnchá, kàn wǒ yǒu méi yǒu fèi _____.

7) 要是需要验病人的血，他得先给病人_____。
   Yàoshi xūyào yàn bìngrén de xuè, tā děi xiān gěi bìngrén _____.

8) 每次我去看病，医生都会给我开_____。
   Měi cì wǒ qù kànbìng, yīshēng dōu huì gěi wǒ kāi _____.

9) 要是你心脏有问题，医生可能会给你做一个_____图。
   Yàoshi nǐ xīnzàng yǒu wèntí, yīshēng kěnéng huì gěi nǐ zuò yí ge _____tú.

10) 要是你得了肠炎，你会_____，还会_____肚子。
    Yàoshi nǐ déle chángyán, nǐ huì _____, hái huì _____dùzi.

6. Select the normal procedures for a medical or physical examination.

1) 医生给你量体温。
   Yīshēng gěi nǐ liáng tǐwēn.

2) 医生给你量血压。
   Yīshēng gěi nǐ liáng xuèyā.

3) 医生给你做手术。
   Yīshēng gěi nǐ zuò shǒushù.

4) 医生给你做肺部X光透视。
   Yīshēng gěi nǐ zuò fèibù X guāng tòushì.

5) 医生给你抽血、验血。
   Yīshēng gěi nǐ chōu xuè, yàn xuè.

6) 医生给你量脉搏。
   Yīshēng gěi nǐ liáng màibó.

7) 医生给你打一针青霉素。
   Yīshēng gěi nǐ dǎ yì zhēn qīngméisù.

8) 医生给你做心电图。
   Yīshēng gěi nǐ zuò xīndiàntú.

9) 医生给你开抗生素。
   Yīshēng gěi nǐ kāi kàngshēngsù.

10) 医生用听诊器为你检查。
    Yīshēng yòng tīngzhěnqì wèi nǐ jiǎnchá.

11) 医生让你化验小便。
    Yīshēng ràng nǐ huàyàn xiǎobiàn.

12) 医生给你做主要脏器的检查。
    Yīshēng gěi nǐ zuò zhǔyào zàngqì de jiǎnchá.

I HAD AN ACCIDENT

我出了一个**意外事故**。   unexpected, accident
Wǒ chūle yí ge *yìwài shìgù.*

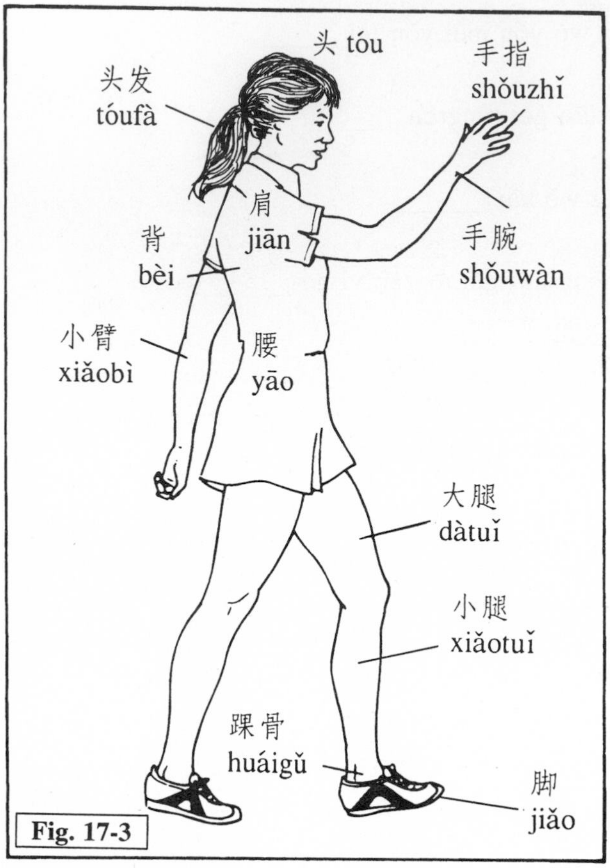

头 tóu

头发
tóufà

手指
shǒuzhǐ

肩
jiān

背
bèi

手腕
shǒuwàn

小臂
xiǎobì

腰
yāo

大腿
dàtuǐ

小腿
xiǎotuǐ

踝骨
huáigǔ

脚
jiǎo

Fig. 17-3

我的**手指骨折**了。 Wǒde *shǒuzhǐ gǔzhé* le.	finger, bone fracture
胳膊/手臂 *gēbo/shǒubì*	arm
胳膊肘 *gēbozhǒu*	elbow
手腕 *shǒuwàn*	wrist
踝骨 *huáigǔ*	ankle
胯骨 *kuàgǔ*	hip
膝盖 *xīgài*	knee
肩膀 *jiānbǎng*	shoulder
我的**腰扭伤**了。 Wǒde *yāo niǔshāng* le.	waist/lower back, sprain
背 *bèi*	back

我这儿疼。   It hurts here
Wǒ zhèr téng.

他的左**脚**骨折了。   foot
Tāde zuǒ *jiǎo* gǔzhé le.

医生得给他**把骨头固定**好，   set the bone
Yīshēng děi gěi tā *bǎ gǔtou gùdìng* hǎo.

然后还得给他**上石膏**。   put it in cast
Ránhòu hái děi gěi tā *shàng shígāo.*

病人只能**拄**着**拐杖**走路。   on crutches
Bìngrén zhǐ néng *zhǔzhe guǎizhàng* zǒulù.

我把**手割破**了。   hand, cut
Wǒ bǎ *shǒu gēpò* le.

           脸   cheek/face
           liǎn

要是**伤口**不**深**，   wound, deep
Yàoshi *shāngkǒu* bù *shēn,*

我可以用**创口贴**。   adhesive bandage
Wǒ kěyǐ yòng *chuāngkǒutiē.*

要是伤口太深，我得去医院。
Yàoshi shāngkǒu tài shēn, wǒ děi qù yīyuàn.

医生会把我的伤口**缝合**。   stitch
Yīshēng huì bǎ wǒde shāngkǒu *fénghé.*

然后再用**绷带**把伤口**包**起来。   bandage, bind up
Ránhòu zài yòng *bēngdài* bǎ shāngkǒu *bāo* qǐlái.

他说五天以后就可以**拆线**了。   take out the stitches
Tā shuō wǔ tiān yǐhòu jiù kěyǐ *chāixiàn* le.

7. Complete.

小王出了一个意外__1__。他跌倒了，摔__2__了右腿。他父母把他送到了__3__。
Xiǎo wáng chū le yí ge yìwài __1__. Tā diēdǎo le, shuāi __2__ le yòu tuǐ. Tā fùmǔ bǎ tā sòngdào le __3__.

医生告诉他们伤口需要照__4__以后才能知道是不是__5__了。
Yīshēng gàosù tāmen shāngkǒu xūyào zhào __4__ yǐhòu cái néng zhīdao shì bú shì __5__ le.

X光检查的结果是骨折。医生要把骨头__6__好，然后再打上__7__。小王
X guāng jiǎnchá de jiéguǒ shi gǔzhé. Yīshēng yào bǎ gǔtóu __6__ hǎo, ránhòu zài dǎshàng __7__. Xiǎo wáng

这几个星期只好拄着__8__走路了。
zhèi jǐ ge xīngqī zhǐhǎo zhǔzhe __8__ zǒulù le.

8. Complete.

他割__1__了手。因为伤口比较__2__，所以医生要先__3__伤口，然后用__4__把
Tā gē __1__ le shǒu. Yīnwèi shāngkǒu bǐjiào __2__, suǒyǐ yīshēng yào xiān __3__ shāngkǒu, ránhòu yòng __4__ bǎ

伤口__5__起来。过几天伤口长好了才能给他__6__。
shāngkǒu __5__ qǐlái. Guò jǐ tiān shāngkǒu zhǎnghǎole cái néng gěi tā __6__.

9. Identify each item in Figure 17-4.

1)_____   2)_____   3)_____   4)_____

5)_____   6)_____   7)_____   8)_____

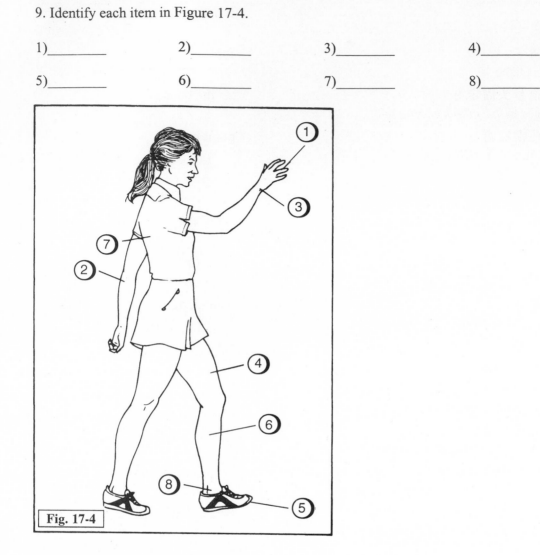

Fig. 17-4

IN THE EMERGENCY ROOM

救护车到了。 *Jiùhùchē* dào le.	ambulance
病人躺在**担架**上。 Bìngrén tǎng zài *dānjià* shàng.	stretcher
病人没有坐**轮椅**。 Bìngrén méiyǒu zuò *lúnyǐ*.	wheelchair
担架被**推**进了**急诊室**。 Dānjià bèi *tuī* jìn le *jízhěnshì*.	push, emergency room
护士给病人量脉搏，量血压 Hùshì gěi bìngrén liáng màibó, liáng xuèyā.	
值班医生给病人做检查。 *Zhíbān yīshēng* gěi bìngrén zuò jiǎnchá.	doctor on duty
实习医生在旁边**观察**。 *Shíxí yīshēng* zài pángbiān *guānchá*.	intern, observe

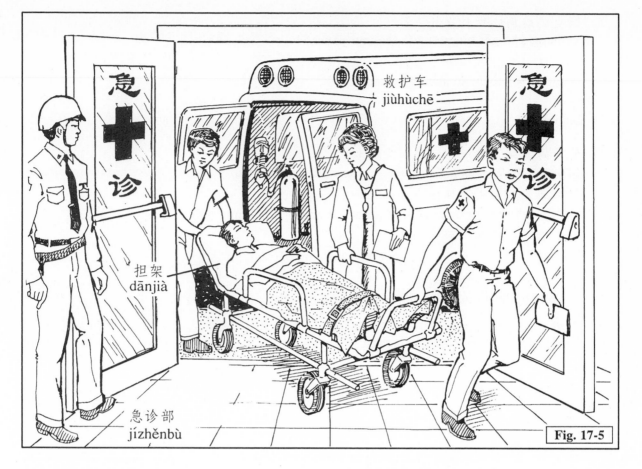

Fig. 17-5

病人**肚子疼**，　　　　　　　　　　　　　　　stomachache
Bìngrén *dùzi téng*.

医生要给病人照X光。
Yīshēng yào gěi bìngrén zhào X guāng.

病人被送到了**放射科**。　　　　　　　　　department of radiology
Bìngrén bèi sòngdào le *fàngshèkē*.

10. Answer.

1)　病人是坐什么车到医院来的？
　　Bìngrén shi zuò shénme chē dào yīyuàn lái de?

2)　病人能走吗？
　　Bìngrén néng zǒu ma?

3)　他怎么进的医院？
　　Tā zěnme jìn de yīyuàn?

4)　护士给病人做什么了？
　　Hùshì gěi bìngrén zuò shénme le?

5)　是谁检查的病人？
　　Shì shéi jiǎnchá de bìngrén?

6)　病人哪儿不舒服？
　　Bìngrén nǎr bù shūfu?

7) 医生要给病人做什么检查?
    Yīshēng yào gěi bìngrén zuò shénme jiǎnchá?

8) 病人被送到什么地方去了?
    Bìngrén bèi sòngdào shénme dìfang qù le?

11. Complete.

1) 急诊病人常常被_____送到医院去。
    Jízhěn bìngrén chángcháng bèi _____ sòngdào yīyuàn qù.

2) 要是病人不能走，他就得躺在_____上或坐在_____上。
    Yàoshi bìngrén bù néng zǒu, tā jiù děi tǎngzài _____ shàng huò zuòzài _____ shàng.

3) 进医院以后，急诊病人会马上被送进_____。
    Jìn yīyuàn yǐhòu, jízhěn bìngrén huì mǎshàng bèi sòngjìn _____.

4) 通常护士会先给病人测量_____和_____。
    Tōngcháng hùshì huì xiān gěi bìngrén cèliáng _____ hé _____.

5) 要是医生不清楚病人有什么病，就会让病人做_____检查。
    Yàoshi yīshēng bù qīngchǔ bìngrén yǒu shénme bìng, jiù huì ràng bìngrén zuò _____ jiǎnchá.

SURGERY

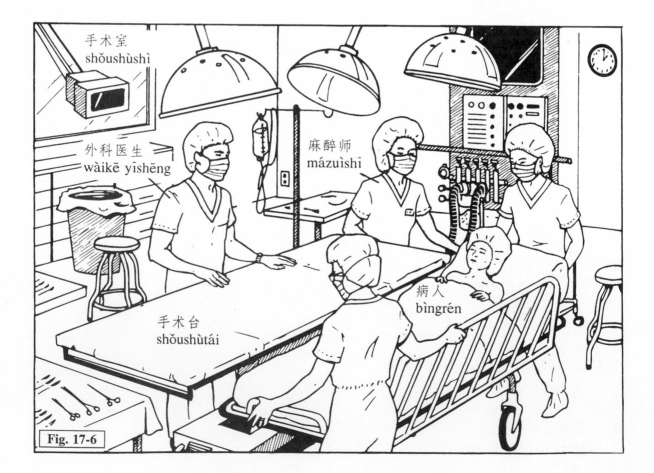

Fig. 17-6

病人要**做手术**了。   have an operation
Bìngrén yào *zuò shǒushù* le.

他们先给病人**注射**一支**镇静剂**。   inject, tranquilizer
Tāmen xiān gěi bìngrén *zhùshè* yì zhī *zhènjìngjì*.

大家正在**做**手术的**准备**。   prepare
Dàjiā zhèngzài *zuò* shǒushù de *zhǔnbèi*.

病人被用担架车送进了**手术室**。   operating room
Bìngrén bèi yòng dānjiàchē sòngjìn le *shǒushùshì*.

病人被**安置**在**手术台**上。   place, operating table
Bìngrén bèi *ānzhì* zài *shǒushùtái* shàng.

麻醉师给病人注射**麻药**。   anesthetist, anesthesia
Mázuìshī gěi bìngrén zhùshè *máyào*.

外科医生开始给病人**动手术**。   surgeon, operate
Wàikē yīshēng kāishǐ gěi bìngrén *dòng shǒushù*.

这是**阑尾切除**手术。   appendix, removal
Zhè shi *lánwěi qiēchú* shǒushù.

病人得的是**急性阑尾炎**。   acute, appendicitis
Bìngrén dé de shi *jíxìng lánwěiyán*.

12. Complete.

医生决定给病人动__1__。为了不让病人太紧张，护士给病人注射了一针__2__。
Yīshēng juédìng gěi bìngrén dòng __1__. Wèile bú ràng bìngrén tài jǐnzhāng, hùshì gěi bìngrén zhùshè le yì zhēn __2__.

病人是用__3__送到手术室来的，因为他不能走。病人被安置在__4__上。
Bìngrén shi yòng __3__ sòngdào shǒushùshì lái de, yīnwèi tā bù néng zǒu. Bìngrén bèi ānzhìzài __4__ shàng.

麻醉师给他打了__5__。接着，医生开始手术。他今天做的是阑尾__6__手术。
Mázuìshī gěi tā dǎle __5__. Jiēzhe, yīshēng kāishǐ shǒushù. Tā jīntiān zuò de shi lánwěi __6__ shǒushù.

IN THE RECOVERY ROOM

手术以后，病人被送到了**观察室**里。   recovery room
Shǒushù yǐhòu, bìngrén bèi sòng dào le *guāncháshì* lǐ.

在观察室里，他们给病人**输氧**。   oxygen therapy
Zài guāncháshì lǐ, tāmen gěi bìngrén *shūyǎng*.

他们还给病人**输液**。   intravenous feeding
Tāmen hái gěi bìngrén *shūyè*.

护士告诉病人，
Hùshì gàosù bìngrén,

他**手术后情况**不错。   prognosis
Tā *shǒushù hòu qíngkuàng* búcuò.

如果手术后，病人情况不好，
Rúguǒ shǒushù hòu, bìngrén qíngkuàng bù hǎo,

就会被送到**特护病房**去。   intensive care unit
Jiù huì bèi sòngdào *tèhù bìngfáng* qù.

13. Complete.

1) 手术后，病人被送到了_____。
   Shǒushù hòu, bìngrén bèi sòngdào le _____.

2) 护士给病人_____，这样病人可以呼吸得好一点。
   Hùshì gěi bìngrén _____, zhèiyàng bìngrén kěyǐ hūxī de hǎo yìdiǎn.

3) 他们给不能吃东西的病人_____。
   Tāmen gěi bù néng chī dōngxi de bìngrén _____.

4) 要是病人_____情况很好，他就不必去_____。
   Yàoshi bìngrén _____ qíngkuàng hěn hǎo, tā jiù bú bì qù _____.

IN THE DELIVERY ROOM

她**怀孕**了。   pregnant
Tā *huáiyùn* le.

她就要**生孩子**了。   give birth
Tā jiùyào *shēng háizi* le.

她正在**分娩中**。   in labor
Tā zhèngzài *fēnmiǎn* zhōng.

阵痛开始了。   labor pain
Zhèntòng kāishǐ le.

她被送进了**产房**。   delivery room
Tā bèi sòngjìnle *chǎnfáng*.

产科医生在为她**接生**。   obstetrician, deliver (a child)
Chǎnkē yīshēng zài wèi tā *jiēshēng*.

14. Complete.

A.   她__1__了。很快就要__2__了，所以被送进了__3__。现在她腹部__4__已经开始了。
     Tā __1__ le, hěnkuài jiùyào __2__ le, suǒyǐ bèi sòngjìn le __3__. Xiànzài tā fùbù __4__ yǐjīng kāishǐ le.

     __5__正在为她接生。
     __5__ zhèngzài wèi tā jiēshēng.

B.   一天小王觉得肚子疼。他躺在床上没法子起来。他不知道应该怎么
     Yì tiān Xiǎo Wáng juéde dùzi téng. Tā tǎngzài chuáng shàng méi fázi qǐlái. Tā bù zhīdao yīnggāi zěnme

     办，只好打电话叫了一辆救护车。几分钟以后救护车就来了。他们把小
     bàn, zhǐhǎo dǎ diànhuà jiào le yí liàng jiùhùchē. Jǐ fēnzhōng yǐhòu jiùhùchē jiù lái le. Tāmen bǎ Xiǎo

     王放在担架上，送到了医院的急诊室。护士给他量了脉搏，也为他量了
     Wáng fàngzài dānjià shàng, sòngdào le yīyuàn de jízhěnshì. Hùshì gěi tā liángle màibó, yě wèi tā liángle

血压。医生也来了。医生问他什么地方不舒服，小王说了一下他的
xuèyā. Yīshēng yě lái le. Yīshēng wèn tā shénmē dìfang bù shūfu, Xiǎo Wáng shuōle yíxià tāde

症状。医生想知道他吐不吐，拉不拉肚子。小王说他只是肚子疼。
zhèngzhuàng. Yīshēng xiǎng zhīdào tā tù bú tù, lā bù lā dùzi. Xiǎo Wáng shuō tā zhǐ shi dùzi téng.

医生给他检查以后，要他去做X光检查。一个护士帮他坐进轮椅，把他
Yīshēng gěi tā jiǎnchá yǐhòu, yào tā qù zuò X guāng jiǎnchá. Yí ge hùshì bāng tā zuòjìn lúnyǐ, bǎ tā

推到了放射科。他在那儿照了几张X光片。一个小时以后，医生告诉他
tuīdàole fàngshèkē. Tā zài nàr zhàole jǐ zhāng X guāng piān. Yí ge xiǎoshí yǐhòu, yīshēng gàosù tā

检查的结果是急性盲肠炎，需要马上动手术。
jiǎnchá de jiéguǒ shi jíxìng mángchángyán, xūyào mǎshàng dòng shǒushù.

小王进了手术室。护士给他打了镇静剂。然后让他躺在手术台上。
Xiǎo Wáng jìnle shǒushùshì. Hùshì gěi tā dǎle zhènjìngjì. Ránhòu ràng tā tǎngzài shǒushùtái shàng.

麻醉师给他注射了麻药，并让他数数。他还没数到100就睡着了。外科
Mázuìshī gěi tā zhùshè le máyào, bìng ràng tā shǔshù. Tā hái méi shǔdào yìbǎi jiù shuìzháo le. Wàikē

医生开始给他动手术。手术很快就做好了。小王醒来以后发现自己
yīshēng kāishǐ gěi tā dòng shǒushù. Shǒushù hěn kuài jiù zuòhǎo le. Xiǎo Wáng xǐng lái yǐhòu fāxiàn zìjǐ

躺在观察室里，鼻子里插着输氧管。他们也在为小王输液。一个护士过来
tǎng zài guānchǎshì lǐ. bízi lǐ chāzhē shūyǎng guǎn. Tāmen yě wèi Xiǎo Wáng shūyè. Yí ge hùshì guòlái

告诉小王，说手术进行得很顺利，手术后情况也很好。两天后
gàosù Xiǎo Wáng, shuō shǒushù jìnxíng de hěn shùnlì, shǒushù hòu qíngkuàng yě hěn hǎo. Liǎng tiān hòu

就可以出院了。出院时他不需要担架，也不需要轮椅。他可以自己走着回家。
jiù kěyǐ chūyuàn le. Chūyuàn shí tā bù xūyào dānjià, yě bù xūyào lúnyǐ. Tā kěyǐ zìjǐ zǒuzhē huíjiā.

15. Complete.

1) 小王肚子_____。
   Xiǎo Wáng dùzi _____.

2) 他是坐_____到医院去的。
   Tā shi zuò _____dào yīyuàn qù de.

3) 小王不能走路，他得躺在_____上。
   Xiǎo Wáng bùnéng zǒulù, tā děi tǎngzài _____shàng.

4) 一到医院，他就被送进了_____。
   Yí dào yīyuàn, tā jiù bèi sòngjìn le _____.

5) 护士给他量了_____和_____。
   Hùshì gěi tā liángle _____he _____.

6) 他告诉医生他有些什么_____。
   Tā gàosù yīshēng tā yǒu xiē shénme _____.

7) 他被送到放射科去_____。
   Tā bèi sòngdào fàngshèkē qù _____.

8) 医生决定给他做_____。
   Yīshēng juédìng gěi tā zuò _____.

9) 到手术室以后，他们先给他打了一针_____。
   Dào shǒushùshì yǐhòu, tāmen xiān gěi tā dǎ le yì zhēn _____.

10) 麻醉医生给他注射了_____。
   Mázuì yīshēng gěi tā zhùshè le _____.

11) 外科医生为他切除了_____。
   Wàikē yīshēng wèi tā qiēchú le _____.

12) 小王醒来以后，发现自己躺在_____里。
   Xiǎo Wáng xǐnglái yǐhòu, fāxiàn zìjǐ tǎngzài _____ lǐ.

13) 医生告诉他他的_____很好。
   Yīshēng gàosù tā tāde _____ hěn hǎo.

14) 要是他的手术后情况不好，就会被送到_____去。
   Yàoshi tāde shǒushù hòu qíngkuàng bù hǎo, jiù huì bèi sòngdào _____ qù.

KEY WORDS

abdomen	小腹	xiǎofù
accident	事故	shìgù
acute	急性	jíxìng
adhesive bandage	创口贴	chuāngkǒutiē
allergic	过敏	guòmǐn
allergy	过敏症	guòmǐnzhèng
ambulance	救护车	jiùhùchē
anesthesia	麻药	máyào
anesthetist	麻醉师	mázuìshī
ankle	踝骨	huáigǔ
antibiotics	抗生素	kàngshēngsù
appendicitis	阑尾炎/盲肠炎	lánwěiyán/mángchángyán
appendix	阑尾/盲肠	lánwěi/mángcháng
arm	胳膊/手臂	gēbo/shǒubì
arthritis	关节炎	guānjiéyán
back	背	bèi
bandage	绷带	bēngdài
bind up	包	bāo
blood	血	xuè
blood pressure	血压	xuèyā
blood test	验血	yànxuè
blood type	血型	xuèxíng
bone fracture	骨折	gǔzhé
call number	叫号	jiàohào
cancer	癌症	áizhèng
catch	得	dé
check	测	cè
cheek/face	脸	liǎn
chest	胸口	xiōngkǒu
chicken pox	水痘	shuǐdòu
chills	发冷	fālěng
congested	不通	bùtōng
cough	咳嗽	késou
cut	割破	gēpò
deep	深	shēn
deep breath	深呼吸	shēn hūxī
deliver	接生	jiēshēng
delivery room	产房	chǎnfáng
diarrhea	拉肚子/腹泻	lā dùzi/fùxiè
dizzy	头晕	tóuyūn
doctor	医生	yīshēng
doctor on duty	值班医生	zhíbān yīshēng
draw, collect	抽	chōu
ear	耳朵	ěrduō
elbow	胳膊肘	gēbozhǒu
electrocardiogram	心电图	xīndiàntú
emergency room	急诊室	jízhěnshì
enteritis	肠炎	chángyán
epilepsy	癫痫	diānxián
every 4 hours	每隔四小时	měi gé sì xiǎoshí
examine	检查	jiǎnchá
feces	大便	dàbiàn
fever	发烧	fāshāo
fill in	填	tián
finger	手指	shǒuzhǐ
flu	流感	liúgǎn
foot	脚	jiǎo
form	表	biǎo
give an injection	打一针	dǎ yì zhēn
give birth	生孩子	shēng háizi
glands	淋巴	línbā
hand	手	shǒu
have a cold	感冒	gǎnmào
have a surgery/operation	做手术	zuò shǒushù
head	头	tóu
heart	心脏	xīnzàng
heart disease	心脏病	xīnzàngbìng
hip	胯骨	kuàgǔ
hospital	医院	yīyuàn
human body	人体	réntǐ

hurt/sore	疼	téng
in labor	分娩中	fēnmiǎn zhōng
inflammation	发炎	fāyán
inject	注射	zhùshè
intensive care unit	特护病房	tèhù bìngfáng
intern	实习医生	shíxí yīshēng
intravenous feeding	输液	shūyè
It hurts here	我这儿疼	wǒ zhèr téng
kidney	肾脏	shènzàng
knee	膝盖	xīgài
labor pain	阵痛	zhèntòng
lab-test	化验	huàyàn
leg	腿	tuǐ
liver	肝脏	gānzàng
lungs	肺部	fèibù
measles	麻疹	mázhěn
measure	量	liáng
medical history	病史	bìngshǐ
medical insurance	医疗保险	yīliáo bǎoxiǎn
medicine	药	yào
menstrual periods	月经	yuèjīng
mental illness	精神病	jīngshénbìng
mouth	嘴	zuǐ
mumps	流行性腮腺炎	liúxíngxìng sāixiànyán
nauseous	恶心	ěxīn
nose	鼻子	bízi
nurse	护士	hùshì
observe	观察	guānchá
obstetrician	产科医生	chǎnkē yīshēng
on crutches	拄拐杖	zhǔ guǎizhàng
open	张开	zhāngkāi
operate	动手术	dòng shǒushù
operating room	手术室	shǒushù shì
operating table	手术台	shǒushù tái
operation/surgery	手术	shǒushù
organs	脏器	zàngqì
oxygen therapy	输氧	shū yǎng
patient	病人	bìngrén
penicillin	青霉素	qīngméisù
place, put	安置	ānzhì
polio	小儿麻痹症	xiǎoér mábìzhèng
pregnant	怀孕	huáiyùn

prepare	做准备	zuò zhǔnbèi
prescribe	开	kāi
prognosis	手术后情况	shǒushù hòu qíngkuàng
pulse	脉搏	màibó
push	推	tuī
put it in cast	上石膏	shàng shígāo
recovery room	观察室	guāncháshì
register	挂号	guàhào
registration (office)	挂号处	guàhàochù
regular	正常	zhèngcháng
removal/remove	切除	qiēchú
roll up	卷起	juǎnqǐ
running nose	流鼻涕	liú bítì
see a doctor	看病	kànbìng
set the bone	固定骨头	gùdìng gǔtóu
shoulder	肩膀	jiānbǎng
sick	难受	nánshòu
sleeve	袖子	xiùzi
sprain	扭伤	niǔshāng
stethoscope	听诊器	tīngzhěnqì
stitch	缝合	fénghé
stomachache	胃疼	wèiténg
stomachache	肚子疼	dùzi téng
stretcher	担架	dānjià
surgeon	外科医生	wàikē yīshēng
swollen	肿	zhǒng
symptoms	症状	zhèngzhuàng
tablet, pill	片	piàn
take temperature	量体温	liáng tǐwēn
throat	嗓子/喉咙	sǎngzi/hóulóng
tonsils	扁桃腺	biǎntáoxiàn
tranquilizer	镇静剂	zhènjìngjì
tuberculosis	肺结核	fèi jiéhé
uncomfortable	不舒服	bù shūfu
unexpected	意外	yìwài
urine	小便	xiǎobiàn
venereal disease	性病	xìngbìng
vital	主要	zhǔyào
vomit	吐	tù
waist/lower back	腰	yāo
waiting room	候诊室	hòuzhěn shì
wheelchair	轮椅	lúnyǐ
wound, injury	伤口	shāngkǒu
wrist	手腕	shǒuwàn
X-ray	X光检查/透视	X guāng jiǎnchá/tòushì

Chapter 18: At the theater and the movies

第十八章: 在剧院和电影院
Zài jùyuàn hé diànyǐngyuàn

SEEING A SHOW

今天晚上我们要去看一场演出。	see a show
Jīntiān wǎnshang wǒmen yào qù *kàn yì chǎng yǎnchū.*	
什么演出? 是歌剧吗?	opera
Shénme yǎnchū? Shi *gējù* ma?	
话剧	drama
huàjù	
舞剧	dance drama
wǔjù	
芭蕾	ballet
bālěi	
歌舞	song and dance
gēwǔ	
音乐会	concert
yīnyuèhuì	
相声	cross talks
xiàngsheng	
杂技	acrobatics
zájì	
演出在首都剧场。	theater
Yǎnchū zài Shǒudū *Jùchǎng.*	
北京青年艺术剧院	theater
Běijīng Qīngnián Yìshù *Jùyuàn.*	
长安大戏院	theater
Cháng'ān Dà*xìyuàn*	
北京音乐厅	concert hall
Běijīng *Yīnyuètīng.*	
我昨天看的那个戏是悲剧。	tragedy
Wǒ zuótiān kàn de nèige xì shi *bēijù.*	
喜剧	comedy
xǐjù	
是谁主演的?	lead

172

Shi shéi *zhǔyǎn* de?

男主角 是谁？   leading male actor

Nán zhǔjué shi shéi?

女主角   leading female actor

nǚ zhǔjué

他是**配角**，   supporting actor

Tā shi *pèijué*,

在戏里**演**一个**歌星**。   play the part, singing star

zài xì lǐ *yǎn yí ge gēxīng*.

那个**男演员演**得真好。   actor, play/act

Nèi ge nán yǎnyuán yǎn de zhēn hǎo.

      女演员   actress

      nǚ yǎnyuán

这个戏一共有三**幕**，每幕有两**场**。   acts, scenes

Zhèi ge xì yígòng yǒu sān *mù,* měi mù yǒu liǎng *chǎng*.

第二幕以后有**幕间休息**。   intermission

Dì èr mù yǐhòu yǒu *mùjiān xiūxi*.

演员**上场/出场**了。   come on stage

Yǎnyuán *shàngchǎng/chūchǎng* le.

观众鼓掌/拍手了。   audience, applaud

Guānzhòng gǔzhǎng/pāishǒu le.

他们很喜欢这出戏。

Tāmen hěn xǐhuān zhèi chū xì.

1. Complete.

1) 我们去_____好吗？我想去看京戏。

    Wǒmen qù _____hǎo ma? Wǒ xiǎng qù kàn jīngxì.

2) 今天晚上在北京音乐厅有一场_____，你去不去？

    Jīntiān wǎnshan zài Běijīng Yīnyuètīng yǒu yì chǎng _____, nǐ qù bú qù?

3) 我不想看悲剧。我想看_____。

    Wǒ bù xiǎng kàn bēijù. Wǒ xiǎng kàn _____.

4) 她在这出戏中_____最重要的角色。她是_____。

    Tā zài zhèi chū xì zhōng _____zuì zhòngyào de juésè. Tā shi _____.

5) 那个女_____很有名。她演得真好。

    Nèi ge nǚ _____hěn yǒumíng. Tā yǎn de zhēn hǎo.

6) 这个戏很长，一共有五_____，每幕有两_____。

    Zhèi ge xì hěn cháng, yígòng yǒu wǔ _____, měi mù yǒu liǎng _____.

7) 在第三幕和第四幕之间有十五分钟的_____时间。

    Zài dì sān mù hé dì sì mù zhījiān yǒu shíwǔ fēnzhōng de _____shíjiān.

8) _____都在拍手，因为他们觉得演员演得很好。

    _____dōu zài pāishǒu, yīnwèi tāmen juéde yǎnyuán yǎn de hěn hǎo.

2. Give the opposite:

1) 喜剧
   xǐjù

2) 男演员
   nán yǎnyuán

3) 女主角
   nǚ zhǔjué

AT THE TICKET WINDOW

有**今天**晚上演出的**票**吗？ Yǒu *jīntiān* wǎnshang yǎnchū de *piào* ma?	today, ticket
明天的票 *míngtiān* de piào	tomorrow
二楼的**座位** èr lóu de zuòwèi	second floor, seat
一楼 yī lóu	first floor
中间 zhōngjiān	middle
左边 zuǒbiān	left side
右边 yòubiān	right side
前排座位的票 qián pái zuòwèi de piào	front rows, seat
对不起，今天晚上的票都**卖完**了。 Duìbuqǐ, jīntiān wǎnshang de piào dōu *màiwán* le.	sold out
一楼前排的票**多少钱**一张？ yīlóu qián pái de piào *duōshǎoqián* yì zhāng?	how much
这是您的票：一楼四**排**十五、十六**座/号**。 Zhè shi nínde piào: yī lóu sì *pái* shíwǔ、shíliù *zuò/hào*.	row, seat
演出什么时候**开始**？ Yǎnchū shénme shíhou kāishǐ?	start/begin
大衣可以放在**存衣处**。 Dàyī kěyǐ fàng zài *cúnyīchù*.	cloakroom
带位员发给我们一张**节目单**。 *Dàiwèiyuán* fāgěi wǒmen yì zhāng *jiémùdān*.	usher, program

3. Complete.

(At the ticket office)

A：还有今天晚上演出的___1___吗?
   Hái yǒu jīntiān wǎnshan yǎnchū de ___1___ ma?

B：对不起，都___2___了。不过我们有明天晚上___3___的票。
   Duìbuqǐ, dōu ___2___ le. Búguò wǒmen yǒu míngtiān wǎnshang ___3___ de piào.

A：明天的也行。
   Míngtiān de yě xíng.

B：您想要一___4___还是二___5___的?
   Nín xiǎngyào yī ___4___ háishi èr ___5___ de?

A：我不要楼上的座。我想要两张___6___中间的票。
   Wǒ bú yào lóu shàng de zuò. Wǒ xiǎngyào liǎng zhāng ___6___ zhōngjiān de piào.

B：真对不起。明天一楼中间的票都没有了。只有左边或___7___的。
   Zhēn duìbuqǐ. Míngtiān yīlóu zhōngjiān de piào dōu méiyǒu le. Zhǐ yǒu zuǒbiān huò ___7___ de.

A：也可以。只要不是楼上就行。___8___钱一张?
   Yě kěyǐ. Zhǐ yào bú shi lóushàng de jiù xíng. ___8___ qián yì zhāng?

B：前排的五十，后排的三十。
   Qián pái de wǔshí, hòu pái de sānshí.

A：我买两张___9___的。这是一百块。
   Wǒ mǎi liǎng zhāng ___9___ de. Zhè shi yìbǎi kuài.

B：一百块正好。这是您的___10___。一楼左边五___11___六、七___12___。
   Yìbǎi kuài zhèng hǎo. Zhè shi nínde ___10___. Yī lóu zuǒbiān wǔ ___11___ liù, qī ___12___.

A：请问___13___几点开始?
   Qǐngwèn ___13___ jǐ diǎn kāishǐ?

B：八点。
   Bā diǎn.

(At home)

A：今天你去买票了吗?
   Jīntiān nǐ qù mǎi piào le ma?

B：买了。
   Mǎi le.

A：是今天晚上的吗?
   Shi jīntiān wǎnshang de ma?

B：不是，今天晚上的票都卖完了。我买了两张明天晚上的。
   Bú shi, Jīntiān wǎnshang de piào dōu màiwán le. Wǒ mǎile liǎng zhāng míngtiān wǎnshàng de.

A：票怎么样?
   Piào zěnmeyàng?

B：一楼中间的没有了。只有左边和右边的。
   Yī lóu zhōngjiān de méiyǒu le. Zhǐ yǒu zuǒbiān de he yòubiān de.

A：是前面的还是后面的？
Shi qiánmiàn de háishi hòumiàn de?

B：前面的。我买的是一楼左边第五排的。
Qiánmiàn de. Wǒ mǎi de shi yī lóu zuǒbiān dì wǔ pái de.

A：不错。看戏我喜欢坐在前面。
Búcuò. Kànxì wǒ xǐhuan zuò zài qiánmiàn.

4. Answer the following questions based on the conversation above:

1)　B 今天做什么了？
　　B jīntiān zuò shénme le?

2)　A 和B今天晚上要去看戏吗？
　　A hé B jīntiān wǎnshang yào qù kànxì ma?

3)　为什么？
　　Wèishénme?

4)　明天的也没有了吗？
　　Míngtiān de yě méiyǒu le ma?

5)　B 买了几张明天的票？
　　B mǎile jǐ zhāng míngtiān de piào?

6)　他买的是楼上的票吗？
　　Tā mǎi de shi lóushàng de piào ma?

7)　为什么？
　　Wèishénme?

8)　他们的座位在哪儿？
　　Tāmen de zuòwèi zài nǎr?

9)　A喜欢他们的座位吗？
　　A xǐhuan tāmen de zuòwèi ma?

10)　为什么？
　　Wèishénme?

5. Correct each statement according to the conversation.

1) B在存衣处买票。
　 B zài cúnyīchù mǎi piào.

2) 售票的人不告诉买票的人演出开始的时间。
　 Shòupiào de rén bú gàosù mǎipiào de rén yǎnchū kāishǐ de shíjiān.

3) B想买楼上的票。
　 B xiǎng mǎi lóushàng de piào.

4) B买了今天晚上的票。
　 B mǎile jīntiān wǎnshan de piào.

5) A看戏喜欢坐在后面。
　 A kànxì xǐhuan zuòzài hòumiàn.

AT THE MOVIES

电影院今天放的是什么电影？   cinema, movie/film
Diànyǐngyuàn jīntiān fàng de shi shénme *diànyǐng*?

谁演的？   play
Shéi *yǎn* de?

还有下午四点的票吗？
Hái yǒu xiàwǔ sì diǎn de piào ma?

我要买一张大人票，两张儿童票。   adult, children
Wǒ yào mǎi yì zhāng *dàrén* piào, liǎng zhāng *értóng* piào.

我不想坐得离银幕太近。   distance to/from, screen, close
Wǒ bù xiǎng zuò de *lí yínmù* tài *jìn*.

电影是中文电影，可是有英文字幕。   subtitle
Diànyǐng shi Zhōngwén diànyǐng, kěshì yǒu Yīngwén *zìmù*.

这个导演很有名。   director
Zhèi ge *dǎoyǎn* hěn yǒumíng.

这部片子是在哪儿拍的？   shoot
Zhèi bù piānzi shi zài nǎr *pāi* de?

你想看这个电影的原版吗？   original release
Nǐ xiǎng kàn zhèi ge diànyǐng de *yuánbǎn* ma?

我喜欢看故事片。   drama
Wǒ xǐhuan kàn *gùshipiān*.

    纪录片   documentary
    jìlùpiān

    爱情片   romance
    àiqíngpiān

    科幻片   science fiction
    kēhuànpiān

    功夫片/武打片   Kung-fu
    gōngfūpiān/wǔdǎpiān

    动作片   action
    dòngzuòpiān

    惊险片   thriller
    jīngxiǎnpiān

    喜剧片   comedy
    xǐjùpiān

    西部片   Western
    xībùpiān

    进口片   imported
    jìnkǒupiān

    外国片   foreign
    wàiguópiān

动画片   cartoon
dònghuàpiān

6. Complete.

1) 我不喜欢看＿＿＿＿片，因为总是打来打去的。
   Wǒ bù xǐhuan kàn ＿＿＿＿piān, yīnwèi zǒngshi dǎ lái dǎ qù de.

2) 这是一部中国电影，是在中国南部＿＿＿＿的。
   Zhè shi yí bù Zhōngguó diànyǐng, shi zài Zhōngguó nánbù ＿＿＿＿de.

3) 我的中文不够好，不知道那部片子有没有英文＿＿＿＿？
   Wǒde Zhōngwén bú gòu hǎo, bù zhīdao nèi bù piānzi yǒu méiyǒu Yīngwén ＿＿＿＿?

4) 我买两张晚上八点的＿＿＿＿。
   Wǒ mǎi liǎng zhāng wǎnshàng bā diǎn de ＿＿＿＿.

5) 我不想坐得＿＿＿＿银幕太近。
   Wǒ bù xiǎng zuò de ＿＿＿＿yínmù tài jìn.

6) 很多人喜欢看外＿＿＿＿电影。
   Hěn duō rén xǐhuan kàn wài ＿＿＿＿diànyǐng.

7) 虽然我听不懂演员说的话，可是我看得懂英文＿＿＿＿。
   Suīrán wǒ tīng bù dǒng yǎnyuán shuō de huà, kěshì wǒ kàn de dǒng Yīngwén ＿＿＿＿.

8) 我很喜欢这部片子的男主角，可是不太喜欢那个女＿＿＿＿。
   Wǒ hěn xǐhuan zhèi bù piānzi de nán zhǔjué, kěshì bú tài xǐhuan nèi ge nǚ ＿＿＿＿.

9) 小孩儿都喜欢看＿＿＿＿片。
   Xiǎoháir dōu xǐhuan kàn ＿＿＿＿piān.

10) 很多人喜欢看＿＿＿＿，大家都看得哈哈大笑。
    Hěn duō rén xǐhuan kàn ＿＿＿＿, dàjiā dōu kàn de hāhā dà xiào.

KEY WORDS

acrobatics	杂技	zájì	cross talks	相声	xiàngshēng
act, play	演	yǎn	dance drama	舞剧	wǔjù
action movie	动作片	dòngzuòpiān	director	导演	dǎoyǎn
actor	男演员	nán yǎnyuán	distance to or from	离	lí
actress	女演员	nǚ yǎnyuán	documentary	纪录片	jìlùpiān
acts	幕	mù	downstairs	楼下	lóuxià
adult	大人	dàrén	drama	话剧	huàjù
applaud	鼓掌/拍手	gǔzhǎng/pāishǒu	drama	故事片	gùshipiān
audience	观众	guānzhòng	first floor	一楼	yī lóu
ballet	芭蕾	bālěi	foreign film	外国片	wàiguópiān
cartoon	动画片	dònghuà piān	front rows	前排	qiánpái
children	儿童	értóng	how much	多少钱	duōshǎoqián
cinema	电影院	diànyǐng yuàn	imported film	进口片	jìnkǒupiān
cloakroom	存衣处	cúnyīchù	intermission	幕间休息	mùjiān xiūxi
close, near	近	jìn	Kung-fu movie	功夫片/	gōngfupiān
come on stage	上/出场	shàng/chūchǎng		武打片	wǔdǎpiān
comedy	喜剧	xǐjù	lead	主演	zhǔyǎn
comedy	喜剧片	xǐjùpiān	leading female actor	女主角	nǚ zhǔjué
concert	音乐会	yīnyuèhuì			
concert hall	音乐厅	yīnyuètīng	leading male actor	男主角	nán zhǔjué

left	左边	zuǒbiān	singing star	歌星	gēxīng
middle	中间	zhōngjiān	sold out	卖完	màiwán
movie/film	电影/片子	diànyǐng/piānzi	song and dance	歌舞	gēwǔ
opera	歌剧	gējù	start/begin	开始/开演	kāishǐ/kāiyǎn
original release	原版	yuánbǎn	subtitle	字幕	zìmù
play the part	演	yǎn	supporting actor	配角	pèijué
program	节目单	jiémùdān	theater	剧场	jùchǎng
right	右边	yòubiān	theater	剧院	jùyuàn
romance	爱情片	àiqíngpiān	theater	戏院	xìyuàn
row	排	pái	thriller	惊险片	jīngxiǎnpiān
scenes	场	chǎng	ticket	票	piào
science fiction	科幻片	kēhuànpiān	today	今天	jīntiān
screen	银幕	yínmù	tomorrow	明天	míngtiān
seat	座(位)	zuò(wèi)	tragedy	悲剧	bēijù
second floor	二楼	èr lóu	upstairs	楼上	lóushàng
see a show	看演出	kàn yǎnchū	usher	带位员	dàiwèiyuán
shoot (a movie)	拍	pāi	Western (movie)	西部片	xībùpiān

Chapter 19: Sports

第十九章：体育运动

Tǐyù yùndòng

SOCCER

我喜欢看**足球比赛**。	soccer, game
Wǒ xǐhuan kàn *zúqiú bǐsài*.	
足球比赛有两个**队**参加。	team
Zúqiú bǐsài yǒu liǎng ge *duì* cānjiā.	
每个队有11个**队员**。	player
Měi ge duì yǒu shíyī ge *duìyuán*.	
现在他们在足球**场**上。	field
Xiànzài tāmen zài zúqiú *chǎng* shàng.	
他们**用脚踢球**。	with foot, kick, ball
Tāmen *yòng jiǎo tī qiú*.	
他们有时候用**头顶**球。	head, butt (with one's head)
Tāmen yǒushíhou yòng *tóu dǐng* qiú.	
守门员守护球门。	goalie, defend, goal
Shǒuményuán shǒuhù qiúmén.	
守门员得**挡住**球。	block/stop
Shǒuményuán děi *dǎngzhù* qiú.	
左后卫把球**传**给一个队员。	left end, pass/toss
Zuǒ hòuwèi bǎ qiú *chuán* gěi yí ge duìyuán.	
对方的队员把球**抢走**了。	the opposing team, steal
Duìfāng de qiúyuán bǎ qiú *qiǎngzǒu* le.	
他**踢进**了一球。	make a goal
Tā *tījìn le yì qiú*.	
北京队**得了一分**。	score a point
Běijīng Duì *déle yì fēn*.	
裁判员判5号**犯规**。	referee, foul
Cáipànyuán pàn wǔhào *fànguī*.	
裁判员**吹哨**子了。	blow, whistle
Cáipànyuán *chuī shàozi* le.	
上半场结束了。	first half (of game), end
Shàngbànchǎng jiéshù le.	

下**半场**开始了。	second half
Xiàbànchǎng kāishǐ le.	
双方都**没有进球**。	both parties, no-score game
Shuāngfāng dōu méiyǒu *jìnqiú*.	
双方踢成了**平局**。	tied
Shuāngfāng tīchéngle *píngjú*.	
记分板上会显示**分数**。	scoreboard, score
Jìfēnbǎn shàng huì xiǎnshì *fēnshù*.	
上一次北京队以三**比**二**赢**了。	three to two, win
Shàng yí cì Běijīng Duì yǐ *sān bǐ èr yíng* le.	
这一次北京队**输**了。	lose
Zhè yí cì Běijīng Duì *shū* le.	

1. Answer.

1) 一个队有多少个队员?
   Yí ge duì yǒu duōshǎo ge duìyuán?

2) 一场比赛中有几个队?
   Yì chǎng bǐsài zhōng yǒu jǐ ge duì?

3) 队员在哪儿比赛?
   Duìyuán zài nǎr bǐsài?

4) 谁守门?
   Shéi shǒumén?

5) 队员把球传给谁?
   Duìyuán bǎ qiú chuán gěi shéi?

6) 守门员看见球来了,会怎么样?
   Shǒuményuán kànjiàn qiú lái le, huì zěnmeyàng?

7) 要是一个队员踢进一个球,这个队得分吗?
   Yàoshi yí ge duìyuán tī jìn yí ge qiú, zhèi ge duì défēn ma?

8) 谁可以判队员犯规?
   Shéi kěyǐ pàn duìyuán fànguī?

9) 上半场结束以后,我们就能知道哪个队赢了吗?
   Shàngbànchǎng jiéshù yǐhòu, wǒmen jiù néng zhīdào nǎ ge duì yíng le ma?

10) 要是双方都没有进球,是不是平局?
   Yàoshi shuāngfāng dōu méiyǒu jìnqiú, shì bú shì píngjú?

2. Complete.

__1__比赛开始了,两个__2__都在__3__上。一个队员把球__4__给另一个队员,可是
1_bǐsài kāishǐ le, liǎng ge __2__ dōu zài __3__ shàng. Yí ge duìyuán bǎ qiú __4__ gěi lìng yí ge duìyuán, kěshì

球被对方的队员__5__了。这名队员起脚__6__,可是球没有__7__,因为对方的
qiú bèi duìfāng de duìyuán __5__ le. Zhè míng duìyuán qǐjiǎo __6__, kěshì qiú méiyǒu __7__, yīnwèi duìfāng de

守门员把球__8__了。__9__结束了,双方都没有__10__。他们的__11__都是0。
shǒuményuán bǎ qiú __8__ le. __9__ jiéshù le, shuāngfāng dōu méiyǒu __10__, Tāmen de __11__ dōu shi líng.

3. Identify each item in Figure 19-1.

1)_____   2)_____   3)_____   4)_____   5)_____   6)_____

Fig. 19-1

TENNIS

这是一场**网球比赛**。 Zhè shi yì chǎng *wǎngqiú bǐsài*.	tennis, tournament
两个**运动员**都在**网球场**上。 Liǎng ge *yùndòngyuán* dōu zài *wǎngqiúchǎng* shàng.	sportsmen, tennis court
他们都拿着**网球拍**。 Tāmen dōu názhe *wǎngqiúpāi*.	racket
这是一场**单打**比赛， Zhè shi yì chǎng *dāndǎ* bǐsài.	singles
不是**双打**比赛。 Bú shi *shuāngdǎ* bǐsài.	doubles
一方现在**发球**， Yì fāng xiànzài *fāqiú*.	serve the ball
另一方**接球**。 Lìng yì fāng *jiēqiú*.	return the serve
他把球**打过网**。 Tā bǎ qiú *dǎguò wǎng*.	over the net

球**出界**了。   out, out of bounds
Qiú *chūjiè* le.

比分是15比0。   score
Bǐfēn shi shíwǔ bǐ líng

他打了一个**擦网球**。   net ball
Tā dǎle yí ge *cāwǎngqiú*.

他们一共打了三**局**。   set
Tāmen yígòng dǎle sān *jú*.

他**胜**了两局。   win
Tā *shèng*le liǎng jú.

4. Complete.

1) 单打比赛时有两个_____。四个运动员一起打的比赛是_____。
   Dāndǎ bǐsài shí yǒu liǎng ge _____. Sì ge yùndòngyuán yìqǐ dǎ de bǐsài shi _____.

2) 打网球得用_____。
   Dǎ wǎngqiú děi yòng _____.

3) 打网球时，你得把球打_____网。
   Dǎ wǎngqiú shí, nǐ děi bǎ qiú dǎ _____wǎng.

4) 他们在_____上比赛。
   Tāmen zài _____shàng bǐsài.

5) 要是一个球落在白线以外，就是____了。
   Yàoshi yí ge qiú luòzài bái xiàn yǐwài, jiù shi _____le.

6) 一个队员_____球，另一个队员____球。
   Yí ge duìyuán _____qiú, lìng yí ge duìyuán _____qiú.

7) 要是球碰到了球网，这就是一个_____球。
   Yàoshi qiú pèngdàole qiúwǎng, zhè jiù shi yí ge _____qiú.

BASKETBALL

篮球队员在**篮球场**上。   basketball, court
Lánqiú duìyuán zài *lánqiúchǎng* shàng.

一个队员在**投篮**。   shoot (a basket)
Yí ge duìyuán zài *tóulán*.

这个队的**防守**很**严密**。   defense, tight (maneuver)
Zhèi ge duì de *fángshǒu* hěn *yánmì*.

他**没投中**。   miss the shot
Tā *méi tǒuzhòng*.

一个队员**扣篮**得分。   slam dunk
Yí ge duìyuán *kòulán* défēn.

每投进一球，就得两分。
Měi tóujìn yì qiú, jiù dé liǎng fēn.

Fig. 19-2

5. Answer on the basis of Fig. 19-2.

1) 这个篮球队员在哪儿?
   Zhèi ge lánqiú duìyuán zài nǎr?

2) 她在做什么?
   Tā zài zuò shénme?

3) 她投的是什么?
   Tā tóu de shi shénme?

4) 她要把球投到哪儿去?
   Tā yào bǎ qiú tóudào nǎr qù?

5) 她投中了没有?
   Tā tóuzhòngle méiyǒu?

6) 她能得分吗?
   Tā néng défēn ma?

TABLE TENNIS

球桌/台两端站着乒乓球选手。   table, end, ping-pong player
Qiú zhuō/tái liǎng duān zhànzhe pīngpāngqiú xuǎnshǒu.

他们手里拿的是乒乓球拍。   ping-pong paddle
Tāmen shǒu lǐ ná de shi *pīngpāngqiú pāi.*

一名选手**发球**，　　　　　　　　　　　　　serve the ball
Yì míng xuǎnshǒu *fāqiú*.

他发的是**转球**，　　　　　　　　　　　　　spinning ball
Tā fā de shi *zhuànqiú*.

另一名选手接球。
Lìng yì míng xuǎnshǒu jiēqiú.

他**削**球不过网，丢了一分。　　　　　　　slice, lose
Tā *xiāo*qiú bú guò wǎng, *diū*le yì fēn.

现在**换发球**。　　　　　　　　　　　　　　change serves
Xiànzài *huànfāqiú*

接球的队员发球**抢攻**，**抽**球得分。　　　quick attack, slam
Jiēqiú de duìyuán fāqiú *qiǎnggōng*, *chōu*qiú défēn.

男子单打比赛后是**女子双打**。　　　　　　male singles, female doubles
Nánzi dāndǎ bǐsài hòu shi *nǚzi shuāngdǎ*.

最后是**混合双打**。　　　　　　　　　　　　mixed doubles
Zuìhòu shi *hùnhé shuāngdǎ*.

6. Match the words and their definitions.

1) 男子单打　　　　　　　　　　　a. 乒乓球选手用的拍子
　　nánzi dāndǎ　　　　　　　　　　　pīngpāng qiú xuǎnshǒu yòng de pāizi

2) 抽球　　　　　　　　　　　　　b. 每方都是一男一女的比赛
　　chōuqiú　　　　　　　　　　　　　měi fāng dōu shi yì nán yì nǚ de bǐsài

3) 发球　　　　　　　　　　　　　c. 四名女选手的比赛
　　fāqiú　　　　　　　　　　　　　　sì míng nǚ xuǎnshǒu de bǐsài

4) 乒乓球拍　　　　　　　　　　　d. 两名男选手的比赛
　　pīngpāngqiú pāi　　　　　　　　　liǎng míng nán xuǎnshǒu de bǐsài

5) 女子双打　　　　　　　　　　　e. 开始打球
　　nǚzi shuāngdǎ　　　　　　　　　　kāishǐ dǎ qiú

6) 男女混合双打　　　　　　　　　f. 用球拍用力打过去的球
　　nánnǚ hùnhé shuāngdǎ　　　　　　yòng qiúpāi yònglì dǎ guòqù de qiú

TAI CHI

太极拳是中国**武术**的一种。　　　　　　　Tai Chi, martial arts
Tàijíquán shi Zhōngguó *wǔshù* de yì zhǒng.

　　　　一种**拳术**　　　　　　　　　　　art of boxing
　　　　yì zhǒng *quánshù*

　　　　一种很**流行**的**健身运动**　　　　　popular, workout
　　　　yì zhǒng hěn *liúxíng* de *jiànshēn yùndòng*

Fig. 19-3

掌 zhǎng
拳 quán
实步 shíbù   虚步 xūbù
直 zhí   弯 wān
弓步 gōngbù

太极拳的**动作**看起来比较慢， Tàijíquán de *dòngzuò* kàn qǐlai bǐjiào màn,	movement
可是能**运动**身体的各个部分。 Kěshì néng *yùndòng* shēntǐ de gè ge bùfen.	exercise
太极拳的**手型**有**拳**和**掌**等， Tàijíquán de *shǒuxíng* yǒu quán he zhǎng děng,	hand form, fist, palm
手位也很多，比方说：**推、按**等等。 *Shǒuwèi* yě hěn duō, bǐfāngshuō: *tuī, àn* děngděng.	hand position, push, press
步法可以**前移**， *Bùfǎ* kěyǐ *qiányí*,	footwork, move forward
也可以**后退**。 yě kěyǐ *hòutuì*.	step backward/retreat
脚步有**实步**， *Jiǎobù* yǒu *shíbù*,	step, weighted step,
也有**虚步**。 yě yǒu *xūbù*.	nonweighted step
腿有时**弯**，有时**直**。 *Tuǐ* yǒushí *wān*, yǒushí *zhí*.	leg, bent, straight
太极拳有很多**基本动作**， Tàijíquán yǒu hěn duō *jīběn dòngzuò*.	basic, movement
比方说，前腿弯，后腿直，叫**弓步**。 Bǐfāngshuō, qiántuǐ wān, hòutuǐ zhí, jiào *gōngbù*.	bow stance
身体的**重心**随着动作的变化， Shēntǐ de *zhòngxīn* suízhe dòngzuò de biànhuà,	weight
向前、后、左、右**移动**。 xiàng qián, hòu, zuǒ, yòu *yídòng*.	shift
总的来说，打太极拳的时候， Zǒngdeláishuō, dǎ tàijíquán de shíhou,	

呼吸要自然，　　　　　　　　　　　　　　breathe, natural

hūxī yào zìrán,

身体要稳定，　　　　　　　　　　　　　　stable

shēntǐ yào wěndìng,

动作要协调。　　　　　　　　　　　　　　coordinated

dòngzuò yào xiétiáo.

7. Identify each item in Figure 19-4.

1)_____　　　　2)_____　　　　3)_____　　　　4)_____

5)_____　　　　6)_____　　　　7)_____

Fig. 19-4

KEY WORDS

art of boxing	拳术	quánshù	
ball	球	qiú	
basic	基本	jīběn	
basket	篮	lán	
basketball	篮球	lánqiú	
basketball court	篮球场	lánqiúchǎng	
bent	弯	wān	
block/stop	挡住	dǎngzhù	
blow	吹	chuī	
both parties	双方	shuāngfāng	
bow stance	弓步	gōngbù	
breathe	呼吸	hūxī	
butt (with one's head)	顶	dǐng	
change of service	换发球	huànfāqiú	
coordinated	协调	xiétiáo	
defend	守护	shǒuhù	
defense	防守	fángshǒu	
doubles	双打	shuāngdǎ	
end (of object)	端	duān	
end, close	结束	jiéshù	
exercise	运动	yùndòng	

female	女子	nǚzi	
first half	上半场	shàngbànchǎng	
fist	拳	quán	
foot	脚	jiǎo	
foot work	步法	bùfǎ	
foul	犯规	fànguī	
game	比赛	bǐsài	
goal	球门	qiúmén	
goalie	守门员	shǒuményuán	
hand form	手型	shǒuxíng	
hand position	手位	shǒuwèi	
head	头	tóu	
judge	判	pàn	
kick	踢	tī	
left end	左后卫	zuǒ hòuwèi	
leg	腿	tuǐ	
lose (a game)	输	shū	
lose (a point)	丢	diū	
make a goal	踢进一球	tījìn yì qiú	
male	男子	nánzi	
male single	男子单打	nánzi dāndǎ	

martial arts	武术	wǔshù
miss the shot	没投中	méi tóuzhòng
mixed doubles	混合双打	hùnhé shuāngdǎ
move forward	前移	qiányí
movement	动作	dòngzuò
natural	自然	zìrán
net ball	擦网球	cāwǎngqiú
nonweighted step	虚步	xū bù
no-score game	没有进球	méiyǒu jìnqiú
opponent	对方	duìfāng
out	出界	chūjiè
over the net	打过网	dǎ guò wǎng
palm	掌	zhǎng
pass/toss	传	chuán
pingpong paddle	乒乓球拍	pīngpāngqiú pāi
player	队员	duìyuán
player	选手	xuǎnshǒu
popular	流行	liúxíng
press	按	àn
push	推	tuī
quick attack	抢攻	qiǎnggōng
racket	网球拍	wǎngqiúpāi
referee	裁判员	cáipànyuán
return	接球	jiēqiú
score	分数	fēnshù
score	比分	bǐfēn
score a point	得一分	dé yìfēn
scoreboard	记分板	jìfēnbǎn
second half	下半场	xiàbànchǎng
serve the ball	发球	fāqiú

shift	移动	yídòng
shoot a basket	投篮	tóulán
singles	单打	dāndǎ
slam	抽	chōu
slam dunk	扣篮	kòulán
slice the ball	削球	xiāoqiú
soccer	足球	zúqiú
soccer field	足球场	zúqiúchǎng
spinning ball	转球	zhuàn qiú
sports	体育运动	tǐyù yùndòng
sportsmen	运动员	yùndòngyuán
stable	稳定	wěndìng
steal	抢走	qiǎngzǒu
step	脚步	jiǎobù
step backward	后退	hòutuì
straight	直	zhí
table	球桌/台	qiúzhuō/tái
table tennis	乒乓球	pīngpāng qiú
Tai Chi	太极拳	tàijíquán
team	队	duì
tennis	网球	wǎngqiú
tennis court	网球场	wǎngqiúchǎng
three to two	三比二	sān bǐ èr
tied	平局	píngjú
tight (maneuver)	严密	yánmì
tournament	比赛	bǐsài
weight	重心	zhòngxīn
weighted step	实步	shí bù
whistle	哨子	shàozi
win	赢/胜	yíng/ shèng
workout	健身运动	jiànshēn yùndòng

Chapter 20: Computer and Internet

第二十章：电脑和因特网

        Diànnǎo hé Yīntèwǎng

COMPUTER PARTS AND FUNCTIONS

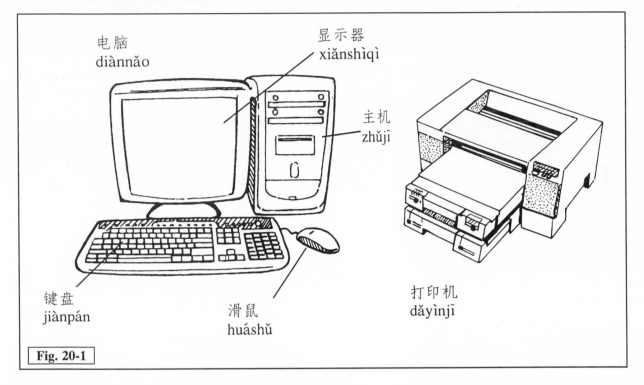

电脑
diànnǎo

显示器
xiǎnshìqì

主机
zhǔjī

键盘
jiànpán

滑鼠
huáshǔ

打印机
dǎyìnjī

Fig. 20-1

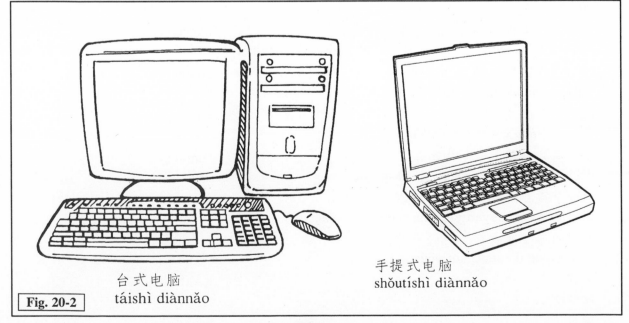

台式电脑
táishì diànnǎo

手提式电脑
shǒutíshì diànnǎo

Fig. 20-2

一般家里和公司用的**电脑**叫**个人电脑**。　　　　　　　computer, PC
Yìbān jiā lǐ hé gōngsī yòng de diànnǎo jiào *gèrén diànnǎo*.

电脑有**台式**电脑和**手提式/**电脑。　　　　　　　　　　desktop, laptop
Diànnǎo yǒu *táishì* diànnǎo he *shǒutíshì* diànnǎo.

手提式电脑又叫**笔记本**电脑　　　　　　　　　　　　　　notebook
Shǒutíshì diànnǎo yòu jiào *bǐjìběn* diànnǎo.

电脑**处理资料/数据**。　　　　　　　　　　　　　　　　process, data
Diànnǎo *chǔlǐ zīliào/shùjù*.

电脑**储存信息**。　　　　　　　　　　　　　　　　　　store, information
Diànnǎo *chǔcún xìnxī*.

电脑根据**指令**来储存信息。　　　　　　　　　　　　　instruction
Diànnǎo gēnjù *zhǐlìng* lái chǔcún xìnxī.

电脑有**硬件系统**和**软件**系统。　　　　　　　hardware, system, software
Diànnǎo yǒu *yìngjiàn xìtǒng* hé *ruǎnjiàn* xìtǒng.

电脑机和其他**有形设备**一起叫硬件。　　　　　　tangible, equipment
Diànnǎojī he qítā *yǒuxíng shèbèi* yìqǐ jiào yìngjiàn.

从外面能看到的电脑的几个**部件**是：　　　　　　component/part
Cóng wàimiàn néng kàndào de diànnǎo de jǐ ge *bùjiàn* shi:

主机　　　　　　　　　　　　　　　　　　　　main machine/tower
zhǔjī

显示器　　　　　　　　　　　　　　　　　　　monitor
xiǎnshìqì

键盘　　　　　　　　　　　　　　　　　　　　keyboard
jiànpán

滑鼠　　　　　　　　　　　　　　　　　　　　mouse
huáshǔ

主机内的**主板**和CPU是最重要的硬件。　　　　　motherboard
Zhǔjī nèi de *zhǔbǎn* he CPU shi zuì zhòngyào de yìngjiàn.

CPU就好像是电脑的"**大脑**"。　　　　　　　　　brain
CPU jiù hǎoxiàng shi diànnǎo de "*dànǎo*".

CPU的**速度**越来越快。　　　　　　　　　　　　speed
CPU de *sùdù* yuè lái yuè kuài.

比方说，**奔腾** I、II、III等等。　　　　　　　　Pentium
Bǐfāngshuō, *Bēnténg* I, II, III děngděng.

另一个重要硬件设备是**存储器**。　　　　　　　　memory
Lìng yí ge zhòngyào yìngjiàn shèbèi shi *cúnchǔqì*.

常用的存储器有：
Chángyòng de cúnchǔqì yǒu:

内存　　　　　　　　　　　　　　　　　　　　RAM
nèicún

硬盘　　　　　　　　　　　　　　　　　　　　hard disk
yìngpán

软盘 *ruǎnpán*	floppy disk
光盘 *guāngpán*	CD
内存越大，电脑的**运行**速度就越快。 Nèicún yuè dà, diànnǎo de *yùnxíng* sùdù jiù yuè kuài.	operating
用硬盘、软盘和光盘时 Yòng yìngpán, ruǎnpán he guāngpán shí,	
需要有**驱动器装置**。 xūyào yǒu *qūdòngqì zhuāngzhì.*	drive, device
起**输入**作用的硬件设备有： Qǐ *shūrù* zuòyòng de yìngjiàn shèbèi yǒu:	input
键盘、滑鼠和**扫描仪**等。 jiànpán, huáshǔ he *sǎomiáoyí* děng.	scanner
起**输出**作用的硬件设备有： Qǐ *shūchū* zuòyòng de yìngjiàn shèbèi yǒu:	output
显示器、**打印机**等。 xiǎnshìqì, *dǎyìnjī* děng.	printer

1. Identify each item in Figure 20-3.

1)_____   2)_____   3)_____   4)_____

5)_____   6)_____   7)_____   8)_____

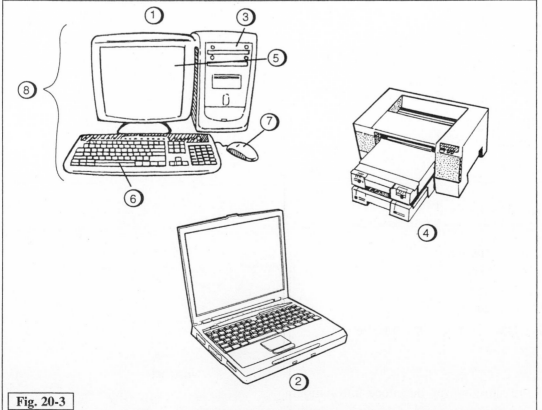

Fig. 20-3

2. Complete.

1) _____电脑又小又轻。
   _____ diànnǎo yòu xiǎo yòu qīng.

2) 电脑根据_____来处理_____。
   Diànnǎo gēnjù _____lái chǔlǐ _____.

3) 电脑有_____系统和软件系统。
   Diànnǎo yǒu _____xìtǒng hé ruǎnjiàn xìtǒng.

4) 主机、_____、键盘和滑鼠都是硬件。
   Zhǔjī, _____, jiànpán hé huáshǔ dōu shi yìngjiàn.

5) _____III是速度很快的CPU。
   _____III shi sùdù hěnkuài de CPU.

6) 现在电脑的_____越来越大，128MB已经很常见了。
   Xiànzài diànnǎo de _____yuè lái yuè dà, 128MB yǐjing hěn chángjiàn le.

7) 你可以把信息存到一个_____上，再存到另一个电脑里。
   Nǐ kěyǐ bǎ xìnxī cúndào yí ge _____shàng, zài cúndào lìng yí ge diànnǎo lǐ.

8) _____有不同的种类，比方说，CD、VCD、DVD等等。
   _____yǒu bùtóng de zhǒnglèi, bǐfāngshuō, CD, VCD, DVD děngděng.

9) 输出设备包括显示器，_____等。
   Shūchū shèbèi bāokuò xiǎnshìqì, _____děng.

10) 除了键盘和滑鼠以外，_____也常常被用来输入信息。
    Chúle jiànpán hé huáshǔ yǐwài, _____yě chángcháng bèi yòng lái shūrù xìnxī.

3. Define the following:

1) 硬件
   yìngjiàn

2) 个人电脑
   gèrén diànnǎo

3) 存储器
   cúnchǔqì

4) 台式电脑
   táishì diànnǎo.

5) 手提式电脑
   shǒutíshì diànnǎo.

MORE COMPUTER FUNCTIONS

指示电脑工作的系统叫软件。   instruct
Zhǐshì diànnǎo gōngzuò de xìtǒng jiào ruǎnjiàn.

控制电脑**操作**的一**系列**指令叫**程序**。   control, operate, series, program
Kòngzhì diànnǎo *cāozuò* de *yí xìliè* zhǐlìng jiào *chéngxù.*

操作系统是电脑中最重要的软件。   operating system
Cāozuò xìtǒng shi diànnǎo zhōng zuì zhòngyào de ruǎnjiàn.

最常用的操作系统是**视窗**系统。   Windows
Zuì chángjiàn de cāozuò xìtǒng shi *Shìchuāng* xìtǒng.

比方说视窗98中文**版**。   version
Bǐfāngshuō Shìchuāng 98 Zhōngwén *bǎn.*

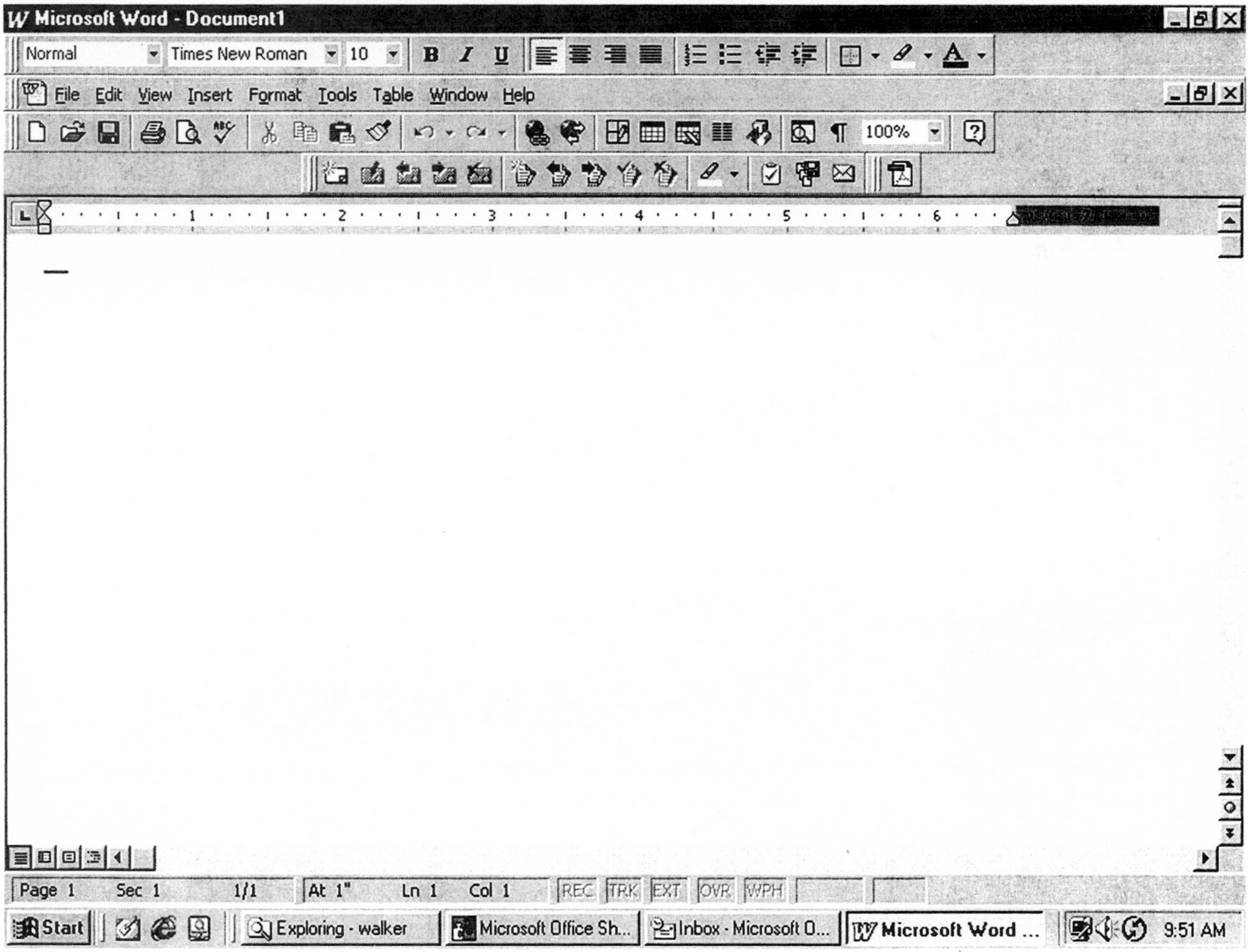

Fig. 20-4

电脑**桌面/屏幕**上有些**图标**：   desktop/screen, icon
Diànnǎo *zhuōmiàn/píngmù* shàng yǒu xiē *túbiāo*:

我的电脑   My computer
wǒde diànnǎo.

我的文档   My documents
wǒde wéndàng

回收站   Recycle Bin
huíshōuzhàn

我的公文包   My Briefcase
wǒde gōngwénbāo

双击一个图标可以开启一个程序。   double click, open
Shuāngjī yí ge túbiāo kěyǐ kāiqǐ yí ge chéngxù.

桌面的左下角是"开始"按钮。   start, button
Zhuōmiàn de zuǒ xià jiǎo shi "kāishǐ" ànjiàn.

单击"开始"会看到"开始"菜单/选项单。   single click, menu
Dānjī "kāishǐ" huì kàndào "kāishǐ" càidān/xuǎnxiàng dān.

视窗98的微软字处理窗口主要有：   Microsoft Word
Shìchuāng 98 de wēiruǎn zìchǔlǐ chuāngkǒu zhǔyào yǒu:

标题栏   title bar
biāotí lán

菜单/选项栏   menu bar
càidān/xuǎnxiàng lán

工具栏   toolbar
gōngjù lán

状态栏   status bar
zhuàngtài lán

工作区   working area
gōngzuò qū

滚动条   scroll bar
gǔndòng tiáo

4. Define the following:

1) 软件
    ruǎnjiàn

2) 程序
    chéngxù

5. Complete.

1) _____电脑工作的系统叫软件。
    _____diànnǎo gōngzuò de xìtǒng jiào ruǎnjiàn.

2) 程序是控制电脑_____的一系列指令。
    Chéngxù shi kòngzhì diànnǎo _____de yí xìliè zhǐlìng.

3) 在视窗98的桌面上有很多_____。
    Zài Shìchuāng 98 de zhuōmiàn shàng yǒu hěnduō _____.

4) _____一个图标可以打开这个程式。
    _____yí ge túbiāo kěyǐ dǎkāi zhèige chéngshì.

5) 要想打开文件，用_____栏或者_____栏都可以。
    Yào xiǎng dǎkāi wénjiàn, yòng _____lán huòzhě _____lán dōu kěyǐ.

COMPUTER APPLICATIONS

电脑可以用来做**文字处理**。 word processing
Diànnǎo kěyǐ yòng lái zuò *wénzì chǔlǐ*.

最常用的文字处理软件有
Zuì chángyòng de wénzì chǔlǐ ruǎnjiàn yǒu

美国微软公司的文字处理软件。
Měiguó Wēiruǎn Gōngsī de wénzìchǔlǐ ruǎnjiàn.

微软字处理有各种**编辑**功能。 edit
Wēiruǎn zìchǔlǐ yǒu gè zhǒng *biānjí* gōngnéng.

比方说：
Bǐfāngshuō:

保存	save
bǎocún	
另存	save as
lìngcún	
复制	copy
fùzhì	
剪切	cut
jiǎnqiē	
粘贴	paste
zhāntiē	
删除	delete
shānchú	
查找	search
cházhǎo	
拼写检查	spell check
pīnxiě jiǎnchá	

电脑还可以用来处理**数据表格**。 spreadsheet
Diànnǎo hái kěyǐ yòng lái chǔlǐ *shùjù biǎogé*.

最常用的软件是Excel和Access。
Zuì cháng yòng de ruǎnjiàn shi Excel hé Access.

只要你输入数据和**运算公式**， formula
Zhǐ yào nǐ shūrù shùjù he *yùnsuàn gōngshì*,

你就可以得到想要的数据表格。
Nǐ jiù kěyǐ dédào xiǎngyào de shùjù biǎogé.

用电脑储存信息节约很大的**空间**。 space
Yòng diànnǎo chǔcūn xìnxī jiéyuē hěn dà de *kōngjiān*.

管理信息也很简单。 manage
Guǎnlǐ xìnxī yě hěn jiǎndān.

查找资料也很方便。
Cházhǎo zīliào yě hěn fāngbiàn.

6. Complete.

1) 人们写文章的时候可以用电脑来处理_____。
   Rénmen xiě wénzhāng de shíhou kěyǐ yòng diànnǎo lái chǔlǐ _____.

2) 微软字处理是最常用的处理文档的_____。
   Wēiruǎn zìchǔlǐ shi zuì cháng yòng de chǔlǐ wéndàng de _____.

3) 用_____这个文档功能可以把一个文件存到另一个名字下。
   Yòng _____zhèige wéndàng gōngnéng kěyǐ bǎ yí ge wénjiàn cúndào lìng yí ge míngzì xià.

4) _____这个文档功能可以去掉你不想要的文字。
   _____zhèige wéndàng gōngnéng kěyǐ qùdiào nǐ bù xiǎngyào de wénzì.

5) 要想移动文本，应该先_____再_____。
   Yào xiǎng yídòng wénběn, yīnggāi xiān _____zài _____.

6) 电脑可以帮助你_____你的拼写。
   Diànnǎo kěyǐ bāngzhù nǐ _____nǐde pīnxiě.

7) 电脑也常用来处理数据_____。
   Diànnǎo yě cháng yòng lái chǔlǐ shùjù _____.

8) 做表格时得先输入数据和_____。
   Zuò biǎogé shí děi xiān shūrù shùjù hé _____.

9) 把信息存在电脑里_____起来很简单。
   Bǎ xìnxī cúnzài diànnǎo lǐ _____qǐlái hěn jiǎndān.

10) _____存在电脑里的资料也很方便。
    _____cún zài diànnǎo lǐ de zīliào yě hěn fāngbiàn.

SOME USEFUL COMPUTER EXPRESSIONS

开机   start
kāijī

关机   shut down
guānjī

退出   exit
tuìchū

重新开机   restart
chóngxīn kāijī

打印   print
dǎyìn

取消   cancel
qǔxiāo

关闭   close
guānbì

文件   file
wénjiàn

文件夹   folder
wénjiànjiá

密码   password
mìmǎo

7. Complete.

1) 使用电脑以前，你得先_____。
   Shǐyòng diànnǎo yǐqián, nǐ děi xiān _____.

2) 用完电脑以后，你就可以_____了。
   Yòng wán diànnǎo yǐhòu, nǐ jiù kěyǐ _____le.

3) 要是你给错了指令，你可以_____。
   Yàoshi nǐ gěicuòle zhǐlìng, nǐ kěyǐ _____.

4) 你可以把很多_____放在文件夹里。
   Nǐ kěyǐ bǎ hěn duō _____fàng zài wénjiànjiá lǐ.

5) 用完了一个程序，你可以从里头_____来。
   Yòngwánle yí ge chéngxù, nǐ kěyǐ cóng lǐtou _____lái.

6) _____只有你一个人知道。
   _____zhǐ yǒu nǐ yí ge rén zhīdào.

7) 打印机可以_____文件。
   Dǎyìnjī kěyǐ _____wénjiàn.

INTERNET

因特网是一个电脑的国际互联网。   Internet, international, inter-, network
Yīntèwǎng shi yí ge diànnǎo de *guójì hùlián wǎng*.

为全世界的网上用户提供信息服务。   consumer, provide, service
Wèi quán shìjiè de wǎngshàng *yònghù tígōng* xìnxī *fúwù*.

信息资料来自各国，各领域，   come from, each, field
Xìnxī zīliào *lái zì gè* guó, gè *lǐngyù*.

有文字的，声音的，图像的，   words/text, audio, visual
Yǒu *wénzì* de, *shēngyīn* de, *túxiàng* de.

最常用的万维网上有很多资料   www (worldwide web)
Zuì chángyòng de *wànwéiwǎng* shàng yǒu hěn duō zīliào.

想上网的用户要：   go on line
Xiǎng *shàngwǎng* de yònghù yào:

选择一家网上服务提供商   choose, ISP (internet service provider)
xuǎnzé yì jiā *wǎngshàng fūwù tígōng shāng*

安装调制解调器(猫)   install, modem
ānzhuāng tiáozhì jiětiáoqì (māo).

建立一个帐户   set up, account
jiànlì yí ge *zhànghù*

每次上网要：
Měi cì shàng wǎng yào:

    拨号连接   dial, connect
    bōhào liánjiē

    输入用户**姓名**和**密码**   insert, user name
    shūrù yònghù xìngmíng hé mìmǎ

    启动**浏览器**   browser
    qǐdòng *liúlǎnqì*

    比方说：Internet Explorer, Netscape
    bǐfāngshuō, Internet Explorer, Netscape

    决定要**访问**的**网站**   visit, Web site
    juédìng yào *fǎngwèn* de *wǎngzhàn*

    填入网站的**网址**。   fill in, URL
    tiánrù wǎngzhàn de *wǎngzhǐ*

浏览网页时可以   browse, Web page
Liúlǎn wǎngyè shí kěyǐ

用**后退**、**前进**去想去的网页，   back, forward
yòng *hòutuì, qiánjìn* qù xiǎng qù de wǎngyè.

也可以**下载**需要的资料。   download
yě kěyǐ *xiàzǎi* xūyào de zīliào

8. Complete.

1)   因特网是一个电脑的国际_____。
     Yīntèwǎng shi yí ge diànnǎo de guójì _____.

2)   因特网上有各种_____，比方说各国的新闻。
     Yīntèwǎng shàng yǒu gè zhǒng _____, bǐfāngshuō gè guó de xīnwén.

3)   有些资料是有声音，有_____的。
     Yǒuxiē zīliào shi yǒu shēngyīn, yǒu _____de.

4)   _____是很常用的因特网。
     _____shi hěn chángyòng de yīntèwǎng.

5)   想要上网，除了要有电脑以外，还要安装_____。
     Xiǎngyào shàng wǎng, chúle yào yǒu diànnǎo yǐwài, háiyào ānzhuāng _____.

6)   你可以向网上服务提供商申请_____。
     Nǐ kěyǐ xiàng wǎngshàng fūwù tígōng shāng shēnqǐng _____.

7)   每个用户都有一个只有自己知道的_____。
     Měi ge yònghù dōu yǒu yí ge zhí yǒu zìjǐ zhīdào de _____.

8)   Internet Explorer 是常用的_____。
     Internet Explorer shi chángyòng de _____.

9)   每一个网站都有一个_____。
     Měi yí ge wǎngzhàn dōu yǒu yí ge _____.

10) 我们可以从网上_____自己需要的资料。
     Wǒmen kěyǐ cóng wǎng shàng _____zìjǐ xūyào de zīliào.

9. Match.

1)	提供 tígōng	a.	调剂解调器 tiáojì jiětiáoqì
2)	输入 shūrù	b.	网站 wǎngzhàn
3)	浏览 liúlǎn	c.	信息服务 xìnxī fúwù
4)	安装 ānzhuāng	d.	资料 zīliào
5)	访问 fǎngwèn	e.	密码 mìmǎ
6)	下载 xiàzǎi	f.	网页 wǎngyè

EMAIL

电子邮件(电邮)就是网上的信件。 *Diànzǐ yóujiàn (diànyóu)* jiù shi wǎngshàng de xìnjiàn.	e-mail
写电子邮件时要先打开"**新邮件**" Xiě diànzǐ yóujiàn shí yào xiān dǎkāi "*xīn yóujiàn*".	new mail
填好**收件人**的**电子邮箱地址**。 Tiánhǎo *shōujiànrén* de *diànzi yóuxiāng dìzhǐ*.	recipient, e-mail address
打好邮件的**题目**， Dǎhǎo yóujiàn de *tímù*,	subject
再写好信，就可以**发送**了。 Zài xiěhǎo xìn, jiù kěyǐ *fāsòng* le.	send
来信在**收信箱**里。 Láixìn zài *shōuxìnxiāng* lǐ.	in-box
你也可以给别人**回信**。 Nǐ yě kěyǐ gěi biérén *huíxìn*.	reply
不需要的邮件可以删除。 Bù xūyào de yóujiàn kěyǐ shānchú.	

10. Answer.

1) 电子邮件和普通邮件有什么不同？
   Diànzǐ yóujiàn he pǔtōng yóujiàn yǒu shénme bùtóng?

2) 收件人的地址叫什么？
   Shōujiànrén de dìzhǐ jiào shénme?

3) 在什么地方可以找到别人给你的电子邮件？
   Zài shénme dìfang kěyǐ zhǎodào biérén gěi nǐ de diànzǐ yóujiàn?

4) 写好的信件怎么办?
   Xiěhǎo de xìnjiàn zěnme bàn?

5) 朋友给你写信你应该怎么办?
   Péngyǒu gěi nǐ xiěxìn nǐ yīnggāi zěnme bàn?

5) 不需要的信件怎么办?
   Bù xūyào de xìnjiàn zěnme bàn?

KEY WORDS

account	帐户	zhànghù	go on line	上网	shàngwǎng
audio	声音	shēngyīn	hard disk	硬盘	yìngpán
back	后退	hòutuì	hardware	硬件	yìngjiàn
brain	大脑	dànǎo	icon	图标	túbiāo
browse	浏览	liúlǎn	in-box	收信箱	shōuxìnxiāng
browser	浏览器	liúlǎnqì	information	信息	xìnxī
button	按钮	ànniǔ	input	输入	shūrù
cancel	取消	qǔxiāo	insert	插入、填入	chārù, tiánrù
CD	光盘	guāngpán			
choose	选择	xuǎnzé	install	安装	ānzhuāng
close	关闭	guānbì	instruct	指示	zhǐshì
come from	来自	lái zì	instruction	指令	zhǐlìng
component	部件	bùjiàn	inter-	互联	hùlián
connect	连接	liánjiē	international	国际	guójì
consumer	用户	yònghù	Internet	因特网	yīntèwǎng
control	控制	kòngzhì	ISP	网上服务	wǎngshàng fúwù
copy	复制	fùzhì	(internet	提供商	tígōng shāng
cut	剪切	jiǎnqiē	service		
data	资料/数据	zīliào/shùjù	provider)		
delete	删除	shānchú	keyboard	键盘	jiànpán
desktop	台式	táishì	laptop	手提式	shǒutíshì
desktop/screen	桌面/屏幕	zhuōmiàn/píngmù	main machine,	主机	zhǔjī
device	装置	zhuāngzhì	tower		
dial	拨号	bōhào	manage	管理	guǎnlǐ
double click	双击	shuāngjí	memory	存储器	cǔnchǔqì
download	下载	xiàzǎi	menu	菜单/选项单	càidān/xuǎnxiàng dān
drive	驱动器	qūdòngqì			
each	各	gè	menu bar	菜单/选项栏	càidān/xuǎnxiàng lán
edit	编辑	biānjí			
e-mail	电子邮件(电邮)	diànzǐ yóujiàn (diànyóu)	Microsoft Word	微软字处理	Wēiruǎn Zìchǔlǐ
e-mail address	电子邮箱地址	diànzǐ yóuxiāng dìzhǐ	modem	调制解调器(猫)	tiáozhì jiětiáoqì (māo)
equipment	设备	shèbèi	monitor	显示器	xiǎnshìqì
exit	退出	tuìchū	motherboard	主板	zhǔbǎn
field	领域	lǐngyù	mouse	滑鼠	huáshǔ
file, document	文件	wénjiàn	My Briefcase	我的公文包	wǒde gōngwénbāo
fill in	填入	tiánrù			
floppy disk	软盘	ruǎnpán	My Computer	我的电脑	wǒde diànnǎo
folder	文件夹	wénjiànjiá	My Documents	我的文档	wǒde wéndàng
formula	运算公式	yùnsuàn gōngshì	Net, network	网	wǎng
forward	前进	qiánjìn	new mail	新邮件	xīn yóujiàn
function	功能	gōngnéng	notebook	笔记本	bǐjìběn

open	开启/打开	kāiqǐ/dǎkāi	shut down	关机	guānjī
operate	操作	cāozuò	single click	单击	dān jī
operating	运行	yùnxíng	software	软件	ruǎnjiàn
operating system	操作系统	cāozuò xìtǒng	space	空间	kōngjiān
			speed	速度	sùdù
output	输出	shūchū	spell check	拼写检查	pīnxiě jiǎnchá
paste	粘贴	zhāntiē	spreadsheet	数据表格	shùjù biǎogé
PC	个人电脑	gèrén diànnǎo	start	开始/开机	kāishǐ/kāijī
Pentium	奔腾	Bēnténg	status bar	状态栏	zhuàngtài lán
print	打印	dǎyìn	store	储存	chǔcún
printer	打印机	dǎyìnjī	subject	题目	tímù
process	处理	chǔlǐ	system	系统	xìtǒng
program	程序	chéngxù	tangible	有形的	yǒuxíng de
provide	提供	tígōng	title bar	标题栏	biāotí lán
RAM	内存	nèicún	toolbar	工具栏	gōngjù lán
recipient	收件人	shōujiàn rén	URL	网址	wǎngzhǐ
Recycle Bin	回收站	huíshōu zhàn	user name	用户姓名	yònghù xìngmíng
reply	回信	huíxìn	version	版	bǎn
restart	重新开机	chóngxīn kāijī	visit	访问	fǎngwèn
save	保存	bǎocún	visual	图像	túxiàng
save as	另存	lìngcún	Web page	网页	wǎngyè
scanner	扫描仪	sǎomiáoyí	Web site	网站	wǎngzhàn
scroll bar	滚动条	gǔndòng tiáo	Windows	视窗	Shìchuāng
search	查找	cházhǎo	word processing	文字处理	wénzì chǔlǐ
sent	发送	fāsòng			
series	系列	xìliè	words/text	文字	wénzì
service	服务	fúwù	working area	工作区	gōngzuò qū
set up	建立	jiànlì	www	万维网	wànwéiwǎng

Chapter 21: The weather
第二十一章：天气
Tiānqì

今天**天气很好**。 Jīntiān *tiānqi hěn hǎo.*	nice weather
不好 *bù hǎo.*	bad
很**冷** hěn *lěng*	cold
很**热** hěn *rè*	hot
很**凉快** hěn *liángkuài*	cool
很**暖和** hěn *nuǎnhuo*	warm
很**闷热** hěn *mēnrè*	humid
很**晴朗** hěn *qínglǎng*	sunny
明天**风很大**。 Míngtiān *fēng hěn dà*	windy
摄氏30度 *shèshì sānshí dù*	30 degrees centigrade
是**晴天** shi *qíngtiān.*	fine, clear
阴天 *yīntiān*	overcast
多云 *duōyún*	cloudy
有**大风** yǒu *dàfēng*	gusty wind
有**台风** yǒu *táifēng*	typhoon
有**雨** yǒu *yǔ*	rain
有**阵雨** yǒu *zhènyǔ*	shower

有**雷雨**   thunderstorm
yǒu *léiyǔ*

有**雪**   snow
yǒu *xuě*

有**暴风雪**   snowstorm, blizzard
yǒu *bàofēngxuě*

有**雾**   fog
yǒu *wù*

现在正在**下雨**。   rain
Xiànzài zhèng zài *xiàyǔ*.

下小雨   drizzle
xià xiǎoyǔ

下雪   snow
xiàxuě

下冰雹   hail
xià bīngbáo

打雷   thunder
dǎléi

闪电   lightning
shǎndiàn

1. Complete.

1) 这儿夏天很_____，也很_____。
 Zhèr xiàtiān hěn _____, yě hěn _____.

2) 冬天这儿很_____，常常_____。
 Dōngtiān zhèr hěn _____, chángcháng _____.

3) 每年夏天这儿都很热，可是今年夏天这儿很_____。
 Měi nián xiàtiān zhèr dōu hěn rè, kěshì jīnnián xiàtiān zhèr hěn _____.

4) 春天来了，天气开始_____了。
 Chūntiān lái le, tiānqi kāishǐ _____ le.

5) 明天没有雨，明天是_____。
 Míngtiān méiyǒu yǔ, míngtiān shi _____.

6) 今天上午多云，下午有小_____。
 Jīntiān shàngwǔ duōyún, xiàwǔ yǒu xiǎo _____.

7) 明天是_____，没有太阳。
 Míngtiān shi _____, méiyǒu tàiyang.

8) 现在_____很大，我什么都看不见。
 Xiànzài _____ hěn dà, wǒ shénme dōu kàn bú jiàn.

9) 外头在闪电。你听见打_____了吗?
 Wàitou zài shǎndiàn. Nǐ tīngjiàn dǎ _____ le ma?

10) 今天＿＿＿＿38度，非常热。
Jīntiān ＿＿＿＿sānshibā dù, fēicháng rè.

2. Tell more about the weather.

1) 今天是晴天，＿＿＿＿＿＿＿＿＿＿＿＿＿＿＿＿＿＿＿＿＿＿＿＿＿＿＿＿＿。
Jīntiān shi qíngtiān,

2) 明天是阴天，＿＿＿＿＿＿＿＿＿＿＿＿＿＿＿＿＿＿＿＿＿＿＿＿＿＿＿＿＿。
Míngtiān shi yīntiān.

3) 明天天气很不好，＿＿＿＿＿＿＿＿＿＿＿＿＿＿＿＿＿＿＿＿＿＿＿＿＿。
Míngtiān tiānqi hěn bù hǎo,

3. Give a word or phrase related to each of the following:

1) 晴朗
qínglǎng

2) 摄氏40度
shèshì sìshí dù

3) 下雨
xiàyǔ

4) 台风
táifēng

5) 摄氏0度
shèshì líng dù

6) 雷雨
léiyǔ

7) 闷
mēn

8) 云
yún

4. Write true (T), or false (F).

1) 晴天的时候，有很多云。
Qíngtiān de shíhou, yǒu hěn duō yún.

2) 晴天的时候，没什么云，阳光很好。
Qíngtiān de shíhou, méi shénme yún, yángguāng hěn hǎo.

3) 下暴风雪的时候，又打雷，又闪电。
Xià bàofēngxuě de shíhou, yòu dǎléi, yòu shǎndiàn.

4) 下小雨的时候，常常有雹子。
Xià xiǎoyǔ de shíhou, chángcháng yǒu báozi.

5) 台风来的时候，常常风很大，雨也很大。
Táifēng lái de shíhou, chángcháng fēng hěn dà, yǔ yě hěn dà.

6) 今天摄氏37度，人们都觉得很凉快。
   Jīntiān shèshì sānshíqī dù, rénmen dōu juéde hěn liángkuài.

7) 有雾的时候，最好不要开车。
   Yǒu wù de shíhou, zuìhǎo bú yào kāichē.

8) 下阵雨的时候，一会儿有雨，一会儿没有雨。
   Xià zhènyǔ de shíhou, yí huǐr yǒu yǔ, yí huǐr méiyǒu yǔ.

5. Read the following weather reports, and then answer the questions:

Report 1

今天白天多云转阴，有阵雨。今天傍晚有雷雨，东南风，风力
Jīntiān báitiān duōyún zhuǎn yīn, yǒu zhènyǔ. Jīntiān bàngwǎn yǒu léiyǔ, dōngnán fēng, fēnglì
5-6级[1]。最高温度摄氏28度。最低温度22度。
wǔ dào liù jí. Zuì gāo wēndù shèshì èrshíbā dù. Zuì dī wēndù èrshíèr dù.

1) 今天天气怎么样？
   Jīntiān tiānqi zěnmeyàng?

2) 今天会一直多云吗？
   Jīntiān huì yìzhí duōyún ma?

3) 有太阳吗？
   Yǒu tàiyáng ma?

4) 有雪吗？
   Yǒu xuě ma?

5) 晚上天气怎么样？
   Wǎnshang tiānqi zěnmeyàng?

6) 风从什么方向来？
   Fēng cóng shénme fāngxiàng lái?

7) 风多大？
   Fēng duō dà?

8) 最高温度是多少？
   Zuì gāo wēndù shi duōshǎo?

9) 最低温度是多少？
   Zuì dī wēndù shi duōshǎo?

10) 今天冷不冷？
    Jīntiān lěng bù lěng?

Report 2

今天夜间晴，风力1-2级，最低气温摄氏3度。明天白天多云
Jīntiān yèjiān qíng, fēnglì yī dào èr jí, zuì dī qìwēn shèshì sān dù. Míngtiān báitiān duōyún

---

[1] In weather reports in China , "级" denotes measure of degrees regarding wind force on the Beaufort Scale.

转阴，下午有雪。最高气温0度，最低气温0下4度。
zhuǎn yīn. Xiàwǔ yǒu xuě. Zuì gāo qìwēn líng dù, zuì dī qìwēn língxià sì dù.

1) 今天夜里比明天白天冷，对不对？
   Jīntiān yèlǐ bǐ míngtiān báitiān lěng, duì bú duì?

2) 今天夜里有雨没有？
   Jīntiān yèli yǒu yǔ méiyǒu?

3) 明天从早上开始下雪，对不对？
   Míngtiān cóng zǎoshang kāishǐ xiàxuě, duì bú duì?

4) 明天冷还是热？
   Míngtiān lěng háishi rè?

5) 明天最高气温是多少？
   Míngtiān zuì gāo qìwēn shi duōshǎo?

6) 明天最低气温是多少？
   Míngtiān zuì dī qìwēn shi duōshǎo?

7) 明天有太阳吗？
   Míngtiān yǒu tàiyang ma?

8) 今天夜里有大风吗？
   Jīntiān yèli yǒu dàfēng ma?

9) 今天夜里的最低气温比明天白天的最低气温高7度，对不对？
   Jīntiān yèlǐ de zuì dī qìwēn bǐ míngtiān báitiān de zuì dī qìwēn gāo qīdù, duì bú duì?

10) 现在是冬天还是夏天？
    Xiànzài shi dōngtiān háishi xiàtiān?

KEY WORDS

bad	不好	bùhǎo	lightning	闪电	shǎndiàn
centigrade	摄氏	shèshì	nice	很好	hěn hǎo
cloudy	多云	duōyún	overcast	阴天	yīntiān
cold	冷	lěng	rain	雨,下雨	yǔ, xiàyǔ
cool	凉快	liángkuài	shower	阵雨	zhènyǔ
degree (temperature)	度	dù	snow	雪,下雪	xuě, xiàxuě
degree (wind force)	级	jí	snowstorm, blizzard	暴风雪	bàofēngxuě
drizzle	下小雨	xià xiǎoyǔ	sunny	晴朗	qínglǎng
fine, clear	晴天	qíngtiān	thunder	雷,打雷	léi, dǎléi
fog	雾	wù	thunderstorm	雷雨	léiyǔ
gusty wind	大风	dàfēng	typhoon	台风	táifēng
hail	冰雹	bīngbáo	warm	暖和	nuǎnhuó
hot	热	rè	weather	天气	tiānqì
humid	闷热, 湿热	mēnrè, shīrè	windy	风很大	fēng hěn dà

Chapter 22: Education

第二十二章：教育
Jiàoyù

ELEMENTARY SCHOOL

这儿有**公立学校**也有**私立**学校。 public school, private
Zhèr yǒu *gōnglì xuéxiào* yě yǒu *sīlì* xuéxiào.

6岁以下的孩子/儿童上**幼儿园**。 nursery school, kindergarten
Liù suì yǐxià de háizi/értóng shàng *yòuéryuán*.

6岁开始上**小学**。 elementary school
Liù suì kāishǐ shàng *xiǎoxué*.

小学有一**年级**到六年级。 first grade
Xiǎoxué yǒu *yī niánjí* dào liù niánjí.

小学**老师**教小学生。 teacher, teach, students
Xiǎoxué *lǎoshī jiāo* xiǎo *xuéshēng*.

学生天天**学习**。 study
Xuéshēng tiāntiān *xuéxí*.

老师天天**教课/教书**。 teach
Lǎoshī tiāntiān *jiāokè/jiāoshū*.

他们在**黑板**上写字。 blackboard
Tāmen zài *hēibǎn* shàng xiězì.

学生的**课本**在**课桌**上。 textbook, desk
Xuéshēng de *kèběn* zài *kèzhuō* shàng.

老师**念课文**。 read aloud, the text
Lǎoshī *niàn kèwén*.

校长到**教室**里来了。 principal, classroom
Xiàozhǎng dào *jiàoshì* lǐ lái le.

1. Match.

1) 小学生   a. 六岁以下的孩子学习的地方
    xiǎoxuéshēng   liùsuì yǐxià de háizi xuéxí de dìfang

2) 教室   b. 管理一个学校的人
    jiàoshì   guǎnlǐ yí ge xuéxiào de rén

3) 教课   c. 小学生在学校里做的事
    jiāokè   xiǎoxuéshēng zài xuéxiào lǐ zuò de shì

4) 小学   d. 在小学学习的学生
    xiǎoxué   zài xiǎoxué xuéxí de xuéshēng

5) 幼儿园   e. 学生上课用的书
    yòuéryuán   xuéshēng shàngkè yòng de shū

6) 老师   f. 一到六年级的学校
    lǎoshī   yī dào liù niánjí de xuéxiào

7) 学习   g. 学生上课的地方
    xuéxí   xuéshēng shàngkè de dìfang

8) 课本   h. 老师的工作
    kèběn   lǎoshī de gōngzuò

9) 校长   i. 在学校教书的人
    xiàozhǎng   zài xuéxiào jiāoshū de rén

10) 私立学校   j. 学生自己交钱的学校
    sīlì xuéxiào   xuéshēng zìjǐ jiāo qián de xuéxiào

2. Complete.

六岁以下的孩子上 __1__。小学生一般从一 __2__ 上到六 __3__。在小学教书
Liù suì yǐxià de háizi shàng __1__. Xiǎoxuéshēng yìbān cóng yī __2__ shàng dào liù __3__. Zài xiǎoxué jiāoshū

的人叫 __4__。老师教学生 __5__。老师在 __6__ 上写字。
de rén jiào __4__. Lǎoshī jiāo xiǎo xuéshēng __5__. Lǎoshī zài __6__ shàng xiězì.

MIDDLE /HIGH /SECONDARY SCHOOL

学生上完小学，就上**中学**。   high/middle/secondary school
Xuéshēng shàngwán xiǎoxué, jiù shàng *zhōngxué*.

中学有**初中**和**高中**。   junior high, senior high
Zhōngxué yǒu *chūzhōng* hé *gāozhōng*.

先上初中，再上高中。
Xiān shàng chūzhōng, zài shàng gāozhōng.

学生有**走读生**也有**寄宿生**。   day student, boarder/resident student
Xuéshēng yǒu *zǒudúshēng* yě yǒu *jìsùshēng*.

有些私立学校要求学生穿**校服**。   school uniform
Yǒuxiē sīlì xuéxiào yāoqiú xuéshēng chuān *xiàofú*.

学生的**书包**里有很多书。   schoolbag
Xuéshēng de *shūbāo* lǐ yǒu hěn duō shū.

他们每天都**上课**。   attend class
Tāmen měi tiān dōu *shàngkè*.

他们得上很多门**课**。   subject, course
Tāmen děi shàng hěn duō mén *kè*.

每一门课有一个不同的**老师讲课**。   lecture
Měi yì mén kè yǒu yí ge bùtóng de lǎoshī *jiǎngkè*.

学生一边**听课**，一边**记笔记**。   listen to lecture, take notes
Xuéshēng yìbiān *tīngkè*, yìbiān *jì bǐjì*.

学生**放学以后**常常要**做功课**。   after school, do homework
Xuéshēng *fàngxué* yǐhòu chángcháng yào *zuò gōngkè*.

他们常常用**铅笔**或者是**圆珠笔**写字。   pencil, ballpoint pen
Tāmen chángcháng yòng *qiānbǐ* huòzhě shi *yuánzhūbǐ* xiězì.

他们常常有**考试**。   test/exam
Tāmen chángcháng yǒu *kǎoshì*.

人人都想考好**分数**。100分是最高分。   grade/score
Rénrén dōu xiǎng kǎo hǎo *fēnshù*. Yìbǎi fēn shi zuì gāo fēn.

3. Answer.

1) 谁上中学？
   Shéi shàng zhōngxué?

2) 谁教中学？
   Shéi jiāo zhōngxué?

3) 什么样的学生住在学校里？
   Shénmeyàng de xuéshēng zhù zài xuéxiào lǐ?

4) 什么样的学生天天回家？
   Shénmeyàng de xuéshēng tiāntiān huíjiā?

5) 装书的包叫什么？
   Zhuāng shū de bāo jiào shénme?

6) 中学生只上英文课吗？
   Zhōngxuéshēng zhǐ shàng Yīngwén kè ma?

7) 上课的时候老师做什么？学生做什么？
   Shàngkè de shíhòu lǎoshī zuò shénme? Xuéshēng zuò shénme?

8) 上学穿的一样的衣服叫什么？
   Shàngxué chuān de yíyàng de yīfu jiào shénme?

9) 放学以后学生还要做什么事？
   Fàngxué yǐhòu xuéshēng hái yào zuò shénme shì?

10) 他们用什么写字？
    Tāmen yòng shénme xiězì?

11) 他们有考试吗？
    Tāmen yǒu kǎoshì ma?

12) 他们都想得什么分数？
    Tāmen dōu xiǎng dé shénme fēnshù?

4. Choose the appropriate word.

1) 上完_____上中学。   a. 幼儿园   b. 小学
   Shàngwán _____ shàng zhōngxué.   yòuéryuán   xiǎoxué

2) _____不每天回家。   a. 走读生   b. 寄宿生
   _____ bù měi tiān huíjiā.   zǒudúshēng   jìsùshēng

3) _____讲课。   a. 老师   b. 学生
   _____jiǎngkè.   lǎoshī   xuéshēng

4) 学生把书放在_____里。   a. 校服   b. 书包
   Xuéshēng bǎ shū fàng zài _____ lǐ.   xiàofú   shūbāo

5) 学生下课以后要_____。   a. 考试   b. 做功课
   Xuéshēng xiàkè yǐhòu yào _____.   kǎoshì   zuò gōngkè

5. Complete.

1) 在中国，一个中学常常有初中，也有_____。
   Zài Zhōngguó, yí ge zhōngxué chángcháng yǒu chūzhōng, yě yǒu _____.

2) _____常常是三年，高中也是三年。
   _____chángcháng shì sān nián, gāozhōng yě shì sān nián.

3) 初中一年级的学生叫初一_____。高中二年级的学生叫高二学生。
   Chūzhōng yī niánjí de xuéshēng jiào chūyī _____. Gāozhōng èr niánjí de xuéshēng jiào gāoèr xuéshēng.

4) 中学生每天都要上很多_____课。
   Zhōng xuéshēng měi tiān dōu yào shàng hěn duō _____kè.

5) 大家都觉得_____分是好分数。
   Dàjiā dōu juéde _____fēn shi hǎo fēnshù.

UNIVERSITY

他参加了**高考**。   college entrance exam
Tā cānjiā le *gāokǎo.*

他**考上**了北京**大学**。   be admitted by, university/college
Tā *kǎoshàng* le Běijīng *Dàxué.*

他是中文**系文学专业**的学生。   department, literature, major
Tā shi Zhōngwén *xì wénxué zhuānyè* de xuéshēng.

他要在大学学四年。
Tā yào zài dàxué xué sì nián.

学校**开学**了。   school starts
Xuéxiào *kāixué* le.

他到学校去**注册**。   register
Tā dào xuéxiào qù *zhùcè.*

他**申请**了**奖学金**。   apply for, scholarship
Tā *shēnqǐng*le *jiǎngxuéjīn.*

学费很贵。   tuition
Xuéfèi hěn guì.

一年有两个**学期**。   semester
Yì nián yǒu liǎng ge *xuéqī.*

这个学期他一共有**5门课**。   five courses
Zhèi ge xuéqī tā yígòng yǒu *wǔ mén kè.*

他还想**旁听**一门课。   audit
Tā hái xiǎng *pángtīng* yì mén kè.

一个**教授**正在讲课。   professor
Yí ge *jiàoshòu* zhèngzài jiǎngkè.

学生在**笔记本**上记笔记。   notebook
Xuéshēng zài *bǐjì běn* shàng jì bǐjì.

他快**毕业**了。   graduate
Tā kuài *bìyè* le.

毕业的时候，他可以得到**毕业证书**。   diploma
Bìyè de shíhòu, tā kěyǐ dédào *bìyè zhèngshū*.

他得到了**学士学位**。   bachelor, degree
Tā dédàole *xuéshì xuéwèi*.

他还想读**硕士**。   master
Tā hái xiǎng dú *shuòshì*.

      博士   doctor/Ph.D.
      bóshì

大学常常分成不同的**学院**。   school
Dàxué chángcháng fēnchéng bùtóng de *xuéyuàn*.

比方说：**文学院**   school of arts and humanities
Bǐfāngshuō, *wén xuéyuàn*

      理学院   school of science
      lǐ xuéyuàn

      工学院   engineering school
      gōng xuéyuàn

      法学院   law school
      fǎ xuéyuàn

      医学院   medical school
      yī xuéyuàn

各个学院有不同的系。
Gè ge xuéyuàn yǒu bùtóng de xì.

大学生住在学生**宿舍**里。   dormitory
Dà xuéshēng zhù zài xuéshēng *sùshè* lǐ.

大学里有学生**食堂**。   canteen/cafeteria
Dàxué lǐ yǒu xuéshēng *shítáng*.

6. Give the word being defined.

1) 大学的入学考试
    dàxué de rùxué kǎoshì

2) 学生交给学校的钱
    xuéshēng jiāo gěi xuéxiào de qián

3) 上课的第一天
    shàngkè de dì yī tiān

4) 申请到的帮你交学费的钱
   shēnqǐng dào de bāng nǐ jiāo xuéfèi de qián

5) 念完学士以后的学位
   niànwán xuéshì yǐhòu de xuéwèi

6) 教大学的人
   jiāo dàxué de rén

7) 毕业时得到的东西
   bìyè shí dédào de dōngxi

8) 在大学里得到的最高学位
   zài dàxué lǐ dédào de zuì gāo xuéwèi

9) 学生住的地方
   xuéshēng zhù de dìfang

10) 学校里学生吃饭的地方
    xuéxiào lǐ xuéshēng chīfàn de dìfang

7. Complete.

1) 要是你想上大学，你就得参加_____。
   Yàoshi nǐ xiǎng shàng dàxué, nǐ jiù děi cānjiā _____.

2) 他想当律师，就得上_____。
   Tā xiǎng dāng lǜshī, jiù děi shàng _____.

3) 她是学文学的，在念_____院。
   Tā shì xué wénxué de, zài niàn _____yuàn.

4) 现在大学的____很贵，所以很多学生都申请了_____。
   Xiànzài dàxué de _____hěn guì, suǒyǐ hěn duō xuéshēng dōu shēnqǐngle _____.

5) 在中国，九月一号常常是_____的第一天。
   Zài Zhōngguó, jiǔ yuè yī hào cháng cháng shi _____de dì yī tiān.

6) 开学的时候，学生们都得回校_____。
   Kāixué de shíhòu, xuéshēngmen dōu děi huíxiào _____.

8. Answer.

1) 学生在开学的时候要做什么？
   Xuéshēng zài kāixué de shíhòu yào zuò shénme?

2) 如果上大学的钱不够，你怎么办？
   Rúguǒ shàng dàxué de qián bú gòu, nǐ zěnme bàn?

3) 上课的时候，学生要做什么？
   Shàngkè de shíhòu, xuéshēng yào zuò shénme?

4) 毕业的时候学生得到的文件叫什么？
   Bìyè de shíhòu xuéshēng dé dào de wénjiàn jiào shénme?

5) 硕士生毕业时拿到的学位是什么？
   Shuòshìshēng bìyè de shíhòu nádào de xuéwèi shi shénme?

9. Tell in which school one would enroll if one wished to become the following.

1) 医生
   yīshēng

2) 律师
   lùshī

3) 电脑工程师
   diànnǎo gōngchéngshī

4) 文学教授
   wénxué jiàoshòu

5) 数学家
   shùxuéjiā

KEY WORDS

after school	放学以后	fàngxué yǐhòu	literature	文学	wénxué
apply for	申请	shēnqǐng	major	专业	zhuānyè
attend class	上课	shàngkè	master	硕士	shuòshì
audit	旁听	pángtīng	medical school	医学院	yīxuéyuàn
bachelor	学士	xuéshì	notebook	笔记本	bǐjì běn
ballpoint pen	圆珠笔	yuánzhū bǐ	nursery school/	幼儿园	yòuéryuán
be admitted by	考上	kǎoshàng	kindergarten		
blackboard	黑板	hēibǎn	pencil	铅笔	qiānbǐ
boarder, resident	寄宿生	jìsùshēng	principal	校长	xiàozhǎng
student			private	私立	sīlì
canteen/cafeteria	食堂	shítáng	professor	教授	jiàoshòu
classroom	教室	jiàoshì	public	公立	gōnglì
college entrance	高考	gāokǎo	read aloud	念	niàn
exam			register (at schhol)	注册	zhùcè
day student	走读生	zǒudúshēng	scholarship	奖学金	jiǎngxuéjin
degree	学位	xuéwèi	school	学校	xuéxiào
department	系	xì	school	学院	xuéyuàn
desk	课桌	kèzhuō	school of arts and	文学院	wénxuéyuàn
diploma	毕业证书	bìyè zhèngshū	humanities		
do homework	做功课	zuò gōngkè	school of science	理学院	lǐxuéyuàn
doctor/Ph.D.	博士	bóshì	school starts	开学	kāixué
dormitory	宿舍	sùshè	school uniform	校服	xiàofú
education	教育	jiàoyù	schoolbag	书包	shūbāo
elementary school	小学	xiǎoxué	semester	学期	xuéqī
engineering	工学院	gōngxuéyuàn	senior high	高中	gāozhōng
school			student	学生	xuéshēng
first grade	一年级	yì niánjí	study	学习	xuéxí
five courses	5门课	wǔ mén kè	subject/course	(一门)课	(yì mén) kè
grade/score	分数	fēnshù	take notes	做/记笔记	zuò/jì bǐjì
graduate	毕业	bìyè	teach	教(书)/(课)	jiāo(shū)/(kè)
high/middle	中学	zhōngxué	teacher	老师	lǎoshī
school			test/exam	考试	kǎoshì
junior high	初中	chūzhōng	textbook	课本	kèběn
law school	法学院	fǎxuéyuàn	the text	课文	kèwén
lecture	讲课	jiǎngkè	tuition	学费	xuéfèi
listen to lecture	听课	tīngkè	university/college	大学	dàxué

Chapter 23: Business

第二十三章：商业
Shāngyè

BUSINESS

商业经营主要是指生产和销售产品。   business, produce, sell, products
Shāngyè jīngyíng zhǔyào shi zhǐ *shēngchǎn* hé *xiāoshòu* chǎnpǐn.

买方买，卖方卖。   buyer, seller
Mǎifāng mǎi, *màifāng* mài.

买东西的人是消费者。   consumer
Mǎi dōngxi de rén shi *xiāofèizhě*.

消费者为商品花钱，也为服务花钱。   goods, service
Xiāofèizhě wèi *shāngpǐn* huāqián, yě wèi *fúwù* huāqián.

卖东西的人可以批发，也可以零售。   wholesale, retail
Mài dōngxi de rén kěyǐ *pīfā,* yě kěyǐ *língshòu*.

批发商品货物的人叫批发商。   wholesalers
Pīfā shāngpǐn huòwù de rén jiào *pīfāshāng*.

零售商品货物的人叫零售商。   retailers
Língshòu shāngpǐn huòwù de rén jiào *língshòushāng*.

从国外进口商品的人叫进口商。   import
Cóng guówài *jìnkǒu* shāngpǐn de rén jiào jìnkǒushāng.

出口商品的人叫出口商。   export
Chūkǒu shāngpǐn de rén jiào chūkǒushāng.

做生意的方式有很多：   do business
Zuò shēngyì de fāngshì hěn duō.

有大公司，   corporation (big company)
yǒu *dà gōngsī,*

有合股公司。   partnership
yǒu *hégǔ gōngsī.*

合股公司有两个或者更多的合股人。   partner
Hégǔ gōngsī yǒu liǎng ge huòzhě gèng duō de *hégǔrén.*

有国营企业也有私营公司。   state-owned enterprise, private
Yǒu *guóyíng qǐyè* yě yǒu *sīyíng* gōngsī.

在一个大公司里，
Zài yí ge dà gōngsī lǐ,

所有重要的决定都由董事会来做。   board of directors

suǒyǒu zhòngyào de juédìng dōu yóu *dǒngshìhuì* lái zuò.

有些事情由公司**主管**和**经理**来决定。   chief executive, manager
Yǒu xiē shìqing yóu gōngsī *zhǔguǎn* hé *jīnglǐ* lái juédìng.

董事会永远遵照**股东**的利益来**做决定**。   stock holders, make decisions
Dǒngshìhuì yǒngyuǎn zūnzhào *gǔdōng* de lìyì lái *zuò juédìng*.

股东们**拥有股份**。   own, share
Gǔdōngmen *yōngyǒu gǔfèn*.

股票可以**盈利**。   stocks, make profit
Gǔpiào kěyǐ *yínglì*.

股票根据企业的**经营情况**而上下**浮动**。   management performance, fluctuate
Gǔpiào gēnjù qǐyè de *jīngyíng qíngkuàng* ér shàngxià *fúdòng*.

人们在**股票市场买卖/交易**股票。   stock market, trade
Rénmen zài *gǔpiào shìchǎng mǎimài/jiāoyì* gǔpiào.

1. Match the synonyms.

1) 卖东西   a. 做生意
   mài dōngxi   zuò shēngyì

2) 批发商品的人   b. 消费者
   pīfā shāngpǐn de rén   xiāofèizhě

3) 经营商业   c. 零售商
   jīngyíng shāngyè   língshòushāng

4) 买东西的人   d. 交易
   mǎi dōngxi de rén   jiāoyì

5) 零售商品的人   e. 销售产品
   língshòu shāngpǐn de rén   xiāoshòu chǎnpǐn

6) 买卖   f. 批发商
   mǎimài   pīfāshāng

2. Complete.

1) _____卖, _____买。
   _____mài, _____mǎi.

2) 买东西的人是_____。
   Mǎi dōngxi de rén shi _____.

3) 做批发生意的人叫_____。
   Zuò pīfā shēngyì de rén jiào _____.

4) 做零售生意的人叫_____。
   Zuò língshòu shēngyì de rén jiào _____.

5) 进出口货物的公司叫_____公司。
   Jìnchūkǒu huòwù de gōngsī jiào _____ gōngsī.

6) 公司有大有小。IBM是一家_____公司。
   Gōngsī yǒu dà yǒu xiǎo, IBM shi yì jiā _____ gōngsī.

7) 一个合股公司常常有两个或者更多的_____。

Yí ge hégǔ gōngsī chángcháng yǒu liǎng ge huòzhě gèng duō de _____.

8) 一个公司的主管和_____常常可以决定很多事情。

Yí ge gōngsī de zhǔguǎn hé _____ chángcháng kěyǐ juédìng hěn duō shìqing.

9) _____遵照_____的利益来做决定。

_____ zūnzhào _____ de lìyì lái zuò juédìng.

10) 人们在股票市场_____股票。

Rénmen zài gǔpiào shìchǎng _____ gǔpiào.

MARKETING

每一种产品或服务都有自己的**市场**。 Měi yì zhǒng chǎnpǐn huò fúwù dōu yǒu zìjǐ de *shìchǎng*.	market
公司的市场部负责产品的**广告**和**促销**。 Gōngsī de shìchǎng bù fùzé chǎnpǐn de *guǎnggào* hé *cùxiāo*.	advertisement, promotion
在生产新产品以前 Zài shēngchǎn xīn chǎnpǐn yǐqián,	
他们要考虑市场的**供应和需求**。 Tāmen yào kǎolù shìchǎng de *gōngyìng* hé *xūqiú*.	supply and demand
他们要**定价格**。 Tāmen yào *dìng jiàgé*.	establish a price
办企业是为了**盈利**，当然也有**支出**。 Bàn qǐyè shi wèile *yínglì*, dāngrán yě yǒu *zhīchū*.	gain profit, expense
生产产品的支出叫**成本**。 Shēngchǎn chǎnpǐn de zhīchū jiào *chéngběn*.	production cost
除去所有支出后的所得部分就是**利润**。 Chúqù suǒyǒu zhīchū hòu de suǒdé bùfèn jiù shi *lìrùn*.	profit
企业和个人一样，也要**纳税(交税、上税)**。 Qǐyè hé gèrén yíyàng, yě yào *nàshuì* (*jiāoshuì/shàngshuì*).	pay tax
他们要根据**应纳税**的收入交税。 Tāmen yào gēnjù *yīng nàshuì de shōurù* jiāo shuì.	taxable income

3. Answer.

1) 每一种产品或者服务都有什么？

Měi yì zhǒng chǎnpǐn huòzhě fúwù dōu yǒu shénme?

2) 市场部负责什么？

Shìchǎngbù fùzé shénme?

3) 企业在生产新产品以前要考虑什么？

Qǐyè zài shēngchǎn xīn chǎnpǐn yǐqián yào kǎolù shénme?

4) 办企业的目的是什么？
Bàn qǐyè de mùdì shi shénme?

5) 企业要向政府上交什么？
Qǐyè yào xiàng zhèngfǔ shàngjiāo shénme?

4. Give the word being defined.

1) 企业和个人向政府上交的钱
qǐyè hé gèrén xiàng zhèngfǔ shàngjiāo de qián

2) 负责产品宣传和促销的部门
fùzé chǎnpǐn xuānchuán hé cùxiāo de bùmén

3) 生产产品的费用
shēngchǎn chǎnpǐn de fèiyòng

4) 企业除去生产和销售支出费用后的所得部分
qǐyè chúqù shēngchǎn hé xiāoshòu zhīchū fèiyòng hòu de suǒdé bùfèn

ACCOUNTING

会计师准备财务报告。   accountant, financial statement
Kuàijìshī zhǔnbèi cáiwù bàogào.

财务报告显示公司的资产和债务。   assets, liabilities
Cáiwù bàogào xiǎnshì gōngsī de zīchǎn hé zhàiwù.

资产负债表是很重要的财务报表   balance sheet
Zīchǎn fùzhài biǎo shi hěn zhòngyào de cáiwù bàobiǎo.

如果一家企业不盈利，
Rúguǒ yì jiā qǐyè bù yínglì,

它可能会有亏损。   loss/deficit
Tā kěnéng huì yǒu kuīsǔn.

最后它就要破产。   bankruptcy
Zuìhòu tā jiù yào pòchǎn.

5. Complete.

1) 会计师在一个企业的＿＿＿＿部门工作。
Kuàijìshī zài yí ge qǐyè de ＿＿＿＿bùmén gōngzuò.

2) 会计师准备各式各样的＿＿＿＿报告。
Kuàijìshī zhǔnbèi gèshìgèyàng de ＿＿＿＿bàogào.

3) ＿＿＿＿表很重要。
＿＿＿＿biǎo hěn zhòngyào.

4) 从＿＿＿＿报告上可以看到公司的资产和债务。
Cóng ＿＿＿＿bàogào shàng kěyǐ kàndào gōngsī de zīchǎn hé zhàiwù.

5) 一个企业除掉支出以后赚的钱叫＿＿＿＿。
Yí ge qǐyè chúdiào zhīchū yǐhòu zhuàn de qián jiào ＿＿＿＿.

KEY WORDS

accountant	会计师	kuàijìshī	
advertisement	广告	guǎnggào	
assets	资产	zīchǎn	
balance sheet	资产负债表	zīchǎn fùzhài biǎo	
bankruptcy	破产	pòchǎn	
board of directors	董事会	dǒngshìhuì	
business	商业	shāngyè	
buyer	买方	mǎifāng	
chief executive	主管	zhǔguǎn	
consumer	消费者	xiāofèizhě	
corporation (big company)	大公司	dà gōngsī	
decision making	做决定	zuò juédìng	
do business	做生意	zuò shēngyì	
enterprise	企业	qǐyè	
establish a price	定价格	dìng jiàgé	
expense	支出	zhīchū	
export	出口	chūkǒu	
financial statement	财务报告	cáiwù bàogào	
fluctuate	浮动	fúdòng	
goods	商品	shāngpǐn	
import	进口	jìnkǒu	
liabilities	债务	zhàiwù	
loss, deficit	亏损	kuīsǔn	
make profit	盈利	yínglì	
management/ performance	经营情况	jīngyíng qíngkuàng	
manager	经理	jīnglǐ	

market	市场	shìchǎng	
own	拥有	yōngyǒu	
partner	合股人	hégǔrén	
partnerships	合股公司	hégǔ gōngsī	
pay tax	纳/交/上税	nà/jiāo/shàng shuì	
privately owned	私营	sīyíng	
produce	生产	shēngchǎn	
production cost	成本	chéngběn	
products	产品	chǎnpǐn	
profit	利润	lìrùn	
promotion	促销	cùxiāo	
retail	零售	língshòu	
retailer	零售商	língshòushāng	
sell	销售	xiāoshòu	
seller	卖方	màifāng	
service	服务	fúwù	
share	股份	gǔfèn	
state-owned	国营	guóyíng	
stock	股票	gǔpiào	
stock market	股票市场	gǔpiào shìchǎng	
stockholders	股东	gǔdōng	
supply and demand	供应和需求	gōngyìng hé xūqiú	
taxable income	应纳税的收入	yīng nàshuì de shōurù	
trade	买卖/交易	mǎimài/jiāoyì	
wholesale	批发	pīfā	
wholesalers	批发商	pīfāshāng	

Appendix 1: Numbers

附录1： 数 shù

一	yī	1	一百	yìbǎi	100
二	èr	2	一百零一	yìbǎilíngyī	101
三	sān	3	一百一十	yìbǎiyìshí	110
四	sì	4	一百一十一	yìbǎiyìshíyī	111
五	wǔ	5	二百	èrbǎi	200
六	liù	6	三百	sānbǎi	300
七	qī	7	四百	sìbǎi	400
八	bā	8	九百	jiǔbǎi	900
九	jiǔ	9	一千	yìqiān	1,000
十	shí	10	一千零一	yìqiānlíngyī	1,001
十一	shíyī	11	一千零二十一	yìqiānlíngèrshíyī	1,021
十二	shíèr	12	一千一百	yìqiānyìbǎi	1,100
二十	èrshí	20	一千一百零一	yìqiānyìbǎilíngyī	1,101
二十一	èrshíyī	21	一千一百一十一	yìqiānyìbǎiyìshíyī	1,111
三十	sānshí	30	二千	èrqiān	2,000
三十一	sānshíyī	31	二千零二十	èrqiānlíngèrshí	2,020
四十	sìshí	40	九千九百九十九	jiǔqiānjiǔbǎijiǔshíjiǔ	9,999
五十	wǔshí	50	一万	yíwàn	10,000
六十	liùshí	60	一万零一	yíwànlíngyī	10,001
七十	qīshí	70	十万	shíwàn	100,000
八十	bāshí	80	一百万	yìbǎiwàn	1,000,000
九十	jiǔshí	90	一千万	yìqiānwàn	10,000,000
			一亿	yíyì	100,000,000

Appendix 2: Time expressions

附录2: 时间用语 shíjiānyòngyǔ

Days of the week

今天(是)星期几?	jīntiān (shi) xīngqījǐ ?	What day (of the week) is it today?
星期一	xīngqīyī	Monday
星期二	xīngqīèr	Tuesday
星期三	xīngqīsān	Wednesday
星期四	xīngqīsì	Thursday
星期五	xīngqīwǔ	Friday
星期六	xīngqīliù	Saturday
星期天/日	xīngqītiān/rì	Sunday
星期	xīngqī	week
周末	zhōumò	weekend
周日	zhōurì	weekday
生日	shēngrì	birthday

Holidays

January 1	新年/元旦	xīnnián/yuándàn	New Year's Day
February 14	情人节	qíngrén jié	Valentine's Day
March 8	妇女节	fùnǔ jié	Women's Day
May 1	劳动节	láodòng jié	Labor Day
May 4	青年节	qīngnián jié	Youth's Day (Mainland)
June 1	儿童节	értong jié	Children's Day
October 1	国庆节	guóqìng jié	National Day (Mainland)
*January 1	春节	chūn jié	Spring Festival/ Chinese New Year
*January 15	元宵节	yuánxiāo jié	Lantern Festival
*May 5	端午节	duānwǔ jié	Dragon Boat Festival
*August 15	中秋节	zhōngqiū jié	Mid-Autumn Festival

Note: Dates marked with * are traditional holidays counted by the Lunar Calendar. Western calendar dates may differ from dates shown.

Months of the year and dates

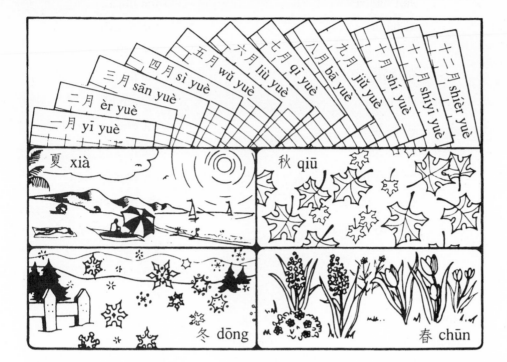

今天是几月几号/日？	Jīntiān shi jǐ yuè jǐhào/rì?	What's today's date?
今天是十二月二号/日。	Jīntiān shi shíèr yuè èr hào/rì.	It's December 2.
二零零一年八月三十号/日	èrlínglíngyī nián bāyuè sānshí hào/rì	August 30, 2001
阳历	yánglì	solar calendar
阴历	yīnlì	lunar calendar
一月	yīyuè	January
二月	èryuè	February
三月	sānyuè	March
四月	sìyuè	April
五月	wǔyuè	May
六月	liùyuè	June
七月	qīyuè	July
八月	bāyuè	August
九月	jiǔyuè	September
十月	shíyuè	October
十一月	shíyīyuè	November
十二月	shíèryuè	December
一号/日	yī hào/rì	the first

二号/日	èr hào/rì	the second
三号/日	sān hào/rì	the third
四号/日	sì hào/rì	the fourth
五号/日	wǔ hào/rì	the fifth
九号/日	jiǔ hào/rì	the ninth
十号/日	shí hào/rì	the tenth
十一号/日	shíyī hào/rì	the eleventh
二十号/日	èrshí hào/rì	the twentieth
二十一号/日	èrshíyī hào/rì	the twenty-first
三十号/日	sānshí hào/rì	the thirtieth
三十一号/日	sānshíyī hào/rì	the thirty-first

Seasons

春天	chūntiān	spring
夏天	xiàtiān	summer
秋天	qiūtiān	autumn
冬天	dōngtiān	winter

Telling time

请问现在几点?	Qǐngwèn xiànzài jǐdiǎn?	What time is it now, please?
早上	zǎoshang	morning (before 8:00am)
上午	shàngwǔ	morning (eight to twelve)
中午	zhōngwǔ	noon
下午	xiàwǔ	afternoon
晚上	wǎngshang	evening
夜里	yèlǐ	night
半夜	bànyè	midnight
凌晨	língchén	early morning (before daybreak)
一点	yī diǎn	1 o'clock
下午一点	xiàwǔ yī diǎn	1 pm
六点十分	liù diǎn shí fēn	6:10
八点差五分	bā diǎn chà wǔ fēn	five to eight (7:55)
八点零五分	bā diǎn líng wǔ fēn	8:05
三点十五分	sān diǎn shíwǔ fēn	3:15

三点一刻	sān diǎn yí kè	a quarter past three
两点三十(分)	liǎng diǎn sānshí (fēn)	2:30
两点半	liǎng diǎn bàn	half past two
十二点整	shíèr diǎn zhěng	12 o'clock sharp
差不多九点	chàbuduō jiǔ diǎn	about nine
早	zǎo	early
晚	wǎn	late
准时	zhǔnshí	punctual, on time
迟到	chídào	late (for appointment/scheduled time)

Length of time

*六十秒(钟)	liùshí miǎo (zhōng)	60 seconds
*十五分(钟)	shíwǔ fēn (zhōng)	15 minutes
一个钟头/小时	yí ge zhōngtóu/ xiǎoshí	1 hour
半个钟头/小时	bàn ge zhōngtóu/ xiǎoshí	1/2 hour
两个半钟头/小时	liǎng ge bàn zhōngtóu	2.5 hours
三小时四十分(钟)	sān xiǎoshí sìshí fēn (zhōng)	3 hours and 40 minutes
*一天	yì tiān	1 day
两个星期	liǎng ge xīngqī	2 weeks
三个月	sān ge yuè	3 months
*四年	sì nián	4 years
一个世纪	yí ge shìjì	1 century
二十一世纪	èrshíyī shìjì	21st century

Note: seconds, minutes, days, years (marked with *) are nouns that do not require measure words when they are used with numerals.

Other time expressions

今天	jīntiān	today
明天	míngtiān	tomorrow
昨天	zuótiān	yesterday
后天	hòutiān	the day after tomorrow
前天	qiántiān	the day before yesterday
昨天早上/中午	zuótiān zǎoshang/zhōngwǔ	yesterday morning/noon
昨天晚上	zuótiān wǎnshang	last night

每天	měi tiān	every day
每隔一天	měi gé yì tiān	every other day
每天晚上	měi tiān wǎnshang	every evening
这个星期	zhèi ge xīngqī	this week
上个星期	shàng ge xīngqí	last week
下个星期	xià ge xīngqī	next week
下下个星期	xià xià ge xīngqī	the week after next
每个星期	měi ge xīngqī	every week
每隔两个星期	mě gé liǎng ge xīngqī	every two weeks
这个月	zhèige yuè	this month
上个月	shàng ge yuè	last month
下个月	xià ge yuè	next month
每个月	měi ge yuè	every month
今年	jīnnián	this year
去年	qùnián	last year
明年	míngnián	next year
前年	qiánnián	the year before last
后年	hòunián	the year after next
每年	měi nián	every year
月初	yuèchū	the beginning of the month
月中	yuèzhōng	the middle of the month
月底	yuèdǐ	the end of the month
年初	niánchū	the beginning of the year
年中	niánzhōng	the middle of the year
年底	niándǐ	the end of the year
一年以前	yì nián yǐqián	a year ago
两年以后	liǎng nián yǐhòu	in two years/ two years later
今年夏天	jīnnián xiàtiān	this (year's) summer
去年秋天	qùnián qiūtiān	last (year's) autumn
明年春天	míngnián chūntiān	next (year's) spring
前年冬天	qiánnián dōngtiān	winter in the year before last

Appendix 3: Food
附录3: 食物 shíwù

Vegetables 蔬菜 shūcài

asparagus	芦笋	lúsǔn
bamboo shoots	竹笋	zhúsǔn
bean sprouts	豆芽	dòuyá
bean curd	豆腐	dòufǔ
black fungus	木耳	mùěr
broccoli	西兰花	xīlánhuā
cabbage	卷心菜	juǎnxīncài
carrot	胡罗卜	húluóbo
cauliflower	菜花	càihuā
celery	芹菜	qíncài
Chinese cabbage	白菜	báicài
Chinese chive	韭菜	jiǔcài
Chinese water-spinach	空心菜	kōngxīncài
corn	玉米	yùmǐ
cucumber	黄瓜	huángguā
eggplant	茄子	qiézi
garlic	蒜	suàn
ginger	姜	jiāng
green pepper	青椒	qīngjiāo
green peas	青豆	qīngdòu
kidney beans	蚕豆	cándòu
leek	大葱	dàcōng
lettuce	莴笋	wōsǔn
lotus root	藕	ǒu
mushroom	蘑菇	mógū
mustard green	榨菜	zhàcài
onion	洋葱	yángcōng
peanut	花生	huāshēng
potato	土豆/洋芋	tǔdòu/yángyù
pumpkin	南瓜	nánguā
radish	小罗卜	xiǎo luóbo
red bean	红豆	hóng dòu
red pepper	红柿子椒	hóng shìzijiāo
red chili	红尖椒	hóng jiānjiāo
scallion	葱	cōng
seaweed	海带	hǎidài
sesame	芝麻	zhīma
spinach	菠菜	bōcài
squash	西葫芦	xī húlu
string beans	四季豆	sìjìdòu
sweet potato	白薯/红薯	báishǔ/hóngshǔ
taro	芋头	yùtóu
tomato	西红柿	xīhóngshì
towel gourd	丝瓜	sīguā
turnip	白罗卜	bái luóbo
watercress	西洋菜	xīyángcài
water chestnut	荸荠	bóqí
white gourd	冬瓜	dōngguā
zucchini	青瓜	qīngguā

Fruit 水果 shuǐguǒ

almond	杏仁	xìngrén
apple	苹果	píngguǒ
apricot	杏	xìng
avocado	鳄梨	èlí
banana	香蕉	xiāngjiāo
blueberry	蓝莓	lánméi
cherry	樱桃	yīngtáo
chestnut	栗子	lìzi
coconut	椰子	yēzi
date	枣	zǎo
fig	无花果	wúhuāguǒ
grape	葡萄	pútao
grapefruit	柚子	yòuzi
kiwi	猕猴桃	míhóutáo
lemon	柠檬	níngméng
lime	酸橙	suānchéng
lychee	荔枝	lìzhī
mango	芒果	mángguǒ
melon	瓜	guā
nectarine	油桃	yóutáo
olive	橄榄	gǎnlǎn
orange	橙	chéng
papaya	木瓜	mùguā
peach	桃	táo
pear	梨	lí
persimmon	柿子	shìzi
pineapple	菠萝	bōluó
plum	李子	lǐzi
pomegranate	石榴	shíliǔ
prune	梅子	méizi
raison	葡萄干	pútaogān
raspberry	木莓/山莓	mùméi/shānméi
strawberry	草莓	cǎoméi
tangerine	橘子	júzi
walnut	核桃	hétao
watermelon	西瓜	xīguā

Meat	肉类	ròulèi
bacon	咸肉	xiánròu
beef	牛肉	niúròu
brisket	胸肉	xiōngròu
chicken	鸡肉	jīròu
(chicken) eggs	鸡蛋	jīdàn
duck	鸭	yā
frog	青蛙肉	qīngwāròu
ground meat	肉末	ròumò
ham	火腿	huǒtuǐ
kidney	腰	yāo
lamb	小羊肉	xiǎoyángròu
leg	腿	tuǐ
liver	肝	gān
mutton	羊肉	yángròu
pork	猪肉	zhūròu
rib	排骨	páigǔ
sausage	香肠	xiāngcháng
shoulder	肘肉	zhǒuròu
snake	蛇肉	shéròu
thigh	大腿	dàtuǐ
tongue	舌头	shétou
turkey	火鸡	huǒjī
veal	小牛肉	xiǎoniúròu
wing	翅膀	chìbǎng

Seafood	海鲜	hǎixiān
carp	鲤鱼	lǐyú
clams	蛤	gě
crab	螃蟹	pángxiè
cuttlefish	墨鱼	mòyú
eel	鳝鱼	shànyú
flatfish	比目鱼	bǐmùyú
lobster	龙虾	lóngxiā
mussel	淡菜	dàncài
octopus	章鱼	zhāngyú
oyster	生蚝	shēngháo
prawn	对虾	duìxiā
salmon	鲑鱼/三文鱼	guīyú/sānwényú
sardine	沙丁鱼	shādīngyú
scallops	扇贝	shànbèi
sea cucumber	海参	hǎishēn
shrimp	虾	xiā
snail	蜗牛	wōniú
soft-shelled turtle	甲鱼	jiǎyú
squid	鱿鱼	yóuyú
trout	鳟鱼	zūnyú
tuna	金枪鱼	jīnqiāngyú
turtle	乌龟	wūguī

Dessert	甜食	tiánshí
cake	蛋糕	dàngāo
candy	糖果	tángguǒ
chocolate	巧克力	qiǎokelì
cookie	饼干	bǐnggān
custard	牛奶蛋糊	niúnǎi dànhú
honey	蜂蜜	fēngmì
ice cream	冰淇淋	bīngqílín
jam	果酱	guǒjiàng
jelly	果冻	guǒdòng
pancakes	薄饼	báobǐng
pie	馅饼	xiànbǐng
pudding	布丁	bùdīng
syrup	糖浆	tángjiāng

Beverage	饮料	yǐnliào
beer	啤酒	píjiǔ
champagne	香槟酒	xiāngbīnjiǔ
cider	苹果酒	píngguǒjiǔ
coke	可口可乐	kěkǒukělè
cocoa	可可	kěkě
coffee	咖啡	kāfēi
iced coffee	冰咖啡	bīngkāfēi
ice	冰	bīng
juice	果汁	guǒzhī
lemonade	柠檬水	níngméngshuǐ
liquor	白酒	báijiǔ
milk	牛奶	niúnǎi
mineral water	矿泉水	kuàngquánshuǐ
soda	汽水	qìshuǐ
tea	茶	chá
green tea	绿茶	lùchá
black tea	红茶	hóngchá
iced tea	冰茶	bīngchá
jasmine tea	茉莉花茶	mòlìhuā chá
Maotai spirits	茅台酒	Máotái jiǔ
Oolong tea	乌龙茶	wūlóng chá
water	水	shuǐ
wine	葡萄酒	pútaojiǔ
red wine	红葡萄酒	hóng pútaojiǔ
dry red wine	干红葡萄酒	gān hóng pútaojiǔ
white wine	白葡萄酒	bái pútaojiǔ

Spices	调味作料	tiáowèi zuóliào
basil	九重塔	jiǔchóngtǎ
cinnamon	桂皮	guìpí
cooking wine	料酒	liàojiǔ
coriander	芫荽/香菜	yánsuì/xiāngcài
fennel	茴香	huíxiāng
garlic	蒜	suàn
ginger	姜	jiāng
mint	薄荷	bòhe
MSG	味精	wèijīng
mustard	芥末	jièmò
pepper	胡椒	hújiāo

peppercorn	花椒	huājiāo
red pepper	红椒	hóngjiāo
salt	盐	yán
sauce	酱	jiàng
sesame oil	麻油	máyóu
scallion	葱	cōng
soy sauce	酱油	jiàngyóu
sugar	糖	táng
tomato sauce	番茄酱	fānqiéjiàng
vinegar	醋	cù
rice vinegar	米醋	mǐcù

Others 其他 qítā

bread	面包	miànbāo
butter	黄油	huángyóu
cheese	奶酪	nǎilào
cornstarch	淀粉	diànfěn
cream	奶油	nǎiyóu
dumplings	饺子	jiǎozi
egg white	蛋白	dànbái
egg yolk	蛋黄	dànhuáng
flour	面粉	miànfěn
fried bread stick	油条	yóutiáo
lard	猪油	zhūyóu
noodles	面条	miàntiáo
nut	果仁	guǒrén
oil	油	yóu
olive oil	橄榄油	gǎnlǎn yóu
pancake	煎饼	jiānbǐng
pickles	泡菜	pàocài
porridge	稀饭/粥	xīfàn/zhōu
rice	米饭	mǐfàn
rice noodles	米粉	mǐfěn
sandwich	三明治	sānmíngzhì
snack	点心/小吃	diǎnxīn/xiǎochī
steamed buns	馒头	mántou
steamed rolls	花卷	huājuǎn
steamed meat buns	包子	bāozi
toast	土司	tǔsī
vegetable oil	菜油	cài yóu
waffle	华夫饼干	huáhū bǐnggān
yeast powder	发酵粉	fājiàofěn
yogurt	酸奶	suānnǎi

Methods of cooking 烹调方法 pēngtiáo fāngfǎ

add	放/加	fàng/jiā
bake	烤	kǎo
blend	搅拌	jiǎobàn
boil	煮	zhǔ
braise	炖/烧	dùn/shāo
braise in soy sauce	红烧	hóngshāo
broil	烤焙	kǎobèi
chill	凉	liáng
chop	切(碎)	qiē(suì)
crispy deep-fry	香酥	xiāngsū
deep-fry	炸	zhá
defrost	解冻	jiědòng
dissolve	溶解	róngjiě
drain	沥干	lìgān
filling	馅	xiàn
grill	烤	kǎo
heat	热	rè
melt	溶化	rónghuà
mince	肉末	ròumò
pan-fry	煎	jiān
peel	削皮	xiāopí
pour	倒	dào
rinse	冲洗	chōngxǐ
roast	烤	kǎo
sauté	油焖	yóumèn
season	调味	tiáowèi
shred	切丝	qiēsī
simmer	焖	mèn
slice	切片	qiēpiàn
smoked	熏	xūn
soak	浸泡	jìnpào
sprinkle	撒	sǎ
steam	(清)蒸	(qīng) zhēng
stew	炖	dùn
stir fry	炒	chǎo
strain	滤	lù
sweet and sour	糖醋	tángcù
whip	搅打	jiǎodǎ

Answers to exercises
练习答案

Chapter 1: At the airport

1. 1. 公共汽车　　2. 总站　　　3. 出发
      gōnggòng qìchē   zǒng zhàn   chūfā

2. 1. 登机楼　　2. 航班　　　3. 国内　　4. 航班　　5. 东楼
      dēngjīlóu   hángbān   guónèi   hángbān   dōng lóu

3. 1. 航空公司的接待柜台　　　　　　2. 排队　　　3. 手续　　4. 机票
      hángkōng gōngsī de jiēdài guìtái   páiduì   shǒuxù   jīpiào

   5. 航班　　　6. 护照　　　7. 签证
      hángbān   hùzhào   qiānzhèng

4. 1. 国际　　2. 登机楼　　3. 机票，护照，签证　　　　　　4. 手提行李　　5. 公文包
      guójì   dēngjīlóu   jīpiào, hùzhào, qiānzhèng   shǒutí xíngli   gōngwénbāo

   6. 登机牌，登机牌　　7. 班机/航班，牌，座　　8. 行李领取单，领取
      dēngjīpái, dēngjīpái   bānjī/hángbān, pái, zuò   xínglǐ lǐngqǔ dān, lǐngqǔ

   9. 底下，座位上头　　10. 进去，托运
      dǐxia, zuòwèi shàngtóu   jìnqù, tuōyùn

5. 1. 航空公司的接待柜台。
      Hángkōng gōngsī de jiēdài guìtái.

   2. 航空公司的职员小姐。
      Hángkōng gōngsī de zhíyuán xiǎojiě.

   3. 机票。
      Jīpiào.

   4. 三件。
      Sān jiàn.

   5. 不都是手提行李。
      Bù dōu shi shǒutí xíngli.

   6. 公文包。
      Gōngwénbāo.

   7. 能。
      Néng.

   8. 一张登机牌和两张行李领取单。
      Yì zhāng dēngjīpái hé liǎng zhāng xínglì lǐngqǔ dān.

   9. 22排C座。
      Èrshíèrpái C zuò.

   10. 两件。
      Liǎng jiàn.

6. 1. a　　2. c　　3. a　　4. b　　5. a

7. 1. 广播　2. 班机　3. 飞往　　4. 通过　　5. 安全门　　6. 8号　　7. 登机口　　8. 起飞
      guǎngbō   bānjī   fēiwǎng   tōngguò   ānquánmén   bāhào   dēngjīkǒu   qǐfēi

8. 1. 通知　　2. 到港　　3. 从　　4. 航班
      tōngzhī   dàogǎng   cóng   hángbān

9. 1. 离开　　2. 下飞机　　3. 到…去
      líkāi   xià fēijī   dào…qù

10. 1. 误　　2. 班机　　3. 满员　　4. 座位　　5. 票价
       wù   bānjī   mǎnyuán   zuòwèi   piàojià

228

6. 价钱   7. 转让   8. 直飞航班   9. 停
   jiàqián   zhuǎnràng   zhífēi hángbān   tíng

11.   1. 登机楼，登机楼，国内
         dēngjīlóu, dēngjīlóu, guónèi

      2. 职员，航空，柜台
         zhíyuán, hángkōng, guìtái

      3. 机票
         jīpiào

      4. 护照
         hùzhào

      5. 行李
         xíngli

      6. 行李领取单，领取
         xínglǐ lǐngqǔdān, lǐngqǔ

      7. 手提行李
         shǒutí xíngli

      8. 靠走道
         kào zǒudào

      9. 预订
         yùdìng

     10. 满员，座位
         mǎnyuán, zuòwèi

     11. 登机牌，排，座
         dēngjīpái, pái, zuò

     12. 飞往，停
         fēiwǎng, tíng

     13. 转机
         zhuǎnjī

     14. 起飞
         qǐfēi

     15. 登机口
         dēngjīkǒu

12.   1. 史密斯先生到了飞机场。
         Shǐmìsī xiānsheng dào le fēijīchǎng.

      2. 有两个登机楼。
         Yǒu liǎng ge dēngjīlóu.

      3. 因为一个是国际航班登机楼，一个是国内航班登机楼。
         Yīnwèi yí ge shi guójì hángbān dēngjīlóu, yí ge shi guónèi hángbān dēngjīlóu.

      4. 他去了航空公司的接待柜台。
         Tā qùle hángkōng gōngsi de jiēdài guìtái.

      5. 他要去那儿办理登机手续。
         Tā yào qù nàr bànlǐ dēngjī shǒuxù.

      6. 他有两件托运行李。
         Tā yǒu liǎng jiàn tuōyùn xíngli.

      7. 他可以在纽约领取行李。
         Tā kěyǐ zài Niǔyuē lǐngqǔ xíngli.

      8. 他得凭行李领取单领取行李。
         Tā děi píng xínglǐ lǐngqǔ dān lǐngqǔ xíngli.

9. 他要带一个公文包上飞机。
   Tā yào dài yí ge gōngwénbāo shàng fēijī.

10. 放在前面座位的底下，或者座位上头的行李舱里。
    Fàng zài qiánmiàn zuòwèi de dǐxia, huòzhě zuòwèi shàngtou de xínglicāng lǐ.

11. 他预订了座位，可是电脑上没显示。
    Tā yùdìngle zuòwèi, kěshì diànnǎo shàng méi xiǎnshì.

12. 因为飞机不满，还有座位。
    Yīnwèi fēijī bù mǎn, hái yǒu zuòwèi.

13. 他得到了一个靠走道的座位。
    Tā déidàole yí ge kào zǒudào de zuòwèi.

14. 他得从6号登机口登机。
    Tā děi cóng liù hào dēngjīkǒu dēngjī.

15. 这班飞机不是直飞航班。
    Zhè bān fēijī bú shi zhífēi hángbān.

13. 1. 飞机不能正点起飞。
        Fēijī bù néng zhèngdiǎn qǐfēi.

     2. 飞机要推迟45分钟起飞。
        Fēijī yào tuīchí sìshíwǔ fēnzhōng qǐfēi.

     3. 有。
        Yǒu.

     4. 因为天气问题。
        Yīnwèi tiānqì wèntí.

Chapter 2: On the airplane

1. | 1. 机组人员 | 2. 飞行员 | 3. 乘务员 | 4. 后舱 | 5. 头等舱 |
    |---|---|---|---|---|
    | jīzǔ rényuán | fēixíngyuán | chéngwùyuán | hòucāng | tóuděngcāng |

6. 经济舱	7. 安全	8. 驾驶舱	9. 起飞	10. 着陆
jīngjìcāng	ānquán	jiàshǐcāng	qǐfēi	zhuólù

2. | 1. 机组人员 | 2. 欢迎 | 3. 起飞 | 4. 飞行时间 | 5. 高度 | 6. 速度 | 7. 小时 |
    |---|---|---|---|---|---|---|
    | jīzǔ rényuán | huānyíng | qǐfēi | fēixíng shíjiān | gāodù | sùdù | xiǎoshí |

3. | 1. 在座位底下 | 2. 氧气罩会自动降下 | 3. 在前舱、后舱和机翼附近 |
    |---|---|---|
    | zài zuòwèi dǐxia | yǎngqìzhào huì zìdòng jiàngxià | zài qiáncāng, hòucāng he jīyì fùjìn |

4. | 1. 起飞 | 2. 着陆 | 3. 坐好 | 4. 系好 |
    |---|---|---|---|
    | qǐfēi | zhuólù | zuòhǎo | jìhǎo |

5. 安全带	6. 湍流	7. 颠簸
ānquándài	tuānliú	diānbǒ

5. | 1. 抽烟 | 2. 抽烟探测器，洗手间 | 3. 罚款 | 4. 抽烟区 |
    |---|---|---|---|
    | chōuyān | chōuyān tàncèqì, xǐshǒujiān | fákuǎn | chōuyānqū |

6. | 1. 走道上 | 2. 前面的座位底下 | 3. 头顶上方的行李舱 |
    |---|---|---|
    | zǒudào shàng | qiánmiàn de zuòwèi dǐxia | tóudǐng shàngfāng de xínglǐcāng |

4. 靠背	5. 托盘餐桌
kàobèi	tuōpán cānzhuō

7. | 1. 饮料和餐点 | 2. 音乐 | 3. 频道 | 4. 电影 |
    |---|---|---|---|
    | yǐnliào he cāndiǎn | yīnyuè | píndào | diànyǐng |

5. 租	6. 耳机	7. 枕头	8. 毛毯
zū	ěrjī	zhěntou	máotǎn

8. | 1. 枕头 | 2. 毛毯 |
    |---|---|
    | zhěntou | máotǎn |

9.   1. 舱
       cāng

    2. 前，舱，经济
       qián, cāng, jīngjì

    3. 乘务员，机票
       chéngwùyuán, jipiào

    4. 氧气面罩
       yǎngqì miànzhào

    5. 手提行李，座位上头的行李舱里
       shǒutí xínglǐ, zuòwèi shàngtou de xínglicāng lǐ

    6. 抽烟，抽烟探测器
       chōuyān, chōuyān tàncèqì

    7. 罚款
       fákuǎn

    8. 着陆，放直
       zhuólù, fàngzhí

    9. 安全带
       ānquándài

    10. 饮料，餐点
        yǐnliào, cāndiǎn

    11. 耳机
        ěrjī

    12. 驾驶舱
        jiàshǐ cāng

10.   1. 乘务员会在门口欢迎他们。
       Chéngwùyuán huì zài ménkǒu huānyíng tāmen.

    2. 前舱是头等舱，后舱是经济舱。
       Qiáncāng shi tóuděngcāng, Hòucāng shi jīngjìcāng.

    3. 氧气面罩和救生衣
       Yǎngqì miànzhào hé jiùshēngyī.

    4. 放在前面座位的底下或者座位上头的行李舱里。
       Fàngzài qiánmiàn zuòwèi de dǐxia huòzhě zuòwèi shàngtou de xínglicāng lǐ.

    5. 不可以。
       Bù kěyǐ.

    6. 因为探测器可以查出在洗手间抽烟的人。
       Yīnwèi tàncèqì kěyǐ cháchū zài xǐshǒujiān chōuyān de rén.

    7. 他们得把座椅靠背放直，系好安全带。
       Tāmen děi bǎ zuòyǐ kàobèi fàngzhí, jìhǎo ānquándài.

    8. 因为飞机有时会遇上突然的湍流。
       Yīnwèi fēijī yǒu shí huì yùshàng tūrán de tuānliú.

    9. 饮料和餐点。
       Yǐnliàò he cāndiǎn.

    10. 飞行时间，航线，飞行高度，速度等等。
        Fēixíng shíjiān, hángxiàn, fēixíng gāodù, sùdù děngděng.

11.

1. 机组人员	2. 氧气面罩	3. 登机牌	4. 座椅靠背	5. 安全带
jīzǔ rényuán	yǎngqì miànzhào	dēngjīpái	zuòyǐ kàobèi	ānquándài
6. 乘务员	7. 紧急出口	8. 座位底下	9. 航线	10. 飞行员
chéngwùyuán	jǐnjí chūkǒu	zuòwèi dǐxia	hángxiàn	fēixíngyuán

Chapter 3: Passport control and customs

1. 　1. 护照　2. 护照　3. 多久　4. 待　　5. 往　6. 公务　　7. 旅游
　　　 hùzhào　　hùzhào　duōjiǔ　dāi　　wǎng　gōngwù　　lǚyóu

2. 　1. 申报，通道
　　　 shēnbào, tōngdào

　　2. 红色通道
　　　 hóngsè tōngdào

　　3. 两
　　　 liǎng

　　4. 申报，税
　　　 shēnbào, shuì

　　5. 海关申报单
　　　 hǎiguān shēnbào dān

　　6. 个人物品
　　　 gèrén wùpǐn

Chapter 4: At the train station

1. 　1. 火车站　　　2. 软卧　　　3. 硬卧　　　4. 上　　　5. 单程　　6. 下
　　　 huǒchēzhàn　　ruǎnwò　　　yìngwò　　　shàng　　dānchéng　xià

2. 　1. 火车票　　　2. 软卧　　　3. 下铺　　　4. 几
　　　 huǒchē piào　　ruǎnwò　　　xiàpù　　　jǐ

　　5. 来回票　　　6. 单程票　　　7. 单程票
　　　 láihuí piào　　dānchéng piào　dānchéng piào

3. 　1. 火车　　　　2. 售票处　　　3. 售票　　　4. 软卧　　　5. 硬卧
　　　 huǒchē　　　shòupiàochù　　shòupiào　　ruǎnwò　　　yìngwò

　　6. 软卧　　　　7. 硬卧　　　　8. 快车　　　9. 特快　　　10. 硬卧
　　　 ruǎnwò　　　yìngwò　　　kuàichē　　tèkuài　　　yìngwò

4. 　1. 长途　　2. 在电子屏幕上　　　　3. 两点　　4. 不会，因为有一个事故
　　　 chángtú　zài diànzǐ píngmù shàng　liǎng diǎn　búhuì, yīnwèi yǒu yí ge shìgù

　　5. 三点　　6. 会　　　7. 晚点一个钟头　　　8. 在候车室等候
　　　 sāndiǎn　huì　　wǎndiǎn yí ge zhōngtóu　zài hòuchēshì děnghòu

5. 　1. 事故　　2. 正点　　　3. 一个　　4. 候车室
　　　 shìgù　　zhèngdiǎn　　yí ge　　hòuchēshì

6. 　1. 站台/月台　　2. 车箱，号　　　3. 列车员　4. 上车，下车
　　　 zhàntái/yuètái　　chēxiāng, hào　　lièchēyuán　shàng chē, xià chē

7. 　1. 列车员　　2. 打扫，整理　3. 餐车　　4. 盒饭
　　　 lièchēyuán　dǎsǎo, zhěnglǐ　cānchē　　héfàn

8. 　1. T　2. F　3. F　4. F　5. T　6. F　7. T　8. F　9. T　10. F

9. 　1. 他们是坐出租车去的。
　　　 Tāmen shi zuò chūzūchē qù de.

　　2. 不会正点发车。
　　　 Bú huì zhèngdiǎn fāchē.

　　3. 要晚点一个半小时。
　　　 Yào wǎndiǎn yíge bàn xiǎoshí.

　　4. 售票处。
　　　 Shòupiàochù.

5. 两张硬卧票。
Liǎng zhāng yìngwò piào.

6. 候车室。
Hòuchēshì

7. 八号月台。
Bā hào yuètái.

8. 因为从北京到上海要坐很久的火车，他们得在火车上睡觉。
Yīnwèi cóng Běijīng dào Shànghǎi yào zuò hěn jiǔ de huǒchē, tāmen děi zài huǒchē shàng shuìjiào.

9. 列车员给乘客送报纸杂志，零食和饮料。他们也打扫车厢，整理卧具。
Lièchēyuán gěi chéngkè sòng bàozhǐ zázhì, língshí he yǐnliào. Tāmen yě dǎsǎo chēxiāng, zhěnglǐ wòjù.

10. 他们在餐车上吃饭。
Tāmen zài cānchē shàng chīfàn.

10. 1. c   2. h   3. e   4. b   5. a   6. f   7. g   8. d

Chapter 5: Public transportation

1. 1. 公共交通   2. 公共汽车站   3. 地铁   4. 路   5. 站
    gōnggòng jiāotōng   gōnggòng qìchē zhàn   dìtiě   lù   zhàn

    6. 去   7. 停   8. 月票   9. 方向   10. 到站
    qù   tíng   yuèpiào   fāngxiàng   dào zhàn

2. 1. 车票   2. 去   3. 坐   4. 下车   5. 换   6. 到   7. 乘客   8. 下车
    chēpiào   qù   zuò   xiàchē   huàn   dào   chéngkè   xiàchē

3. 1. 广场   2. 车   3. 地铁   4. 地铁上   5. 售票员   6. 地铁站   7. 坐   8. 票   9. 以内
    guǎngchǎng   chē   dìtiě   dìtiě shàng   shòupiàoyuán   dìtiězhàn   zuò   piào   yǐnèi

4. 1. 打的   2. 计时器   3. 包   4. 租   5. 押金   6. 师傅   7. 慢   8. 小费
    dǎdī   jìshíqì   bāo   zū   yājīn   shīfu   màn   xiǎofèi

5. 1. 汽车   2. 车   3. 要   4. 哪儿   5. 去   6. 车
    qìchē   chē   yào   nǎr   qù   chē

6. 1. 去   2. 多久   3. 交通   4. 快   5. 到了   6. 多少   7. 小费
    qù   duōjiǔ   jiāotōng   kuài   dàole   duōshǎo   xiǎofèi

Chapter 6: Automobile

1. 1. 自动挡   2. 租   3. 里程   4. 公里   5. 信用卡   6. 驾照
    zìdòngdǎng   zū   lǐchéng   gōnglǐ   xìngyòngkǎ   jiàzhào

2. 1. 租   2. 车   3. 车   4. 租   5. 多少钱   6. 里程
    zū   chē   chē   zū   duōshǎo qián   lǐchéng

    7. 保险   8. 驾照   9 押金   10. 信用卡   11. 签字
    bǎoxiǎn   jiàzhào   yājīn   xìnyòngkǎ   qiānzì

3. 1. b   2. a   3. c   4. a   5. c   6. b   7. c   8. b   9. a   10. c

4. 1 空档   2. 转向灯   3. 安全带   4. 备用胎   5. 后视镜
    kōngdàng   zhuǎngxiàngdēng   ānquándài   bèiyòng tāi   hòushìjìng

5. 1. e   2. c   3. g   4. b

6. 1. 油箱, 加油站   2. 冷却液   3. 电池   4. 轮胎
    yóuxiāng, jiāyóuzhàn   lěngquèyè   diànchí   lúntāi

    5. 挡风玻璃   6. 发动机, 变速器润滑
    dǎngfēng bōli   fādòngjī, biànsùqì rùnhuá

7.　1. 停　　2. 火　　3. 拖车　　4. 拖　　5. 备用零件　　6. 修好
　　　tíng　　huǒ　　tuōchē　　tuō　　bèiyòng língjiàn　　xiūhǎo

Chapter 7: Asking for directions

1.　1. 迷路　　2. 街　　3. 大道　　4. 远　　5. 远
　　　mílù　　jiē　　dàdào　　yuǎn　　yuǎn

　　6. 近　　7. 走路　　8. 方向　　9. 后　　10. 向前
　　　jìn　　zǒulù　　fāngxiàng　　hòu　　xiàngqián

　　11. 路口　　12. 转　　13. 再　　14. 到了　　15. 这儿
　　　lùkǒu　　zhuǎn　　zài　　dàole　　zhèr

　　16. 后　　17. 一直　　18. 路口　　19. 右　　20. 过
　　　hòu　　yìzhí　　lùkǒu　　yòu　　guò

2.　1. 大道　　2. 走路　3. 公共汽车　　4. 车站　5. 路口　6. 路　　7. 车站　8. 第十路　9. 下车
　　　dàdào　　zǒulù　　gōnggòng qìchē　　chēzhàn　lùkǒu　lù　　chēzhàn　dì shí lù　xiàchē

3.　1. 郊区　　2. 国道，高速公路　　3. 高峰，塞车　　4. 高峰时期　　5. 国道
　　　jiāoqū　　guódào, gāosù gōnglù　　gāofēng, sāichē　　gāofēng shíqī　　guódào

　　6. 高速公路费　　7. 车道　　8. 车道，出口　　9. 单行道　　10. 红灯
　　　gāosù gōnglù fèi　　chēdào　　chēdào, chūkǒu　　dānxíngdào　　hóngdēng

4.　1. 红绿灯　　2. 收费公路　　3. 车道　　4. 出口　　5. 收费站
　　　hónglùdēng　　shōufèi gōnglù　　chēdào　　chūkǒu　　shōufèizhàn

5.　1. d　　2. f　　3. a　　4. g　　5. b　　6. h　　7. e　　8. c

Chapter 8: Making a telephone call

1.　1. 电话　　2. 号码　　3. 电话号码簿　　4. 市内　　5. 地区号码
　　　diànhuà　　hàomǎ　　diànhuà hàomǎ bù　　shì nèi　　dìqū hàomǎ

　　6. 听筒　　7. 拨号音　　8. 拨号盘　　9. 按　　10. 电话铃　　11. 接
　　　tīngtǒng　　bōhàoyīn　　bōhàopán　　àn　　diànhuàlíng　　jiē

2.　1. 市外/长途　　2. 地区　　3. 国家号码　　4. 接线员　　5. 对方付费
　　　shìwài/chángtú　　dìqū　　guójiā hàomǎ　　jiēxiànyuán　　duìfāng fùfèi

3.　1. 无绳电话　　2. 电话绳　　3. 无绳　　4. 手机　　5. 电话
　　　wúshéng diànhuà　　diànhuà shéng　　wúshéng　　shǒujī　　diànhuà

4.　1. 公用电话　　2. 公用电话　　3. 电话卡　　4. 拿起　　5. 插入
　　　gōngyòng diànhuà　　gōngyòng diànhuà　　diànhuà kǎ　　náqǐ　　chārù

　　6. 拨号音　　7. 拨号　　8. 对方　　9. 接
　　　bōhàoyīn　　bōhào　　duìfāng　　jiē

5.　1. 您好　　2. 请问　　3. 在吗　　4. 您是哪位　　5. 我姓X，是他朋友。
　　　nín hǎo　　qǐngwèn　　zài ma　　nín shi něi wèi　　wǒ xìng X, shi tā péngyǒu.

　　6. 稍等　　7. 他不在　　8. 挂电话　　9. 留话
　　　shāo děng　　tā bú zài　　guà diànhuà　　liúhuà

6.　1. 拨号音　　2. 坏了　　3. 忙音　　4. 拨错了号码　　5. 再打回去
　　　bōhàoyīn　　huàile　　mángyīn　　bōcuòle hàomǎ　　zài dǎ huíqù

　　6. 杂音/干扰音　　7. 断了
　　　záyīn/gānrǎoyīn　　duànle

7.　1. d　　2. a　　3. e　　4. c　　5. f　　6. g　　7. b

8.　1. 呼机号码　　2. 呼　　3. 姓　　4. 留言　　5. 回电话
　　　hūjī hàomǎ　　hū　　xìng　　liúyán　　huí diànhuà

Chapter 9: At the hotel

1.　　1. 预订　　　　　2. 单人间　　　　　3. 双人间　　　　4. 院子，街　　5. 海
　　　　yùdìng　　　　 dānrénjiān　　　　shuāngrénjiān　　yuànzi, jiē　　hǎi

　　　6. 包括早餐　　　7. 空调　　　　　　8. 暖气　　　　　9. 客满，空　　10. 办理入住手续，证件
　　　　bāokuò zǎocān　kōngtiáo　　　　nuǎnqì　　　　　kèmǎn, kōng　　bànlǐ rùzhù shǒuxù, zhèngjiàn

　　　11. 护照　　　　 12. 行李员　　　　13. 信用卡　　　14. 钥匙
　　　　hùzhào　　　　 xínglǐyuán　　　　xìnyòngkǎ　　　yàoshi

2.　　1. 房间　　　　　2. 预订　　　　　3. 客满　　　　　4. 空　　　　　5. 单人床
　　　　fángjiān　　　　yùdìng　　　　　kèmǎn　　　　　kōng　　　　　dānrén chuáng

　　　6. 双人床　　　　7. 单人床　　　　8. 朝　　　　　　9. 房价　　　　10. 包括
　　　　shuāngrénchuáng　dānrénchuáng　cháo　　　　　fángjià　　　　bāokuò

　　　11. 空调　　　　 12. 多久　　　　　13. 到　　　　　14. 填　　　　　15. 证件　　　16. 行李
　　　　kōngtiáo　　　　duōjiǔ　　　　　dào　　　　　　tián　　　　　zhèngjiàn　　xínglǐ

3.　　1. 客房服务员　　2. 洗衣服务　　　3. 洗/烫　　　　4. 干洗　　　　5. 加急费
　　　　kèfáng fúwùyuán　xǐyī fúwù　　　xǐ/tàng　　　　gānxǐ　　　　jiājí fèi

　　　6. 插座　　　　　7. 毛毯　　　　　8. 浴巾　　　　　9. 衣架　　　　10. 卫生纸
　　　　chāzuò　　　　 máotǎn　　　　　yùjīn　　　　　yījià　　　　　wèishēngzhǐ

4　　　1. 盥洗池　　　　2. 马桶　　　　　3. 毛毯　　　　　4. 床　　　　　5. 淋浴　　　　6. 毛巾
　　　　guànxǐchí　　　mǎtǒng　　　　　máotǎn　　　　　chuáng　　　　línyù　　　　máojīn

　　　7. 插座　　　　 8. 卫生纸　　　　9. 衣架　　　　　10. 壁橱　　　　 11. 浴缸　　　 12. 客房服务员
　　　　chāzuò　　　　wèishēngzhǐ　　　yījià　　　　　bìchú　　　　　yùgāng　　　　kèfáng fúwùyuán

5.　　1. 坏了　　　　　2. 水龙头　　　　3. 堵住　　　　　4. 热水　　　　5. 不开　　　　6. 丢了
　　　　huàile　　　　 shuǐlóngtóu　　　dǔzhù　　　　　rèshuǐ　　　　bùkāi　　　　diūle

6.　　1. 盥洗池　　　　2. 水龙头　　　　3. 灯　　　　　　4. 灯泡　　　　5. 开关
　　　　guànxǐchí　　　shuǐlóngtóu　　　dēng　　　　　dēngpào　　　　kāiguān

7.　　1. 结帐　　　　　2. 房间　　　　　3. 帐单　　　　　4. 电话　　　　5. 信用卡　　　6. 信用卡
　　　　jiézhàng　　　 fángjiān　　　　zhàngdān　　　　diànhuà　　　　xìnyòngkǎ　　xìnyòngkǎ

8.　　1. 前台，入住手续　　　　　2. 填，证件　　　3. 单人　　4. 双人　　5. 单人，双人
　　　　qiántái, rùzhù shǒuxù　　 tián, zhèngjiàn　dānrén　　shuāngrén　dānrén, shuāngrén

　　　6. 包括　　　　 7. 朝，朝，安静　　8. 预订　　　　9. 空，客满　10. 行李员
　　　　bāokuò　　　　cháo, cháo, ānjìng　yùdìng　　　　kōng, kèmǎn　xínglǐyuán

　　　11. 服务员　　　12. 暖气，空调　　　13. 毛毯　　　14. 衣架　　　15. 洗衣
　　　　fúwùyuán　　　nuǎnqì, kōngtiáo　　máotǎn　　　　yījià　　　　xǐyī

　　　16. 结帐　　　　17. 电话帐单　　　 18. 信用卡　　19. 收　　　　20. 叫
　　　　jiézhàng　　　 diànhuà zhàngdān　xìnyòngkǎ　　shōu　　　　jiào

9.　　1. 这个房间不朝街，它朝海。
　　　　Zhèi ge fángjiān bù cháo jiē, tā cháo hǎi.

　　　2. 这个房间有阳台。
　　　　Zhèi ge fángjiān yǒu yángtái.

　　　3. 这个房间有一张双人床。
　　　　Zhèi ge fángjiān yǒu yì zhāng shuāngrénchuáng.

　　　4. 这是一个双人房间。
　　　　Zhè shi yí ge shuāngrén fángjiān.

　　　5. 这个房间有卫生间。
　　　　Zhèi ge fángjiān yǒu wèishēngjiān.

　　　6. 卫生间里有马桶，盥洗池和淋浴。
　　　　Wèishēngjiān lǐ yǒu mǎtǒng, guànxǐchí he línyù.

7. 房间里有空调。
Fángjiān lǐ yǒu kōngtiáo.

8. 床上有枕头和毛毯。
Chuáng shàng yǒu zhěntóu he máotǎn.

10.   1. 这些人在旅馆。
Zhèixiē rén zài lǚguǎn.

2. 他们要办理入住手续。
Tāmen yào bànlǐ rùzhù shǒuxù.

3. 他们在跟前台服务员说话。
Tāmen zài gēn qiántái fúwùyuán shuōhuà.

4. 那个男的在填表。
Nèi ge nánde zài tiánbiǎo.

5. 行李员手里拿着客房钥匙。
Xínglǐyuán shǒu lǐ názhe kèfáng yàoshi.

6. 那个女的手里拿着信用卡。
Nèi ge nǚde shǒu lǐ názhe xìnyòngkǎ.

11.   1. 这是旅馆的一个房间。
Zhè shi lǚguǎn de yí ge fángjiān.

2. 床上有枕头和毛毯。
Chuáng shàng yǒu zhěntou he máotǎn.

3. 客房服务员在房间里工作。
Kèfáng fúwùyuán zài fángjiān lǐ gōngzuò.

4. 她在打扫房间。
Tā zài dǎsǎo fángjiān.

5. 壁橱里有衣架。
Bìchú lǐ yǒu yījià.

6. 盥洗池在卫生间里。
Guànxǐchí zài wèishēngjiān lǐ.

7. 卫生间里有淋浴。
Wèishēngjiān lǐ yǒu línyù.

8. 卫生间里有电动剃须刀插座。
Wèishēngjiān lǐ yǒu diàndòng tìxūdāo chāzuò.

9. 卫生间里有两条毛巾。
Wèishēngjiān lǐ yǒu liǎng tiáo máojīn.

10. 卫生间里有一卷卫生纸。
Wèishēngjiān lǐ yǒu yì juǎn wèishēngzhǐ.

Chapter 10: At the bank

1.	1. 人民币	2. 换	3. 手续费	4. 银行	5. 手续费
	rénmínbì	huàn	shǒuxùfèi	yínháng	shǒuxùfèi

2.	1. 换	2. 兑换率	3. 旅行支票	4. 兑换率	5. 出纳窗口
	huàn	duìhuànlǜ	lǚxíng zhīpiào	duìhuànlǜ	chūnà chuāngkǒu

3.	1. 付帐	2. 现金	3. 兑现
	fùzhàng	xiànjīn	duìxiàn

4.	1. 旅行支票	2. 兑换率	3. 换	4. 出纳窗口	5. 人民币	6. 零钱
	lǚxíng zhīpiào	duìhuànlǜ	huàn	chūnà chuāngkǒu	rénmínbì	língqián

5.   1. 存款户头   2. 存   3. 钱   4. 银行存折   5. 存钱
       cúnkuǎn hùtóu   cún   qián   yínháng cúnzhé   cúnqián

       6. 取钱   7. 自动提款机   8. 银行卡   9. 密码
       qǔqián   zìdòng tíkuǎnjī   yínhángkǎ   mìmǎo

6.   1. 兑现   2. 收   3. 付帐   4. 找开   5. 开
       duìxiàn   shōu   fùzhàn   zhǎokāi   kāi

       6. 存   7. 换   8. 取   9. 存钱，取钱，查户头结余   10. 取钱
       cún   huàn   qǔ   cúnqián, qǔqián, chá hùtóu jiēyú   qǔqián

Chapter 11: At the post office

1.   1. 寄   2. 信筒   3. 邮局   4. 邮资   5. 邮票   6. 邮局   7. 邮票
       jì   xìntǒng   yóujú   yóuzī   yóupiào   yóujú   yóupiào

2.   1. 寄   2. 邮资   3. 航空信   4. 航空信   5. 邮资   6. 特快专递   7. 特快专递
       jì   yóuzī   hángkōng xìn   hángkōng xìn   yóuzī   tèkuài zhuāndì   tèkuài zhuāndì

3.   1. 三块   2. 航空信   3. 王大明   4. 100082
       sān kuài   hángkōngxìn   Wáng Dàmíng

       5. 李小林   6. 北京   7. 200030
       Lǐ Xiǎolín   Běijīng

4.   1. 包裹，多重   2. 称   3. 保险   4. 易碎   5. 航空   6. 海运   7. 海运，航空
       bāoguǒ, duōzhòng   chēng   bǎoxiǎn   yìsuì   hángkōng   hǎiyùn   hǎiyùn, hángkōng

5.   1. 邮局   2. 邮递员   3. 信箱   4. 邮政汇票
       yóujú   yóudìyuán   xìnxiāng   yóuzhèng huìpiào

Chapter 12: At the clothing store

1.   1. 皮鞋   2. 平跟   3. 有
       píxié   pínggēn   yǒu

2.   1. 皮鞋   2. 号   3. 号   4. 高跟鞋   5. 颜色   6. 大小   7. 小   8. 大
       píxié   hào   hào   gāogēn xié   yánsè   dàxiǎo   xiǎo   dà

3.   (Answers may vary)

4.   1. 什么   2. 化纤   3. 棉   4. 丝   5. 多大   6. 号   7. 短袖
       shénme   huàxiān   mián   sī   duōdà   hào   duǎnxiù

       8. 袖   9. 条纹   10. 格子   11. 条纹   12. 颜色   13. 配   14. 领带
       xiù   tiáowén   gézi   tiáowén   yánsè   pèi   lǐngdài

5.   1. d   2. c   3. a   4. b

6.   1. 配   2. 高   3. 雨衣   4. 短裤，汗衫   5. 量量，尺寸
       pèi   gāo   yǔyī   duǎnkù, hànshān   liángliáng, chǐcùn

       6. 防皱   7. 化纤，舒服   8. 紧
       fángzhòu   huàxiān, shūfu   jǐn

7.   (Answers may vary)

8.   1. 条纹   2. 格子   3. 带点儿的
       tiáowén   gézi   dài diǎnr de

9.   1. 内裤，连裤袜，胸罩   2. 配   3. 大一点儿   4. 防皱
       nèikù, liánkùwà, xiōngzhào   pèi   dà yìdiǎnr   fángzhòu

10.   1. b   2. a   3. b   4. c   5. a

Chapter 13: At the dry cleaner

1.
   1. 缩水，干洗   2. 洗，烫   3. 开,缝   4. 补   5. 扣子，缝   6. 污渍，去掉
   suōshuǐ, gānxǐ   xǐ, tàng   kāi, féng   bǔ   kòuzi, féng   wūzì, qùdiào

2.
   1. 洗   2. 烫   3. 浆   4. 浆   5. 污渍   6. 去掉   7. 去掉
   xǐ   tàng   jiāng   jiāng   wūzì   qùdiào   qùdiào

   8. 去掉   9. 洗   10. 缩水   11. 干洗   12. 取   13. 取
   qùdiào   xǐ   suōshuǐ   gānxǐ   qǔ   qǔ

Chapter 14: At the restaurant

1.
   1. 订，位 2. 豪华   3. 普通   4. 外头
   dìng, wèi háohuá   pǔtōng   wàitou

   5. 小姐/服务员，菜单   6. 包间   7. 酒单   8. 中餐，餐馆
   xiǎojiě/fúwùyuán, càidān   bāojiān   jiǔdān   zhōngcān, cānguǎn

2.
   1. 几   2. 位   3. 订位   4. 坐   5. 靠   6. 包
   jǐ   wèi   dìngwèi   zuò   kào   bāo

3.
   1. 餐厅   2. 服务员   3. 桌子   4. 菜单   5. 菜单
   cāntīng   fúwùyuán   zhuōzi   càidān   càidān

4.
   1. 豪华酒楼   2. 四位   3. 窗户旁边   4. 服务员 5. 酒 6. 菜单 7. 西餐
   háohuá jiǔlóu   sì wèi   chuānghu pángbiān   fúwùyuán   jiǔ   càidān   xī cān

5.
   1. 中，西   2. 服务员   3. 推荐，拿手   4. 汤   5. 菜单   6. 素   7. 素菜
   zhōng, xī   fúwùyuán   tuījiàn, náshǒu   tāng   càidān   sù   sùcài

6.
   1. 烤   2. 烤   3. 炖   4. 熏   5. 老   6. 嫩
   kǎo   kǎo   dùn   xūn   lǎo   nèn

7.
   1. 炸   2. 炖   3. 糖醋   4. 凉拌
   zhá   dùn   tángcù   liángbàn

   5. 素   6. 酸辣   7. 红烧   8. 炒
   sù   suānlà   hóngshāo   chǎo

8.   1. d   2. c   3. a   4. b

9.   Answer may vary

10.   1. d   2. a   3. c   4. b

11.
   1. 少   2. 盐瓶   3. 醋   4. 味精   5. 好   6. 老
   shǎo   yán píng   cù   wèijīng   hǎo   lǎo

12.
   1. 酒杯/玻璃杯   2. 糖罐   3. 盐瓶   4. 胡椒瓶   5. 茶杯/咖啡杯   6. 盘子
   jiǔbēi/bōlibēi   tángguàn   yánpíng   hújiāopíng   chábēi/kāfēibēi   pánzi

   7. 餐巾   8. 叉子   9. 餐刀   10. 茶匙   11. 汤匙   12. 桌布   13. 盘子   14. 饭碗
   cānjīn   chāzi   cāndāo   cháchǐ   tāngchǐ   zhuōbù   pánzi   fànwǎn

   15. 茶壶   16. 醋/酱油瓶   17. 汤碗   18. 小碟   19. 筷子   20. 汤匙
   cháhú   cù/jiàngyóu píng   tāngwǎn   xiǎodié   kuàizi   tāngchǐ

13.
   1. 饭馆   2. 订位   3. 外头   4. 靠窗   5. 菜单，酒单
   fànguǎn   dìng wèi   wàitou   kào chuāng   càidān, jiǔdān

   6. 红酒   7. 凉菜，热菜，汤   8. 素菜   9. 推荐   10. 清蒸
   hóng jiǔ   liáng cài, rè cài, tāng   sù cài   tuījiàn   qīngzhēng

14.
   1. 窗户旁边
   Chuānghu pángbiān

   2. 因为他们来以前订了位。
   Yīnwèi tāmen lái yǐqián dìngle wèi.

3. 因为他的朋友不爱喝红酒。
Yīnwèi tāde péngyǒu bú ài hē hóngjiǔ.

4. 少了一个酒杯。
Shǎole yí ge jiǔbēi.

5. 吃了凉菜。
Chīle liáng cài.

6. 不错。
Búcuò.

7. 青菜。
Qīngcài.

8. 点了(汤)。
Diǎn le (tāng).

9. 没点(甜点)。
Méi diǎn (tiándiǎn).

10. 一壶菊花茶。
Yì hú júhuā chá.

Chapter 15: Shopping for food

1.
1. 糕点 gāodiǎn	2. 肉 ròu	3. 水果 shuǐguǒ	4. 熟食 shóushí	5. 饮料 yǐnliàò	6. 水产 shuǐchǎn
7. 菜 cài	8. 调味品 tiáowèipǐn	9. 豆制品 dòuzhìpǐn	10. 粮食 liángshi	11. 推车 tuīchē	12. 自由 zìyóu

2.
1. 糕点部 gāodiǎn bù	2. 糖果部 tángguǒ bù	3. 蔬菜部 shūcài bù	4. 水果部 shuǐguǒ bù	5. 饮料部 yǐnliào bù
6. 水产部 shuǐchǎn bù	7. 肉食部 ròushí bù	8. 熟食部 shóushí bù	9. 粮食部 liángshi bù	10. 冷冻部 lěngdòng bù

3.
1. 东西 dōngxi	2. 市场 shìchǎng	3. 食品 shípǐn	4. 副食品店 fùshípǐn diàn	5. 食品 shípǐn	6. 自由市场 zìyóu shìchǎng

4.
1. 想买点什么? Xiǎng mǎi diǎn shénme?		2. 水果 shuǐguǒ	3. 苹果 píngguǒ	4. 荔枝 lìzhī	5. 贵 guì
6. 便宜一点 piányì yìdiǎn	7. 多少钱一斤? Duōshǎo qián yì jīn?	8. 卖完了 mài wán le	9. 一共 yī gòng	10. 找 zhǎo	

Chapter 16: At home

1.
1. 洗碗 xǐwǎn	2. 盘子 pánzi	3. 洗涤池 xǐdíchí	4. 水龙头 shuǐlóngtóu
5. 洗碗剂 xǐwǎnjì	6. 洗 xǐ	7. 冲洗 chōngxǐ	8. 擦干 cāgān

2.
1. 有 yǒu	2. 水龙头 shuǐlóngtóu	3. 筷筒 kuài tǒng	4. 冰箱旁边的储物柜里 bīngxiāng pángbiān de chǔwù guì lǐ
5. 没有 méiyǒu	6. 煤气炉 méiqìlú	7. 四个 sì ge	8. 有 yǒu

3.
1. 开水壶 kāishuǐ hú	2. 炒锅 chǎoguō	3. 电饭锅 diànfànguō	4. 蒸锅 zhēngguō	5. 大锅 dàguō	6. 平底锅 píngdǐguō
7. 削皮刀 xiāopídāo	8. 菜刀和案板 càidāo he ànbǎn	9. 洗菜盆 xǐcàipén	10. 沥水盆 lìshuǐpén	11开罐刀 kāiguàndāo	12. 启瓶器 qǐpíngqì

4. 1. 锅
        guō
    2. 平底锅
        píngdǐguō
    3. 开水壶
        kāishuǐhú
    4. 锅盖
        guōgài
    5. 开罐刀
        kāiguàndāo
    6. 启瓶器
        qǐpíngqì

    7. 锅铲
        guōchǎn
    8. 洗菜盆
        xǐcàipén
    9. 沥水盆
        lìshuǐpén
    10. 菜刀
        càidāo
    11. 案板
        ànbǎn
    12. 电饭锅
        diànfànguō

    13. 搅拌机
        jiǎobànjī
    14. 炒锅
        chǎoguō

5. a) 1. 削皮刀
        xiāopídāo
    2. 洗
        xǐ
    3. 案板
        ànbǎn
    4. 菜刀
        càidāo

    b) 1. 水池
        shuǐchí
    2. 洗
        xǐ
    3. 沥水盆
        lìshuǐpén
    4. 炒锅
        chǎoguō
    5. 青菜
        qīngcài

6. 1. 蒸
        zhēng
    2. 炸
        zhá
    3. 炒
        chǎo
    4. 煮
        zhǔ
    5. 烙
        lào

7. 1. 盥洗池，肥皂
        guànxǐchí, féizào
    2. 肥皂盒，
        féizào hé
    3. 淋浴，浴缸
        línyù, yùgāng

    4. 浴巾，浴衣
        yùjīn, yùyī
    5. 镜子，头发
        jìngzi, tóufà
    6. 刷牙，橱
        shuāyá, chú

8. 1. 浴衣
        yùyī
    2. 洗面巾
        xǐmiànjīn
    3. 马桶
        mǎtǒng
    4. 小橱
        xiǎo chú
    5. 浴缸
        yùgāng

    6. 淋浴
        línyù
    7. 毛巾
        máojīn
    8. 镜子
        jìngzi
    9. 卫生纸
        wèishēngzhǐ
    10. 肥皂/香皂
        féizào/xiāngzào

    11. 毛巾架
        máojīn jià
    12. 浴帽
        yùmào
    13. 肥皂盒
        féizào hé
    14. 浴垫
        yùdiàn
    15. 盥洗池
        guànxǐchí

9. 1. 窗帘
        chuānglián
    2. 台灯
        táidēng
    3. 书架，音响
        shūjià, yīnxiǎng
    4. 茶几
        chájī

    5. 画
        huà
    6. 电视上，像框
        diànshì shàng, xiàngkuàng
    7. 椅子
        yǐzi
    8. 单人沙发
        dānrén shāfā

    9. 双人沙发
        shuāngrén shāfā
    10. 三人沙发
        sānrén shāfā
    11 地毯
        dìtǎn

10. 1. 卧室，床头柜
        wòshì, chuángtóuguì
    2. 闹钟
        nàozhōng
    3. 双人床
        shuāngrén chuáng

    4. 枕头，枕套
        zhěntou, zhěntào
    5. 抽屉
        chōutì
    6. 衣架
        yījià

11. 1. 枕头
        zhěntou
    2. 枕头套
        zhěntou tào
    3. 毛毯
        máotǎn
    4. 床垫
        chuángdiàn
    5. 床罩
        chuángzhào
    6. 被子
        bèizi

12. 1. 我晚上在卧室睡觉。
        Wǒ wǎnshang zài wòshì shuìjiào.

    2. 我晚上十一点上床睡觉。
        Wǒ wǎnshang shíyī diǎn shàngchuáng shuìjiào.

    3. 我睡觉前得拨好闹钟。
        Wǒ shuìjiào qián děi bōhǎo nàozhōng.

    4. 我每天睡八个小时。
        Wǒ měi tiān shuì bā ge xiǎoshí.

    5. 我很快就能睡着。
        Wǒ hěn kuài jiù néng shuì zháo.

    6. 闹钟一响，我就醒来了。
        Nàozhōng yì xiǎng, wǒ jiù xǐnglái le.

    7. 我早上七点起床
        Wǒ zǎoshang qī diǎn qǐchuáng.

    8. 铺床。
        Pūchuáng.

13.
1. 洗衣服 xǐ yīfu	2. 熨斗 yùndǒu	3. 吸尘 xīchén	4. 洗衣机 xǐyījī
5. 吸尘器 xīchénqì	6. 抹 mā	7. 垃圾 lājī	

14. 1. b   2. d   3. e   4. a   5. f   6. c

15.
1. 灯泡 dēngpào	2. 插头 chātóu	3. 保险丝 bǎoxiǎnsī	4. 电工 diàngōng

16.
1. 排水 páishuǐ	2. 下水道 xiàshuǐ dào	3. 管工 guǎnggōng	4. 修理 xiūlǐ

Chapter 17: At the hospital

1.
1. 看病 kànbìng	2. 挂号 guàhào	3. 填 tián	4. 候诊室 hòuzhěnshì	5. 号 hào

6. 医生 yīshēng

2.
1. 疼 téng	2. 发冷 fālěng	3. 不通 bùtōng	4. 肿 zhǒng
5. 感冒 gǎnmào	6. 流感 liúgǎn	7. 看病 kànbìng	

3.
1. 感冒 gǎnmào	2. 流感 liúgǎn	3. 症状 zhēngzhuàng	4. 疼 téng	5. 鼻涕 bítì
6. 嘴 zuǐ	7. 喉咙 hóulóng	8. 疼 téng	9. 咳嗽 késou	10. 体温 tǐwēn
11. 过敏 guòmǐn	12. 袖子 xiùzi	13. 针 zhēn	14. 药 yào	15. 抗生素 kàngshēngsù
16. 次 cì	17. 片 piàn			

4.
1. 头疼，鼻子 tóuténg, bízi	2. 冷 lěng	3. 喉咙 hóulóng	4. 打针，袖子 dǎzhēn, xiùzi

5.
1. 过敏 guòmǐn	2. 哮喘 xiàochuǎn	3. 脏器 zàngqì	4. 型 xíng	5. 正常 zhèngcháng
6. X光，结核 Xguāng, jiéhé	7. 抽血 chōu xuě	8. 药 yào	9. 心电 xīndiàn	10. 吐，拉 tù, lā

6. 2, 4, 5, 6, 8, 10, 11, 12

7.
1. 事故 shìgù	2. 伤 shāng	3. 医院 yīyuàn	4. X光 X guāng
5. 骨折 gǔzhé	6. 固定 gùdìng	7. 石膏 shígāo	8. 拐杖 guǎizhàng

8.
1. 破 pò	2. 深 shēn	3. 缝合 fénghé	4. 绷带 bēngdài	5. 包 bāo

6. 拆线 chāixiàn

9.
1. 手 shǒu	2. 胳膊 gēbo	3. 手腕 shǒuwǎn	4. 腿 tuǐ	5. 脚 jiǎo	6. 小腹 xiǎofù	7. 背 bèi

10.
1. 救护车 jiùhùchē	2. 不能 bù néng	3. 用担架推进来的 yòng dānjià tuī jìnlái de	4. 量脉搏，量血压 liáng màibó, liáng xuèyā
5. 值班医生 zhíbān yīshēng	6. 肚子疼 dùzi téng	7. 照X光 zhào X guāng	8. 放射科 fàngshè kē

11.
1. 救护车 jiùhùchē	2. 担架,轮椅 dānjià, lúnyǐ	3. 急诊室 jízhěnshì	4. 量脉搏，血压 liáng màibó, xuèyā	5. X光 X guāng

12.   1. 手术   2. 镇静剂   3. 担架车   4. 手术台   5. 麻药   6. 切除
         shǒushù   zhènjìngjì   dānjiàchē   shǒushùtái   máyào   qiēchú

13.   1. 观察室   2. 输氧   3. 输液   4. 手术后，特护病房
         guāncháshì   shūyǎng   shūyè   shǒushù hòu, tèhù bìngfáng

14.   1. 怀孕   2. 分娩   3. 产房   4. 阵痛   5. 产科医生
         huáiyùn   fēnmiǎn   chǎnfáng   zhèntòng   chǎnkē yīshēng

15.   1. 疼   2. 救护车   3. 担架   4. 急诊室   5. 脉搏，血压
         téng   jiùhùchē   dānjià   jízhěnshì   màibó, xuèyā

      6. 症状   7. 照X光   8. 手术   9. 镇静剂   10. 麻药
         zhèngzhuàng   zhào X guāng   shǒushù   zhènjìngjì   máyào

      11. 盲肠   12. 观察室   13. 手术后情况   14. 特护病房
         mángcháng   guāncháshì   shǒushù hòu qíngkuàng   tèhù bìngfán

Chapter 18: At the theater and the movies

1.   1. 看戏   2. 音乐会   3. 喜剧   4. 演，主角
        kànxì   yīnyuèhuì   xǐjù   yǎn, zhǔjué

     5. 演员   6. 幕，场   7. 幕间休息   8. 观众
        yǎnyuán   mù, chǎng   mùjiān xiūxi   guānzhòng

2.   1. 悲剧   2. 女演员   3. 男主角
        bēijù   nǚ yǎnyuán   nán zhǔjué

3.   1. 票   2. 卖完   3. 演出   4. 楼   5. 楼
        piào   màiwán   yǎnchū   lóu   lóu

     6. 一楼   7. 右边   8. 多少   9. 前   10. 票
        yī lóu   yòubiān   duōshǎo   qián   piào

     11. 排   12. 座   13. 演出
        pái   zuò   yǎnchū

4.   1. B今天去买票了。
        B jīntiān qù mǎi piào le.

     2. 不去。
        Bú qù.

     3. 今天晚上的票卖完了。
        Jīntiān wǎnshang de piào màiwán le.

     4. 明天的还有。
        Míngtiān de hái yǒu.

     5. 两张。
        Liǎng zhāng.

     6. 不是。
        Bú shì.

     7. 他不喜欢楼上的票。
        Tā bù xǐhuan lóu shàng de piào.

     8. 一楼左边五排六、七座。
        yī lóu zuǒbiān wǔ pái liù, qī zuò.

     9. 喜欢。
        Xǐhuan.

     10. 因为看戏时他们喜欢坐在前面。
        Yīnwèi kàn xì shí tāmen xǐhuan zuò zài qiánmiàn.

5.   1. B在售票处买票。
        B zài shòupiàochù mǎi piào.

2. 售票处的人会告诉买票的人演出开始的时间。
Shòupiàochù de rén huì gàosù mǎi piào de rén yǎnchū kāishǐ de shíjiān.

3. B不想买楼上的票。
B bù xiǎng mǎi lóushàng de piào.

4. B买了明天晚上的票。
B mǎi le míngtiān wǎnshang de piào.

5. A看戏喜欢坐在前面。
A kànxì xǐhuan zuòzài qiánmiàn.

6.
1. 功夫/武打	2. 拍	3. 字幕	4. 电影票	5. 离
gōngfu/wǔdǎ	pāi	zìmù	diànyǐngpiào	lí
6. 国	7. 字幕	8. 主角	9. 动画片	9. 喜剧片
guó	zìmù	zhǔjué	dònghuà piān	xǐjù piān

Chapter 19: Sports

1.
1. 一个队有11个队员。
Yí ge duì yǒu shíyī ge duìyuán.

2. 一场比赛中有两个队。
Yì chǎng bǐsài zhōng yǒu liǎng ge duì.

3. 队员在足球场上比赛。
Duìyuán zài zúqiúchǎng shàng bǐsài.

4. 守门员守门。
Shǒuményuán shǒumén.

5. 队员把球传给自己队的队员。
Duìyuán bǎ qiú chuángěi zìjǐ duì de duìyuán.

6. 守门员看见球来了，会挡住球。
Shǒuményuán kànjiàn qiú lái le, huì dǎngzhù qiú.

7. 要是一个队员踢进一个球，这个队就得分了。
Yàoshi yí ge duìyuán tījìn yí ge qiú, zhèi ge duì jiù défēn le.

8. 裁判员可以判队员犯规。
Cáipànyuán kěyǐ pàn duìyuán fànguī.

9. 上半场结束以后，我们还不能知道哪个队赢了。
Shàng bàn chǎng jiéshù yǐhòu, wǒmen hái bù néng zhīdao nǎ ge duì yíng le.

10. 要是双方都没有进球，就是平局。
Yàoshi shuāngfāng dōu méiyǒu jìn qiú, jiù shi píngjú.

2.
1. 足球	2. 队	3. 足球场	4. 传	5. 抢	6. 射门
zúqiú	duì	zúqiúchǎng	chuán	qiǎng	shèmén
7. 踢进	8. 挡住	9. 上半场	10. 进球	11. 得分/分数	
tījìn	dǎngzhù	shàngbànchǎng	jìnqiú	défēn/fēnshù	

3.
1. 球门	2. 队员	3. 记分板	4. 球	5. 裁判	6. 哨子
qiúmén	duìyuán	jìfēnbǎn	qiú	cáipàn	shàozi

4.
1. 运动员，双打		2. 网球拍	3. 过	4. 网球场
yùndòngyuán, shuāngdǎ		wǎngqiúpāi	guò	wǎngqiúchǎng
5. 出界	6. 发，接	7. 擦网		
chūjiè	fā, jiē	cāwǎng		

5.
1. 篮球场上	2. 投篮	3. 篮球	4. 篮里头	5. 投中了	6. 能
lánqiúchǎng shàng	tóulán	lánqiú	lán lǐtou	tóuzhòngle	néng

6. 1. d   2. f   3. e   4. a   5. c   6. b

7.　1. 拳　　2. 掌　　3. 实步　　4. 虚步　　5. 弯腿　　6. 直腿　　7. 弓步
　　　quán　　zhǎng　　shíbù　　xūbù　　wāntuǐ　　zhítuǐ　　gōngbù

Chapter 20: Computer and Internet

1.　1. 台式电脑　　2. 手提式电脑　　3. 主机　　4. 打印机
　　　táishì diànnǎo　　shǒutíshì diànnǎo　　zhǔjī　　dǎyìnjī

　　5. 显示器　　6. 键盘　　7. 滑鼠　　8. 硬件
　　　xiǎnshìqì　　jiànpán　　huáshǔ　　yìngjiàn

2.　1. 笔记本　　2. 指令，信息　　3. 硬件　　4. 显示器　　5. 奔腾
　　　bǐjìběn　　zhǐlìng, xìnxī　　yìngjiàn　　xiǎnshìqì　　bēnténg

　　6. 内存　　7. 软盘　　8. 光盘　　9. 打印机　　10. 扫描仪
　　　nèicún　　ruǎnpán　　guāngpán　　dǎyìnjī　　sǎomiáoyí

3.　1. 电脑机和其他有形设备
　　　diànnǎo jī he qítā yǒuxíng shèbèi

　　2. 一般公司和个人用的电脑
　　　yìbān gōngsi he gèrén yòng de diànnǎo

　　3. 储存信息的硬件设备
　　　chǔcún xìnxī de yìngjiàn shèbèi

　　4. 放在桌子上的电脑
　　　fàngzài zhuōzi shàng de diànnǎo

　　5. 可以随身携带的小型电脑
　　　kěyǐ suíshēn xiédài de xiǎoxíng diànnǎo

4.　1. 指示电脑工作的系统
　　　zhǐshì diànnǎo gōngzuò de xìtǒng

　　2. 控制电脑操作的一系列指令
　　　kòngzhì diànnǎo cāozuò de yí xìliè zhǐlìng

5.　1. 指示　　2. 操作　　3. 图标　　4. 双击　　5. 菜单，工具
　　　zhǐshì　　cāozuò　　túbiāo　　shuāngjī　　càidān, gōngjù

6.　1. 文字　　2. 软件　　3. 另存　　4. 删除　　5. 复制，粘贴
　　　wénzì　　ruǎnjiàn　　lìng cún　　shānchú　　fùzhì, zhāntiē

　　6. 检查　　7. 表格　　8. 公式　　9. 管理　　10. 查找
　　　jiǎnchá　　biǎogé　　gōngshì　　guǎnlǐ　　cházhǎo

7.　1. 开机　　2. 关机　　3. 取消　　4. 文件　　5. 退出　　6. 密码　　7. 打印
　　　kāi jī　　guān jī　　qǔxiāo　　wénjiàn　　tuìchū　　mìmǎ　　dǎyìn

8.　1. 互联网　　2. 信息　　3. 图象　　4. 万维网　　5. "猫"
　　　hùliánwǎng　　xìnxī　　túxiàng　　wànwéiwǎng　　"māo"

　　6. 帐户　　7. 密码　　8. 浏览器　　9. 网址　　10. 下载
　　　zhànghù　　mìmǎ　　liúlǎnqì　　wǎngzhǐ　　xiàzǎi

9.　1 - C　　2 - E　　3 - F　　4 - A　　5 - B　　6 - D

10.　1. 电子邮件是在网上交流的邮件。
　　　Diànzǐ yóujiàn shi zài wǎng shàng jiāoliú de yóujiàn.

　　2. 收件人的地址叫电子邮箱地址。
　　　Shōujiànrén de dìzhǐ jiào diànzǐ yóuxiāng dìzhǐ.

　　3. 在收信箱里可以找到别人给你的电子邮件。
　　　Zài shōuxìnxiāng lǐ kěyǐ zhǎodào biérén gěi nǐ de diànzǐ yóujiàn.

　　4. 写好的信件就可以发送出去了。
　　　Xiéhǎo de xìnjiàn jiù kěyǐ fāsòng chūqù le.

5. 朋友给你写信你就应该回信。
Péngyǒu gěi nǐ xiě xìn nǐ jiù yīnggāi huíxìn.

6. 不需要的信件可以删除。
Bù xūyào de xìnjiàn kěyǐ shānchú.

Chapter 21: The weather

1. 1. 热，闷   2. 冷，下雪   3. 凉快   4. 暖和   5. 晴天
    rè, mēn   lěng, xiàxuě   liángkuài   nuǎnhuo   qíngtiān

    6. 雨   7. 阴天   8. 雾   9. 雷   10. 摄氏
    yǔ   yīntiān   wù   léi   shèshì

2. 1. 太阳很大，可是不热，有风。
    Tàiyáng hěn dà, kěshì bú rè, yǒu fēng.

    2. 明天是阴天，没有太阳，可能会下雨。
    Míngtiān shi yīntiān, méiyǒu tàiyáng, kěnéng huì xià yǔ.

    3. 会下大雪，很冷。
    Huì xià dà xuě, hěn lěng.

3. 1. 有太阳   2. 热   3. 天气不好   4. 大风大雨
    yǒu tàiyáng   rè   tiānqì bù hǎo   dà fēng dà yǔ

    5. 冷   6. 闪电   7. 热   8. 阴
    lěng   shǎndiàn   rè   yīn

4. 1. F   2. T   3. F   4. F   5. T   6. F   7. T   8. T

5. Report 1:

    1. 天气不太好   2. 不是一直多云   3. 没有   4. 没有   5. 很不好
    tiānqì bú tài hǎo bú shì yìzhí duōyún méiyǒu   méiyǒu   hěn bù hǎo

    6. 东南   7. 5-6级   8. 摄氏28度   9. 摄氏22度   10. 不冷
    dōngnán   wǔ dào liù jí   shèshì 28 dù   shèshì 22 dù   bù něng

    Report 2:

    1. 不对   2. 没有   3. 不对   4. 冷   5. 0度
    bú duì   méiyǒu   bú buì   lěng   líng dù

    6. 0下4度   7. 没有   8. 没有   9. 对   10. 冬天
    líng xià sì dù   méiyǒu   méiyǒu   duì   dōngtiān

Chapter 22: Education

1. 1. d   2. g   3. h   4. f   5. a   6. i   7. c   8. e   9. b   10. j

2. 1. 幼儿园   2. 年级   3. 年级   4. 小学老师   5. 念书，写字   6. 黑板
    yòuéryuán   niánjí   niánjí   xiǎoxué lǎoshī   niànshū, xiězì   hēibǎn

3. 1. 中学生   2. 中学老师   3. 寄宿生
    zhōngxué shēng   zhōngxué lǎoshī   jìsù shēng

    4. 走读生   5. 书包   6. 不对，也上别的课。
    zǒudúshēng   shūbāo   bú duì, yě shàng biéde kè

    7. 老师讲课，学生听课，做笔记   8. 校服
    lǎoshī jiǎngkè, xuéshēng tīngkè, zuò bǐjì   xiàofú

    9. 做功课   10. 铅笔或圆珠笔   11. 有   12. 好分数
    zuò gōngkè   qiānbǐ huò yuánzhūbǐ   yǒu   hǎo fēnshù

4.   1. b   2. b   3. a   4. b   5. b

5.   1. 高中   2. 初中   3. 学生   4. 门   5. 100
         gāozhōng   chūzhōng   xuéshēng   mén   yìbǎi

6.   1. 高考   2. 学费   3. 开学   4. 奖学金   5. 硕士
         gāokǎo   xuéfèi   kāixué   jiǎngxuéjīn   shuòshì

      6. 教授   7. 学位   8. 博士   9. 宿舍   10. 食堂
         jiàoshòu   xuéwèi   bóshì   sùshè   shítáng

7.   1. 高考   2. 法学院   3. 文学   4. 学费，奖学金   5. 开学   6. 注册
         gāokǎo   fǎxuéyuàn   wénxué   xuéfèi, jiǎngxuéjīn   kāixué   zhùcè

8.   1. 注册   2. 申请奖学金   3. 记笔记   4. 毕业证书   5. 硕士
         zhùcè   shēnqǐng jiǎngxuéjīn   jì bǐjì   bìyè zhèngshū   shuòshì

9.   1. 医学院   2. 法学院   3. 工学院   4. 文学院   5. 理学院
         yīxuéyuàn   fǎxuéyuàn   gōngxuéyuàn   wénxuéyuàn   lǐxuéyuàn

Chapter 23: Business

1.   1. e   2. f   3. a   4. b   5. c   6. d

2.   1. 卖方，买方   2. 消费者   3. 批发商   4. 零售商   5. 进出口
         màifāng, mǎifāng   xiāofèizhě   pīfāshāng   língshòushāng   jìnchūkǒu

      6. 大   7. 合股人   8. 经理   9. 董事会，股东   10. 交易
         dà   hégǔrén   jīnglǐ   dǒngshìhuì, gǔdōng   jiāoyì

3.   1. 市场
         shìchǎng

      2. 产品的广告和促销
         chǎnpǐn de guǎnggào he cùxiāo

      3. 市场的供应和需求
         shìchǎng de gōngyìng he xūqiú

      4. 盈利
         yínglì

      5. 税
         shuì

4.   1. 税   2. 市场部   3. 成本   4. 利润
         shuì   shìchǎng bù   chéngběn   lìrùn

5.   1. 财务   2. 财务   3. 资产负债   4. 财务   5. 利润
         cáiwù   cáiwù   zīchǎn fùzhài   cáiwù   lìrùn

Glossary: Chinese -English
索引： 中文-英文

爱情片	àiqíngpiān	romance
癌症	áizhèng	cancer
安静	ānjìng	quiet
安全带	ānquándài	seat belt
安全	ānquán	safety, security
安置	ānzhì	place, put
安装	ānzhuāng	install
按	àn	press
案板/切菜板	ànbǎn/qiēcàibǎn	chopping board
按键电话	ànjiàn diànhuà	touchtone
按钮，键	ànniǔ, jiàn	button
按下	ànxià	press down
按(照)	àn(zhào)	according to
熬	áo	simmer
8号	bā hào	number 8
芭蕾	bālěi	ballet
白	bái	white
白兰地	báilándì	brandy
白葡萄酒	bái pútaojiǔ	white wine
版	bǎn	version
办理登机(入住)手续	bànlǐ dēngjī (rùzhù) shǒuxù	check in
包	bāo	bag
包	bāo	bind up
包	bāo	hire/charter
包(括)	bāo (kuò)	include
包裹	bāoguǒ	package
包间	bāojiān	private room
包子	bāozi	steamed meat bun
保存	bǎocún	save
保险丝	bǎoxiǎnsī	fuse
保险	bǎoxiǎn	insurance
爆	bào	quick-fry
暴风雪	bàofēngxuě	snowstorm, blizzard
报(纸)	bào(zhǐ)	newspaper
背	bèi	back
被发现	bèi fāxiàn	be found out
悲剧	bēijù	tragedy
背心	bèixīn	vest
备用	bèiyòng	spare
杯子	bēizi	cup/glass
被子	bèizi	quilt
本市电话	běnshì diànhuà	local call
奔腾	Bēnténg	Pentium
绷带	bēngdài	bandage
壁橱	bìchú	closet
比分	bǐfēn	score
比赛	bǐsài	game
比赛	bǐsài	tournament
笔记本	bǐjì běn	notebook
必须	bìxū	must
毕业	bìyè	graduate
毕业证书	bìyè zhèngshū	diploma
鼻子	bízi	nose
编辑	biānjí	edit

变速箱润滑油	biànsùxiāng rùnhuáyóu	transmission oil
扁桃腺	biǎntáoxiàn	tonsils
表	biǎo	form
标签	biāoqiān	label
标题栏	biāotí lán	title bar
瘪	biě	flat
别的	biéde	other
冰	bīng	ice
冰雹	bīngbáo	hail
冰箱	bīngxiāng	refrigerator
病史	bìngshǐ	medical history
病人	bìngrén	patient
拨	bō	dial
拨到	bōdào	set to (clock time)
拨号	bōhào	dial
拨号盘	bōhào pán	dial pad
拨号音	bōhàoyīn	dial tone
玻璃器皿	bōli qìmǐn	glassware
博士	bóshì	doctor/Ph.D.
补	bǔ	mend
部	bù	section
步法	bùfǎ	foot work
部件	bùjiàn	component
不好	bùhǎo	bad
不舒服	bù shūfu	uncomfortable
不通	bùtōng	congested
不准抽烟	bùzhǔn chōuyān	no smoking
擦	cā	wipe (clean)
擦干	cā gān	dry, towel dry
擦网球	cāwǎngqiú	net ball
踩	cǎi	step on
菜单	càidān	menu
菜单/选项单	càidān/ xuǎnxiàng dān	menu
菜单栏/选项栏	càidānlán /xuǎnxiàng lán	menu bar
菜刀	càidāo	kitchen knife
菜店	cài diàn	green grocer
裁缝师傅	cáifeng shīfu	tailor
裁判员	cáipànyuán	referee
财务报告	cáiwù bàogào	financial statement
餐车	cānchē	dining car
餐点	cāndiǎn	meal
餐巾纸	cānjīn zhǐ	napkin
餐厅	cāntīng	restaurant
舱	cāng	compartment
操作	cāozuò	operate
操作系统	cāozuò xìtǒng	operating system
测	cè	check
厕所	cèsuǒ	toilet
超级市场(超市)	chāo jí shìchǎng	supermarket
叉(子)	chā(zi)	fork
查	chá	check

查票	chápiào	check ticket
查找	cházhǎo	search
茶	chá	tea
茶几	chájī	coffee table
插入、填入	chārù, tiánrù	insert
插上	chāshang	plug in
插座	chāzuò	socket
产房	chǎnfáng	delivery room
产科医生	chǎnkē yīshēng	obstetrician
产品	chǎnpǐn	products
长	cháng	long
长裤	chángkù	pants/trousers
长丝袜/	chángsīwà/	panty hose
连裤袜	liánkùwà	
长途	chángtú	long distance
长途电话	chángtú diànhuà	long-distance call
长袖	chángxiù	long sleeve
场	chǎng	scenes
尝	cháng	taste
肠炎	chángyán	enteritis
朝	cháo	face
炒	chǎo	stir fry
炒饭	chǎo fàn	fried rice
炒粉	chǎo fěn	fried rice noodles
炒锅	chǎoguō	wok
炒面	chǎo miàn	fried noodles
车	chē	car
车道	chēdào	lane
车厢	chēxiāng	(train) car
衬裙	chènqún	slip
衬衫/衬衣	chènshān/chènyī	shirt, blouse
称	chēng	weigh
成本	chéngběn	production cost
乘客	chéngkè	passenger
乘务员	chéngwùyuán	flight attendants
程序	chéngxù	program
池	chí	pool
尺寸	chǐcùn	measurement
吃素	chīsù	vegetarian
冲洗	chōngxǐ	rinse
重新开机	chóngxīn kāijī	restart
抽	chōu	draw, collect
抽球	chōu qiú	slam the ball
抽屉	chōutì	drawer
抽烟区	chōuyān qū	smoking area
储存	chǔcún	store
厨房	chúfáng	kitchen
出港	chūgǎng	disembark
出界	chūjiè	out
出口	chūkǒu	exit
出口	chūkǒu	export
除了...以外	chúle...yǐwài	except for
处理	chǔlǐ	process
出纳	chūnà	teller
出纳窗口	chūnà chuāngkǒu	cashier's window
出示	chūshì	show
初中	chūzhōng	junior high
出租车/计程车/的士	chūzūchē, jìchéngchē,	taxi

	díshì	
传	chuán	pass/toss
床	chuáng	bed
床单	chuángdān	bed sheet
床垫	chuāngdiàn	mattress
床头柜	chuángtóuguì	bedside table
床罩	chuángzhào	bedspread
窗户	chuānghu	window
窗口	chuāngkǒu	window
窗帘	chuānglián	curtain
创口贴	chuāngkǒutiē	adhesive bandage
吹	chuī	blow
瓷器	cíqì	ceramics
从	cóng	from
葱	cōng	scallion
醋	cù	vinegar
促销	cùxiāo	promotion
存储器	cǔnchǔqì	memory
存款	cúnkuǎn	savings
存钱	cún qián	deposit money
存衣处	cúnyīchù	cloakroom
存一笔钱	cún yì bǐ qián	make a deposit
存折	cúnzhé	bankbook
打不开	dǎ bù kāi	can't open
打不着火	dǎ bù zháo huǒ	won't start
打"的"	dǎ dī	take a taxi
打(电话)	dǎ diànhuà	make (a call)
打过网	dǎ guò wǎng	over the net
打开	dǎ kāi	turn on
打扫	dǎsǎo	clean
打算	dǎsuàn	plan
打一针	dǎ yì zhēn	give an injection
打印	dǎyìn	print
打印机	dǎyìnjī	printer
大便	dàbiàn	feces
大道	dàdào	avenue
大风	dàfēng	gusty wind
大公司	dà gōngsī	corporation (big company)
大号	dàhào	large
大火	dà huǒ	high heat
大街	dàjiē	street
大陆	dàlù	mainland
大脑	dànǎo	brain
大票子	dà piàozi	large bills
大人	dàrén	adult
大学	dàxué	university/college
大衣	dàyī	coat
待	dāi	stay
带	dài	with
带点儿的	dài diǎnr	polka-dotted
带位员	dàiwèiyuán	usher
淡	dàn	plain, bland
单程票	dānchéngpiào	one way ticket
单打	dāndǎ	singles
单击	dān jī	single click
单人床	dānrénchuáng	single bed
单人房	dānrénfáng	single room
素色	dān sè	solid colored
单行道	dānxíngdào	one-way street
担架	dānjià	stretcher

挡住	dǎngzhù	block/stop
挡风玻璃	dǎngfēng bōli	windshield
刀	dāo	knife
到	dào	arrive in/at
到	dào	until (time)
到达/到港	dàodá/ dàogǎng	arrive
到站	dàozhàn	arrive at a station
倒档	dàodǎng	reverse gear
道路变窄	dàolù biàn zhǎi	Road narrows!
导演	dǎoyǎn	director
得	dé	catch
得一分	dé yìfēn	score a point
登机楼	dēngjīlóu	terminal
登机	dēngji	board the plane
登机口	dēngjīkǒu	boarding gate
登机牌	dēngjīpái	boarding pass
灯	dēng	light
灯泡	dēngpào	light bulb
灯芯绒	dēngxīnróng	corduroy
等	děng	wait
低	dī	low
底	dǐ	sole
地区号(码)	dìqūhào(mǎ)	area code
地毯	dìtǎn	carpet
地铁	dìtiě	subway
地铁站	dìtiězhàn	subway station
地址	dìzhǐ	address
颠簸	diānbǒ	bounce/bump
点菜	diǎncài	order dishes
点火	diǎn huǒ	start the engine
点火器	diǎnhuǒqì	ignition switch
电车	diànchē	trolley
电池	diànchí	battery
电吹风	diànchuīfēng	hair drier
电灯	diàndēng	lamp
电饭锅	diàn fànguō	electric rice cooker
电工	diàngōng	electrician
电话卡	diànhuàkǎ	telephone card
电话号码	diànhuà hàomǎ	phone number
电话号码簿	diànhuà hàomǎbù	phone book
电炉	diànlú	electric stove
电视	diànshì	TV
电视	diànshì	television
电影	diànyǐng	movie
电影/片子	diànyǐng/piānzi	movie/film
电影院	diànyǐng yuàn	cinema
电源插头	diànyuán chātóu	plug
电子屏幕	diànzǐ píngmù	electronic screen
电子邮箱 地址	diànzǐ yóuxiāng dìzhǐ	e-mail address
电子邮件 (电邮)	diànzǐ yóujiàn (diànyóu)	e-mail
癫痫	diānxián	epilepsy
掉了	diào le	lost
顶	dǐng	butt (with one's head)
定价格	dìng jiàgé	establish a price
丢了	diūle	lost
洞	dòng	hole
董事会	dǒngshìhuì	board of directors
动画片	dònghuà piān	cartoon
动手术	dòng shǒushù	operate
动作	dòngzuò	movement
动作片	dòngzuòpiān	action movie
豆制品	dòu zhìpǐn	soybean product
度	dù	degree (temperature)
堵车/塞车	dǔchē/sāichē	traffic jam
堵住	dǔzhù	clogged up
肚子疼	dùzi téng	stomachache
端	duān	end (of object)
短	duǎn	short
短裤	duǎnkù	shorts
短途	duǎntú	short distance
短袖	duǎnxiù	short sleeve
断了	duànle	disconnected
队	duì	team
队员	duìyuán	player
对方	duìfāng	the other party
对方/对手	duìfāng/duìshǒu	opponent
对方付费 电话	duìfāng fùfèi diànhuà	collect call
兑换处	duìhuànchù	exchange bureau
兑换率	duìhuànlù	exchange rate
兑现(支票)	duìxiàn zhīpiào	cash (a check)
炖	dùn	stew
多/超过	duō/chāoguò	more than
多大(号)	duōdà (hào)	what size
多久	duōjiǔ	how long (time)
多久来 一趟?	Duōjiǔ lái yí tàng?	How often does it come?
多少钱	duōshǎoqián	how much
多云	duōyún	cloudy
多重	duōzhòng	how heavy
饿	è	hungry
恶心	ěxīn	nauseous
耳朵	ěrduō	ear
耳机	ěrjī	headset
二楼	èr lóu	second floor
儿童	értóng	children
发动机盖	fādòngjī gài	hood of a car
发动机油	fādòngjīyóu	engine oil
发冷	fālěng	chills
发球	fāqiú	serve the ball
发烧	fāshāo	fever
发刷	fàshuā	hairbrush
发送	fāsòng	sent
发炎	fāyán	inflammation
罚款	fákuǎn	fine
法兰绒	fǎlánróng	flannel
法学院	fǎxuéyuàn	law school
饭店	fàndiàn	hotel
犯规	fànguī	foul
饭馆/餐馆	fànguǎn/ cānguǎn	restaurant
房间	fángjiān	room
防守	fángshǒu	defense
访问	fǎngwèn	visit
方向	fāngxiàng	direction

方向盘	fāngxiàngpán	steering wheel	高中	gāozhōng	senior high
放学以后	fàngxué yǐhòu	after school	各	gè	each
放直	fàngzhí	straighten	胳膊/手臂	gēbo/shǒubì	arm
防皱	fángzhòu	wrinkle-resistant	胳膊肘	gēbozhǒu	elbow
肥	féi	wide/big (for clothing)	歌剧	gējù	opera
			割破	gēpò	cut
肺部	fèibù	lungs	个人(的)	gèrén (de)	personal
飞机	fēijī	airplane	个人电脑	gèrén diànnǎo	PC
飞机场	fēijīchǎng	airport	歌舞	gēwǔ	song and dance
飞机票	fēijīpiào	airline ticket	歌星	gēxīng	singing star
飞往	fēiwǎng	bound for	格子	gézi	checked
飞行时间	fēixíng shíjiān	flying time	宫保鸡丁	gōngbǎo jīdīng	spicy diced
飞行员	fēixíngyuán	pilot			chicken with
肥皂盒	féizào hé	soapdish			peanuts
肥皂/香皂	féizào/xiāngzào	soap	弓步	gōngbù	bow stance
肺结核	fèi jiéhé	tuberculosis	功夫片/	gōngfupiān	Kung-fu movie
分机	fēnjī	extension	武打片	wǔdǎpiān	
分机号码	fēnjī hàomǎ	extension number	公共	gōnggòng	public
分开算	fēn kāi suàn	split the bill/go Dutch	公共厕所	gōnggòng cèsuǒ	public restroom
			公共电话亭	gōnggòng diànhuà tíng	telephone booth
分娩中	fēnmiǎn zhōng	in labor			
分数	fēnshù	grade/score	公共汽车	gōnggòng qìchē	bus
分钟	fēnzhōng	minute	(公共)汽车站	(gōnggòng) qìchē zhàn	bus stop
缝	fèng	seam			
缝	féng	sew	工具栏	gōngjù lán	toolbar
缝合	fénghé	stitch	公斤	gōngjīn	kilo
风很大	fēng hěn dà	windy	公立	gōnglì	public
风衣	fēngyī	trench coat	公里	gōnglǐ	kilometer
浮动	fúdòng	fluctuate	功能	gōngnéng	function
附近	fùjìn	nearby	公文包	gōngwénbāo	briefcase
副食品店	fùshípǐn diàn	grocery store	公务	gōngwù	on business
伏特加	fútèjiā	vodka	工学院	gōngxuéyuàn	engineering school
服务	fúwù	service	供应	gōngyìng	serve
服务费	fúwù fèi	service fee	供应和需求	gōngyìng hé xūqiú	supply and demand
服务员	fúwùyuán	waiter			
付帐	fù zhàng	pay a bill	公园	gōngyuán	park
复制	fùzhì	copy	工作区	gōngzuò qū	working area
服装店	fúzhuāng diàn	clothing store	购物	gòuwù	shopping
房价	fángjià	room charge	股东	gǔdōng	stockholders
擀	gǎn	roll	股份	gǔfèn	share
擀面杖	gǎnmiànzhàng	rolling pin	股票	gǔpiào	stock
盖上	gàishang	cover	股票市场	gǔpiào shìchǎng	stock market
干	gān	dry	固定骨头	gùdìng gǔtóu	set the bone
干洗	gānxǐ	dry clean	故事片	gùshipiān	drama
干洗店	gānxǐdiàn	dry cleaner's	鼓掌/拍手	gǔzhǎng/pāishǒu	applaud
感冒	gǎnmào	have a cold			
肝脏	gānzàng	liver	骨折	gǔzhé	bone fracture
高	gāo	high	刮胡子	guā húzi	shave
糕点	gāodiǎn	bakery	挂	guà	hang up
高度	gāodù	altitude, height	挂号	guàhào	register
高峰期	gāofēngqī	rush hour	挂号处	guàhàochù	registration (office)
高跟	gāogēn	high heel			
高光灯	gāoguāng dēng	high beam	挂号信	guàhàoxìn	registered mail
高级	gāojí	first class	挂一挡	guà yīdǎng	put in first gear
高考	gāokǎo	college entrance exam	关闭	guānbì	close
			关不上	guān bú shàng	can't close
高速公路	gāosù gōnglù	express way	关机	guānjī	shut down
高速公路费	gāosù gōnglù fèi	toll	观察	guānchá	observe
			观察室	guāncháshì	recovery room
高速公路 入口	gāosù gōnglù rùkǒu	highway entrance	关节炎	guānjiéyán	arthritis
			管理	guǎnlǐ	manage

盥洗池	guànxǐchí	basin	后视镜	hòushìjìng	rearview mirror
观众	guānzhòng	audience	后退	hòutuì	step backward
广播	guǎngbō	broadcast	后退	hòutuì	back
广告	guǎnggào	advertisement	候车室	hòuchēshì	waiting room
光盘	guāngpán	CD	候诊室	hòuzhěn shì	waiting room
光线好	guāngxiàn hǎo	bright	呼	hū	beep
贵	guì	expensive	呼机	hūjī	beeper
柜台	guì tái	counter	呼机号码	hūjī hàomǎ	beeper number
规则	guīzé	regulation	壶	hú	pot
滚动条	gǔndòng tiáo	scroll bar	胡椒	hújiāo	pepper
锅	guō	pot	互联	hùlián	inter-
锅铲	guōchǎn	turner, spatula	护士	hùshì	nurse
锅盖	guōgài	lid	户头	hùtóu	account
锅贴	guōtiē	fried dumplings	呼吸	hūxī	breathe
国道	guódào	national highway	护照	hùzhào	passport
国际	guójì	international	回信	huíxìn	reply
国际电话	guójì diànhuà	international call	化纤料	huà xiān liào	synthetic fabric
国家号码	guójiā hàomǎ	country code	花	huā	flowers
国内	guónèi	domestic	花	huā	patterned
国营	guóyíng	state-owned	花边儿	huābiānr	lace
过敏	guòmǐn	allergic	画	huà	painting
过敏症	guòmǐnzhèng	allergy	话剧	huàjù	drama
过热	guò rè	overheating	滑鼠	huáshǔ	mouse (with computer)
果汁	guǒzhī	fruit juice			
海	hǎi	sea	化验	huàyàn	lab-test
海拔	hǎibá	above sea level	化妆	huàzhuāng	put on make-up
海关官员	hǎiguān guānyuán	customs officer	踝骨	huáigǔ	ankle
			坏	huài	breakdown
海绵	hǎimián	sponge	坏了	huài le	broken
海鲜	hǎixiān	seafood	怀孕	huáiyùn	pregnant
海运	hǎiyùn	by sea	换	huàn	change, exchange
汗衫/汗背心	hànshān/hàn bèixīn	undershirt	换车	huàn chē	transfer
			换挡杆	huàndǎnggǎn	gear shift lever
航空公司	hángkōng gōngsī	airline company	换挡	huàn dǎng	change gears
			换发球	huànfāqiú	change of service
航空信	hángkōngxìn	airmail	换开	huànkāi	break (a large bill), make change
航班/班机	hángbān/bānjī	flight			
好	hǎo	ready	欢迎	huānyíng	welcome
号	hào	size	黄瓜	huángguā	cucumber
豪华	háohuá	luxurious	回电话	huí diànhuà	return call
号码错了	hàomǎ cuòle	wrong number	回收站	huíshōu zhàn	Recycle Bin
好在	hǎozài	fortunately	汇票	huìpiào	money order
喝	hē	drink	混纺	hùnfǎng	blend
盒饭	héfàn	boxed meal	混合双打	hùnhé shuāngdǎ	mixed doubles
合股公司	hégǔ gōngsī	partnerships	火车站	huǒchēzhàn	train station
合股人	hégǔrén	partner	火鸡	huǒjī	turkey
合身,合适	héshēn, héshì	fit	火腿	huǒtuǐ	ham
合同	hétóng	contract	几	jǐ	a few
黑	hēi	black	鸡	jī	chicken
黑板	hēibǎn	blackboard	(鸡)蛋	(jī) dàn	eggs
很好	hěn hǎo	nice	级	jí	degree (wind force)
红	hóng	red			
红茶	hóngchá	black tea	寄	jì	send
红绿灯	hónglùdēng	traffic light	基本	jīběn	basic
红葡萄酒	hóng pútaojiǔ	red wine	寄出去	jì chūqù	send out
红色通道	hóngsè tōngdào	red channel	机场费	jīchǎng fèi	airport departure tax
红烧	hóngshāo	braise in soy sauce			
后	hòu	later	机翼	jīyì	wing
后备箱	hòubèixiāng	trunk	机组人员	jīzǔ rényuán	crew
后舱	hòucāng	rear cabin	计程表	jìchéngbiǎo	meter
后面	hòumiàn	back	记分板	jìfēnbǎn	scoreboard

系紧	jìjǐn	fasten
挤脚	jǐjiǎo	hurt the feet
几路	jǐ lù	which route
纪录片	jìlùpiān	documentary
寄宿生	jìsùshēng	boarder, resident student
寄信人	jìxìnrén	sender
继续,保持	jìxù, bǎochí	keep (doing), continue
急性	jíxìng	acute
急诊室	jízhěnshì	emergency room
家具	jiājù	furniture
加	jiā	add. fill
加大号	jiādàhào	extra-large
加急费	jiājífèi	fee for express service
加速	jiāsù	accelerate
加油站	jiāyóuzhàn	gas station
夹克	jiákè	jacket
价钱	jiàqián	price
驾(驶执)照	jià(shǐ zhí)zhào	driver's license
驾驶舱	jiàshǐcāng	cockpit
肩膀	jiānbǎng	shoulder
检查	jiǎnchá	examine, check
建立	jiànlì	set up
键盘	jiànpán	keyboard
剪切	jiǎnqiē	cut
健身运动	jiànshēn yùndòng	workout
减速让行!	jiǎnsù ràngxíng	Yield!
浆	jiāng	starch
将	jiāng	will (formal), about to
讲课	jiǎngkè	lecture
奖学金	jiǎngxuéjīn	scholarship
酱油	jiàngyóu	soy sauce
叫	jiào	call
叫号	jiàohào	call number
脚	jiǎo	foot
脚步	jiǎobù	step
搅拌机	jiǎobànjī	blender
交叉	jiāochā	cross
郊区	jiāoqū	suburb
交税	jiāo shuì	pay duty
交通，运输	jiāotōng, yùnshū	transportation
交通标志	jiāotōng biāozhì	traffic sign
教育	jiàoyù	education
教室	jiàoshì	classroom
教授	jiàoshòu	professor
教(书)/(课)	jiāo(shū)/(ke)	teach
饺子	jiǎozi	dumplings
饺子皮	jiǎozi pí	dumpling wrap
接	jiē	connect
接待	jiēdài	reception
接电话	jiē diànhuà	answer a phone
接球	jiēqiú	return
接生	jiēshēng	deliver (a child)
接线员	jiēxiànyuán	operator
街	jiē	street

街口/街角	jiēkǒu/jiējiǎo	street corner
节目单	jiémùdān	program
结束	jiéshù	end, close
结余	jiéyú	balance
结帐	jié zhàng	figure out the bill
结帐/买单	jiézhàng/mǎidān	pay check/bill in restaurants
斤	jīn	half-kilo
近	jìn	close, near
紧	jǐn	tight
紧身裤	jǐnshēnkù	tights
紧急出口	jǐnjí chūkǒu	emergency exit
紧急情况	jǐnjí qíngkuàng	emergency
进口	jìnkǒu	import
进口片	jìnkǒupiān	imported film
今天	jīntiān	today
禁止超车!	jìnzhǐ chāochē	No passing!
禁止调头!	jìnzhǐ diàotóu	No U turn!
禁止机动车通行!	jìnzhǐ jīdòngchē tōngxíng	No thoroughfare for vehicles!
禁止鸣喇叭	jìnzhǐ míng lǎbā	No honking!
禁止驶入	jìnzhǐ shǐrù	Do not enter!
禁止停车!	jìnzhǐ tíngchē	No parking!
禁止通行!	jìnzhǐ tōngxíng	No thoroughfare!
禁止左转弯	jìnzhǐ zuǒzhuǎnwān	No left turn!
经过	jīngguò	pass
经济(舱)	jīngjì (cāng)	economy class
经理	jīnglǐ	manager
经营情况	jīngyíng qíngkuàng	management/ performance
精神病	jīngshénbìng	mental illness
惊险片	jīngxiǎnpiān	thriller
镜子	jìngzi	mirror
酒	jiǔ	alcohol
酒单	jiǔ dān	wine list
酒楼/酒家	jiǔlóu/jiǔjiā	restaurant
救护车	jiùhùchē	ambulance
救生衣	jiùshēngyī	life vest
菊花	júhuā	chrysanthemum
桔子汁/ 橙汁	júzi zhī/chéngzhī	orange juice
剧场	jùchǎng	theater
剧院	jùyuàn	theater
卷	juǎn	roll (of paper)
卷起	juǎnqǐ	roll up
决定	juédìng	decide
烤	kǎo	roast
咖啡	kāfēi	coffee
咖啡色	kāfēisè	brown
开	kāi	leave/drive
开	kāi	open
开	kāi	prescribe
开(车)	kāi (chē)	drive
开关	kāiguān	light switch
开罐刀	kāiguàndāo	can opener
开启/打开	kāiqǐ/dǎkāi	open
开始/开机	kāishǐ/kāijī	start
开始/开演	kāishǐ/kāiyǎn	start/begin
开水	kāishuǐ	boiled water

开水壶	kāishuǐhú	kettle	阑尾/盲肠	lánwěi/	appendix
开胃菜	kāiwèi cài	appetizer		mángcháng	
开线	kāixiàn	torn	阑尾炎/	lánwěiyán/	appendicitis
开学	kāixué	school starts	盲肠炎	mángchángyán	
看病	kànbìng	see a doctor	老	lǎo	overdone
看演出	kàn yǎnchū	see a show	烙饼	làobǐng	make pancakes
抗生素	kàngshēngsù	antibiotics	老师	lǎoshī	teacher
烤	kǎo	baked	雷雨	léiyǔ	thunderstorm
烤/焗	kǎo/jū	grilled	雷,打雷	léi, dǎléi	thunder
烤箱	kǎoxiāng	oven	冷	lěng	cold
考试	kǎoshì	test/exam	冷冻	lěngdòng	frozen
考上	kǎoshàng	be admitted by	冷冻室	lěngdòngshì	freezer
靠窗座位	kàochuāng zuò wèi	window seat	冷却液	lěngquèyè	coolant
			离	lí	distance to or from
靠窗	kào chuāng	by the window	离港时间	lígǎng shíjiān	departure time
靠墙角	kào qiángjiǎo	at the corner	离合器	líhéqì	clutch
靠走道座位	kào zǒudào zuò wèi	aisle seat	离合器踏板	líhéqì tàbǎn	clutch pedal
			梨	lí	pear
咳嗽	késou	cough	里程	lǐchéng	mileage
课本	kèběn	textbook	里程表	lǐchéngbiǎo	odometer
课(程)	kè (chéng)	subject, course	里脊	lǐji	tenderloin
客房服务员	kèfáng fúwùyuán	(hotel) housekeeper	利润	lìrùn	profit
			立升	lìshēng	liter
科幻片	kēhuànpiān	science fiction	沥水	lìshuǐ	strain
可乐	kělè	coke	沥水盆	lìshuǐpén	strainer
客满	kèmǎn	full (no vacancy)	理学院	lǐxuéyuàn	school of science
客人	kèrén	guest	荔枝	lìzhī	lychee
客厅	kètīng	living room	脸	liǎn	cheek/face
课文	kèwén	the text	连接	liánjiē	connect
课桌	kèzhuō	desk	连通	liántōng	connection
空	kōng	empty/vacant	连衣裙	liányīqún	dress
空档	kōngdǎng	neutral gear	量	liáng	measure
空间	kōngjiān	space	亮	liàng	shine/on
空调	kōngtiáo	air conditioner	凉拌	liángbàn	cold and dressed with sauce
空位	kōng wèi	available seat/table			
空座位	kòng zuòwèi	vacant seat	凉菜	liángcài	cold dish
控制	kòngzhì	control	凉快	liángkuài	cool
口袋	kǒudài	pocket	凉鞋	liángxié	sandal
扣篮	kòulán	slam dunk	粮食	liángshi	grain
扣子	kòuzi	button	量体温	liáng tǐwēn	take temperature
胯骨	kuàgǔ	hip	聊天	liáotiān	chat
块	kuài	bar	料子	liàozi	fabric
快	kuài	fast	列车员	lièchēyuán	conductor
会计师	kuàijìshī	accountant	淋巴	línbā	glands
筷子	kuàizi	chopsticks	淋浴	línyù	shower
筷子筒	kuàizi tǒng	chopstick holder	另存	lìngcún	save as
矿泉水	kuàngquánshuǐ	mineral water	领带	lǐngdài	tie
亏损	kuīsǔn	loss, deficit	零件	língjiàn	parts
垃圾	lājī	garbage	零钱	língqián	small change
拉肚子/腹泻	lā dùzi/fùxiè	diarrhea	领取	lǐngqǔ	claim
垃圾筒	lājītǒng	garbage can	领取单	lǐngqǔ dān	claim stub
喇叭	lǎbā	horn	零售	língshòu	retail
辣	là	spicy/hot	零售商	língshòushāng	retailer
辣椒	làjiāo	chili/hot pepper	领域	lǐngyù	field
辣椒酱	làjiāo jiàng	chili sauce	留	liú	leave
来回票	láihuípiào	round trip ticket	留话	liúhuà	leave a message
来自	lái zì	come from	留言	liúyán	message
蓝	lán	blue	流鼻涕	liú bítì	running nose
篮(子)	lán(zi)	basket	流感	liúgǎn	flu
篮球	lánqiú	basketball	流行	liúxíng	popular
篮球场	lánqiúchǎng	basketball court	流行性	liúxíngxìng	mumps

腮腺炎	sāixiànyán	mumps
浏览	liúlǎn	browse
浏览器	liúlǎnqì	browser
龙虾	lóngxiā	lobster
楼上	lóushàng	upstairs
楼下	lóuxià	downstairs
漏(水/油)	lòu (shuǐ/yóu)	dripping/ leaking
绿茶	lùchá	green tea
路过	lùguò	pass through
路滑!	lù huá	Slippery road!
路口	lùkǒu	cross road/ intersection
炉眼	lúyǎn	burner
轮胎	lúntāi	tire
轮椅	lúnyǐ	wheelchair
绿色通道	lùsè tōngdào	green channel
旅途愉快!	lǚtú yúkuài	Bon Voyage!
旅行支票	lǚxíng zhīpiào	traveler's check
旅游	lǚyóu	tour
旅游鞋	lǚyóuxié	sneaker
卖完	màiwán	sold out
煤气炉	méiqìlú	gas stove
抹	mā	wipe
抹布	mābù	rag (to wipe things)
马上	mǎshàng	immediately
马桶	mǎtǒng	toilet
麻药	máyào	anesthesia
麻疹	mázhěn	measles
麻醉师	mázuìshī	anesthetist
买	mǎi	buy
卖	mài	sell
卖方	màifāng	seller
买方	mǎifāng	buyer
买卖/交易	mǎimài/jiāoyì	trade
卖完了	màiwán le	sold out
脉搏	màibó	pulse
慢	màn	slow
慢车	mànchē	local train
馒头	mántou	steamed buns
满员	mǎnyuán	full
占线	máng	(line is) busy
忙音	mángyīn	busy signal
毛巾	máojīn	towel
毛巾架	máojīn jià	towel bar
茅台	máotái	Maotai (a strong Chinese spirits)
毛毯	máotǎn	blanket
毛衣	máo yī	sweater
帽子	màozi	hat
每隔四小时	měi gé sì xiǎoshí	every 4 hours
没投中	méi tóuzhòng	miss the shot
没问题	méi wènti	no problem.
没进球	méi jìnqiú	no-score game
美元	měiyuán	dollar (U. S.)
闷热，湿热	mēnrè, shīrè	humid
米	mǐ	meter
米饭	mǐfàn	cooked rice
迷路	mílù	lost
密码	mìmǎ	PIN
(纯)棉	(chún) mián	(all) cotton
面包	miànbāo	bread
面条	miàntiáo	noodles
明天	míngtiān	tomorrow
明信片	míngxìnpiàn	postcard
茉莉花	mòlìhuā	jasmine
幕	mù	acts
幕间休息	mùjiān xiūxi	intermission
沐浴液	mùyùyè	body wash lotion
纳/交/上税	nà/jiāo/shàng shuì	pay tax
拿起	náqǐ	pick up
拿手菜/ 招牌菜	náshǒu cài/ zhāopáicài	house specialty
难受	nánshòu	sick
男演员	nán yǎnyuán	actor
男主角	nán zhǔjué	leading male actor
男子	nánzǐ	male
男子单打	nánzǐ dāndǎo	male single
闹钟	nàozhōng	alarm clock
内存	nèicún	RAM
内短裤/ 三角裤	nèiduǎnkù/ sānjiǎokù	underwear, briefs
内衣	nèiyī	underclothes
嫩	nèn	rare
能放进	néng fàngjìn	fit
你就到了	Nǐ jiù dào le.	You'll be there.
尼龙	nílóng	nylon
呢子	nízi	heavy woolen
念	niàn	read aloud
您慢慢吃	nín mànmàn chī	Enjoy!
牛奶	niú nǎi	milk
牛排	niúpái	steak
牛肉	niúròu	beef
扭伤	niǔshāng	sprain
牛仔裤	niúzǎikù	jeans
女演员	nǚ yǎnyuán	actress
女主角	nǚ zhǔjué	leading female actor
女子	nǚzi	female
暖和	nuǎnhuó	warm
暖气	nuǎnqì	heat
拍	pāi	shoot (a movie)
排	pái	row
排队	páiduì	line up
排水	pái shuǐ	drain
判	pàn	judge
盘子	pánzi	plate
旁听	pángtīng	audit
螃蟹	pángxiè	crab
抛锚	pāomáo	stalled
泡澡	pào zǎo	take a bath
配	pèi	match
配角	pèi jué	supporting actor
皮	pí	leather, skin
皮带	pídài	belt
批发	pīfā	wholesale
批发商	pīfāshāng	wholesalers
啤酒	píjiǔ	beer
片	piàn	sliced

片	piàn	tablet, pill	球桌/台	qiúzhuō/tái	table
便宜	piányi	inexpensive	驱动器	qūdòngqì	drive
便宜一点儿	piányi yìdiǎnr	sell it cheaper	取	qǔ	pick up
票	piào	ticket	取钱	qǔ qián	withdraw money
票价	piàojià	fare	取消	qǔxiāo	cancel
频道	píndào	channel	去	qù	bound for/to
拼盘	pīnpán	starter, assorted cold dishes	去掉	qùdiào	remove
			拳	quán	fist
拼写检查	pīnxiě jiǎnchá	spell check	拳术	quánshù	art of boxing
瓶	píng	bottle	全天	quán tiān	all day long
平底锅	píngdǐguō	frying pan	裙子	qúnzi	skirt
平跟	pínggēn	flat heel	热	rè	hot
平局	píngjú	tied	人(造)棉	rén (zào) mián	rayon
平信	píngxìn	regular mail	人民币	rénmínbì	RMB(Chinese currency)
苹果	píngguǒ	apple			
乒乓球	pīngpāng qiú	table tennis	人体	réntǐ	human body
乒乓球拍	pīngpāngqiú pāi	pingpong paddle	人员	rényuán	personnel
破产	pòchǎn	bankruptcy	肉	ròu	meat
铺床	pūchuáng	make the bed	肉丝	ròusī	shredded meat
普通	pǔtōng	ordinary	肉食	ròushí	meat product
气	qì	air	让人	ràng rén	have someone (do something)
汽车号牌	qìchēhàopái	license plate			
起床	qǐchuáng	get up	如果	rúguǒ	in case of
起动	qǐdòng	start	软件	ruǎnjiàn	software
起飞	qǐfēi	take off	软盘	ruǎnpán	floppy disk
旗袍	qípáo	Mandarin dress	软卧	ruǎnwò	soft sleeper
启瓶器	qǐpíngqì	bottle opener	三比二	sān bǐ èr	three to two
七喜	Qīxǐ	seven up	三明治	sānmíngzhì	sandwich
企业	qǐyè	enterprise	三文鱼	sānwényú	salmon
汽油	qìyóu	gas	嗓子/喉咙	sǎngzi/hóulóng	throat
气压	qìyā	air pressure	扫地	sǎo dì	sweep the floor
铅笔	qiānbǐ	pencil	扫描仪	sǎomiáoyí	scanner
千斤顶	qiānjīndǐng	jack	扫帚	sàozhǒu	broom
前	qián	forward, ahead	事故	shìgù	accident
前(大)灯	qián (dà) dēng	headlight	刹车	shāchē	brake
前保险杠	qián bǎoxiǎngàng	bumper	刹车闸	shāchē zhá	brake pedal
			沙发	shāfā	sofa
前进	qiánjìn	forward	沙拉	shālā	salad
前排	qiánpái	front rows	山	shān	mountain
前台	qiántái	reception	删除	shānchú	delete
前台服务员	qiántái fúwùyuán	receptionist	闪电	shǎndiàn	lightning
			上	shàng	get (on)to
前移	qiányí	move forward	上半场	shàngbànchǎng	first half
签字	qiān zì	sign (a name)	上(车)	shàngchē	get on, board
签证	qiānzhèng	visa	上场/出场	shàngchǎng/chūchǎng	come on stage
抢攻	qiǎnggōng	quick attack			
抢走	qiǎngzǒu	steal	上课	shàngkè	attend class
切	qiē	chop/cut	上铺	shàngpù	upper berth
切除	qiēchú	removal/remove	上石膏	shàng shígāo	put it in cast
请	qǐng	please...	上网	shàngwǎng	go on line
青菜	qīngcài	green-leaf vegetables	伤口	shāngkǒu	wound, injury
			商品	shāngpǐn	goods
青岛	Qīngdǎo	Qingdao	商业	shāngyè	business
晴朗	qínglǎng	sunny	少	shǎo	lack
青霉素	qīngméisù	penicillin	少一点儿	shǎo yìdiǎnr	lower the price (in bargaining)
轻松	qīngsōng	relax			
晴天	qíngtiān	fine, clear	勺	sháo	spoon
请问是哪位?	Qǐngwèn shi nǎwèi?	who's calling?	稍等	shāoděng	hold on
			烧断	shāoduàn	blow (fuse)
球	qiú	ball	烧坏	shāohuài	burn out
球门	qiúmén	goal	烧水	shāo shuǐ	boil water

哨子	shàozi	whistle	熟食	shóu shí	cooked food
设备	shèbèi	equipment	售邮票机	shòuyóupiàojī	stamp machine
摄氏	shèshì	centigrade	输	shū	lose (a game)
深	shēn	deep	输出	shūchū	output
深呼吸	shēn hūxī	deep breath	输入	shūrù	input
申报	shēnbào	declare	输氧	shū yǎng	oxygen therapy
申请	shēnqǐng	apply for	输液	shūyè	intravenous
肾脏	shènzàng	kidney			feeding
生	shēng	rare	书包	shūbāo	schoolbag
生产	shēngchǎn	produce	书架	shūjià	bookcase
生孩子	shēng háizi	give birth	蔬菜	shūcài	vegetable
声音	shēngyīn	audio	数据表格	shùjù biǎogé	spreadsheet
试	shì	try	梳子	shūzi	comb
实步	shí bù	weighted step	刷	shuā	brush
市场	shìchǎng	market	双	shuāng	pair
视窗	Shìchuāng	Windows	双打	shuāngdǎ	doubles
师傅	shīfu	master (skilled worker)	双方	shuāngfāng	both parties
			双击	shuāngjí	double click
施工	shīgōng	Under construction!	双人床	shuāngrén chuáng	double bed
时刻表	shíkèbiǎo	time schedule	双人房	shuāngrén fáng	double room
十路	shí lù	Number 10/ Route 10(bus)	双向交通	shuāngxiàng jiāotōng	Two-way traffic
市内总站	shìnèi zǒngzhàn	city terminal	睡	shuì	sleep
市区地图	shìqū dìtú	city map	水	shuǐ	water
食品	shípǐn	food	水产	shuǐchǎn	seafood
食堂	shítāng	canteen/cafeteria	水痘	shuǐdòu	chicken pox
实习医生	shíxí yīshēng	intern	水果	shuǐguǒ	fruit
收	shōu	accept, charge	水管	shuǐguǎn	pipe
收到	shōudào	receive	水管工	shuǐguǎngōng	plumber
收费公路	shōufèi gōnglù	turnpike	水龙头	shuǐlóngtóu	faucet
收费站	shōufèi zhàn	tollbooth	睡觉	shuìjiào	go to bed
收(费)	shōu (fèi)	charge	睡衣	shuìyī	pajamas
收件人	shōujiàn rén	recipient	睡着	shuìzháo	fall asleep
收起来	shōu qǐlai	put back	硕士	shuòshì	master
收信人	shōuxìnrén	addressee	(真)丝	(zhēn) sī	(pure) silk
收信箱	shōuxìnxiāng	in-box	司机	sījī	driver
手	shǒu	hand	私立	sīlì	private
手机	shǒujī	cellular	私营	sīyíng	privately owned
手排挡	shǒupáidǎng	manual transmission	40号	sìshíhào	size 40
			送	sòng	deliver
手术	shǒushù	operation/ surgery	素菜	sùcài	vegetarian dish
手术后情况	shǒushù hòu qíngkuàng	prognosis	速度	sùdù	speed
			速度表	sùdù biǎo	speedometer
手术室	shǒushù shì	operating room	塑料袋	sùliào dài	plastic bag
手术台	shǒushù tái	operating table	宿舍	sùshè	dormitory
手套	shǒutào	gloves	算	suàn	calculate
手套箱	shǒutào xiāng	glove compartment	酸	suān	sour
手提式	shǒutíshì	laptop	酸辣	suānlà	sour and spicy
手提行李	shǒutí xíngli	carry-on luggage	缩水	suōshuǐ	shrink
手腕	shǒuwàn	wrist	T恤	tī xù	T shirt
手位	shǒuwèi	hand position	糖醋	táng cù	sweet and sour
手型	shǒuxíng	hand form	糖果	tángguǒ	candy
手续费	shǒuxù fèi	commission	台灯	táidēng	desk lamp
手闸	shǒuzhá	hand brake	台风	táifēng	typhoon
手指	shǒuzhǐ	finger	台式	táishì	desktop
瘦/窄	shòu/zhǎi	narrow	太极拳	tàijíquán	Tai Chi
守护	shǒuhù	defend	探测器	tàncèqì	detector
守门员	shǒuményuán	goalie	汤	tāng	soup
售票处	shòupiàochù	ticket office	糖	táng	sugar
售票员	shòupiàoyuán	conductor			

汤面	tāng miàn	noodle soup	推荐	tuījiàn	recommend
汤勺	tāng sháo	soup ladle	退出	tuìchū	exit
烫/熨	tàng/yùn	to iron, press	退房	tuì fáng	check out
烫衣板	tàngyībǎn	ironing board	拖把	tuōbǎ	mop
桃	táo	peach	拖车	tuōchē	tow truck
套间	tàojiān	suite	拖地板	tuō dìbǎn	mop the floor
特护病房	tèhù bìngfáng	intensive care unit	托盘餐桌	tuōpán cānzhuō	tray table
特快	tèkuài	express train	拖鞋	tuōxié	slipper
特快专递	tèkuài zhuāndì	express mail	托运(行李)	tuōyùn (xíngli)	check in (luggage)
疼	téng	hurt/sore	拖走	tuōzǒu	tow away
腾出	téngchū	vacate	袜子	wàzi	socks
替	tì	for	外币	wàibì	foreign currency
踢	tī	kick	外国片	wàiguópiān	foreign film
踢进一球	tījìn yì qiú	make a goal	外科医生	wai kē yīshēng	surgeon
提供	tígōng	provide	外头	wàitou	outside
题目	tímù	subject	弯	wān	bent
剃须刀	tìxūdāo	razor	碗	wǎn	bowl
体育运动	tǐyù yùndòng	sports	晚点	wǎndiǎn	delay
甜	tián	sweet	万维网	wànwéiwǎng	www
甜点	tiándiǎn	dessert	丸子	wánzi	meatballs
天	tiān	day	忘	wàng	forget
天安门广场	Tiānānmén Guǎngchǎng	Tian'anmen Square	网	wǎng	Net, network
天气	tiānqì	weather	网球	wǎngqiú	tennis
填	tián	fill (a form)	网球场	wǎngqiúchǎng	tennis court
填入	tiánrù	fill in	网球拍	wǎngqiúpāi	racket
挑	tiāo	select	网上服务提供商	wǎngshàng fūwù tígōng shāng	ISP (internet service provider)
条纹	tiáowén	striped			
调味品	tiáowèipǐn	spice	网页	wǎngyè	Web page
调整	tiáozhěng	adjust	网址	wǎngzhǐ	URL
调制解调器(猫)	tiáozhì jiětiáoqì (māo)	modem	网站	wǎngzhàn	Web site
			微波炉	wēibōlú	microwave
铁路道口	tiělù dàokǒu	Railroad crossing!	微软字处理	Wēiruǎn Zìchǔlǐ	Microsoft Word
听	tīng	can			
听课	tīngkè	listen to lecture	围巾	wéijīn	scarf
听诊器	tīngzhěnqì	stethoscope	味精	wèijīng	MSG
停	tíng	stop	卫生	wèishēng	hygiene
停车(场)	tíngchē (chǎng)	Parking	卫生纸	wèishēngzhǐ	toilet paper
通过	tōngguò	pass through	卫生间	wèishēngjiān	bathroom
通知	tōngzhī	announce	威士忌	wēishìjì	whiskey
头	tóu	head	胃疼	wèiténg	stomachache
头班/末班地铁	tóubān/mòbān dìtiě	first /last subway	稳定	wěndìng	stable
			文件	wénjiàn	file, document
头等(舱)	tóuděng (cāng)	first class	文件夹	wénjiànjiá	folder
头顶舱	tóudǐngcāng	overhead compartment	问路	wènlù	ask for direction
			文学院	wénxuéyuàn	school of arts and humanities
头顶上方	tóudǐng shàngfāng	overhead			
			文学	wénxué	literature
头发	tóufa	hair	文字	wénzì	words/text
头晕	tóuyūn	dizzy	文字处理	wénzì chǔlǐ	word processing
投篮	tóulán	shoot a basket	我的电脑	wǒde diànnǎo	My Computer
吐	tù	vomit	我的公文包	wǒde gōngwénbāo	My Briefcase
图标	túbiāo	icon			
图像	túxiàng	visual	我的文档	wǒde wéndàng	My Documents
土豆	tǔdòu	potato	卧具	wòjù	bedding
突然	tūrán	unexpected	卧铺	wòpù	sleeper
湍流	tuānliú	turbulence	卧室	wòshì	bedroom
腿	tuǐ	leg	我这儿疼	wǒ zhèr téng	It hurts here
推	tuī	push	雾	wù	fog
推车	tuīchē	cart	五斗柜	wǔdǒuguì	chest of drawers
推迟	tuīchí	postpone	舞剧	wǔjù	dance drama

乌龙茶	wūlóng chá	Woolong tea
误了	wùle	missed
5门课	wǔ mén kè	five courses
物品	wùpǐn	article, thing
无铅	wúqiān	unleaded
无绳	wúshéng	cordless
武术	wǔshù	martial arts
污渍/脏东西	wūzì /zāng dōngxi	stain
X光检查/ 透视	X guāng jiǎnchá/ tòushì	X-ray
西部片	xībùpiān	Western (movie)
西餐	xīcān	Western meal
西装	xīzhuāng	suit
吸尘	xīchén	vacuum-clean
吸尘器	xīchénqì	vacuum cleaner
膝盖	xīgài	knee
熄火	xī huǒ	stop the engine
洗	xǐ	wash
洗脸巾	xǐliǎnjīn	face cloth
洗菜盆	xǐcài pén	washbowl
洗涤	xǐdí	cleanse
洗涤池	xǐdíchí	sink, basin
洗发香波	xǐfà xiāngbō	shampoo
洗手间	xǐshǒujiān	toilet/washroom
洗手间	xǐshǒujiān	washroom
洗碗布	xǐwǎn bù	dish towel
洗碗剂	xǐwǎn jì	dishwashing liquid
洗衣机	xǐyījī	washing machine
洗衣	xǐyī	laundry
洗衣服	xǐ yīfu	do laundry
喜剧	xǐjù	comedy
喜剧片	xǐjùpiān	comedy
系	xì	department
系列	xìliè	series
系统	xì tǒng	system
戏院	xìyuàn	theater
小儿麻痹症	xiǎoér mábìzhèng	polio
虾	xiā	shrimp
下半场	xiàbànchǎng	second half
下(车)	xiàchē	get off
下铺	xiàpù	lower berth
下水道	xiàshuǐdào	drainage pipe
下小雨	xià xiǎoyǔ	drizzle
下一个	xià yī ge	next
下一站	xià yí zhàn	next stop
下载	xiàzǎi	download
先	xiān	first
线	xiàn	line
咸	xián	salty
现金	xiànjīn	cash
显示	xiǎnshì	display
显示器	xiǎnshìqì	monitor
现代	xiàndài	modern
现在	xiànzài	now; right away
限制	xiànzhì	limits
限制速度	xiànzhì sùdù	Speed limit
响	xiǎng	ring
香槟	xiāngbīn	champagne
香蕉	xiāngjiāo	banana
香酥鸭	xiāngsū yā	crispy duck
相反	xiāngfǎn	opposite
向后转	xiàng hòu zhuǎn	turn back
向右转弯	xiàng yòu zhuǎnwān	Right turn
向左转/拐	xiàng zuǒ zhuǎn/guǎi	turn to the left
向左急转弯	xiàng zuǒ jí zhuǎnwān	Sharp left turn!
橡胶	xiàngjiāo	rubber
像框	xiàngkuàng	picture frame
想买点什么?	xiǎng mǎi diǎn shénme?	May I help you?
相声	xiàngshēng	cross talks
箱子	xiāngzi	suitcase
削	xiāo	peel
消费者	xiāofèizhě	consumer
削球	xiāoqiú	slice the ball
销售	xiāoshòu	sell
小便	xiǎobiàn	urine
小吃/零食	xiǎochī/língshí	snacks
小吃店	xiǎochīdiàn	snack shop
小橱/柜	xiǎochú/guì	medicine cabinet, kitchen closet
小费	xiǎofèi	tip
小腹	xiǎofù	abdomen
小号	xiǎohào	small (size)
小火	xiǎo huǒ	low heat
小声	xiǎoshēng	be quiet
小时/钟头	xiǎoshí/zhōngtou	hour
小学	xiǎoxué	elementary school
校服	xiàofú	school uniform
校长	xiàozhǎng	principal
鞋	xié	shoe
鞋带	xiédài	shoelace
鞋跟	xiégēn	heel
鞋油	xiéyóu	shoe polish
协调	xiétiáo	coordinated
信	xìn	letter
信封	xìnfēng	envelop
信息	xìnxī	information
信用卡	xìnyòngkǎ	credit card
新邮件	xīn yóujiàn	new mail
心电图	xīndiàntú	electrocardiogram
心脏	xīnzàng	heart
心脏病	xīnzàngbìng	heart disease
新鲜	xīnxiān	fresh
性病	xìngbìng	venereal disease
醒来	xǐng lái	wake up
行李	xíngli	luggage
行李员	xíngliyuán	porter
星期	xīngqi	week
胸口	xiōngkǒu	chest
胸罩	xiōngzhào	brassiere
修(理)	xiū(lǐ)	repair
袖子	xiùzi	sleeve
削皮刀	xiāopídāo	peeler
虚步	xū bù	nonweighted step

选手	xuǎnshǒu	player
选择	xuǎnzé	choose
学费	xuéfèi	tuition
学期	xuéqī	semester
学生	xuéshēng	student
学士	xuéshì	bachelor
学位	xuéwèi	degree (academic)
学习	xuéxí	study
学校	xuéxiào	school
学院	xuéyuàn	school
血	xuè	blood
血型	xuèxíng	blood type
血压	xuèyā	blood pressure
靴子	xuēzi	boot
雪,下雪	xuě, xiàxuě	snow
熏	xūn	smoked
鸭	yā	duck
牙	yá	tooth
牙膏	yágāo	toothpaste
牙签	yáqiān	toothpick
牙刷	yáshuā	toothbrush
押金	yājīn	deposit
演	yǎn	act, play
烟,香烟	yān, xiāngyān	cigarettes
盐	yán	salt
严密	yánmì	tight (maneuver)
颜色	yánsè	color
验血	yànxuè	blood test
洋酒	yáng jiǔ	foreign drinks
羊肉	yángròu	lamb
阳台	yángtái	balcony
氧气罩	yǎngqìzhào	oxygen mask
腰	yāo	waist
药	yào	medicine
要是	yàoshì	if
钥匙	yàoshi	key
移动	yídòng	shift
仪表盘	yíbiǎopán	dashboard
衣橱/柜	yīchú/guì	wardrobe
衣服	yīfu	clothes
衣架	yījià	hanger
一个菜	yí ge cài	one dish
一共	yígòng	altogether
一楼	yī lóu	first floor
一年级	yì niánjí	first grade
一起算	yìqǐ suàn	one check for everyone
一直向前	yìzhí xiàngqián	straight ahead
医生	yīshēng	doctor
医疗保险	yīliáo bǎoxiǎn	medical insurance
医学院	yīxuéyuàn	medical school
医院	yīyuàn	hospital
以内	yǐnèi	within
易碎	yìsuì	fragile
意外	yìwài	unexpected
椅子	yǐzi	chair
银行	yínháng	bank
银行卡	yínhángkǎ	bank card
饮料	yǐnliào	drinks, beverage
银幕	yínmù	screen
因特网	yīntèwǎng	Internet
阴天	yīntiān	overcast
音响	yīnxiǎng	stereo
音乐	yīnyuè	music
音乐会	yīnyuèhuì	concert
音乐厅	yīnyuètīng	concert hall
硬	yìng	tough
硬币	yìngbì	coin
硬件	yìngjiàn	hardware
硬盘	yìngpán	hard disk
硬卧	yìngwò	hard sleeper
硬座	yìngzuò	hard seat
盈利	yínglì	make profit
应纳税的收入	yìng nàshuì de shōurù	taxable income
赢/胜	yíng/ shèng	win
用	yòng	use
用餐	yòngcān	have a meal
用户	yònghù	consumer
用户姓名	yònghù xìngmíng	user name
用品	yòngpǐn	articles
用现金	yòng xiànjīn	in cash
拥有	yōngyǒu	own
油	yóu	oil
油量表	yóuliàngbiǎo	fuel gauge
油门	yóumén	gas pedal
油腻	yóunì	oily/greasy
游泳	yóu yǒng	swimming
游泳衣	yóuyǒngyī	bathing suit
邮递员	yóudìyuán	mail carrier
邮件	yóujiàn	mail
邮局	yóujú	post office
邮票	yóupiào	stamp
邮筒/信筒	yóutǒng/xìntǒng	postbox
油箱	yóuxiāng	tank
邮箱/信箱	yóuxiāng/xìnxiāng	mailbox
邮资	yóuzī	postage
邮政编码	yóuzhèng biānmǎ	postal code
有形的	yǒuxíng de	tangible
鱿鱼	yóuyú	squid
右	yòu	right
右边	yòubiān	right side
幼儿园	yòuéryuán	nursery school/ kindergarten
鱼	yú	fish
雨衣	yǔyī	rain coat
雨,下雨	yǔ, xiàyǔ	rain
雨刷	yǔshuā	windshield wiper
浴垫	yùdiàn	bath mat
浴缸	yùgāng	bathtub
浴巾	yùjīn	bath towel
浴帽	yùmào	bath cap
浴室	yùshì	bathroom
浴衣	yùyī	bath robe
预订	yùdìng	reserve, book
遇上	yùshàng	encounter
原版	yuánbǎn	original release
原来位置	yuánlái wèizhì	original position
圆珠笔	yuánzhū bǐ	ballpoint pen

远	yuǎn	far
院子	yuànzi	courtyard
月	yuè	month
月经	yuèjīng	menstrual periods
月票	yuè piào	monthly pass
运动	yùndòng	exercise
运动员	yùndòngyuán	sportsmen
运算公式	yùnsuàn gōngshì	formula
运行	yùnxíng	operating
熨斗机	yùndǒu	iron
晕机	yūnjī	air sickness
总机	zǒng jī	switchboard
杂技	zájì	acrobatics
杂音/ 干扰音	záyīn/gānrǎoyīn	static
杂志	zázhì	magazine
再	zài	again
在这儿	zài zhèr	Here you are.
在…上	zài…shàng	on
脏	zāng	dirty
脏器	zàngqì	organs
早餐	zǎocān	breakfast
怎么走	zěnmē zǒu	how to go
…怎么卖?	…zěnme mài?	How do you sell …?
肿	zhǒng	swollen
症状	zhèng zhuàng	symptoms
炸	zhá	deep fry
债务	zhàiwù	liabilities
站	zhàn	stop, station
站台/月台	zhàntái/yuètái	platform
粘贴	zhāntiē	paste
占线	zhànxiàn	the line is busy
掌	zhǎng	palm
帐单	zhàngdān	bill
帐户	zhànghù	account
张开	zhāngkāi	open
找	zhǎo	give change
镇静剂	zhènjìngjì	tranquilizer
枕头	zhěntou	pillow
枕套	zhěntoutào	pillowcase
阵痛	zhèntòng	labor pain
阵雨	zhènyǔ	shower
蒸	zhēng	steam
蒸锅	zhēngguō	steamer
正常	zhèngcháng	regular
正点	zhèngdiǎn	on time
证件	zhèngjiàn	ID
整理	zhěnglǐ	tidy up
只	zhǐ	only
直	zhí	straight
直飞	zhífēi	nonstop
值班医生	zhíbān yīshēng	doctor on duty
支出	zhīchū	expense
纸袋	zhǐdài	paper bag
指定的	zhǐdìng de	assigned
指令	zhǐlìng	instruction
指示	zhǐshì	instruct
中餐	zhōngcān	Chinese meal
中国	Zhōngguó	China
中号	zhōnghào	medium (size)

中间	zhōngjiān	middle
中学	zhōngxué	high/middle school
重心	zhòngxīn	weight
猪肉	zhūròu	pork
猪油	zhūyóu	lard
煮	zhǔ	boil, cook
主板	zhǔbǎn	motherboard
主菜	zhǔcài	entrée
主管	zhǔguǎn	chief executive
主机	zhǔjī	main machine, (computer) tower
主食	zhǔshí	staple principal food
注射	zhùshè	inject
主要	zhǔyào	vital
主演	zhǔyǎn	lead
注意	zhùyì	attention, pay attention to
注意交通 信号灯!	zhùyì jiāotōng xìnhàodēng	Traffic light!
注册	zhùcè	register (at schhol)
拄拐杖	zhǔ guǎizhàng	on crutches
转机	zhuǎn jī	change planes
转盘电话	zhuànpán diànhuà	rotary dial
转球	zhuàn qiú	spinning ball
转让	zhuǎnràng	endorse
转向灯	zhuǎnxiàngdēng	turn signal
专业	zhuānyè	major
状态栏	zhuàngtài lán	status bar
装置	zhuāngzhì	device
准时/正点	zhǔnshí/zhèngdiǎn	on time
着陆	zhuólù	land
桌面/屏幕	zhuōmiàn/píngmù	desktop/screen
桌子	zhuōzi	table
资产	zīchǎn	assets
资产负债表	zīchǎn fùzhài biǎo	balance sheet
自动	zìdòng	automatically
自动挡	zìdòngdǎng	automatic transmission
自动提款机	zìdòng tíkuǎnjī	ATM
资料/数据	zīliào/shùjù	data
字幕	zìmù	subtitle
自然	zìrán	natural
自由	zìyóu	free
走读生	zǒudúshēng	day student
走路	zǒu lù	walk/on foot
租	zū	rent
租金	zūjīng	rent charge
租一天	zū yì tiān	rent for a day
足	zú	enough
足球	zúqiú	soccer
足球场	zúqiúchǎng	soccer field
嘴	zuǐ	mouth
左边	zuǒbiān	left
左反光镜	zuǒ fǎnguāngjìng	left mirror
左后卫	zuǒ hòuwèi	left end

坐(车)	zuò (chē)	take (vehicle)	做/记笔记	zuò/jì bǐjì	take notes
坐出租车	zuò chū zūchē	take a taxi	做决定	zuò juédìng	decision making
坐好	zuòhǎo	seated	做米饭	zuò mǐfàn	cook rice
座(位)	zuò(wèi)	seat	做生意	zuò shēngyì	do business
座位下	zuòwèi xià	under the seat	做手术	zuò shǒushù	have a surgery/
座椅靠背	zuòyǐ kàobèi	seat back			operation
做饭	zuòfàn	cook	做准备	zuò zhǔnbèi	prepare
做功课	zuò gōngkè	do homework			

Glossary: English- Chinese
索引： 英文-中文

English	Chinese	Pinyin
a few	几	jǐ
abdomen	小腹	xiǎofù
above sea level	海拔	hǎibá
accelerate	加速	jiāsù
accept	收	shōu
accident	事故	shìgù
according to	按	àn
account	户头/帐户	hùtóu/ zhànghù
accountant	会计师	kuàijìshī
acrobatics	杂技	zájì
act, play	演	yǎn
action movie	动作片	dòngzuòpiān
actor	男演员	nán yǎnyuán
actress	女演员	nǚ yǎnyuán
acts	幕	mù
acute	急性	jíxìng
add	加	jiā
address	地址	dìzhǐ
addressee	收信人	shōuxìnrén
adhesive bandage	创口贴	chuàngkǒutiē
adjust	调整	tiáozhěng
adult	大人	dàrén
advertisement	广告	guǎnggào
after school	放学以后	fàngxué yǐhòu
again	再	zài
air	气	qì
air conditioner	空调	kōngtiáo
air pressure	气压	qìyā
air sickness	晕机	yūnjī
airline company	航空公司	hángkōng gōngsī
airline ticket	飞机票	fēijīpiào
airmail	航空信	hángkōngxìn
airplane	飞机	fēijī
airport	飞机场	fēijīchǎng
airport departure tax	机场费	jīchǎng fèi
aisle seat	靠走道座位	kào zǒudào zuò wèi
alarm clock	闹钟	nàozhōng
alcohol	酒	jiǔ
all day long	全天	quán tiān
allergic	过敏	guòmǐn
allergy	过敏症	guòmǐnzhèng
altitude, height	高度	gāodù
altogether	一共	yígòng
ambulance	救护车	jiùhùchē
anesthesia	麻药	máyào
anesthetist	麻醉师	mázuìshī
ankle	踝骨	huáigǔ
announce	通知	tōngzhī
answer a phone	接电话	jiē diànhuà
antibiotics	抗生素	kàngshēngsù
appendicitis	阑尾炎/盲肠炎	lánwěiyán/ mángchángyán
appendix	阑尾/盲肠	lánwěi/ mángcháng
appetizer	开胃菜	kāiwèi cài
applaud	鼓掌/拍手	gǔzhǎng/pāishǒu
apple	苹果	píngguǒ
apply for	申请	shēnqǐng
area code	地区号(码)	dìqūhào(mǎ)
arm	胳膊/手臂	gēbo/shǒubì
arrive	到/到达/	dào/dàodá/
	到港/到站	dàogǎng/ dàozhàn
art of boxing	拳术	quánshù
arthritis	关节炎	guānjiéyán
article, thing	物品/用品	wùpǐn/ yòngpǐn
ask for direction	问路	wènlù
assets	资产	zīchǎn
assigned	指定的	zhǐdìng de
at the corner	靠墙角	kào qiángjiǎo
ATM	自动提款机	zìdòng tíkuǎnjī
attend class	上课	shàngkè
attention, pay attention to	注意	zhùyì
audience	观众	guānzhòng
audio	声音	shēngyīn
audit	旁听	pángtīng
automatic transmission	自动挡	zìdòngdǎng
automatically	自动	zìdòng
available seat/table	空位	kōng wèi
avenue	大道	dàdào
bachelor	学士	xuéshì
back	后面	hòumiàn
back	背	bèi
back	后退	hòutuì
bad	不好	bùhǎo
bag	包	bāo
baked	烤	kǎo
bakery	糕点	gāodiǎn
balance	结余	jiéyú
balance sheet	资产负债表	zīchǎn fùzhài biǎo
balcony	阳台	yángtái
ball	球	qiú
ballet	芭蕾	bāléi
ballpoint pen	圆珠笔	yuánzhū bǐ
banana	香蕉	xiāngjiāo
bandage	绷带	bēngdài
bank	银行	yínháng
bank card	银行卡	yínhángkǎ
bankbook	存折	cúnzhé
bankruptcy	破产	pòchǎn
bar	块	kuài
basic	基本	jīběn
basin	盥洗池	guànxǐchí
basket	篮(子)	lán(zi)
basketball	篮球	lánqiú
basketball court	篮球场	lánqiúchǎng
bath cap	浴帽	yùmào
bath mat	浴垫	yùdiàn
bath robe	浴衣	yùyī

bath towel	浴巾	yùjīn
bathing suit	游泳衣	yóuyǒngyī
bathroom	卫生间/浴室	wèishēngjiān/ yùshì
bathtub	浴缸	yùgāng
battery	电池	diànchí
be admitted by	考上	kǎoshàng
be found out	被发现	bèi fāxiàn
be quiet	小声	xiǎoshēng
bed	床	chuáng
bed sheet	床单	chuángdān
bedding	卧具	wòjù
bedroom	卧室	wòshì
bedside table	床头柜	chuángtóuguì
bedspread	床罩	chuángzhào
beef	牛肉	niúròu
beep	呼	hū
beeper	呼机	hūjī
beeper number	呼机号码	hūjī hàomǎ
beer	啤酒	píjiǔ
belt	皮带	pídài
bent	弯	wān
beverage	饮料	yǐnliào
bill	帐单	zhàngdān
bind up	包	bāo
black	黑	hēi
black tea	红茶	hóngchá
blackboard	黑板	hēibǎn
blanket	毛毯	máotǎn
blend (fabric)	混纺	hùnfǎng
blender	搅拌机	jiǎobànjī
block/stop	挡住	dǎngzhù
blood	血	xuè
blood pressure	血压	xuèyā
blood test	验血	yànxuè
blood type	血型	xuèxíng
blouse	衬衫/衬衣	chènshān/chènyī
blow	吹	chuī
blow (fuse)	烧断	shāoduàn
blue	蓝	lán
board	上车	shàngchē
board of directors	董事会	dǒngshìhuì
board the plane	登机	dēngjī
boarder, resident student	寄宿生	jìsùshēng
boarding gate	登机口	dēngjīkǒu
boarding pass	登机牌	dēngjīpái
body wash lotion	沐浴液	mùyùyè
boil water	烧水	shāo shuǐ
boil, cook	煮	zhǔ
boiled water	开水	kāishuǐ
Bon Voyage!	旅途愉快!	lǔtú yúkuài
bone fracture	骨折	gǔzhé
bookcase	书架	shūjià
boot	靴子	xuēzi
both parties	双方	shuāngfāng
bottle	瓶	píng
bottle opener	启瓶器	qǐpíngqì
bounce/bump	颠簸	diānbǒ
bound for/to	去/飞往	qù/fēiwǎng
bow stance	弓步	gōngbù
bowl	碗	wǎn
boxed meal	盒饭	héfàn
brain	大脑	dànǎo
braise in soy sauce	红烧	hóngshāo
brake	刹车	shāchē
brake pedal	刹车闸	shāchē zhá
brandy	白兰地	báilándì
brassiere	胸罩	xiōngzhào
bread	面包	miànbāo
break (a large bill), make change	换开	huànkāi
breakdown	坏	huài
breakfast	早餐	zǎocān
breathe	呼吸	hūxī
briefcase	公文包	gōngwénbāo
bright	光线好	guāngxiàn hǎo
broadcast	广播	guǎngbō
broken	坏了	huài le
broom	扫帚	sàozhǒu
brown	咖啡色	kāfēisè
browse	浏览	liúlǎn
browser	浏览器	liúlǎnqì
brush	刷	shuā
bumper	前保险杠	qián bǎoxiǎngàng
burn out	烧坏	shāohuài
burner	炉眼	lúyǎn
bus	公共汽车	gōnggòng qìchē
bus stop	公共汽车站	gōnggòng qìchē zhàn
business	商业	shāngyè
(line is) busy	占线	zhànxiàn
busy signal	忙音	mángyīn
butt (with one's head)	顶	dǐng
button	扣子	kòuzi
button	按钮	ànniǔ
buy	买	mǎi
buyer	买方	mǎifāng
by sea	海运	hǎiyùn
by the window	靠窗	kào chuāng
calculate	算	suàn
call	叫	jiào
call number	叫号	jiàohào
can	听，罐头	tīng, guàntóu
can opener	开罐刀	kāiguàndāo
cancel	取消	qǔxiāo
cancer	癌症	áizhèng
candy	糖果	tángguǒ
can't close	关不上	guān bú shàng
can't open	打不开	dǎ bù kāi
canteen/cafeteria	食堂	shítáng
car	车	chē
(train) car	车厢	chēxiāng
carpet	地毯	dìtǎn
carry-on luggage	手提行李	shǒutí xíngi
cart	推车	tuīchē
cartoon	动画片	dònghuà piān
cash	现金	xiànjīn
cash (a check)	兑现(支票)	duìxiàn zhīpiào
cashier's window	出纳窗口	chūnà chuāngkǒu
catch	得	dé
CD	光盘	guāngpán
cellular phone	手机	shǒujī

English	Chinese	Pinyin
centigrade	摄氏	shèshì
ceramics	瓷器	cíqì
chair	椅子	yǐzi
champagne	香槟	xiāngbīn
change	换	huàn
change gears	换挡	huàn dǎng
change of service	换发球	huànfāqiú
change planes	转机	zhuǎn jī
change train	换车	huànchē
channel	频道	píndào
charge	收(费)	shōu (fèi)
chat	聊天	liáotiān
check	检(查)/测	jiǎnchá/ cè
check in	办理登机/	bànlǐ dēngjī/
	住店手续	zhùdiàn shǒuxù
check in (luggage)	托运(行李)	tuōyùn (xíngli)
check out	退房	tuì fáng
check ticket	查票	chápiào
checked	格子	gézi
cheek/face	脸	liǎn
chest	胸口	xiōngkǒu
chest of drawers	五斗柜	wǔdǒuguì
chicken	鸡	jī
chicken pox	水痘	shuǐdòu
chief executive	主管	zhǔguǎn
children	儿童	értóng
chili sauce	辣椒酱	làjiāo jiàng
chili/hot pepper	辣椒	làjiāo
chills	发冷	fālěng
China	中国	Zhōngguó
Chinese meal	中餐	zhōngcān
choose	选择	xuǎnzé
chop/cut	切	qiē
chopping board	案板/切菜板	ànbǎn, qiēcàibǎn
chopstick holder	筷子筒	kuàizi tǒng
chopsticks	筷子	kuàizi
chrysanthemum	菊花	júhuā
cigarettes	香烟	xiāngyān
cinema	电影院	diànyǐng yuàn
city map	市区地图	shìqū dìtú
city terminal	市内总站	shìnèi zǒngzhàn
claim	领取	lǐngqǔ
claim stub	领取单	lǐngqǔ dān
classroom	教室	jiàoshì
clean	打扫	dǎsǎo
cleanse	洗涤	xǐdí
cloakroom	存衣处	cúnyīchù
clogged up	堵住	dǔzhù
close	关闭	guānbì
close, near	近	jìn
closet	壁橱	bìchú
clothes	衣服	yīfu
clothing store	服装店	fúzhuāng diàn
cloudy	多云	duōyún
clutch	离合器	líhéqì
clutch pedal	离合器踏板	líhéqì tàbǎn
coat	大衣	dàyī
cockpit	驾驶舱	jiàshǐcāng
coffee	咖啡	kāfēi
coffee table	茶几	chájī
coin	硬币	yìngbì
coke	可乐	kělè
cold	冷	lěng
cold and dressed with sauce	凉拌	liángbàn
cold dish	凉菜	liángcài
collect call	对方付费电话	duìfāng fùfèi diànhuà
college entrance exam	高考	gāokǎo
color	颜色	yánsè
comb	梳子	shūzi
come from	来自	lái zì
come on stage	上/出场	shàng/chūchǎng
comedy	喜剧	xǐjù
commission	手续费	shǒuxù fèi
compartment	舱	cāng
component	部件	bùjiàn
concert	音乐会	yīnyuèhuì
concert hall	音乐厅	yīnyuètīng
conductor	列车员/ 售票员	lièchēyuán/ shòupiàoyuán
congested	不通	bùtōng
connect	(连)接	(lián)jiē
connection	连通	liántōng
consumer	用户	yònghù
consumer	消费者	xiāofèizhě
contract	合同	hétóng
control	控制	kòngzhì
cook	做饭	zuòfàn
cook rice	做米饭	zuò mǐfàn
cooked food	熟食	shóu shí
cooked rice	米饭	mífàn
cool	凉快	liángkuài
coolant	冷却液	lěngquèyè
coordinated	协调	xiétiáo
copy	复制	fùzhì
cordless	无绳	wúshéng
corduroy	灯芯绒	dēngxīnróng
corporation (big company)	大公司	dà gōngsī
(all) cotton	纯棉	chúnmián
cough	咳嗽	késou
counter	柜台	guì tái
country code	国家号码	guójiā hàomǎ
courtyard	院子	yuànzi
cover	盖上	gàishang
crab	螃蟹	pángxiè
credit card	信用卡	xìnyòngkǎ
crew	机组人员	jīzǔ rényuán
crispy duck	香酥鸭	xiāngsū yā
cross	交叉	jiāochā
cross road/ intersection	路口	lùkǒu
cross talks	相声	xiàngshēng
cucumber	黄瓜	huángguā
cup/glass	杯子	bēizi
curtain	窗帘	chuānglián
customs officer	海关官员	hǎiguān guānyuán
cut	割/剪/切	gē/jiǎn/qiē
dance drama	舞剧	wǔjù
dashboard	仪表盘	yíbiǎopán
data	资料/数据	zīliào/shùjù
day	天	tiān

day student	走读生	zǒudúshēng	
decide	决定	juédìng	
decision making	做决定	zuò juédìng	
declaration	申报	shēnbào	
declare	申报	shēnbào	
deep	深	shēn	
deep breath	深呼吸	shēn hūxī	
deep fry	炸	zhá	
defend	守护	shǒuhù	
defense	防守	fángshǒu	
degree (academic)	学位	xuéwèi	
degree (temperature)	度	dù	
degree (wind force)	级	jí	
delay	晚点	wǎndiǎn	
delete	删除	shānchú	
deliver	送	sòng	
deliver (a child)	接生	jiēshēng	
delivery room	产房	chǎnfáng	
department	系	xì	
departure time	离港时间	lígǎng shíjiān	
deposit	押金	yājīn	
deposit money	存钱	cún qián	
desk	课桌	kèzhuō	
desk lamp	台灯	táidēng	
desktop	台式	táishì	
desktop/screen	桌面/屏幕	zhuōmiàn/píngmù	
dessert	甜点	tiándiǎn	
detector	探测器	tàncèqì	
device	装置	zhuāngzhì	
dial	拨号	bōhào	
dial pad	拨号盘	bōhào pán	
dial tone	拨号音	bōhàoyīn	
diarrhea	拉肚子/腹泻	lā dùzi/fùxiè	
dining car	餐车	cānchē	
diploma	毕业证书	bìyè zhèngshū	
direction	方向	fāngxiàng	
director	导演	dǎoyǎn	
dirty	脏	zāng	
disconnected	断了	duànle	
disembark	出港	chūgǎng	
dish towel	洗碗布	xǐwǎn bù	
dishwashing liquid	洗碗剂	xǐwǎn jì	
display	显示	xiǎnshì	
distance to or from	离	lí	
dizzy	头晕	tóuyūn	
do business	做生意	zuò shēngyì	
do homework	做功课	zuò gōngkè	
do laundry	洗衣服	xǐ yīfu	
Do not enter!	禁止驶入	jìnzhǐ shǐrù	
doctor	医生	yīshēng	
doctor on duty	值班医生	zhíbān yīshēng	
doctor/Ph.D.	博士	bóshì	
document(s)	文件	wénjiàn	
documentary	纪录片	jìlùpiān	
doesn't work	坏了	huàile	
dollar (U. S.)	美元	měiyuán	
domestic	国内	guónèi	
dormitory	宿舍	sùshè	
double bed	双人床	shuāngrén chuáng	
double click	双击	shuāngjí	
double room	双人房	shuāngrén fáng	
doubles	双打	shuāngdǎ	
download	下载	xiàzǎi	
downstairs	楼下	lóuxià	
drain	排水	pái shuǐ	
drainage pipe	下水道	xiàshuǐdào	
drama	话剧	huàjù	
drama (movie)	故事片	gùshipiān	
draw, collect	抽	chōu	
drawer	抽屉	chōutì	
dress	连衣裙	liányīqún	
drink	喝	hē	
drinks	饮料	yǐnliào	
dripping/leaking	漏水	lòushuǐ	
drive	开(车)	kāi (chē)	
drive (in computer)	驱动器	qūdòngqì	
driver	司机	sījī	
driver's license	驾(驶执)照	jià(shǐ zhí) zhào	
drizzle	下小雨	xià xiǎoyǔ	
dry	干	gān	
dry	擦干	cā gān	
dry clean	干洗	gānxǐ	
dry cleaner's	干洗店	gānxǐdiàn	
duck	鸭	yā	
dumpling wrap	饺子皮	jiǎozi pí	
dumplings	饺子	jiǎozi	
each	各	gè	
ear	耳朵	ěrduō	
economy class	经济(舱)	jīngjì (cāng)	
edit	编辑	biānjí	
education	教育	jiàoyù	
eggs	(鸡)蛋	(jī)dàn	
elbow	胳膊肘	gēbozhǒu	
electric razor	剃须刀	tìxūdāo	
electric rice cooker	电饭锅	diàn fànguō	
electric stove	电炉	diànlú	
electrician	电工	diàngōng	
electrocardio-gram	心电图	xīndiàntú	
electronic screen	电子屏幕	diànzǐ píngmù	
elementary school	小学	xiǎoxué	
e-mail	电子邮件 (电邮)	diànzǐ yóujiàn (diànyóu)	
e-mail address	电子邮箱地址	diànzǐ yóuxiāng dìzhǐ	
emergency	紧急情况	jǐnjí qíngkuàng	
emergency exit	紧急出口	jǐnjí chūkǒu	
emergency room	急诊室	jízhěnshì	
empty/vacant	空	kōng	
encounter	遇上	yùshàng	
end (of object)	端	duān	
end, close	结束	jiéshù	
endorse	转让	zhuǎnràng	
engine oil	发动机油	fādòngjīyóu	
engineering school	工学院	gōngxuéyuàn	
Enjoy!	您慢慢吃	nín mànmàn chī	
enough	足	zú	
enteritis	肠炎	chángyán	
enterprise	企业	qǐyè	
entrée	主菜	zhǔcài	
envelope	信封	xìnfēng	
epilepsy	癫痫	diānxián	

English	Chinese	Pinyin	English	Chinese	Pinyin
equipment	设备	shèbèi	floppy disk	软盘	ruǎnpán
establish a price	定价格	dìng jiàgé	flowers	花	huā
every 4 hours	每隔四小时	měi gé sì xiǎoshí	flu	流感	liúgǎn
examine	检查	jiǎnchá	fluctuate	浮动	fúdòng
except for	除了...以外	chúle...yǐwài	flying time	飞行时间	fēixíng shíjiān
exchange	换	huàn	fog	雾	wù
exchange bureau	兑换处	duìhuànchù	folder	文件夹	wénjiànjiá
exchange rate	兑换率	duìhuànlǜ	food	食品	shípǐn
exercise	运动	yùndòng	foot	脚	jiǎo
exit	出口	chūkǒu	foot work	步法	bùfǎ
exit	退出	tuìchū	for	替	tì
expense	支出	zhīchū	foreign currency	外币	wàibì
expensive	贵	guì	foreign drinks	洋酒	yáng jiǔ
export	出口	chūkǒu	foreign film	外国片	wàiguópiān
express mail	特快专递	tèkuài zhuāndì	forget	忘	wàng
express train	特快	tèkuài	fork	叉(子)	chā(zi)
express way	高速公路	gāosù gōnglù	form	表	biǎo
extension	分机	fēnjī	formula	运算公式	yùnsuàn gōngshì
extension number	分机号码	fēnjī hàomǎ	fortunately	好在	hǎozài
extra-large	加大号	jiādàhào	forward	前进	qiánjìn
fabric	料子	liàozi	foul	犯规	fànguī
face	朝	cháo	fragile	易碎	yìsuì
face	脸	liǎn	free	自由	zìyóu
face cloth	洗脸巾	xǐliǎnjīn	freezer	冷冻室	lěngdòngshì
fall asleep	睡着	shuìzháo	fresh	新鲜	xīnxiān
far	远	yuǎn	fried dumplings	锅贴	guōtiē
fare	票价	piàojià	fried noodles	炒面	chǎo miàn
fast	快	kuài	fried rice	炒饭	chǎo fàn
fasten	系紧	jìjǐn	fried rice noodles	炒粉	chǎo fěn
faucet	水龙头	shuǐlóngtóu	from	从	cóng
feces	大便	dàbiàn	front rows	前排	qiánpái
fee for express	加急费	jiājífèi	frozen	冷冻	lěngdòng
service			fruit	水果	shuǐguǒ
female	女子	nǚzi	fruit juice	果汁	guǒzhī
fever	发烧	fāshāo	fry	炸	zhá
field	领域	lǐngyù	frying pan	平底锅	píngdǐguō
figure out the bill	结帐	jié zhàng	fuel gauge	油量表	yóuliàngbiǎo
file, document	文件	wénjiàn	full	满员	mǎnyuán
fill	加	jiā	full (no vacancy)	客满	kèmǎn
fill (a form)	填	tián	function	功能	gōngnéng
financial statement	财务报告	cáiwù bàogào	furniture	家具	jiājù
fine	罚款	fákuǎn	fuse	保险丝	bǎoxiǎnsī
fine, clear	晴天	qíngtiān	game	比赛	bǐsài
finger	手指	shǒuzhǐ	garbage	垃圾	lājī
first	先	xiān	garbage can	垃圾筒	lājītǒng
first /last subway	头班/末班	tóubān/mòbān	gas	汽油	qìyóu
	地铁	dìtiě	gas pedal	油门	yóumén
first class (cabin)	头等(舱)	tóuděng (cāng)	gas station	加油站	jiāyóuzhàn
first class	高级	gāojí	gas stove	煤气炉	méiqìlú
first floor	一楼	yī lóu	gear shift lever	换挡杆	huàndǎnggǎn
first grade	一年级	yì niánjí	get off	下(车)	xiàchē
first half	上半场	shàngbànchǎng	get on	上(车)	shàngchē
fish	鱼	yú	get up	起床	qǐchuáng
fist	拳	quán	give an injection	打一针	dǎ yì zhēn
fit	能放进	néng fàngjìn	give birth	生孩子	shēng háizi
fit	合身,合适	héshēn, héshì	give change	找	zhǎo
five courses	5门课	wǔ mén kè	glands	淋巴	línbā
flannel	法兰绒	fǎlánróng	glassware	玻璃器皿	bōli qìmǐn
flat	瘪	biě	glove compartment	手套箱	shǒutào xiāng
flat heel	平跟	pínggēn	gloves	手套	shǒutào
flight	航班/班机	hángbān/bānjī	go on line	上网	shàngwǎng
flight attendants	乘务员	chéngwùyuán	go to bed	睡觉	shuìjiào

goal	球门	qiúmén	hotel	饭店	fàndiàn
goalie	守门员	shǒuményuán	hour	小时/钟头	xiǎoshí/zhōngtóu
goods	商品	shāngpǐn	(hotel) housekeeper	客房服务员	kèfáng fúwùyuán
grade/score	分数	fēnshù			
graduate	毕业	bìyè	house specialty	拿手菜/	náshǒu cài/
grain	粮食	liángshi		招牌菜	zhāopáicài
green channel	绿色通道	lùsè tōngdào	How do you sell ...?	...怎么卖?	...zěnme mài?
green grocer	菜店	cài diàn	how heavy	多重	duōzhòng
green tea	绿茶	lùchá	how long (time)	多久	duōjiǔ
green-leaf vegetables	青菜	qīngcài	how much	多少钱	duōshǎoqián
			How often does it come?	多久来 一趟?	Duōjiǔ lái yí tàng?
grilled	烤	kǎo			
grocery store	副食品店	fùshípǐn diàn	how to go	怎么走	zěnmē zǒu
guest	客人	kèrén	human body	人体	réntǐ
gusty wind	大风	dàfēng	humid	闷热，湿热	mēnrè, shīrè
hail	冰雹	bīngbáo	hungry	饿	è
hair	头发	tóufa	hurt the feet	挤脚	jǐjiǎo
hair drier	电吹风	diànchuīfēng	hurt/sore	疼	téng
hairbrush	发刷	fàshuā	hygiene	卫生	wèishēng
half-kilo	斤	jīn	ice	冰	bīng
ham	火腿	huǒtuǐ	icon	图标	túbiāo
hand	手	shǒu	ID	证件	zhèngjiàn
hand brake	手闸	shǒuzhá	if	要是	yàoshì
hand form	手型	shǒuxíng	ignition switch	点火器	diǎnhuǒqì
hand position	手位	shǒuwèi	immediately	马上	mǎshàng
hang up	挂	guà	import	进口	jìnkǒu
hanger	衣架	yījià	imported film	进口片	jìnkǒupiān
hard disk	硬盘	yìngpán	in case of	如果	rúguǒ
hard seat	硬座	yìngzuò	in cash	用现金	yòng xiànjīn
hard sleeper	硬卧	yìngwò	in labor	分娩中	fēnmiǎn zhōng
hardware	硬件	yìngjiàn	in-box	收信箱	shōuxìnxiāng
hat	帽子	màozi	include	包(括)	bāo(kuò)
have a meal	用餐	yòngcān	inexpensive	便宜	piányi
have a cold	感冒	gǎnmào	inflammation	发炎	fāyán
have a surgery/ operation	做手术	zuò shǒushù	information	信息	xìnxī
			inject	注射	zhùshè
have someone (do something)	让人	ràng rén	input	输入	shūrù
			insert	插入、填入	chārù, tiánrù
head	头	tóu	install	安装	ānzhuāng
headlight	前(大)灯	qián (dà) dēng	instruct	指示	zhǐshì
headset	耳机	ěrjī	instruction	指令	zhǐlìng
heart	心脏	xīnzàng	insurance	保险	bǎoxiǎn
heart disease	心脏病	xīnzàngbìng	intensive care unit	特护病房	tèhù bìngfáng
heat	暖气	nuǎnqì	inter-	互联	hùlián
heavy woolen	呢子	nízi	intermission	幕间休息	mùjiān xiūxi
heel	鞋跟	xiégēn	intern	实习医生	shíxí yīshēng
Here you are.	在这儿	zài zhèr	international	国际	guójì
high	高	gāo	international call	国际电话	guójì diànhuà
high beam	高光灯	gāoguāng dēng	Internet	因特网	yīntèwǎng
high heat	大火	dà huǒ	intravenous feeding	输液	shūyè
high heel	高跟	gāogēn			
high/middle school	中学	zhōngxué	iron	熨斗	yùndǒu
highway entrance	高速公路入口	gāosù gōnglù rùkǒu	iron, press	烫	tàng
			ironing board	烫衣板	tàngyībǎn
hip	胯骨	kuàgǔ	ISP (internet service provider)	网上服务提供商	wǎngshàng fúwù tígōng shāng
hire/charter	包	bāo			
hold on	稍等	shāoděng	It hurts here	我这儿疼	wǒ zhèr téng
hole	洞	dòng	jack	千斤顶	qiānjīndǐng
hood of a car	发动机盖	fādòngjī gài	jacket	夹克	jiákè
horn	喇叭	lǎbā	jasmine	茉莉花	mòlìhuā
hospital	医院	yīyuàn	jeans	牛仔裤	niúzǎikù
hot	热	rè	judge	判	pàn

junior high	初中	chūzhōng
keep, continue	继续	jìxù
kettle	开水壶	kāishuǐhú
key	钥匙	yàoshi
keyboard	键盘	jiànpán
kick	踢	tī
kidney	肾脏	shènzàng
kilo	公斤	gōngjīn
kilometer	公里	gōnglǐ
kitchen	厨房	chúfáng
kitchen knife	菜刀	càidāo
knee	膝盖	xīgài
knife	刀	dāo
Kung-fu movie	功夫片/	gōngfupiān
	武打片	wǔdǎpiān
label	标签	biāoqiān
labor pain	阵痛	zhèntòng
lab-test	化验	huàyàn
lace	花边儿	huābiānr
lack	少	shǎo
lamb	羊肉	yángròu
lamp	电灯	diàndēng
land	着陆	zhuólù
lane	车道	chēdào
laptop	手提式	shǒutíshì
lard	猪油	zhūyóu
large	大号	dàhào
large bills	大票子	dà piàozi
later	后	hòu
laundry	洗衣	xǐyī
law school	法学院	fǎxuéyuàn
lead	主演	zhǔyǎn
leading female actor	女主角	nǚ zhǔjué
leading male actor	男主角	nán zhǔjué
leaking/ dripping	漏油	lòu yóu
leather	皮	pí
leave	留	liú
leave a message	留话	liúhuà
leave/drive	开	kāi
lecture	讲课	jiǎngkè
left	左边	zuǒbiān
left end	左后卫	zuǒ hòuwèi
left mirror	左反光镜	zuǒ fǎnguāngjìng
leg	腿	tuǐ
letter	信	xìn
liabilities	债务	zhàiwù
license plate	汽车号牌	qìchēhàopái
lid	锅盖	guōgài
life vest	救生衣	jiùshēngyī
light	灯	dēng
light bulb	灯泡	dēngpào
light switch	开关	kāiguān
lightning	闪电	shǎndiàn
limits	限制	xiànzhì
line	线	xiàn
line up	排队	páiduì
listen to lecture	听课	tīngkè
liter	立升	lìshēng
literature	文学	wénxué
liver	肝脏	gānzàng
living room	客厅	kètīng

lobster	龙虾	lóngxiā
local call	本市电话	běnshì diànhuà
local train	慢车	mànchē
long	长	cháng
long distance	长途	chángtú
long sleeve	长袖	chángxiù
long-distance call	长途电话	chángtú diànhuà
lose (a game)	输	shū
lose (a point)	丢	diū
loss, deficit	亏损	kuīsǔn
lost (one's way)	迷路	mílù
lost (something)	丢了/掉了	diūle/ diào le
low	低	dī
low heat	小火	xiǎo huǒ
lower berth	下铺	xiàpù
lower the price (in bargaining)	少一点儿	shǎo yìdiǎnr
luggage	行李	xíngli
lungs	肺部	fèibù
luxurious	豪华	háohuá
lychee	荔枝	lìzhī
magazine	杂志	zázhì
mail	邮件	yóujiàn
mail carrier	邮递员	yóudìyuán
mailbox	邮箱/信箱	yóuxiāng/ xìnxiāng
main machine, tower	主机	zhǔjī
mainland	大陆	dàlù
major	专业	zhuānyè
make (a call)	打(电话)	dǎ diànhuà
make a deposit	存一笔钱	cún yì bǐ qián
make a goal	踢进一球	tījìn yì qiú
make pancakes	烙饼	làobǐng
make profit	盈利	yínglì
make the bed	铺床	pūchuáng
male	男子	nánzǐ
male single	男子单打	nánzǐ dāndǎo
manage	管理	guǎnlǐ
management/ performance	经营情况	jīngyíng qíngkuàng
manager	经理	jīnglǐ
Mandarin dress	旗袍	qípáo
manual transmission	手排挡	shǒupáidǎng
Maotai (a strong Chinese spirit)	茅台	máotái
market	市场	shìchǎng
martial arts	武术	wǔshù
master (degree)	硕士	shuòshì
master (skilled worker)	师傅	shīfu
match	配	pèi
mattress	床垫	chuángdiàn
May I help you?	想买点什么?	xiǎng mǎi diǎn shénme?
meal	餐点	cāndiǎn
measles	麻疹	mázhěn
measure	量	liáng
measurement	尺寸	chǐcùn
meat	肉	ròu
meat product	肉食	ròushí

meatballs	丸子	wánzi	
medical history	病史	bìngshǐ	
medical insurance	医疗保险	yīliáo bǎoxiǎn	
medical school	医学院	yīxuéyuàn	
medicine	药	yào	
medicine cabinet, kitchen closet	小橱/柜	xiǎochú/guì	
medium (size)	中号	zhōnghào	
memory	存储器	cǔnchǔqì	
mend	补	bǔ	
menstrual periods	月经	yuèjīng	
mental illness	精神病	jīngshénbìng	
menu	菜单/选项单	càidān/xuǎnxiàng dān	
message	留言	liúyán	
meter	米	mǐ	
meter	计程表	jìchéngbiǎo	
Microsoft Word	微软字处理	Wēiruǎn Zìchǔlǐ	
microwave	微波炉	wēibōlú	
middle	中间	zhōngjiān	
mileage	里程	lǐchéng	
milk	牛奶	niú nǎi	
mineral water	矿泉水	kuàngquánshuǐ	
minute	分钟	fēnzhōng	
mirror	镜子	jìngzi	
miss the shot	没投中	méi tóuzhòng	
missed	误了	wùle	
mixed doubles	混合双打	hùnhé shuāngdǎ	
modem	调制解调器(猫)	tiáozhì jiětiáoqì (māo)	
modern	现代	xiàndài	
money order	汇票	huìpiào	
monitor	显示器	xiǎnshìqì	
month	月	yuè	
monthly pass	月票	yuè piào	
mop	拖把	tuōbǎ	
mop the floor	拖地板	tuō dìbǎn	
more than	多/超过	duō/chāoguò	
motherboard	主板	zhǔbǎn	
mountain	山	shān	
mouse	滑鼠	huáshǔ	
mouth	嘴	zuǐ	
move forward	前移	qiányí	
movement	动作	dòngzuò	
movie/film	电影/片子	diànyǐng/piānzi	
MSG	味精	wèijīng	
mumps	流行性腮腺炎	liúxíngxìng sāixiànyán	
music	音乐	yīnyuè	
must	必须	bìxū	
My Briefcase	我的公文包	wǒde gōngwénbāo	
My Computer	我的电脑	wǒde diànnǎo	
My Documents	我的文档	wǒde wéndàng	
napkin	餐巾纸	cānjīn zhǐ	
narrow	瘦/窄	shòu/zhǎi	
national highway	国道	guódào	
natural	自然	zìrán	
nauseous	恶心	ěxīn	
near	近	jìn	
nearby	附近	fùjìn	
net ball	擦网球	cāwǎngqiú	
Net, network	网	wǎng	
neutral gear	空档	kōngdǎng	
new mail	新邮件	xīn yóujiàn	
newspaper	报纸	bàozhǐ	
next	下一个	xià yí ge	
next stop	下一站	xià yí zhàn	
nice	很好	hěn hǎo	
No honking!	禁止鸣喇叭	jìnzhǐ míng lǎbā	
No left turn!	禁止左转弯	jìnzhǐ zuǒ zhuǎnwān	
No parking!	禁止停车!	jìnzhǐ tíngchē	
No passing!	禁止超车!	jìnzhǐ chāochē	
no problem.	没问题	méi wèntí	
no smoking	不准抽烟	bùzhǔn chōuyān	
No thoroughfare for vehicles!	禁止机动车通行!	jìnzhǐ jīdòngchē tōngxíng	
No thoroughfare!	禁止通行!	jìnzhǐ tōngxíng	
No U turn!	禁止调头!	jìnzhǐ diàotóu	
nonstop	直飞	zhífēi	
nonweighted step	虚步	xū bù	
noodle soup	汤面	tāng miàn	
noodles	面条	miàntiáo	
no-score game	没有进球	méiyǒu jìnqiú	
nose	鼻子	bízi	
notebook	笔记本	bǐjì běn	
now, right away	现在	xiànzài	
Number 10/ Route 10(bus)	十路	shí lù	
number 8	8号	bā hào	
nurse	护士	hùshì	
nursery school/ kindergarten	幼儿园	yòuéryuán	
nylon	尼龙	nílóng	
observe	观察	guānchá	
obstetrician	产科医生	chǎnkē yīshēng	
odometer	里程表	lǐchéngbiǎo	
oil	油	yóu	
oily/greasy	油腻	yóunì	
on	在...上	zài...shàng	
on business	公务	gōngwù	
on crutches	拄拐杖	zhǔ guǎizhàng	
on time	准时/正点	zhǔnshí/zhèngdiǎn	
one check for everyone	一起算	yìqǐ suàn	
one dish	一个菜	yí ge cài	
one way ticket	单程票	dānchéngpiào	
one-way street	单行道	dānxíngdào	
only	只	zhǐ	
open	开/张开/打开	kāi/ zhāngkāi/ dǎkāi	
opera	歌剧	gējù	
operate	动手术	dòng shǒushù	
operate	操作	cāozuò	
operating	运行	yùnxíng	
operating room	手术室	shǒushù shì	
operating system	操作系统	cāozuò xìtǒng	
operating table	手术台	shǒushù tái	
operation/ surgery	手术	shǒushù	
operator	接线员	jiēxiànyuán	
opponent	对方	duìfāng	
opposite	相反	xiāngfǎn	
orange juice	桔子汁/	júzi zhī/	

English	Chinese	Pinyin
order dishes	点菜	diǎncài
ordinary	普通	pǔtōng
organs	脏器	zàngqì
original position	原来位置	yuánlái wèizhì
original release	原版	yuánbǎn
other	别的	biéde
out	出界	chūjiè
output	输出	shūchū
outside	外头	wàitou
oven	烤箱	kǎoxiāng
over the net	打过网	dǎ guò wǎng
overcast	阴天	yīntiān
overdone	老	lǎo
overhead	头顶上方	tóudǐng shàngfāng
overhead compartment	头顶舱	tóudǐngcāng
overheating	过热	guò rè
own	拥有	yōngyǒu
oxygen mask	氧气罩	yǎngqìzhào
oxygen therapy	输氧	shū yǎng
package	包裹	bāoguǒ
painting	画	huà
pair	双	shuāng
pajamas	睡衣	shuìyī
palm	掌	zhǎng
pants/trousers	长裤	chángkù
panty hose	长丝袜/连裤袜	chángsīwà/liánkùwà
paper bag	纸袋	zhǐdài
park	公园	gōngyuán
Parking	停车(场)	tíngchē (chǎng)
partner	合股人	hégǔrén
partnerships	合股公司	hégǔ gōngsī
parts	零件	língjiàn
pass	经过	jīngguò
pass by	路过	lùguò
pass through	通过	tōngguò
pass/toss	传	chuán
passenger	乘客	chéngkè
passport	护照	hùzhào
paste	粘贴	zhāntiē
patient	病人	bìngrén
patterned	花	huā
pay	付帐	fù zhàng
pay a bill	付帐	fù zhàng
pay check/bill	结帐/买单	jiézhàng/mǎidān
pay duty	交税	jiāo shuì
pay tax	纳/交/上税	nà/jiāo/shàng shuì
PC	个人电脑	gèrén diànnǎo
peach	桃	táo
pear	梨	lí
peel	削	xiāo
peeler	削皮刀	xiāopídāo
pencil	铅笔	qiānbǐ
penicillin	青霉素	qīngméisù
Pentium	奔腾	Bēnténg
pepper	胡椒	hújiāo
personal	个人(的)	gèrén (de)
personnel	人员	rényuán
phone book	电话号码簿	diànhuà hàomǎbù
phone number	电话号码	diànhuà hàomǎ
pick up	拿起	náqǐ
pick up	取	qǔ
picture frame	像框	xiàngkuàng
pillow	枕头	zhěntou
pillowcase	枕套	zhěntào
pilot	飞行员	fēixíngyuán
PIN	密码	mìmǎ
pingpong paddle	乒乓球拍	pīngpāngqiú pāi
pipe	水管	shuǐguǎn
place, put	安置	ānzhì
plain, bland	淡	dàn
plan	打算	dǎsuàn
plastic bag	塑料袋	sùliào dài
plate	盘子	pánzi
platform	站台/月台	zhàntái/yuètái
play the part	演	yǎn
player	队员/选手	duìyuán/xuǎnshǒu
please...	请	qǐng
plug	电源插头	diànyuán chātóu
plug in	插上	chāshang
plumber	水管工	shuǐguǎngōng
pocket	口袋	kǒudài
polio	小儿麻痹症	xiǎoér mábìzhèng
polka-dotted	带点儿的	dài diǎnr
pool	池	chí
popular	流行	liúxíng
pork	猪肉	zhūròu
porter	行李员	xíngliyuán
post office	邮局	yóujú
postage	邮资	yóuzī
postal code	邮政编码	yóuzhèng biānmǎ
postbox	邮筒/信筒	yóutǒng/xìntǒng
postcard	明信片	míngxìnpiàn
postpone	推迟	tuīchí
pot	锅/壶	guō/hú
potato	土豆	tǔdòu
pregnant	怀孕	huáiyùn
prepare	做准备	zuò zhǔnbèi
prescribe	开	kāi
press	按	àn
press down	按下	ànxià
price	价钱	jiàqián
principal	校长	xiàozhǎng
print	打印	dǎyìn
printer	打印机	dǎyìnjī
private	私立	sīlì
private room	包间	bāojiān
privately owned	私营	sīyíng
process	处理	chǔlǐ
produce	生产	shēngchǎn
production cost	成本	chéngběn
products	产品	chǎnpǐn
professor	教授	jiàoshòu
profit	利润	lìrùn
prognosis	手术后情况	shǒushù hòu qíngkuàng
program (computer) program	节目单 程序	jiémùdān chéngxù
promotion	促销	cùxiāo
provide	提供	tígōng

English	Chinese	Pinyin
public	公共/公立	gōnggòng/ gōnglì
public restroom	公共厕所	gōnggòng cèsuǒ
pulse	脉搏	màibó
push	推	tuī
put back	收起来	shōu qǐlai
put in first gear	挂一挡	guà yīdǎng
put it in cast	上石膏	shàng shígāo
put on make-up	化妆	huàzhuāng
Qingdao	青岛	qīngdǎo
quick attack	抢攻	qiǎnggōng
quick-fry	爆	bào
quiet	安静	ānjìng
quilt	被子	bèizi
racket	网球拍	wǎngqiúpāi
rag (to wipe things)	抹布	mābù
Railroad crossing!	铁路道口	tiělù dàokǒu
rain	雨,下雨	yǔ, xiàyǔ
rain coat	雨衣	yǔyī
RAM	内存	nèicún
rare	嫩	nèn
rare	生	shēng
rayon	人(造)棉	rén (zào) mián
razor	剃须刀	tìxūdāo
read aloud	念	niàn
ready	好	hǎo
rear cabin	后舱	hòucāng
rearview mirror	后视镜	hòushìjìng
receive	收到	shōudào
reception	前台/接待	qiántái/jiēdài
receptionist	前台服务员	qiántái fúwùyuán
recipient	收件人	shōujiàn rén
recommend	推荐	tuījiàn
recovery room	观察室	guāncháshì
Recycle Bin	回收站	huíshōu zhàn
red	红	hóng
red channel	红色通道	hóngsè tōngdào
red wine	红葡萄酒	hóng pútaojiǔ
referee	裁判员	cáipànyuán
refrigerator	冰箱	bīngxiāng
register	挂号	guàhào
register (at schhol)	注册	zhùcè
registered mail	挂号信	guàhàoxìn
registration (office)	挂号处	guàhàochù
regular	正常	zhèngcháng
regular mail	平信	píngxìn
regulation	规则	guīzé
relax	轻松	qīngsōng
remain	继续,保持	jìxù, bǎochí
removal/remove	切除	qiēchú
remove	去掉	qùdiào
rent	租	zū
rent charge	租金	zūjīng
rent for a day	租一天	zū yì tiān
repair	修(理)	xiū(lǐ)
reply	回信	huíxìn
reserve, book	预订	yùdìng
restart	重新开机	chóngxīn kāijī
restaurant	酒楼/酒家/饭馆/餐厅/餐馆	jiǔlóu/jiǔjiā/fànguǎn/cāntīng/cānguǎn
retail	零售	língshòu
retailer	零售商	língshòushāng
return	接球	jiēqiú
return call	回电话	huí diànhuà
reverse gear	倒档	dàodǎng
right	右(边)	yòu(biān)
Right turn	向右转弯	xiàng yòu zhuǎnwān
ring	响	xiǎng
rinse	冲洗	chōngxǐ
RMB(Chinese currency)	人民币	rénmínbì
Road narrows!	道路变窄	dàolù biàn zhǎi
roast	烤	kǎo
roll	擀	gǎn
roll (of paper)	卷	juǎn
roll up	卷起	juǎnqǐ
rolling pin	擀面杖	gǎnmiànzhàng
romance	爱情片	àiqíngpiān
room	房间	fángjiān
room charge	房价	fángjià
rotary dial	转盘电话	zhuànpán diànhuà
round trip ticket	来回票	láihuípiào
row	排	pái
rubber	(橡)胶	(xiàng)jiāo
running nose	流鼻涕	liú bítì
rush hour	高峰期	gāofēngqī
safety	安全	ānquán
safety belt	安全带	ānquándài
salad	沙拉	shālā
salmon	三文鱼	sānwényú
salt	盐	yán
salty	咸	xián
sandal	凉鞋	liángxié
sandwich	三明治	sānmíngzhì
save	保存	bǎocún
save as	另存	lìngcún
savings	存款	cúnkuǎn
scallion	葱	cōng
scanner	扫描仪	sǎomiáoyí
scarf	围巾	wéijīn
scenes	场	chǎng
scholarship	奖学金	jiǎngxuéjīn
school	学校/学院	xuéxiào, xuéyuàn
school of arts and humanities	文学院	wénxuéyuàn
school of science	理学院	lǐxuéyuàn
school starts	开学	kāixué
school uniform	校服	xiàofú
schoolbag	书包	shūbāo
science fiction	科幻片	kēhuànpiān
score	分数, 比分	fēnshù, bǐfēn
score a point	得一分	dé yìfēn
scoreboard	记分板	jìfēnbǎn
screen	银幕	yínmù
scroll bar	滚动条	gǔndòng tiáo
sea	海	hǎi
seafood	海鲜, 水产	hǎixiān, shuǐchǎn
seam	缝	fèng
search	查找	cházhǎo
seat	座(位)	zuò(wèi)

English	Chinese	Pinyin	English	Chinese	Pinyin
seat back	座椅靠背	zuòyǐ kàobèi	single room	单人房	dānrénfáng
seat belt	安全带	ānquándài	singles	单打	dāndǎ
seated	坐好	zuòhǎo	sink, basin	洗涤池	xǐdíchí
second floor	二楼	èr lóu	size	号	hào
second half	下半场	xiàbànchǎng	size 40	40 号	sìshíhào
section	部	bù	skin	皮	pí
security	安全	ānquán	skirt	裙子	qúnzi
see a doctor	看病	kànbìng	slam	抽	chōu
see a show	看演出	kàn yǎnchū	slam dunk	扣篮	kòulán
select	挑	tiāo	sleep	睡	shuì
sell	卖,销售	mài, xiāoshòu	sleeper	卧铺	wòpù
sell it cheaper	便宜一点儿	piányi yìdiǎnr	sleeve	袖子	xiùzi
seller	卖方	màifāng	slice the ball	削球	xiāoqiú
semester	学期	xuéqī	sliced	片	piàn
send	寄	jì	slip	衬裙	chènqún
send out	寄出去	jì chūqù	slipper	拖鞋	tuōxié
sender	寄信人	jìxìnrén	Slippery road!	路滑!	lù huá
senior high	高中	gāozhōng	slow	慢	màn
sent	发送	fāsòng	small (size)	小号	xiǎohào
series	系列	xìliè	small change	零钱	língqián
serve	供应	gōngyìng	smoked	熏	xūn
serve the ball	发球	fāqiú	smoking area	抽烟区	chōuyān qū
service	服务	fúwù	snack shop	小吃店	xiǎochīdiàn
service fee	服务费	fúwù fèi	snacks	小吃,零食	xiǎochī/língshí
set the bone	固定骨头	gùdìng gǔtóu	sneaker	旅游鞋	lǚyóuxié
set to (clock time)	拨到	bōdào	snow	雪,下雪	xuě, xiàxuě
set up	建立	jiànlì	snowstorm, blizzard	暴风雪	bàofēngxuě
Seven Up	七喜	Qīxǐ			
sew	缝	féng	soap	肥皂,香皂	féizào/xiāngzào
shampoo	洗发香波	xǐfà xiāngbō	soapdish	肥皂盒	féizào hé
share	股份	gǔfèn	soccer	足球	zúqiú
Sharp left turn!	向左急转弯	xiàng zuǒ jí zhuǎnwān	soccer field	足球场	zúqiúchǎng
			socket	插座	chāzuò
shave	刮胡子	guā húzi	socks	袜子	wàzi
shift	移动	yídòng	sofa	沙发	shāfā
shine/on	亮	liàng	soft sleeper	软卧	ruǎnwò
shirt	衬衫/衬衣	chènshān/chènyī	software	软件	ruǎnjiàn
shoe	鞋	xié	sold out	卖完了	màiwán le
shoe polish	鞋油	xiéyóu	sole	底	dǐ
shoelace	鞋带	xiédài	solid colored	单色	dān sè
shoot (a movie)	拍	pāi	song and dance	歌舞	gēwǔ
shoot a basket	投篮	tóulán	soup	汤	tāng
shopping	购物	gòuwù	soup ladle	汤勺	tāng sháo
short	短	duǎn	sour	酸	suān
short distance	短途	duǎntú	sour and spicy	酸辣	suānlà
short sleeve	短袖	duǎnxiù	soy sauce	酱油	jiàngyóu
shorts	短裤	duǎnkù	soybean product	豆制品	dòu zhìpǐn
shoulder	肩膀	jiānbǎng	space	空间	kōngjiān
show	出示	chūshì	spare	备用	bèiyòng
shower	淋浴	línyù	speed	速度	sùdù
shower	阵雨	zhènyǔ	Speed limit	限制速度	xiànzhì sùdù
shredded meat	肉丝	ròusī	speedometer	速度表	sùdù biǎo
shrimp	虾	xiā	spell check	拼写检查	pīnxiě jiǎnchá
shrink	缩水	suōshuǐ	spice	调味品	tiáowèipǐn
shut down	关机	guānjī	spicy diced chicken with peanuts	宫保鸡丁	gōngbǎo jīdīng
sick	难受	nánshòu			
sign (a name)	签字	qiān zì			
(pure) silk	真丝	zhēnsī	spicy/hot	辣	là
simmer	熬	áo	spinning ball	转球	zhuàn qiú
singing star	歌星	gēxīng	split the bill/go Dutch	分开算	fēn kāi suàn
single bed	单人床	dānrénchuáng			
single click	单击	dān jī	sponge	海绵	hǎimián

spoon	勺	sháo	
sports	体育运动	tǐyù yùndòng	
sportsmen	运动员	yùndòngyuán	
sprain	扭伤	niǔshāng	
spreadsheet	数据表格	shùjù biǎogé	
squid	鱿鱼	yóuyú	
stable	稳定	wěndìng	
stain	污渍/脏东西	wūzì/zāng dōngxi	
stalled	抛锚	pāomáo	
stamp	邮票	yóupiào	
stamp machine	售邮票机	shòuyóupiàojī	
staple	主食	zhǔshí	
principal food			
starch	浆	jiāng	
start	起动	qǐdòng	
start	开始/开机	kāishǐ/kāijī	
start the engine	点火	diǎn huǒ	
start/begin	开始/开演	kāishǐ/kāiyǎn	
starter, assorted	拼盘	pīnpán	
cold dishes			
state-owned	国营	guóyíng	
static	杂音/干扰音	záyīn/gānrǎoyīn	
status bar	状态栏	zhuàngtài lán	
stay	呆	dāi	
steak	牛排	niúpái	
steal	抢走	qiǎngzǒu	
steam	蒸	zhēng	
steamed buns	馒头	mántou	
steamed meat bun	包子	bāozi	
steamer	蒸锅	zhēngguō	
steering wheel	方向盘	fāngxiàngpán	
step	脚步	jiǎobù	
step backward	后退	hòutuì	
step on	踩	cǎi	
stereo	音响	yīnxiǎng	
stethoscope	听诊器	tīngzhěnqì	
stew	炖	dùn	
stir fry	炒	chǎo	
stitch	缝合	fénghé	
stock	股票	gǔpiào	
stock market	股票市场	gǔpiào shìchǎng	
stockholders	股东	gǔdōng	
stomachache	胃疼, 肚子疼	wèiténg, dùzi téng	
stop	停	tíng	
stop the engine	熄火	xī huǒ	
stop, station	站	zhàn	
store	储存	chǔcún	
straight	直	zhí	
straight ahead	一直向前	yìzhí xiàngqián	
straighten	放直	fàngzhí	
strain	沥水	lìshuǐ	
strainer	沥水盆	lìshuǐpén	
street	街	jiē	
street corner	街口/街角	jiēkǒu/jiējiǎo	
stretcher	担架	dānjià	
striped	条纹	tiáowén	
student	学生	xuéshēng	
study	学习	xuéxí	
subject	题目	tímù	
subject	(一门)课	(yì mén) kè	
subtitle	字幕	zìmù	
suburb	郊区	jiāoqū	

subway	地铁	dìtiě	
subway station	地铁站	dìtiězhàn	
sugar	糖	táng	
suit	西装	xīzhuāng	
suitcase	箱子	xiāngzi	
suite	套间	tàojiān	
sunny	晴朗	qínglǎng	
supermarket	超级市场	chāojí shìchǎng	
	(超市)		
supply and demand	供应和需求	gōngyìng hé xūqiú	
supporting actor	配角	pèijué	
surgeon	外科医生	wàikē yīshēng	
sweater	毛衣	máoyī	
sweep the floor	扫地	sǎo dì	
sweet	甜	tián	
sweet and sour	糖醋	tángcù	
swimming	游泳	yóuyǒng	
switchboard	总机	zǒngjī	
swollen	肿	zhǒng	
symptoms	症状	zhèngzhuàng	
synthetic fabric	化纤料	huàxiānliào	
system	系统	xìtǒng	
T shirt	T恤	tìxù	
table	桌子	zhuōzi	
table	球桌/台	qiúzhuō/tái	
table tennis	乒乓球	pīngpāng qiú	
tablet, pill	片	piàn	
Tai Chi	太极拳	tàijíquán	
tailor	裁缝师傅	cáifeng shīfu	
take (vehicle)	坐(车)	zuò (chē)	
take a bath	泡澡	pào zǎo	
take a taxi	坐出租车/	zuò chūzūchē/	
	打 "的"	dǎdī	
take notes	做/记笔记	zuò/jì bǐjì	
take off	起飞	qǐfēi	
take temperature	量体温	liáng tǐwēn	
tangible	有形的	yǒuxíng de	
tank	油箱	yóuxiāng	
taste	尝	cháng	
taxable income	应纳税的	yīng nàshuì de	
	收入	shōurù	
taxi	出租车/计程	chūzūchē,	
	车/的士	jìchéngchē, dīshì	
tea	茶	chá	
teach	教(书)/(课)	jiāo(shū)/(ke)	
teacher	老师	lǎoshī	
team	队	duì	
telephone card	电话卡	diànhuàkǎ	
telephone booth	公共电话亭	gōnggòng diànhuà	
		tíng	
television	电视	diànshì	
teller	出纳	chūnà	
tenderloin	里脊	lǐjī	
tennis	网球	wǎngqiú	
tennis court	网球场	wǎngqiúchǎng	
terminal	登机楼	dēngjīlóu	
test/exam	考试	kǎoshì	
textbook	课本	kèběn	
the line is busy	占线	zhànxiàn	
the other party	对方	duìfāng	
the text	课文	kèwén	

English	Chinese	Pinyin
theater	剧场, 剧院, 戏院	jùchǎng, jùyuàn, xìyuàn
three to two	三比二	sān bǐ èr
thriller	惊险片	jīngxiǎnpiān
throat	嗓子/喉咙	sǎngzi/hóulóng
thunder	雷，打雷	léi, dǎléi
thunderstorm	雷雨	léiyǔ
Tian'anmen Square	天安门广场	Tiānānmén Guǎngchǎng
ticket	票	piào
ticket office	售票处	shòupiàochù
tidy up	整理	zhěnglǐ
tie	领带	lǐngdài
tied	平局	píngjú
tight	紧	jǐn
tight (maneuver)	严密	yánmì
tights	紧身裤	jǐnshēnkù
time schedule	时刻表	shíkèbiǎo
tip	小费	xiǎofèi
tire	轮胎	lúntāi
title bar	标题栏	biāotí lán
to iron	烫/熨	tàng/yùn
today	今天	jīntiān
toilet	厕所	cèsuǒ
toilet bowl	马桶	mǎtǒng
toilet paper	卫生纸	wèishēngzhǐ
toilet/washroom	洗手间	xǐshǒujiān
toll	高速公路费	gāosù gōnglù fèi
tollbooth	收费站	shōufèi zhàn
tomorrow	明天	míngtiān
tonsils	扁桃腺	biǎntáoxiàn
toolbar	工具栏	gōngjù lán
tooth	牙	yá
toothbrush	牙刷	yáshuā
toothpaste	牙膏	yágāo
toothpick	牙签	yáqiān
torn	开线	kāixiàn
touchtone	按键电话	ànjiàn diànhuà
tough	硬	yìng
tour	旅游	lǚyóu
tournament	比赛	bǐsài
tow away	拖走	tuōzǒu
tow truck	拖车	tuōchē
towel	毛巾	máojīn
towel bar	毛巾架	máojīn jià
towel dry	擦干	cā gān
trade	买卖/交易	mǎimài/jiāoyì
traffic jam	堵车/塞车	dǔchē/sāichē
traffic light	红绿灯	hónglǜdēng
Traffic light!	注意交通信号灯!	zhùyì jiāotōng xìnhàodēng
traffic sign	交通标志	jiāotōng biāozhì
tragedy	悲剧	bēijù
train station	火车站	huǒchēzhàn
tranquilizer	镇静剂	zhènjìngjì
transfer	换车	huàn chē
transmission oil	变速箱润滑油	biànsùxiāng rùnhuáyóu
transportation	交通，运输	jiāotōng, yùnshū
traveler's check	旅行支票	lǚxíng zhīpiào
tray table	托盘餐桌	tuōpán cānzhuō
trench coat	风衣	fēngyī
trolley	电车	diànchē
trunk	后备箱	hòubèixiāng
try	试	shì
tuberculosis	肺结核	fèi jiéhé
tuition	学费	xuéfèi
turbulence	湍流	tuānliú
turkey	火鸡	huǒjī
turn back	向后转	xiàng hòu zhuǎn
turn on	(打)开	(dǎ) kāi
turn signal	转向灯	zhuǎnxiàngdēng
turn to the left	向左转/拐	xiàng zuǒ zhuǎn/guǎi
turner, spatula	锅铲	guōchǎn
turnpike	收费公路	shōufèi gōnglù
TV	电视	diànshì
Two-way traffic	双向交通	shuāngxiàng jiāotōng
typhoon	台风	táifēng
uncomfortable	不舒服	bù shūfu
Under construction!	施工	shīgōng
under the seat	座位下	zuòwèi xià
underclothes	内衣	nèiyī
undershirt	汗衫/汗背心	hànshān/hàn bèixīn
underwear, briefs	内短裤/三角裤	nèiduǎnkù/sānjiǎokù
unexpected	突然, 意外	tūrán, yìwài
university/college	大学	dàxué
unleaded	无铅	wúqiān
until	到	dào
upper berth	上铺	shàngpù
upstairs	楼上	lóushàng
urine	小便	xiǎobiàn
URL	网址	wǎngzhǐ
use	用	yòng
user name	用户姓名	yònghù xìngmíng
usher	带位员	dàiwèiyuán
vacant seat	空座位	kòng zuòwèi
vacate	腾出	téngchū
vacuum cleaner	吸尘器	xīchénqì
vacuum-clean	吸尘	xīchén
vegetable	蔬菜	shūcài
vegetarian	吃素	chīsù
vegetarian dish	素菜	sùcài
venereal disease	性病	xìngbìng
version	版	bǎn
vest	背心	bèixīn
vinegar	醋	cù
visa	签证	qiānzhèng
visit	访问	fǎngwèn
visual	图像	túxiàng
vital	主要	zhǔyào
vodka	伏特加	fútèjiā
vomit	吐	tù
waist	腰	yāo
wait	等	děng
waiter	服务员	fúwùyuán
waiting room	候诊室	hòuzhěn shì
wake up	醒来	xǐng lái
walk/on foot	走路	zǒu lù
wardrobe	衣橱/柜	yīchú/guì
warm	暖和	nuǎnhuó
wash	洗	xǐ

washbowl	洗菜盆	xǐcài pén	window	窗户	chuānghu
washing machine	洗衣机	xǐyījī	window	窗口	chuāngkǒu
washroom	洗手间	xǐshǒujiān	window seat	靠窗的座位	kàochuāng de zuò wèi
water	水	shuǐ			
weather	天气	tiānqì	Windows	视窗	Shìchuāng
Web page	网页	wǎngyè	windshield	挡风玻璃	dǎngfēng bōli
Web site	网站	wǎngzhàn	windshield wiper	雨刷	yǔshuā
week	星期	xīngqī	windy	风很大	fēng hěn dà
weigh	称	chēng	wine list	酒单	jiǔ dān
weight	重心	zhòngxīn	wing	机翼	jīyì
weighted step	实步	shí bù	wipe	抹	mā
welcome	欢迎	huānyíng	wipe (clean)	擦	cā
well done	老	lǎo	with	带	dài
Western (movie)	西部片	xībùpiān	withdraw money	取钱	qǔ qián
western meal	西餐	xīcān	within	以内	yǐnèi
what size	多大号	duōdà hào	wok	炒锅	chǎoguō
wheelchair	轮椅	lúnyǐ	won't start	打不着火	dǎ bù zháo huǒ
which route	几路	jǐ lù	Woolong tea	乌龙茶	wūlóng chá
whiskey	威士忌	wēishìjì	word processing	文字处理	wénzì chǔlǐ
whistle	哨子	shàozi	words/text	文字	wénzì
white	白	bái	working area	工作区	gōngzuò qū
white wine	白葡萄酒	bái pútaojiǔ	workout	健身运动	jiànshēn yùndòng
wholesale	批发	pīfā	wound, injury	伤口	shāngkǒu
wholesalers	批发商	pīfāshāng	wrinkle-resistant	防皱	fángzhòu
who's calling?	请问是 哪位?	Qǐngwèn shi nǎwèi?	wrist	手腕	shǒuwàn
			wrong number	号码错了	hàomǎ cuòle
wide/big (for clothing)	肥	féi	www	万维网	wànwéiwǎng
			X-ray	X光检查/ 透视	X guāng jiǎnchá/tòushì
will (formal), about to	将	jiāng	Yield!	减速让行!	jiǎnsùràngxíng
win	赢/胜	yíng/ shèng	You'll be there.	你就到了	Nǐ jiù dào le.